7TH EDITION

THE CALIFORNIA

NONPROFIT CORPORATION HANDBOOK

BY ATTORNEY ANTHONY MANCUSO

EDITED BY ATTORNEY BARBARA KATE REPA

NOLO PRESS · BERKELEY

YOUR RESPONSIBILITY WHEN USING A SELF-HELP LAW BOOK

We've done our best to give you useful and accurate information in this book. But laws and procedures change frequently and are subject to differing interpretations. If you want legal advice backed by a guarantee, see a lawyer. If you use this book, it's your responsibility to make sure that the facts and general advice contained in it are applicable to your situation.

KEEPING UP TO DATE

To keep its books up to date, Nolo Press issues new printings and new editions periodically. New printings reflect minor legal changes and technical corrections. New editions contain major legal changes, major text additions or major reorganizations. To find out if a later printing or edition of any Nolo book is available, call Nolo Press at 510-549-1976 or check the catalog in the *Nolo News*, our quarterly newspaper.

To stay current, follow the "Update" service in the *Nolo News*. You can get a free two-year subscription by sending us the registration card in the back of the book. In another effort to help you use Nolo's latest materials, we offer a 25% discount off the purchase of the new edition your Nolo book when you turn in the cover of an earlier edition. (See the "Recycle Offer" in the back of the book.)

This book was last revised in: **August 1996**

SEVENTH EDITION

Second Printing	August 1996
Illustrations	MARI STEIN
Printing	DELTA LITHOGRAPH
Index	SAYRE VAN YOUNG

Mancuso, Anthony
    The California nonprofit corporation handbook / by Anthony Mancuso
; edited by Barbara Kate Repa. -- 7th ed.
        p. cm.
    Includes index.
    ISBN 0-87337-316-2
    1. Nonprofit- organizations--Law and legislation--California-
-Popular works. 2. Incorporation--California--Popular works.
I. Repa, Barbara Kate. II. Title.
KFC342.Z9M36 1995
3469.794'064--dc20   95-34625
[347.940664]   CIP

Quantity sales: For information on bulk purchases or corporate premium sales, please contact the Special Sales department. For academic sales or textbook adoptions, ask for Academic Sales. 800-955-4775, Nolo Press, Inc., 950 Parker St., Berkeley, CA, 94710.

ACKNOWLEDGEMENTS

The author extends a special thanks to Barbara Kate Repa, the editor of the fifth edition of this book; to Jake Warner, the publisher, for helping this book through another major revision; and to all the hardworking people at Nolo Press. A personal thanks to Jackie Mancuso, my friend and companion.

CONTENTS

Chapter 3

FEDERAL 501(C)(3) INCOME TAX EXEMPTION

Chapter 4

501(C)(3) PUBLIC CHARITIES AND PRIVATE FOUNDATIONS

Chapter 5

OTHER NONPROFIT BENEFITS AND REQUIREMENTS

Chapter 6

ORGANIZING A NONPROFIT CORPORATION

Chapter 7

PREPARE YOUR CALIFORNIA TAX EXEMPTION APPLICATION

Chapter 8

FILE YOUR INCORPORATION PAPERS

Chapter 9

APPLY FOR YOUR FEDERAL 501(C)(3) TAX EXEMPTION

Chapter 10

FINAL STEPS IN ORGANIZING YOUR NONPROFIT CORPORATION

Chapter 11

AFTER YOUR CORPORATION IS ORGANIZED

Chapter 12

LAWYERS AND ACCOUNTANTS

Appendix of Tear-Out Forms

California Nonprofit Corporation Resource List

The Nonprofit Corporation Law—Overview of the Changes

INTRODUCTION

INTEREST IN FORMING nonprofit corporations is on the increase. All sorts of groups, from artists, musicians and dancers to people active in education, health, ethnic and community services, women's rights and countless other concerns, wish to operate as nonprofit corporations. Often the reason for doing this is simple—being organized as a nonprofit corporation is commonly a requirement for obtaining funds from government agencies and private foundations. Obtaining grants, however, is not the only reason to incorporate. There are also important federal, state, and local tax exemptions available to the nonprofit corporation as well as significant (20-50%) tax deductions available to people who make contributions to nonprofit groups. Low cost nonprofit mailing rates and, in some cases, exemption from payment of property and sales taxes are also incentives for many groups in deciding to form a nonprofit corporation.

In addition to funding source requirements and tax benefits, there are several other important reasons why people choose to set up nonprofit corporations. Perhaps the most important is limited liability. The nonprofit corporation normally protects its directors, officers and members from personal liability for claims brought against the corporation. This means that lawsuits can only reach the assets of the corporation, not the bank accounts, houses or other property owned by the individuals who manage, work for, or participate as members of the corporation. Many incorporators of nonprofit corporations also feel that the act of setting up the corporation is itself beneficial. Why? Because the act of organizing the corporation serves as a convenient means of focusing on and dealing with initial and ongoing business details, and because the existence of the corporation gives the group increased standing in the community.

In essence, going nonprofit can be a handy means of attracting tax-exempt and tax-deductible support for worthwhile purposes and activities while obtaining the added benefits and incentives associated with corporations generally. The price traditionally paid for these benefits is a bit of red tape and a moderate-to-severe attorney's fee. This book is intended to explain and simplify the former difficulty and avoid the latter.

This book provides the information, forms and instructions needed to organize the most common type of nonprofit corporation—one organized and operated for religious, charitable, scientific, literary or educational purposes. These are activities which are eligible for tax exempt status under Section 501(c)(3) of the Internal Revenue Code—this is the catch-all category of nonprofit tax-exempt status appropriate for all but a few special purpose groups. Even groups which don't fit into this catch-all category will find the corporate law and tax information and several of the forms contained in this book useful, indeed essential, in organizing their nonprofit corporations.

Specifically, this book shows you how to:

• Prepare and submit your federal tax exemption application [under Internal Revenue Code § 501(c)(3)];

• Complete and file a California tax exemption application;

• Prepare and file Articles of Incorporation with the California Secretary of State (forms for both the California public benefit and religious organizations are included);

• Prepare Bylaws reflecting the basic provisions and options available under California's Nonprofit Corporation Law (both membership and non-membership Bylaws are included);

• Prepare Minutes of the First Meeting of Directors.

In addition to providing line-by-line instructions and suggested wording for filling in these forms (tear-out forms are provided in the Appendix), we have included a great deal of background information on federal, state and local tax advantages

and requirements as well as California corporate law provisions. Problem areas are flagged and in some unusual or complicated situations, we tell you to see an accountant or attorney for specific answers to specific questions. For help with this, we have included sections on how to find and hire accountants or attorneys who know what they are talking about and who will charge reasonable prices to share this knowledge with you.

The federal tax material and federal tax exemption application instructions will apply to most nonprofit groups seeking to obtain federal tax exempt status. The corporate material and forms will apply to most groups wishing to organize their nonprofit corporation in California.

National Nonprofit Incorporation Note: If you wish to incorporate in state other than California, you can do so using our national nonprofit title, *How To Form Your Own Nonprofit Corporation*. This book shows you how to form a nonprofit corporation under the specific laws of each of the other 49 states as well as information and instructions on obtaining your federal tax exemption from the IRS.

How To Use This Book

Please scan this entire book at least once before you draw conclusions and fill out papers. It is not difficult to organize a nonprofit corporation, but many of the corporate and tax laws are picky or technical—often both—and you should get an overview of the whole subject before getting down to details. The Incorporation Checklist included in the Appendix provides an overview of the material in this book and a checklist for completing the steps involved in forming a California nonprofit corporation.

Chapter 1

OVERVIEW OF THE CALIFORNIA NONPROFIT CORPORATION

IN THIS CHAPTER we provide a general overview of the California nonprofit corporation and its advantages. Background information on other types of corporations is also included to help you understand where the nonprofit corporation fits in the larger corporate world.

A. What Is a Corporation?

A corporation is simply a "legal fiction"—a way for a group of people to pool energy, time and money for profit or nonprofit activities. Legally, a corporation is treated separately from the people who own, manage and operate it. The law considers a corporation to be a "person" capable of entering contracts, incurring debts and paying taxes. This gives those who control, manage and work for a corporation "limited liability"; their property can't normally be taken to satisfy the corporation's debts.

B. How Corporations Are Labeled

1. Domestic and Foreign Corporations

Corporations formed in California are referred to (by the California Corporations Code) as "domestic" corporations, while corporations formed in other states (even if physically present and engaging in activities in California) are called "foreign" corporations.

If your corporation plans to operate or do business in other states, it will usually have to qualify to do so (by filing forms and paying qualification fees in the other states). Also, your out-of-state activities will be subject, at least to some extent, to the corporation laws of the foreign states and your corporation may have to pay taxes based upon the net income derived from activities in these states.

Federal law applies to all nonprofit corporations, regardless of where they are formed (whether do-

mestic or foreign) or where they do business. Federal statutes affecting nonprofit corporations consist primarily of the Internal Revenue Code (IRC) tax exemption provisions. A federal tax-exempt nonprofit corporation will not have to worry about federal corporate income taxes derived from activities performed in other states—the federal tax exemption applies to corporate income earned in any state. Your state tax exemption, however, applies only to the state in which it is granted. If you wish to be exempt from payment of taxes on corporate income derived from activities in other states, you will have to apply for and obtain a separate tax exemption in each of these states.

Why Not Form an Out-of-State Corporation?

You may wonder—Why not incorporate in another state (most notably Delaware where general corporate law provisions are more flexible) and operate in California? The answer is simple for nonprofit corporations which plan to engage in more than minimal activities in California—it's too costly and too much trouble. The relatively minor benefits which nonprofit corporations may obtain from another state's more flexible corporation laws are more than offset by the inconvenience of obtaining qualifications to operate as a corporation in each state and applying for and obtaining multiple state tax exemptions. Furthermore, California, like several other leading jurisdictions, has been active in promoting and passing legislation which seeks to protect nonprofit directors and officers from personal liability when working for, or on behalf of, a California nonprofit corporation. In other words, if you are looking for a state to form your California-based nonprofit corporation, there's usually no place like home (or at least no place particularly better).

Exception: If you plan to set up corporate offices in more than one state, then you should consider incorporating in other states. Consult an attorney or nonprofit resource center (see the Nonprofit Corporation Resource List in the Appendix) to determine the state which will be most convenient and least costly to use as your corporate home.

2. Business Corporations

In California, profit corporations (which are subject to the California General Corporation Law) are called "business corporations" and are authorized by their Articles to do any lawful business activity. (Nonprofit corporations are restricted to public, charitable, religious, or mutual benefit activities as discussed further below.)

Business corporations are authorized to issue shares of stock to shareholders in return for money, property, or past services to the corporation. Shareholders invest in the corporation and get a return on their investment only if dividends are declared or if they receive a proportionate share of the value of the corporation's assets when it stops doing business.[1] Except for a few "hybrid" nonprofit corporations such as a consumer or producer cooperative, nonprofit corporations cannot issue shares, nor can public benefit or religious nonprofit corporations issue dividends in times of prosperity or distribute assets to members when the corporation ends.

C. What Does It Mean to Be "Nonprofit?"

A nonprofit corporation is simply a corporation that is organized and operated for one of the nonprofit purposes recognized under state corporation law and federal and state tax statutes. We discuss these special nonprofit purposes in later sections. "Nonprofit" does not mean that you cannot make a profit: as long as your corporation is organized and operated for a recognized nonprofit purpose (for ex-

ample, an educational or charitable purpose), your corporation can make a profit from its activities. Nonprofit corporations can also make money in ways completely unrelated to their nonprofit purposes (a strictly for-profit activity not necessary to accomplish your nonprofit purposes). This type of unrelated business income is subject to taxation and special rules but is, nonetheless, permissible (and often essential to the survival of the nonprofit group). Finally, although not typical for the average group, a nonprofit corporation can make money from "passive" sources such as rents, royalties, interest, investments, etc. This income is, moreover, non-taxable in some cases.

A nonprofit corporation has many of the attributes of a profit corporation—for example, it is a separate legal entity which provides its founders, directors, officers and members with limited liability. However, nonprofit corporations must meet special requirements to obtain the special advantages associated with nonprofit status. For example, two basic requirements under state and federal tax exemption rules are that the corporation cannot be set up to benefit a particular person and that, if the corporation is dissolved, any remaining assets be distributed to a similar tax-exempt nonprofit group.

We discuss the specific benefits and requirements associated with nonprofit corporations in the remainder of this book. For now, the most important point to keep in mind is that these requirements vary according to the particular benefit you wish to obtain. For example, meeting the requirements for recognition as a California nonprofit corporation simply entitles you to engage in activities as a California nonprofit corporation. If you wish your nonprofit corporation to be exempt from corporate income taxes at the state and federal levels (most incorporators will), the nonprofit corporation must meet separate tax exemption requirements under California and federal tax laws and regulations.

---

[1]If you would like more information on small profit corporations, see *How to Form Your Own Corporation* (California, Florida, New York & Texas editions), by Mancuso (Nolo Press)— order information is at the back of this book.

Note for Pre-Existing Nonprofit Corporations

The California Nonprofit Corporation Law became effective in 1980 and represents a major restatement and clarification of California's nonprofit corporation provisions. We mention this date because it represents a pivotal point in time for existing California corporations and California nonprofit corporations formed prior to January 1, 1980 need to be aware of the major classifications and provisions of this law.[2]

Although nonprofit corporations in existence prior to 1980 automatically become subject to most of the provisions of the new Nonprofit Corporation Law on January 1, 1980, there is no legal requirement that they amend their pre-1980 Articles of Incorporation or Bylaws.[3] We recommend, however, that you do adopt new Bylaws (contained in this book) to reflect the current provisions of the law. Why is this advisable? Because if you take corporate action following procedures contained in outdated Bylaws, chances are good that you will be acting invalidly.

D. The Nonprofit Corporation Law

The California Nonprofit Corporation Law governs the organization and operations of California nonprofit corporations.[4] This is a comprehensive law which contains detailed rules regulating the organization and operation of California nonprofit corporations. The material and forms in this book are based upon this law and changes which have occurred since its passage.

---

[2]Changes to the California Nonprofit Corporation Law occur each year. Although we update the information and forms in this book with each new printing or edition (see printing history on back of title page), we caution you that legislation pending at the time this issue goes to press (and, possibly, some provisions of new law) may not be reflected in this book.

[3]Pre-1980 nonprofit corporations are allowed to file amended Articles which conform to the 1980 law if they wish—see California Corporations Code 9913. Following this amendment, the Bylaws should be amended to conform to the 1980 law—see Corp. Code § 9915.

[4]This law is contained in the California Corporations Code, Sections 5000-9927.

Tax Note: In addition to state corporation statutes, the California Revenue and Taxation Code, as well as the federal Internal Revenue Code, apply to nonprofit corporations. Tax considerations are discussed in Chapters 3, 4 and 5. In most ways, understanding and complying with tax rules is more important (and more challenging) than fulfilling the corporation code requirements.

E. Types of Nonprofit Corporations

There are three types of California nonprofit corporations: public benefit, religious and mutual benefit.

1. Public Benefit Corporations— What Are They?

These are nonprofit corporations formed for a public or charitable purpose.

The Nonprofit Corporation Law itself is not specific as to what public or charitable purposes are—indeed, the Assembly Committee which analyzed and commented on the Nonprofit Law stated: "If reasonable people could say that the [corporation's] purpose was 'public' or 'charitable,' the organization may be formed and operated as a public benefit Corporation." Most public benefit corporations are organized for scientific, literary, or educational purposes which benefit the public, or for charitable purposes since these specific public or charitable purposes qualify for tax-exempt status under Section 501(c)(3) of the Internal Revenue Code (more on tax-exempt purposes later).[5]

---

[5]Civic leagues and social welfare groups are also considered public benefit corporations. These special groups are not treated specifically in this book since they are exempt from federal corporate taxation under Section 501(c)(4) of the Internal Revenue Code (see Chapter 2A3).

Examples: A group formed to provide shelter for the homeless would be organized as a charitable purpose public benefit corporation. A nonprofit school or educational facility would be organized as a public purpose public benefit corporation.

We show you how to decide on the official designation of your nonprofit purpose or purposes (whether public or charitable) in Chapter 5.

Special Characteristics of Public Benefit Corporations

- They can qualify for an exemption from paying federal corporate income taxes under Section 501(c)(3) of the Internal Revenue Code.

- As long as the corporation exists, none of the gains, profits or dividends may go to those defined in the Articles or Bylaws as members. When and if it decides to dissolve, any assets remaining after the debts and liabilities are paid must go to another public benefit or religious corporation or to a similar nonprofit association —and not to any members of the former corporation.

- Self-dealing rules (regulating action by the board if a director has a financial interest in a transaction) apply to public benefit corporations which are more stringent than those applicable to the other types of nonprofit corporations.

- The California Attorney General has more power to oversee the operations of public benefit corporations than the other two types and can even step in and take the corporation to court to make sure it complies with the law.

- A majority of the Board of Directors cannot be paid, or related to other persons who are paid, by the corporation. Because this restriction is important—and knocks out the close-knit, family orga-

nizations many picture when they think of nonprofit corporations, we discuss this provision in detail later in this chapter.

(2.) Religious Corporations—What Are They?

Just as the name indicates, these nonprofit corporations are formed primarily or exclusively for religious purposes.

You need not be setting up a formal church to form a religious corporation. (The Nonprofit Corporation Law purposely avoids using the word "church" because its meaning is restrictive and fluctuating.) Religious purpose organizations qualify as religious organizations as well as more formal religious groups. For example, a group organized to promote the study and practice of a particular religion would incorporate as a religious corporation. By the way, it is unlikely that the Secretary of State's office (where you file your corporate Articles) will question the religious nature of your activities. This type of debate is more likely to occur (if it occurs at all) when you apply for your state or federal tax exemptions.

Special Characteristics of Religious Corporations

- They can obtain a federal tax exemption under Section 501(c)(3) of the Internal Revenue Code.

- They have the widest flexibility in managing their internal affairs. If a religious corporation does not set up its own operating rules, provisions of the nonprofit law apply that are similar to, but less stringent than, those that apply to public benefit corporations.

---

corporate taxation under Section 501(c)(4) of the Internal Revenue Code (see Chapter 2A3).

3. Mutual Benefit Corporations— What Are They?

Mutual benefit corporations are formed to benefit their members. Although some special rules apply, this is a "catch-all" category which includes, by default, any nonprofit corporation that isn't considered either a public benefit or religious corporation.

Examples: Trade associations, automobile clubs, social groups such as tennis clubs.

Special Characteristics of Mutual Benefit Corporations

- Mutual benefit corporations can often qualify for a federal tax exemption under a subsection of 501 (c) of the Internal Revenue Code other than 501(c)(3) [such as IRC § 501(c)(6)]. However, unlike tax-exempt public benefit and religious corporations, contributions to mutual benefit corporations are normally not tax-deductible and the corporation is normally not eligible for many of the other benefits enjoyed by the other two types of nonprofit corporations (such as nonprofit mailing rates, real and personal property tax exemptions, etc.).

- While mutual benefit corporations are in business, they cannot distribute gains, profits or dividends to those designated in the Articles or Bylaws as members but may provide them with other benefits, such as services and facilities.

- Members of a mutual benefit corporation can own part of it. When the corporation shuts down and all its debts and liabilities are paid, the remaining assets, gains and profits can be distributed to the members.

If You Want to Form a Mutual Benefit Corporation: This book is *not* intended to apply directly to these corporations. These groups must obtain tax-exempt status under different tax laws than the other nonprofit corporations. Forms and instructions for these groups are not included in this book. (For a list of the types of mutual benefit corporations which may obtain an exemption from payment of federal corporate income taxes, see the table in Chapter 3.)

If you wish to form a mutual benefit corporation, this book can provide you with much background information. For mutual benefit corporation forms, just go to your local county law library. The library will likely contain several standard legal volumes with Articles and Bylaws and other mutual benefit incorporation forms. For a short discussion on using the law library, see Chapter 12. Also, the Secretary of State's *Corporation's Check List* contains sample mutual benefit corporation Articles with filing instructions (this publication can be ordered for a small fee from the Sacramento office of the Secretary of State).

F. How To Obtain Nonprofit Corporate Status—An Overview

All California nonprofit corporations must be officially recognized by the California Secretary of State. To do this, you must file Articles of Incorporation with the Secretary of State's office, indicating that your organization is entitled to receive nonprofit corporate status. This section covers the basic requirements of being recognized by California's Secretary of State as a public benefit or religious nonprofit corporation. We will focus on public benefit corporations—those formed for public or charitable purposes which comprise the majority of nonprofit corporations eligible for an exemption from federal corporate income taxes under Section 501(c)(3) of the Internal Revenue Code. Requirements for religious corporations are noted only if they are different from the requirements for public benefit corporations. Mutual benefit corporations will only occasionally be mentioned.

The Articles of Incorporation must indicate the following:

- The corporation must be formed by one or more people, partnerships, associations, or corpora tions. Legally, these people or entities are referred to as the incorporators.

- Each incorporator and director (if directors are named in the Articles) must sign and "acknowledge" the Articles. The acknowledgment may be a formal one signed before a notary or a simple declaration signed by the incorporators/directors.

- The Articles must state the name of the corporation. The name must be legally available for the corporation to use—more about this later.

- They must also include a standard legal statement which indicates which of the three types of nonprofit corporation is being formed (public benefit, religious, or mutual benefit) and what its general purposes are (public, charitable or religious). If it's a public benefit corporation formed for public, as opposed to charitable, purposes, then an additional specific statement describing these public purposes must be included.

  - As part of the purpose clause, the Articles must state that the corporation is not organized for any person's private gain. Technically, this means that no individual associated with the corporation (director, officer, regular employee, member, fundraiser) can receive gains, profits or dividends from the corporation. However, it is okay for those who work to further the tax-exempt purposes of the corporation to be paid reasonably for doing so. The purpose of this limitation is to prevent use of the nonprofit corporation as a regular business profit corporation where the principals receive dividends just for making a corporate investment. As we will see later, there are some limitations as to how much directors of public benefit corporations may be paid. This special limitation on directors' salaries does not apply to religious corporations which, as we've said, are granted greater flexibility in managing their affairs.

- The Articles must also designate the person to whom legal papers should be sent in case of a lawsuit against the corporation.

G. Advantages of the Nonprofit Corporation

1. Tax Exemptions

Nonprofit corporations can be eligible for state and federal tax exemptions from payment of corporate income taxes and other tax exemptions and benefits. These tax benefits and the requirements you must meet to qualify for them are discussed in Chapters 3, 4 and 5.

2. Limited Liability

Limited liability can be a real incentive to forming a nonprofit corporation. It means that corporate directors or trustees, officers, employees and members are not *personally* liable for corporate debts. Creditors can only go after corporate assets to satisfy liabilities incurred by the corporation—not the personal assets (car, home, bank accounts) of the people in the corporation.

Example: A nonprofit symphony incurs liability because someone falls due to a poorly maintained railing, and a judgment is entered for an amount greater than insurance coverage. The amount of the judgment which is unpaid is a debt of the nonprofit corporation, but not of the corporation's directors, members, managers, etc.

Exceptions to the Limited Liability Rule

Watch out. In a few situations, people involved with a nonprofit corporation may be personally liable for the corporation's debts.

banks and commercial lending institutions usually require that the corporation's directors or officers personally guarantee the money will be paid back. The corporate heads will have to sign the note twice—in the name of the corporation and in their own names—making them personally liable for re-paying the money.

Taxes: State and federal governments can hold the corporate employee who is responsible for re-porting and paying corporate taxes (usually the trea-surer) personally liable for any unpaid taxes, penal-ties and interest due for failure to pay taxes or file required tax returns. With proper planning, your nonprofit corporation shouldn't have to pay much, if any, corporate taxes, but you will still be held to an-nual reporting requirements and rules for paying or withholding employment taxes which are strictly enforced by the state and the IRS. Since the IRS has substantial penalties for delinquent tax payments and returns, keep this exception to limited liability in mind—particularly if you will be the treasurer.

Dues: Members of a nonprofit corporation are personally liable for any membership fees and dues they owe the corporation.

Private Foundation Managers: If the nonprofit corporation is classified as a private foundation, foundation managers can be held personally liable for federal excise taxes associated with certain prohibited transactions. They may also be held personally liable for penalties and interest charged for failing to file certain tax returns or pay required excise taxes.

Violations of Statutory Duties: Corporate directors and officers owe the corporation a duty to act in its best interest; this is called their "duty of care." If, because of a breach of this duty, they cause financial harm to the corporation, a court may hold them personally liable for any loss sustained by the corporation.

Special Corporations

A few special types of groups may incorporate as public benefit, mutual benefit or even as regular profit corporations, or come under additional special provisions of the Corporations Code. Here is a list with brief descriptions:

Corporations Sole: A bishop, chief priest, presiding elder, or other presiding officer of any religious denomination may form a corporation sole for the purpose of administering and managing the affairs and property of the denomination, society or church. Special provisions of the Corporations Code apply (see Corporations Code §§ 10000-10015).

Chambers of Commerce, Boards of Trade, Mechanics Institutes: These corporations are generally formed to promote trade and commerce. They must organize as regular profit corporations or mutual benefit nonprofit corporations.

Cooperative Corporations: Nonprofit corporations comprised of producers or consumers organized for their mutual benefit are controlled by the Consumer Cooperative Corporation Law (see Corporations Code, starting with § 12200).

Medical or Legal Service Corporations: Nonprofit corporations operated to assume or defray the cost of medical or legal services. These corporations must be organized as public benefit corporations or mutual benefit corporations. Special provisions of the California Corporations Code apply (see Corporations Code §§ 10810-10841).

Humane Societies: Nonprofit corporations formed by 20 or more people (who must be citizens and residents of California) to prevent cruelty to children or animals. These corporations may be formed as public benefit corporations. The Department of Justice must perform a criminal history check on all incorporators and issue a certificate before the Secretary of State will accept the Articles of Incorporation for filing (see Corporations Code §§ 10400-10406).

Piercing the Corporate Veil: A nonprofit corporation must act so that its separate existence is clear and respected. If it mixes up corporate funds with the personal funds of those in charge, fails to follow legal formalities (operate according to prepared bylaws, hold director meetings, keep minutes of meetings), or risks financial liability without sufficient backup in cash or other assets, a court may disregard the corporate entity. (In legalese, this is known as "piercing the corporate veil.") If this happens, the principals of the nonprofit corporation are personally liable for the debts and other liabilities of the corporation (see Chapter 11, Section A).

3. Perpetual Legal Existence

A corporation is a legal entity separate and apart from the people who manage, operate, work for, or otherwise participate in its activities. It is a legal "person," capable, on its own, of entering into contracts, incurring debts, receiving and maintaining funds, and, generally, doing anything a real person can do. This legal person is, in a sense, immortal, as the nonprofit corporation continues to exist as a legal entity despite changes in management or other corporate personnel caused by the resignation, removal or death of the people associated with it. It may, of course, be dissolved or drastically affected by the loss of key people, but its inherent perpetuality adds an element of certainty regarding the continuance of the group's activities, an attractive feature to the private and public grantor who prefers funding activities which have a reasonable probability of continuing to operate into the foreseeable future.

4. Employee Benefits

Another advantage of the nonprofit corporation is that the principals of the corporation can also be employees of the organization and, therefore, be eligible for tax deductible employee fringe benefits not available as readily, if at all, to the owners or operators of self-employed activities. These include sick pay, group life insurance, accident and health insurance, payment of medical expenses and coverage by an approved corporate employee pension or retirement income plan.

5. Formality

A final advantage of the nonprofit corporation has to do with the formal documents (Articles, Bylaws, Minutes of Meetings, Board Resolutions, etc.) associated with the formation and operation of a nonprofit corporation. These documents outline the organizational and operating rules for the group's activities and, aside from the benefits derived from these documents discussed above (obtaining tax exemptions, grant funds, etc.), provide a built-in set of ground rules and procedures for reaching decisions and resolving disputes. This latter feature is an important advantage for any collective activity, but for nonprofit groups it amounts to a virtual necessity, especially where the composition of the board includes diverse members of the community with correspondingly divergent interests. Without the clear-cut delegation of authority and specific operating rules for reaching collective decisions (which are routinely prepared as part of the formation of a nonprofit corporation), the operation of the organization's activities can often be a divisive, if not futile, affair.

H. Disadvantages of the Nonprofit Corporation

Okay, now let's look at the other side of the ledger. What are the disadvantages of forming a nonprofit corporation?

1. Paperwork

One disadvantage involves complying with the red tape of organizing and operating a corporation. This involves the preparation of initial incorporation documents (Articles of Incorporation, Bylaws, and Minutes of First Meeting of the Board of Directors) and paperwork to document ongoing corporate action (Minutes of regular and special meetings of the board of directors or members). This book provides you with the initial incorporation forms together with information and examples to help you fill in the blanks. Keeping track of future actions by the non-profit board, various committees and the member-ship can be time-consuming but is not difficult. Besides, keeping minutes of meetings is a standard part of operating any nonprofit organization, whether incorporated or not.

Annual nonprofit informational tax returns do present a challenge to a new group unfamiliar with IRS forms and requirements. Other record-keeping and reporting chores, such as double-entry account-ing procedures and payroll tax withholding and re-porting, can be equally daunting. At least to start, most nonprofits rely on the experience of a tax advi-sor, bookkeeper, or other legal or tax specialist on the board or in the community to help them set up their books and establish a system for preparing tax forms on time. See Chapter 12 for recommendations on finding legal and tax professionals to help your nonprofit.

2. Incorporation Costs and Fees

Traditionally, the other main disadvantage of in-corporating a nonprofit organization has been the $1,000 to $2,000 or more that you could expect to pay an attorney for preparing the above forms plus, usu-ally, extra amounts for your tax exemption applica-tions. This book, along with a little time and effort on your part, eliminates this costly disadvantage, leaving you with only the actual cost of incorpora-tion. This includes filing fees for the Articles, tax ex

emption application fees, plus a few miscellaneous fees. The total is approximately $200.[6]

3. Time and Energy

These are important factors to consider prior to incorporating. In most cases, the legal decision to in-corporate is intimately bound to a broader decision to increase not just the structure, but the overall scope, scale and visibility of nonprofit operations. With a larger, more accountable organization comes a number of new tasks: setting up and balancing books and bank accounts, depositing and reporting payroll taxes, meeting with an accountant to extract and report year end figures for annual informational returns, etc. Although these financial, payroll and tax concerns are not, strictly speaking, exclusively corporate chores, they do invariably follow from a decision to incorporate—most unincorporated non-profits keep a low employment, tax and financial profile and get by with minimum attention to legal and tax formalities.

Example: A women's health collective operates as an unincorporated nonprofit organization maintained by the part-time volunteer efforts of its two founders. It keeps an office open a few days per week where people can stop by to read and exchange information on community health services, share patient evaluations of local physi-cians, read medical literature on women's health issues and concerns, etc. The two founders donate their time so there is no payroll. The office space is donated by one of the founders and (non-tax-deductible) contributions made people who stop by the office help defray some of the operating costs (phone, utilities, photocopying, etc). The additional portion of the overhead is paid by the two organizers. Formal meetings are rarely held and the organization is run with an absolute

---

[6]Costs are higher for nonprofits which anticipate gross receipts of more than $10,000. These groups pay a $465 rather than a $150 federal tax exemption application fee (see Chapter 9C).

minimum of paperwork and recordkeeping. The organization has never made a profit and tax returns have never been filed for the unincorporated organization.

The founders could decide to could continue in this fashion into the indefinite future. However, a number of women have expressed interest in helping the founders expand the activities and revenues of the collective in order to provide additional services and serve a wider segment of the community. To be eligible for additional support brought by tax deductible contributions and grant funds made available by the city to tax exempt nonprofits, and to qualify the group to employ student interns and work-study students, the founders decide to form a 501(c)(3) nonprofit corporation. Doing so will require the preparation and filing of Articles of Incorporation and corporate income tax exemption applications. An initial board of directors must be selected and organizational bylaws prepared. Formal written minutes of the first board of directors' meeting documenting the beginning business of the corporation should be prepared and placed in the corporate records.

After incorporation, regular board meetings are held and documented with written minutes, a double-entry bookkeeping system is set up and utilized, regular federal and state payroll and tax procedures and controls are implemented, exempt organization tax returns are filed each year, and the operations of the group are expanded. A full-time staff person is assigned to handle the increased paperwork and book-keeping chores brought about by the change in structure and increased operations of the organization.

This example is intended to underline one essential consideration that should be placed high on your pre-incorporation checklist: You should make sure that you and your co-workers can meet the challenge of the extra time and effort that your incorporated nonprofit organization will require. If the extra incorporational and operational work would overwhelm or overtax your current resources, we suggest you hold off on your incorporation until you have obtained the added help necessary to smoothly (or at least more easily) accomplish this task.

Choosing Not to Incorporate: Can You Continue to Operate As An Unincorporated Association?

Many groups do fine and accomplish their nonprofit purposes as unincorporated nonprofit associations, without formal organizational paperwork and written operational rules. If you can continue to accomplish your nonprofit purposes and goals informally, you may be happier staying small.

Example: A senior citizens botany club is organized informally. Initially, six members take a monthly nature walk to study and photograph regional flora. Everyone chips in to buy gas for whoever drives to the hike's starting point. Recently, however, membership has increased to fifteen and the group has decided to collect dues from members to pay for increased expenses—gas money, guidebooks and maps, printing club T-shirts—associated with more frequent field trips. To avoid commingling club monies with personal funds, a treasurer is designated to open a bank account on behalf of the organization. Several people suggest that it is time to incorporate the club. Does this make sense? Probably not. There is no new pressing need to adopt the corporate form or to obtain formal recognition as a tax exempt nonprofit. (Most banks will allow an unincorporated group without a federal Employer Identification Number or IRS tax exemption to open up a non-interest bearing account.)

If your group does not generate a surplus (does not make a taxable profit), does not need to attract tax deductible contributions, does not need to apply for public or private grant monies, and has no legal need to adopt the corporate form (such as providing nonprofit people with the protection of limited liability), it may decide it's best, at least for the present, not to form a tax exempt nonprofit corporation. For example, the botany club discussed above may decide to incorporate in a few years when it seeks funding and contributions to spearhead a drive to save open space in the community.

Chapter 2

NONPROFIT CORPORATIONS AND THE CALIFORNIA CORPORATION LAW

IN THIS CHAPTER, we discuss the basic legal provisions of the Nonprofit Corporation Law[1] governing the organization and operation of California nonprofit corporations. This material is meant to give you further background in the law of nonprofits and to help explain the content of the forms you will fill out in later chapters. Remember, our focus is on California public benefit and religious corporations.

A. Nonprofit Purposes

As we've seen, nonprofit corporations may be formed under California law for public benefit, religious, or mutual benefit purposes. Your Articles of Incorporation need only contain a short, standard phrase indicating which one of these purposes applies to your corporation. If your public benefit corporation is formed for public purposes, you'll need to add a short description of the nature of these purposes. As we explain later, these public purposes should be geared to qualify under one of the purposes allowable by the Internal Revenue Code for tax-exempt nonprofit organizations (e.g., educational, literary, scientific purposes). A long-winded account of your purposes need not, and should not, be included in your Articles of Incorporation.

B. Nonprofit Powers

Nonprofit corporations have the power to engage in any activity related to the nonprofit purposes of the corporation (as stated in their Articles of Incorporation and Bylaws), plus the legal right to engage in other activities specifically allowed by provisions of the Nonprofit Corporations Law. These other statutory powers are so broad that, for all practical purposes, they amount to carte blanche to engage in any lawful business activity. But remember: you can't distribute gains to members of the nonprofit corporation. And, as you will learn, you won't, for tax reasons, want to "substantially" engage in activities unrelated to your tax-exempt purposes.

The Nonprofit Corporation Law specifically lists many powers that may be exercised by nonprofit corporations. We simply list some of them below and don't include them in the tear-out Articles of Incorporation included in this book. There are several reasons for this: (1) most are fairly obvious powers necessary for the transaction of business in general; (2) some may conflict with state and federal tax exemption requirements, giving rise to tax liability and, possibly, jeopardizing your tax-exempt status; and (3) we don't need to pad the papers.

Specific Nonprofit Corporation Law Corporate Powers[2]

To Use a Corporate Seal. To adopt, use, and alter a corporate seal, but failure to use a seal does not affect the validity of any corporate instrument.

To Alter or Change Bylaws. To adopt, amend, and repeal Bylaws.

To Operate In Other States and Countries. To qualify to conduct its activities in any other state, territory, dependency or foreign country.

To Deal In and With Its Own Bonds, Notes, Etc. To issue, purchase, redeem, receive, take, acquire, own, sell, lend, exchange, transfer, or otherwise dispose of, pledge, use, and deal in and with its own bonds, debentures, notes and debt securities.

To Have Members. To issue memberships.

---

[1]The Nonprofit Corporation Law is part of the California Corporations Code and is divided into the Public Benefit Corporation Law, the Religious Corporation Law and the Mutual Benefit Corporation Law.

[2]Remember, these powers apply to public benefit and religious corporations only (not necessarily to mutual benefit corporations).

To Establish Fringe Benefit and Indemnification Plans. To pay pensions and establish and carry out pension, deferred compensation, saving, thrift and other retirement incentive and benefit plans, trusts and provisions for any or all directors, officers, employees, and persons providing services to it or any of its subsidiary or related corporations. Also to indemnify and purchase and maintain insurance on behalf of any fiduciary of such plans, trusts or provisions.

To Levy Dues, Etc. To levy dues, assessments and admission fees.

To Make Donations. To make donations for the public welfare or for community funds, hospital, charitable, educational, scientific, civic, religious or similar purposes.

To Borrow Money. To assume obligations, enter into contracts, including contracts of guaranty, incur liabilities, borrow or lend money or otherwise use its credit, secure any of its obligations, contracts or liabilities by mortgage, pledge or other encumbrance of all or any part of its property and income.

To Do Business Jointly With Other People and Entities. To participate with others in any partnership, joint venture or other association, transaction or arrangement of any kind, whether or not such participation involves sharing or delegation of control with or to others.

To Act as a Trustee. To act as a trustee under any trust, incidental to the principal objects of the corporation, and receive, hold, administer, exchange and expend funds and property subject to such trust.

To Engage in For-Profit Businesses. To carry on a business at a profit and apply any profit that results from the business activity in which the corporation may lawfully engage.

To Do Just About Anything. To have all the powers of a natural person in carrying out its activities.

C. Corporate People—An Overview

While a corporation is a legal person capable of making contracts, incurring liabilities, etc., it obviously needs real people to carry out its corporate purposes and activities. In this section we discuss the basic statutory rights and responsibilities of the people who organize and operate nonprofit corporations.

Corporate people are classified by the Nonprofit Corporation Law in the following way:[3]

Incorporators
Directors
Officers
Members
Employees

The courts and the Nonprofit Corporation Law have given these corporate people varying powers and responsibilities. In the next several sections of this chapter we discuss these legal provisions and a few court-developed rules which apply to each type of corporate person. (Remember that we are limiting

---

[3]Distinctions between these roles often become blurred for the small nonprofit corporation since, as you'll see, one person can, and often does, simultaneously serve in more than one of these capacities.

our focus to public benefit and religious corporations only.) The legal language governing the basic duties and responsibilities of your directors, officers and members is contained in the tear-out Bylaws included in the Appendix to this book.

D. Incorporators

Incorporators as Promoters: Legally, an incorporator is a person who signs the Articles of Incorporation. In a practical sense, however, the incorporators are the people who make arrangements for obtaining money, property, people, and whatever else the corporation will need to get off the ground. In effect, they are the pre-incorporation promoters of the corporation. A corporate promoter is considered by law to be a fiduciary of the corporation. This means that she has a duty to act in the best interests of the corporation and make full disclosure to the corporation of any personal interest in, and potential benefit to be derived from, any of the business she transacts for the corporation.

> **Example:** If the promoter arranges for the sale of property to the corporation in which she has an ownership interest, the fact of such ownership interest and any potential benefit she plans to make on the sale must be disclosed to the board.

> **Promoter Liability:** The corporation is not bound by the promoter's contracts with third persons prior to actual formation of the corporation unless they are later ratified by the board of directors or the corporation accepts the benefits of the contract (uses office space under a promoter-signed lease). The promoter, on the other hand, may be held personally liable on these pre-incorporation contracts unless they are signed by the promoter for and in the name of the corporation and the promoter clearly informs the third party that the corporation does not yet exist, may never come into existence and, even if it does, may not ratify the contract.

> **So, a Bit of Advice:** If you want to arrange for office space, hire employees, or borrow money

before your corporation is formed, make it clear to the people you are dealing with that any commitments you make are for and in the name of a proposed corporation and are subject to ratification by the corporation when, and if, it comes into existence. The other party may, of course, refuse to do business with you under these conditions and tell you to come back after the nonprofit corporation is formed.

E. Directors

The directors are given the authority and responsibility for managing the nonprofit corporation. The directors meet and make decisions collectively as the board of directors. A California nonprofit corporation must have one or more directors. The Nonprofit Corporation Law does not impose residency or age requirements on directors (you may have out-of-state directors). However, to avoid contractual problems, directors should be over the age of eighteen.

> **Religious Corporations:** Religious corporations may set up their own rules, in the Articles or Bylaws, for the tenure, election, selection, designation, removal and resignation of directors.

> **Delegation of Authority:** The Nonprofit Corporation Law permits the board to delegate, by resolution, most of the management of the nonprofit corporation to an executive committee consisting of two or more directors. This arrangement is often used when one or more directors are unable or unwilling to assume an active voice in corporate affairs and the remaining directors wish to assume full control. The passive directors should still keep an eye on what the other directors are up to since the courts have been known to hold passive directors liable for mismanagement by active directors. The board of directors may also delegate management of the day-to-day operations of the nonprofit corporation to a management company or committee of the corporation or other persons,

provided that these people remain under the ultimate control of the board. (This can be risky—consult a lawyer if you plan to do this.)

Terms of Office: The directors of a nonprofit public benefit corporation with members may serve on the board for a maximum term of three years. The directors of a public benefit corporation without members may be elected for terms of up to six years. Religious corporation directors may have such terms as are specified in their Bylaws. For both public benefit and religious corporations, if no provision is specified in the Bylaws, directors may only serve for one year. Of course, directors whose terms of office have run out may be re-elected immediately to serve an unlimited number of additional consecutive terms.

Designation of Directors: Public benefit corporations can get around this three-year (or six-year) term of office limitation by providing in their Bylaws that one or more persons [usually the more active director(s)] be allowed to designate the other directors for any prescribed term. Generally, however, public benefit membership corporations can only use this procedure to designate, rather than elect, one-third of the authorized number of directors of the corporation.

Quorum Rules: In order for the board of directors to take action at a meeting, a specified number of the total number of directors of the corporation must be present—this specified number is called a quorum. Unless otherwise provided in the Bylaws, a majority of the total number of directors represents a quorum for meetings of the board. Most smaller nonprofit corporations restate this majority quorum rule in their Bylaws, but it is legal for you to provide a lower quorum requirement subject to certain restrictions. Specifically, public benefit corporations may provide for a quorum that is not less than two directors or one-fifth of the total number of directors, whichever is larger. A one-director corporation may, of course, have a one-person quorum. Religious corporations can choose whatever lower quorum requirement they wish.

Example: A 5-director public benefit corporation may have as low as a 2-director quorum while a 15-director corporation must have no lower than a 3-person quorum.

Voting Rules: Once a quorum is present at a meeting, a specified number of votes is necessary to pass a board resolution. Unless otherwise stated in the Articles or Bylaws, the board must pass a resolution by the majority vote of the directors present at a meeting at which a quorum is present.[4]

Example: If the Bylaws of a corporation with ten board members require that a majority of the authorized number of directors be present at a meeting to represent a quorum and, further, that action may be taken by a majority of a quorum, then action at a meeting must be carried by at least four votes—a quorum of at least six (a majority of the ten-person board) must be present at the meeting, and four votes (a majority of the six-person quorum) must pass the resolution.

Note, however, that this is a minimum-vote example. If eight of the ten directors attend the meeting, action must be approved by at least five votes—a majority of those present at the meeting.

One final point: If a quorum is present initially at a meeting and one or more board members leave, resulting in the loss of a quorum, action may, in some cases, still be taken despite the loss of a quorum. The law allows action as long as you can still obtain the votes of a majority of the required quorum stated in the Bylaws. Going back to the example, above, it's clear that four votes at a meeting at which six of the ten board members are present will constitute valid action by the board. Under this initial-quorum rule, two of the six directors can leave the meeting and the four remaining votes will still be sufficient to pass a resolution. Why? Because a quorum was initially present and four board

---

[4]Certain actions taken by the board of directors must be passed without counting the votes of certain "interested" directors, e.g., self-interested transactions, indemnification of directors (more on this later).

members, representing a majority of the required quorum of six, can vote to pass the resolution.

Action by Written Consent or Conference Call: Directors may also take action without a meeting by unanimous written consent or by regular voting rules using a conference telephone hookup.

Duty of Loyalty: A director has a duty of loyalty to the corporation and usually must give the corporation a "right of first refusal" as to business opportunities he becomes aware of in his capacity as corporate director. If the corporation fails to take advantage of the opportunity after full disclosure (purchase of inexpensive land, for example) or if the corporation clearly would not be interested in the opportunity, the director can go ahead for himself.

Duty of Care: Directors have a "duty of care" to act in the best interests of the corporation. What does this mean? The Nonprofit Corporation Law doesn't help much. It says that a director must act in good faith, in a manner which such director believes to be in the best interest of the corporation, using such care, including reasonable inquiry, "as an ordinarily prudent person in a like position would use under similar circumstances" (Ever wonder what law students find to talk about for three years?) In effect, the Code leaves it up to the courts to define what type of duty a director owes a corporation. Courts, in turn, usually decide cases on an individual basis. Broadly speaking, however, the courts say honest errors in business judgment do not result in personal liability for a director, while fraudulent or grossly negligent behavior does.

Reliance on Reports: The Code allows a director to rely on the apparently reliable reports of attorneys, accountants, corporate officers, employees and committees in arriving at decisions, unless there is some indication of the need for independent inquiry by the director.

Investment Standard: A stricter standard of care applies with regard to investment decisions made by the boards of public benefit corporations (as we've already indicated, nonprofit corporations may, and often do, rely on investments for additional "tax-free" revenue). Generally, when investing assets, the directors must avoid speculation, looking instead to the permanent disposition of funds, considering the probable income, as well as the probable safety, of the corporation's capital. This stricter standard applies to the assets held by a public benefit corporation for investment. The more relaxed duty of care discussed above applies to the investment of assets by directors that are directly related to the corporation's public or charitable programs. Religious corporation directors are simply held to a duty of care for all investments of assets.

Self-Dealing Rules: Directors must also follow specific, stricter procedures in approving transactions involving the corporation and one or more directors who have a material financial interest in the transaction. If such transactions are not approved by the California Attorney General or a "disinterested" board (or committee of the board), upon a showing of certain facts, the transaction will be deemed a self-dealing transaction and may subject the directors to substantial monetary damages.

Examples: A vote by the board authorizing the corporation to lease or buy property owned by a director, or to purchase services or goods from another corporation in which a director owns a substantial amount of stock, might be considered self-dealing transactions if not properly approved since a director has a material financial interest in each transaction.

Generally, to avoid a transaction from being classified as self-dealing, the following actions must be taken or facts established:

1. The transaction is approved by the California Attorney General either before or after it is consummated; or

2. The transaction is fair and benefits the corporation and, before the transaction is actually entered into, the board (or a properly authorized

committee which obtains board ratification of its decision as soon as is practical) determines that it is the best business deal that the corporation can make and approves it with full knowledge of the economic benefit to the "interested" director. For religious corporations, the board or committee must simply determine that the transaction is fair or in furtherance of the religious purposes of the corporation.

Important: Board action to approve a deal in which a director has a personal stake must be taken without counting the interested director's vote. However, the interested director may be counted in determining whether a quorum is present in order to hold the meeting.

The safest way to handle a situation where there is an interested director is to obtain the Attorney General's approval[5] ahead of time. If you do this you will know that your transaction is legal before it goes through.

If you don't seek the approval of the Attorney General, you may wish to notify the Attorney General (as opposed to getting outright approval) of the potential self-dealing transaction. While doing this is not as good as getting approval, it does have the effect of limiting lawsuits by other directors, officers, members, or the Attorney General to two years from the date of the written notice. Without such approval or notice, a lawsuit by the Attorney General can be filed anytime up to ten years after the date of the transaction. (There is a three-year deadline for lawsuits by other parties.) In all cases involving potential self-dealing transactions, consult a lawyer as to the advisability and the best means of taking such self-interested actions.

Loans and Guarantees: A loan of money or property or a guarantee of an obligation of a director of a public benefit corporation must be approved by the Attorney General. Excluded from this requirement is the payment by the corporation of the premiums, in whole or part, on a life insurance policy for a director (this is considered a "loan") so long as repayment to the corporation of the amount of premiums paid is secured by the proceeds of the policy and its cash surrender value. Also excluded are loans made to an officer which, in the opinion of the board, are necessary to provide financing for the purchase of the principal residence of the officer in order to secure the services or continued services of the officer, as long as the loan is secured by real property in California.

Loans and guarantees given to the directors of religious corporations are not subject to this Attorney General approval requirement—they simply must be made under the general duty of care guidelines discussed above. Again, in such situations you should consult a lawyer.

---

[5]For information on seeking this approval and complying with other nonprofit reporting and filing requirements, obtain the Attorney General's *Guide for Charities*, available free from the Sacramento office of the Attorney General (part of the California Department of Justice) by calling 1-800-952-5225.

Exceptions to Self-Dealing Rules

There are a few exceptions to the self-dealing rules which allow commonplace decisions which benefit the directors to be made. The following actions may be approved by normal board action:

- A board resolution fixing the compensation of a director or officer of the corporation.

- A transaction which is part of the public or charitable (or religious) program of the corporation as long as it is approved without unjustified favoritism and benefits directors or their families because they are in the class of persons intended to be benefitted by the particular corporate program.

- A transaction involving an amount of money which is the lesser of 1% of the corporation's previous year's gross receipts or $100,000—provided that the interested director has no knowledge of the transaction.

- A transaction between the corporation and another corporation on whose board a director also sits (a common directorship), as long as the common director has no material financial interest in the transaction (e.g., doesn't own stock in the other corporation, etc.). This isn't really a self-dealing transaction since there is no financially interested director, but it comes close enough to mention it here. To be on the safe side, this type of transaction should be approved after full disclosure of all the facts and without counting the vote of the common director who sits on both boards, but the Code says it's all right to approve the transaction by normal board action as long as the contract or transaction is just and reasonable as to the corporation at the time it is authorized, approved or ratified.[6] Since dealings between nonprofit corporations and other corporations who have one or more of the same people on their boards are, indeed, common, this extra leeway often makes business dealings a bit easier.

---

[6]For religious corporations, the contract or transaction must be reasonable with respect to the corporation, taking into account the corporation's religious purposes, or must be in furtherance of its religious purposes at the time it is approved.

Tax Note: One last point about these California nonprofit corporation self-dealing rules. Don't confuse them with the more specific and restrictive self-dealing rules under the Internal Revenue Code which apply to tax-exempt nonprofit corporations which are classified as private foundations by the IRS (see Chapter 4).

Compensation: Directors normally serve on the board without compensation, although it is permissible for them to be paid (many nonprofit groups pay directors on a per-meeting basis). If compensation is to be paid, it should be reasonable and provided for in advance by a board resolution. A director may be advanced money for expenses (business travel, meeting fees, necessary publications, etc.) reasonably anticipated to be incurred in the performance of the director's duties. Likewise, a director may be reimbursed for legitimate out-of-pocket expenses authorized by the board—whether expense money is an advancement or reimbursement, it is important that you document the fact that it is authorized by a board resolution.

Special Compensation Rule for Directors of Public Benefit Corporations: Unfortunately, the Nonprofit Corporation Law restricts the practice of small public benefit corporations paying board members regular salaries (or other payments) for simultaneously serving the corporation in another capacity (e.g., directors also serving as salaried officers, employees, etc.) This restriction arises from Corporations Code Section 5227 which states that at least 51% of the board of a public benefit corporation cannot be "interested" persons. A board member is interested if she receives any money for services rendered the corporation in any other capacity (i.e., in a non-director capacity such as an officer, full- or part-time employee, independent contractor, etc.) or is related[7] by blood or marriage to such a paid person.

---

[7]Under the statute, "related" means a brother, sister, ancestor, descendant, spouse, brother-in-law, sister-in-law, son-in-law, daughter-in-law, father-in-law or mother-in-law of any such paid person.

For example, if the board of a public benefit corporation has seven directors, at least four can't be paid by the corporation in a non-director capacity or be related by blood or marriage to any other person paid by the corporation in a non-director capacity.

In other words, a public benefit corporation must have a majority of disinterested directors (51%) who:

1. Serve only on the board, or, if they serve the corporation in some other capacity, are not paid for these services and,

2. In either case, are not related to any persons who are paid for serving in any capacity for the corporation.

But remember, as we learned above, all of the directors may be paid for performing their director duties, as long as such director payment is reasonable. Since board members, generally, only attend managerial meetings (in fulfilling their duties as directors), a reasonable per meeting stipend won't amount to anything approaching a real salary.

Generally, the California Attorney General and Secretary of State interpret (and, with respect to the Attorney General, enforce) this disinterested director rule. The Attorney General's office will look over the corporation's Periodic Report form (Form CT-2) which public benefit groups must file each year and if it is apparent that the board is not constituted according to statute will, at the very least, send out a letter requiring compliance with this Code section.

The Franchise Tax Board utilizes Section 5227 in a slightly different manner to ensure that nonprofit corporations are not engaging in self-inurement (benefiting any individual associated with the corporation). Specifically, the Franchise Tax Board has added question 8(g) to its Exemption Application form (FTB 3500) to make sure that a majority of the directors are not being paid by the corporation (except as directors) and are not related to another paid director—a slightly narrower focus than the statute. Also, the Franchise Tax Board considers any relationship by blood or marriage to a paid director to be an interested relationship, not just those relationships enumerated in the statute.

Example 1: Assume your public benefit corporation has four directors: yourself, your sister Blanche, and two other unrelated persons, Bob and Ray. Also assume that Bob's brother, Alfredo, is one of the paid officers of the corporation. The other paid officers are not related to any board members. If you are getting paid for doing occasional work as an independent contractor, your board is not disinterested and doesn't meet the criteria of the Secretary of State, the Franchise Tax Board or the Attorney General. Why? Because if you are a director and are being paid in another capacity, then you are interested. Similarly, since your sister Blanche is related to a paid director, she is also interested. Consequently, only 50% of the board is disinterested and it doesn't meet the legal requirements.

Example 2: You replace Blanche with another unrelated and unpaid person and you obtain your state tax exemption [since 51% of the board (three out of four) are not paid in any other capacity and are unrelated to any paid director (you are the only paid director)]. Unfortunately, you then realize that your board is improperly constituted under the Attorney General's and Secretary of State's criteria. Why? Because, under their interpretation, two of the four directors are interested: you, because you are paid as an independent contractor; and Bob, because he is related to another person being paid by the corporation—Alfredo. (The Franchise Tax Board didn't care about Alfredo; they only wanted to ensure that Bob wasn't related to another paid director.) Consequently, Bob's brother Alfredo is replaced by another officer who is not related to any board member. Alfredo could have stayed on as an officer, but he didn't want to work for free.

Example 3: Here's another example of how this rule can plague public benefit corporations even after they've set up their initial board of directors properly and obtained their tax exemptions. Let's take the not uncommon example of a two-person board consisting of two unrelated, unpaid people who think it would be a neat idea to set up a small, public-spirited nonprofit public benefit corporation. They file the papers, get their tax exemptions, and spend most of their extra hours working diligently to keep the corporation going. From time to time they consult the spouse of one of the directors who is a lawyer and who, like them, believes in their goals and works for free. Eventually, a major project comes along which requires a lot of outside legal help. This time the board decides that it's only fair to make at least a token payment to the lawyer for all the legal work involved with the new project. Whoops! The spouse of the lawyer just became an interested person since he is related to someone (the lawyer) who was paid (even once) by the corporation. Since there are only two people on the board, only 50% of the board (one person) remains disinterested and the board is now improperly constituted. As you can see, Section 5227 contains more than a few surprises and pitfalls for the unwary.

Larger nonprofit corporations and those which rely on grant funds (where even stricter conflict of interest rules often apply) will already be familiar with director compensation limitations. For smaller groups, however, the 51% rule may require that they look for a few extra (unrelated) people to fill directors' positions so that the more active directors can also be paid salaries as officers, employees, etc. (Remember, no more than 49% can be paid this way.)

Penalties: If a director violates one of the above rules, in that he grossly mismanages or takes advantage of the nonprofit corporation, receives unauthorized or unwarranted compensation, or approves unlawful self-dealing transactions, loans or distributions, the director may be held personally liable to the corporation or members for any financial loss caused by these prohibited activities, and, possibly, be subject to criminal penalties. In some cases, even directors who abstain from voting

on unfair or unlawful transactions can be held financially liable.

Insurance and Indemnification: A nonprofit corporation can purchase insurance to cover a director's legal expenses, judgments, fines and settlements incurred in connection with a lawsuit or other proceeding brought against the director for either a breach of duty to the corporation, or simply because of her status as a director of the corporation (although director-or-officer liability insurance can be costly and is sometimes difficult to obtain). Insurance cannot, as a matter of California law, be purchased to cover any liability which arises from breaking the self-dealing rules discussed above. Insurance coverage or not, a nonprofit corporation must reimburse (indemnify) a director for legal expenses, including attorney's fees, if the director wins the suit.

The rules become a bit more complicated if the director seeks indemnification for expenses incurred in lawsuits involving self-dealing transactions or for other amounts (e.g., judgments, fines, settlements) arising out of actions brought by the corporation itself or the California Attorney General. There are also problems with indemnification whenever a director loses a lawsuit. Generally, however, these amounts may be paid by the corporation if the board, membership, or the court approves such payment and finds that the director was acting in good faith and in a manner he believed to be in the best interests of the nonprofit corporation.

Special Personal Immunity Rules for Volunteer Directors: Many nonprofit corporations will wish to elect outside directors to their boards or policy making committees to take advantage of the special expertise of these individuals, increase community involvement in their corporation, and demonstrate to the IRS that their nonprofit activities are overseen by a cross-section of community leaders. This helps the corporation obtain tax-exempt 501(c)(3) status and public charity status— see Chapters 3 and 4. Furthermore, many smaller public benefit corporations wishing to compensate the active, paid directors of the corporation will have to bring in outside volunteer directors in order to meet the special compensation rule for directors of public benefit corporations as explained above.

Special provisions of the Nonprofit Corporation Law help you do this. There are two basic provisions which provide this protection. Let's look at each.

Section 5239: Here we look at a statute applicable to public benefit corporations.[8] Similar provisions exist which protect the volunteer directors and officers of religious and mutual benefit corporations.[9] Let's look at the basic requirements of this section.

Section 5239 states that there shall be no personal liability to a third party on the part of a volunteer director or volunteer executive officer of a public benefit nonprofit corporation caused by the director's or officer's negligent act or omission in the performance of that person's duties as a director or officer if all of the following conditions are met:

1. The act or omission was within the scope of the director's or executive officer's duties;

2. The act or omission was performed in good faith;

3. The act or omission was not reckless, wanton, intentional or grossly negligent; and

[8]Section 5047.5 is another, somewhat duplicative, section of the California Corporations Code that gives personal immunity to volunteer directors and officers of 501(c)(3) nonprofits. To qualify under this section, a corporation with an annual budget of less than $50,000 must take out a general liability insurance policy of at least $500,000. Larger corporations are required to be insured for at least $1 million.

[9]For similar provisions applicable to California religious corporations, see Section 9247 of the California Corporations Code. Somewhat different volunteer director immunity rules apply to California mutual benefit nonprofit trade, professional and labor organizations—see Section 7231.5 of the Code.

Also Note: Section 425.15 of the California Code of Civil Procedure provides special procedural protections for the volunteer directors and officers of *non-501(c)(3)* nonprofit corporations organized to provide charitable, educational, scientific, social or other forms of public services that are tax exempt under subsections (1), (4), (5), (7) or (19) of Section 501(c) of the Internal Revenue Code (see the table in Chapter 3 for a chart of these special-purpose organizations). Before a lawsuit can be personally filed against directors and officers of these corporations based upon their allegedly negligent acts or omissions, the court must determine that the person seeking to file the lawsuit "has established evidence that substantiates the claim."

4. Damages caused by the act or omission are covered by a liability insurance policy issued to the corporation, either in the form of a general liability policy or a directors' and officers' liability policy, or a policy issued personally to the director or executive officer. Note, however, that even if the damages are not covered by such a liability insurance policy, volunteer directors and executive officers can still be exempt from personal liability for damages to third parties if conditions 1-3 above have been met and if the board of directors and the person (director or executive officer) seeking personal immunity "had made all reasonable efforts in good faith to obtain available liability insurance" but were unable to do so (more on what this means later).

The statute defines a few of the above terms:

• The statute contains a definition of how a small nonprofit corporations can show that it has made "all reasonable efforts in good faith to obtain available liability insurance." Specifically, for 501(c)(3) public benefit nonprofits with annual budgets of less than $25,000 (we know this sounds small but many nonprofits fit within this category), they meet this test if they make at least one inquiry per year to purchase a general liability policy (further defined to mean asking for a premium quote for coverage of at least $500,000), and the policy costs as much as or more than 5% of the nonprofit's annual budget for the previous year.

Example: The Better Books Network has an annual budget of $20,000. The Treasurer calls a nonprofit insurance broker and gets a quote for $500,000 worth of general liability coverage at a cost of more than $1,000 (more than 5% of the nonprofit's previous annual budget). Under the statute, they qualify as having made a reasonable effort to obtain insurance. They don't have to take the policy—they just have to be able to show that they asked for and obtained

this quote (by making a note in the corporate records and, if possible, attaching a faxed or written copy of the quote obtained from their insurance broker).

They must obtain similar quotes for all years in which they hope to take advantage of this statutory escape hatch.

• "Volunteer" means "the rendering of services without compensation." "Compensation" means "remuneration whether by way of salary, fee or other consideration for services rendered." However, the statutes make it clear that the payment of a per diem, mileage, or other reimbursement of expenses to a director or executive officer does not affect the person's status as a volunteer. Therefore, your volunteer directors can be paid these reimbursement amounts and still be considered volunteers for purposes of these personal immunity rules.

• An "executive officer" means the president, vice president, secretary or treasurer of the nonprofit corporation, or an individual who serves in a similar capacity, if the officer also "assists in establishing the policy of the corporation." Therefore, if your corporation has any volunteers fill these top-level officer positions and they help set policy for the corporation (e.g., the board appoints these officers to policy making committees), they can qualify for personal immunity under this section, at least with respect to their policy making decisions (the legislative analysis of the bill enacting this section indicates that this legislation "is not intended to cover day-to-day ministerial actions of corporate employees").

A few additional points to keep in mind:

First, although the volunteer director or officer may be granted personal immunity under this section in a lawsuit brought against the director or officer, the corporation itself is still liable for these damages (whether it is insured or not).

Second, these special rules only apply to third party lawsuits for monetary damages. The volunteer director or officer may still be held personally liable to the corporation under the normal standard of care discussed earlier for his negligent performance of duties, breach of fiduciary duty, violation of the self-dealing rules, etc., in direct corporate lawsuits—those brought by or in the name of the corporation by the other directors, by the members, or by the Attorney General—against the director or officer. Also, personal protection is not provided in lawsuits where another form of relief is sought other than monetary damages (such as restitution). These types of suits are less likely to occur but do happen where directors negligently abuse their corporate responsibilities.

Third, to repeat a point made above, you will want to be able to show a court that you've made all reasonable efforts in good faith to obtain insurance. If you qualify for the small corporation definition covered above (annual budget less than $25,000), and you have not purchased insurance, you will want your corporate records to show that you made at least one inquiry each year for $500,000 in general liability coverage, and that the quotes received equaled or exceed 5% of your annual budget for the prior year. Larger nonprofits that don't qualify for

this special rule should get one or more quotes per year for coverage and, if they are unable to get coverage at a reasonable cost, keep a record of the dates of their contacts with insurance brokers, agents and companies, the types and amounts of coverage sought, and quotes or responses received from each contact. Documentation of this sort should also be kept if a larger nonprofit ends up getting less insurance than it originally sought. The corporate records should also refer to any efforts of the volunteer directors and officers to obtain liability insurance for themselves (remember, the statute says that volunteers must also have made all reasonable efforts to obtain coverage).

Summing Up this Section: This section may come in very handy in the beginning years of your nonprofit corporation's existence (when attracting outside volunteer managerial assistance can be critical to your survival) since underwriters of nonprofit director and officer liability insurance may deny such liability coverage in any amount during the first year of corporate life. In these instances, this section may indeed provide personal immunity for your volunteer directors and officers at a time when you need it most. Note that the fine print in this section says that the small corporation definition of reasonable efforts described above will apply to the first year of operation of a new corporation as long as the corporation's first-year budget does not exceed $25,000.

Warning: Current California nonprofit immunity provisions are a hodgepodge of overlapping requirements, and the Nonprofit Section of the State Bar has been trying to consolidate these important provisions into one section of law. New nonprofit director and officer immunity legislation can be expected each year until these requirements are cleaned up. Please check with your nonprofit insurance broker or agent, look at the California Nonprofit Corporation Code in your local library, or ask a nonprofit lawyer to keep current on these changing rules.

F. Officers

A California nonprofit corporation must have three officers: a President (or chairperson of the board), a Secretary, and a Treasurer (as the chief financial officer in the Nonprofit Corporation Law). One person may fill one or more of the officer positions except that the person or persons who hold(s) the offices of Secretary and Treasurer cannot also be the President (or chairperson of the board). The Nonprofit Corporation Law does not contain officer residency or age requirements.

Authority: Officers (president, vice president, secretary, treasurer) are in charge of carrying out the day-to-day business of the corporation. Their powers, duties and responsibilities are set by the Articles, Bylaws, or by resolution of the board of directors. Officers owe a fiduciary duty to the corporation and must act honestly and in the best interests of the corporation. This day-to-day authority of officers does not automatically include authority to enter into major business transactions (e.g., the mortgage or sale of corporate property— these are left within the province of the board of directors). If the directors desire that the officers have the power to make one or more major business decisions, special authority should be delegated by board resolution. Officers are considered agents of the corporation and can subject the corporation to liability for their negligent or intentional acts which cause damage to people or property if such acts were performed within the course and scope of their employment. The corporation, moreover, is bound by the contracts and obligations entered into or incurred by the corporate officers if they had legal authority to transact the business. This authority can be actual authority (a Bylaw provision or resolution by the board of directors), implied authority (a necessary but unspecified part of duties set out in the Bylaws or a board resolution), or apparent authority (a third party reasonably believes the officer has the authority).

Apparent authority can be far-reaching. Generally, the Nonprofit Corporation Law allows a third party to rely on the signature of the president, vice president, secretary or assistant secretary, treasurer or assistant treasurer on any written instrument, whether or not this officer has any actual or implied authority to sign the instrument on the part of the corporation, as long as the third party did not actually know that the corporate officer didn't have the authority to sign it.

Note: Of course, any act performed by an officer without the legal authority discussed above binds the corporation if the corporation accepts the benefits of the transaction or if the board of directors ratifies it after the fact.

Compensation: Corporate officers may be compensated for services they perform for the nonprofit corporation. Remember, only 49% of the directors of public benefit corporations may also serve as salaried officers. The compensation must be reasonable and given for services actually rendered the corporation.

Loans, Guarantees, Insurance and Indemnification, etc.: The rules that apply to director loans and guarantees (discussed in the preceding section) are also applicable to officers. Officers, like directors, can be insured or indemnified against personal liabilities under the insurance and indemnification rules discussed earlier. Also note that volunteer executive officers (President, Vice President, Secretary, Treasurer) are entitled to the same personal immunity as volunteer directors under the special rules discussed above.

G. Members

Membership vs. Non-Membership Corporations: The term "member" has a special, limited legal definition quite different from its common-usage meaning. Specifically, a member is a person who is given the right in the Articles of Incorporation or Bylaws to vote for the election of directors, for the sale of substantially all of the assets of the

corporation, for a merger or dissolution of the corporation. A legal member is also a person who is specifically referred to as a member in the Articles or Bylaws. These members are, as a matter of law, given other fundamental rights regarding major corporate decisions (see below). In California the majority of nonprofit corporations are set up as non-membership corporations, often to avoid the problem of having major decisions subject to membership approval (e.g., election of directors, amendment of Article and Bylaw provisions, dissolution of the corporation, etc.).

Consequently, although it's common to loosely refer to many "interested people" associated with a nonprofit corporation (who may or may not pay annual dues or other fees) as "members" and to give them certain rights to participate in corporate affairs (positions on advisory committees, special attendance privileges at performances or benefits, discount rates for services, etc.), they are not legal members unless they are specifically granted one or more of the "legal-member" powers set out in the previous paragraph. To add to the confusion, the Nonprofit Corporation Law specifically allows you to refer to these interested people as members in your Bylaws. But, to repeat the basic point, these interested people will not be considered legal members of your corporation (no matter what you call them)—you won't need to get their vote whenever the law says an act must or may be taken or approved by the membership—unless they have the power to vote for the election of directors, for the sale of substantially all of the assets, to merge or dissolve the corporation, or to amend the Articles or Bylaws. Throughout the remainder of this book we will refer to nonprofit corporations with legal members as ones having a "formal membership," or as "membership corporations." We will refer to corporations who have interested people (whether they're called members or not) participating in corporate activities who are not given legal membership voting rights as having a "non-formal" membership or as "non-membership corporations."

Directors May Act as Members: If your corporation does not have formal members, the directors are not considered members but may take their place and vote on matters for which the

Nonprofit Corporation Law would normally require formal membership approval. This legal provision allowing directors to act in the place of members (as opposed to acting also as members) eliminates the need for directors to hold a separate meeting, putting on "membership hats" to approve a matter which is normally subject, under law, to membership approval—only one director meeting is necessary in a non-membership corporation to approve such matters. The directors may, in a non-membership corporation, approve these membership actions by regular board approval—normally by a majority of a quorum vote—even if the Code requires greater membership approval.

Quorum: A quorum for a membership corporation (the number of members necessary to take action at a meeting) is set by the Nonprofit Corporation Law as a majority of all members unless the Bylaws provide for a different number (which may be greater or less than a majority). If you provide for a membership quorum of less than one-third of all the members, then special notice of members' meetings rules will apply if less than one-third of the members actually attend a members' meeting (these are discussed later).

Voting: If you do provide for a formal membership structure, in the absence of a provision to the contrary in the Articles or Bylaws, each member has one vote. You may set up one or more classes of membership with different voting rights, privileges, preferences, restrictions or conditions. You may also set up a formal membership structure and a non-formal membership structure—for example, a large botanical society might have one class of formal members who elect the board of directors, as well as a non-formal membership consisting of persons who receive the society's magazine and newsletters.

Expulsion: A member may not be expelled unless it is done "in good faith and in a fair and reasonable manner." The Nonprofit Corporation

Law[10] provides a specific procedure which public benefit nonprofit corporations may use to be sure that their procedure for expulsion of a member is fair and reasonable. (We've included this procedure in the Bylaw provisions for public benefit membership corporations contained in this book.) Note that the law doesn't answer the question as to what constitutes a good faith reason for expulsion—it only addresses questions of procedure. There have been a number of court cases which have ruled on the fairness of specific bases for expelling members, but there's no general rule. If a question involving the expulsion of members arises, see a lawyer.

Participation in Corporate Decisions: If a member is given the voting rights of a formal member, then the member is empowered, by law, to participate in certain corporate affairs. The following is a list of actions which voting members may take, either unilaterally or in conjunction with the board of directors. (Note that the following rules do not necessarily apply to religious corporations—religious corporations are given considerable flexibility with respect to deciding, on their own, what the members can or cannot do—for further information, see Chapter 6, Step 5D.)[11]

1. **Election and Removal of Directors:** As already mentioned, directors of a membership corporation are elected by the members. The election must take place at a regular membership meeting or, subject to some exceptions, be by written ballot. Regular meetings of members should, therefore, coincide with the time for re-election of directors. The law requires, as mentioned above, that the members be given reasonable nomination and election procedures

and provides explicit rules for such nomination and election procedures.

Special meetings of members for the purpose of removing directors may be called by 5% or more of the members. If the corporation has less than 50 members, removal of directors must be approved by a majority of all members. Normal vote requirements apply to removal of directors if the corporation has 50 or more members.

2. **Amendment of Bylaws:** The voting members may, on their own, adopt, amend, or repeal provisions of the Bylaws. This can be done by unanimous written consent, written ballots received from at least a quorum of members, or by a majority of a quorum vote at a meeting. Since a quorum for a membership meeting (the number of members present at a meeting necessary to take any action) may, as mentioned above, be greater or less than a majority of the total membership voting power, a relatively small percentage of membership votes may be sufficient to change the Bylaws.

---

[10]Corporations Code Sections 5521-5527.

[11]It is important to read the information in this section, but not to get bogged down. Most nonprofit corporations are non-membership corporations, which means that they have no voting members and decision-making is relatively simple.

Example: If a nonprofit corporation has twenty voting members, each with one vote, and the Bylaws require that less than a majority (eight) be present at a meeting to represent a quorum, then five members may change the Bylaws at a meeting.

We think it is wise for the Bylaws to contain higher quorum and voting requirements when it comes to changing the Bylaws—amending the Bylaws is a major decision and should be decided by a substantial number of members of the corporation.

Note: Once formal members have been admitted, a Bylaw or Bylaw amendment fixing or changing the authorized number of directors may only be passed by the members (according to the above rules), and not by the board.

3. **Amendment of Articles:** With few exceptions, members must also approve a board resolution to amend the Articles of Incorporation, following normal membership voting rules.

4. **Approval of Merger or Consolidation:** The principal terms of an agreement to merge or consolidate the nonprofit corporation with another corporation must, generally, be approved by the members.

5. **Election to Wind Up and Dissolve the Corporation:**

   a. Voluntary Dissolution: A majority of all members (not just a majority of members present at a meeting at which a quorum is present) may, unilaterally, elect to voluntarily dissolve the corporation for any reason. The board of directors in conjunction with normal membership approval (the votes of a majority of a quorum) may also elect to voluntarily dissolve the corporation. In a few special cases, the board may, on its own, elect to dissolve the corporation without obtaining

membership approval. Of course, the directors can make the election to dissolve on their own if the corporation has no members.

   b. Involuntary Dissolution: Lesser membership vote requirements are imposed for an involuntary dissolution—one elected for specific reasons, usually indicating a failure on the part of the corporation to effectively carry out its corporate purposes. The grounds for involuntary dissolution and other information relevant to involuntarily dissolving a nonprofit corporation are provided in Section J2 of this chapter. For an involuntary dissolution, at least one-third of the votes of all members is required. (You can't count the votes of members who have participated in any of the acts which form the basis for requesting involuntary dissolution.)

6. **Sale of Corporate Assets:** Members of a nonprofit corporation must approve a board resolution to sell substantially all of the corporation's assets, unless the sale is made for the purpose of securing the payment or performance of any corporate contract, note, bond or obligation, or is in the regular course of business (this latter exception won't normally apply—few nonprofit corporations are organized for the purpose of selling corporate assets).

7. **Approval of Transaction Involving Interested Director or Officer:** The members may approve a resolution allowing indemnification of directors.

Other Membership Attributes: The Nonprofit Corporation Law also contains the following provisions relating to formal members:

• The rights of a member cease upon his death, termination from membership or dissolution of the corporation.

• A member may resign at any time.

• A member cannot transfer for value (sell) his membership or any and all rights which arise from such membership to another person.

• Admission fees, dues or assessments may be levied against a member to initially enroll and maintain membership in the corporation according to provisions contained in the Articles or Bylaws.

• As already mentioned, for the corporation to obtain nonprofit corporate status, members may not receive any of the gains or profits of the corporation. For purposes of the state and federal tax exemptions, moreover, members and any other individuals associated with the nonprofit corporation may not receive any part of the net earnings of the corporation (with some major exceptions such as salaries for working for the corporation, etc.).

• The corporation must maintain a membership book containing the name, address and the class of membership, if applicable, of each member.

Memberships and the Securities Law: Memberships in a nonprofit corporation are considered "securities" and, as such, are regulated by provisions of the Administrative Code overseen by the California Commissioner of Corporations.

The importance of this latter classification of memberships as securities is that, normally, the offer to sell or sale of securities requires the approval of the Commissioner of Corporations, often involving the preparation and filing of complicated and costly documents relating to the sale of securities and the financial condition of the corporation. Obtaining such approval is called "qualifying" the sale of securities with the Commissioner of Corporations and, as you might guess, most small corporations wish to avoid having to qualify their securities.

Fortunately, nonprofit corporations eligible for their federal tax exemption under Section 501(c)(3) of the Internal Revenue Code [and the parallel state tax exemption under Section 23701(d) of the California Revenue & Taxation Code] will, in most cases, be eligible for an automatic exemption from qualifying the issuance of their memberships. The requirements for this automatic exemption are:

1. The issuer (nonprofit corporation) must be organized exclusively for educational, benevolent, fraternal, religious, charitable, social or reformatory purposes, and not for profit;

2. No part of the net earnings of the issuer is allowed to inure to the benefit of any member or other individual; and

3. The promoters of the nonprofit corporation must not expect, intend to, or actually make a profit directly or indirectly from any business or activity associated with the organization or operation of the nonprofit organization or from remuneration received from such nonprofit corporation.

These requirements are basically the same as the requirements for obtaining your federal tax exemption, so you shouldn't have any trouble meeting them. In fact, these requirements are a little looser than the Section 501(c)(3) (the federal tax exemption) requirements in allowing additional purposes (e.g., such as social, fraternal or reformatory purposes). Requirement 3 above simply prohibits the use of paid promoters.

Federal Securities Law Note: Section 3(a)(4) of the federal Securities Act also exempts from registration with the Securities and Exchange Commission securities (memberships) which meet requirements 1 and 2 above (except that memberships issued by a group organized and operated for social purposes are not exempt).

H. Employees

Generally, an employee is a person who works for and under the supervision of the corporation and is paid compensation (a salary) in return for services rendered the corporation. According to this definition, salaried officers are employees of the corporation and are treated as such by the IRS and California tax authorities for purposes of employment taxes and employee benefits. (We have treated the officers separately since they are treated as unique employees by the Nonprofit Corporation Law with special duties and responsibilities.)

Responsibilities: Employees are not subject to the duties associated with director or officer positions. They are, however, expected to perform the services of their position "in good faith." If they cause financial loss to the corporation or to outsiders while acting within the scope of their employment, they are, generally, not personally liable for any financial loss. If the harm is done to outsiders, it is the corporation, not the employees, which must assume the burden of paying for the loss. If they are not acting in good faith (fraudulent transactions) or within the scope of their employment (performing duties outside of the normal job functions given them by the officers), they may be held personally liable for any financial loss caused the corporation or outsiders. This would be the case, for instance, if a teacher at a dance studio went berserk, ran into the street and started choking passers-by with his leotard.

Exception: An important exception to this rule of non-liability exists with respect to any employee whose duties include reporting or paying federal or state corporate or employment taxes. The particular employee who is given this responsibility can be held personally liable for failure to report or pay such taxes. (The IRS takes a broad view as to who is "responsible" for such duties—see Chapter 11C.)

Individual Income Taxes: Employees are, of course, personally liable for, and must report and pay, state and federal individual income taxes for salaries or other compensation paid to them for services rendered the corporation (this includes salaried officers).

Compensation: Salaries, whether paid to officers or regular employees, should be reasonable and given in return for services actually rendered the nonprofit corporation. If salaries are unreasonably high, they are apt to be treated as a simple distribution of the net earnings of the corporation and jeopardize the tax-exempt status of the nonprofit corporation. So, a bit of advice: provide for payment of salaries in advance, making them reasonable—an amount which is roughly equal to that received by employees rendering the same services elsewhere (of course, nonprofit personnel often work for unreasonably low salaries). In any case, try to avoid the payment of discretionary bonuses at the end of a good year—this may look like a payment from the earnings and profits of the corporation, a no-no for nonprofits.

Benefits: Among the major benefits associated with being an employee of a corporation are the employment benefits available to employees. These are, in some cases, more favorable than those allowed non-corporate employees. Benefits (which are deductible by a nonprofit corporation if taxes are owed by the corporation in connection with an activity which uses the services of these employees) include corporate pension plans, corporate medical expense reimbursement plans and corporate group accident, health, life and disability insurance. Generally, amounts paid by the corporation to provide for these benefits (such as the payment of insurance premiums by the corporation) are not included in the employee's individual gross income and, therefore, not taxed to the employee. Also, the benefits themselves (insurance proceeds, etc.) are often not taxed when the employee receives them. These corporate employee benefits can sometimes be an important reason for forming a nonprofit corporation.[13]

Employment Taxes: Generally, nonprofit corporations are subject to the payment of withholding of employment taxes (Social Security,

---

[13]Nonprofits may also establish profit-sharing plans and similar arrangements—see IRC § 401(a)(27). Tax-exempt nonprofits may not, however, set up 401(k) plans (qualified cash or deferred arrangements—§ IRC 401(k)(4)(B). For information on setting up qualified employee plans and other benefits, consult your tax advisor.

unemployment insurance, state disability insurance, state and federal withholding taxes). In some cases, certain nonprofit corporations or employees are exempt from payment of certain employment taxes.

I. How Many People Must Organize a California Nonprofit Corporation?

At Least One Incorporator: The Nonprofit Corporation Law states that a California nonprofit corporation may be formed by one or more persons (incorporators or directors) who must execute (sign and date) the Articles of Incorporation.

At Least One Director: Regardless of who prepares and signs the Articles, a California nonprofit corporation must have at least one director (nonprofit corporations typically have three or more directors). The initial directors of the corporation may be named in, and may execute, the Articles—this is the procedure we use in this book. Preparing the Articles this way avoids having to hold an incorporators' meeting for the purpose of electing the initial directors.

At Least Three Officers: A California nonprofit corporation must have three officers: a President (or Chairperson of the board), a Secretary, and a Treasurer (called, in the Nonprofit Corporation Law, the Chief Financial Officer). Most nonprofit corporations also appoint a Vice President.

Members are Optional: The corporation may or may not have any formal members in addition to the directors, as discussed in Section G above. If the corporation's Articles or Bylaws provide for members, there is no requirement as to the minimum number of members who must be admitted to membership in the corporation.

To Review: A nonprofit corporation must have at least one director and three officers. This doesn't mean that you necessarily need four different people to form and operate your corporation. A director may also fill one or more of the officer positions. See, however, the President restriction discussed below. Remember, however, that a majority of the directors of public benefit corporations cannot be paid, so these corporations need to add unpaid directors to the board if they want a paid director (a director who will be paid as a officer).

Example: If you want your public benefit corporation to have one paid director, you'll need two additional unpaid directors; if you want two paid directors, you'll need additional unpaid directors, etc. Also, these additional unpaid directors must also be unrelated—they cannot be related by blood or marriage to persons who are paid in any capacity by the corporation (again, see Section E above).

President Restriction: There is a restriction, however, on how many officer positions can be filled by one person (e.g., filled by one director). Specifically, one person may fill one or more of the officer positions except that the person or persons who hold(s) the offices of secretary and treasurer cannot also be the president (or chairperson of the board). Therefore, you'll need at least two different people to fill the officer positions, e.g., one to be president and one to be secretary-treasurer.

More Is Often Better: The above discussion concerns itself with only the minimum number of people you'll need to form and operate your

corporation under California law. For practical reasons, almost all nonprofit corporations are managed by at least three directors and have at least four officer positions: a president (or chairperson of the board), a vice president, and a secretary-treasurer—filled by three people who answer to, rather than serve on, the board. We've simply given you the minimum legal requirements you should take into account when you look for people to run and manage your nonprofit corporation. Subject to complying with these minimum requirements, the details here are left to you.

J. How Much Money Must You Start With?

The California Nonprofit Corporation Law corporation law does not contain minimum capitalization requirements—you are not required to have a specified amount of money in the corporate bank account before commencing corporate operations. Nonetheless, your financial resources should be adequate to insure that you can handle any foreseeable initial liabilities arising from your corporation's activities. Why? Because if you wish courts to treat you as a corporation with limited liability for corporate principals, you must plan and carry out your operations with adequate financial reserves.

Except for a few "hybrid" nonprofit corporations such as a consumer or producer cooperative, nonprofit corporations cannot issue shares, nor can public benefit or religious nonprofit corporations make the kind of distributions allowed profit corporations (dividends, liquidation of assets to members upon dissolution). However, the fact that nonprofit corporations cannot provide these investment incentives to members does not mean that they have no way to raise start-up funds. Nonprofit corporations are allowed to include provisions in their Articles or Bylaws for one or more classes of members. This allows the corporation to obtain money in return for membership fees and dues. However, the decision to set up a formal membership nonprofit corporation usually rests more with the desirability of having members participate in corporate affairs than it does with using membership dues as a way to raise money.

Whether or not your nonprofit corporation derives revenue from a formal membership structure, there are still numerous ways of obtaining funds. The most common means include obtaining initial money from the incorporators, "seed" money from outside grant agencies, and by receiving revenue from the public for activities related to your exempt purposes (payments for art lessons, dance courses, etc.). Also, you may decide to borrow funds from a bank (for newly-formed corporations, a bank loan must normally be secured by the personal assets of the incorporators). Finally, you may be incorporating an existing organization—in this case the assets of the pre-existing organization are usually transferred to the new corporation. As you can see, despite the inability to "stock" its coffers with money obtained by issuing shares, there are ways that a nonprofit corporation can, with the usual amount of forbearance and obstinacy required to start any enterprise, raise sufficient money to begin initial operations.

K. Dissolution of a Nonprofit Corporation

We'll end our discussion of the legal provisions affecting California nonprofit corporations with a short summary of the Nonprofit Corporation Law provisions related to dissolving (ending) the corporation. The primary point to keep in mind here is that a California Nonprofit corporation may be dissolved by mutual consent (in a voluntary dissolution) with a minimum of formality. The forms to effect a voluntary dissolution are contained in the Secretary of State's *Corporations Check List*

(available at a small charge from the Sacramento office of the Secretary of State).

We've already looked at membership rights regarding voting to dissolve the corporation, involuntarily or voluntarily. Here we look at these two procedures generally, including director voting requirements as well as the bases upon which these procedures may be invoked.

1. Voluntary Dissolution

Any nonprofit corporation may, on its own motion and out of court, elect to voluntarily wind up and dissolve by the approval of all of the members or by regular membership and board approval, for any reason.

In addition, the board of directors of a public benefit corporation may elect to dissolve the corporation, without membership approval, if any of the following conditions apply (the rules are essentially the same for religious corporations):

- The corporation has no members;

- The corporation has not commenced business and has not issued any memberships;

- The corporation has been adjudged bankrupt;

- The corporation has disposed of all its assets and hasn't conducted any activity for the past five years;

- A subsidiary corporation is required to dissolve because its charter from a head organization has been revoked.

Note: Voluntary dissolution may, upon the request of the nonprofit corporation, at least 5% of the members, three or more creditors, or the Attorney General, be subject to court supervision.

2. Involuntary Dissolution

One-third of the membership votes of a nonprofit corporation, one-half of the directors, or the California Attorney General may file a petition for involuntary dissolution. The petition must be filed in the Superior Court of the county of the corporation's principal office and be based upon the following grounds:

- The nonprofit corporation has abandoned its activities for more than one year;

- The nonprofit corporation has an even number of directors who are equally divided and cannot agree to the management of its affairs, so that the corporation's business cannot be conducted to advantage, or so that there is danger that its property and business (exempt-purpose activities) will be impaired and lost, and the members are so divided into factions that they cannot elect an odd-numbered board;

- The members have been unable, at two consecutive meetings (or in two written ballots), where full voting power has been exercised, or during a four-year period, whichever period is shorter, to elect successors to directors whose term has expired or would have expired upon election of their successors;

- There is internal dissension and two or more factions of members are so deadlocked that the corporation's activities can no longer be conducted to advantage;

- Those in control of the nonprofit corporation (e.g., the directors) have been guilty of or knowingly allowed persistent and pervasive fraud, mismanagement or abuse of authority, or the corporation's property is being misapplied or wasted by its directors or officers;

- Liquidation is reasonably necessary since the corporation is failing and has continuously failed to carry out its purposes;

- The limited period (if this applies) for which the corporation was formed has terminated without extension of such period; or

- In the case of a subordinate corporation created under the authority of a head organization, the Articles of Incorporation of the subordinate corporation require it to dissolve because its charter has been surrendered to, taken away, or revoked by the head organization.

The office of the California Attorney General can also bring an action for involuntary dissolution of the corporation based upon the office's own information or upon the complaint of any private person, for any of the following reasons:[14]

- The corporation has seriously violated any provision of the statutes regulating corporations or charitable organizations;

- The corporation has fraudulently abused or usurped corporate privileges or powers;

- The corporation has, by action or default, violated any provision of law which specifically authorize the forfeiture of corporate existence for noncompliance; or

- The corporation has failed for five years to pay to the California Franchise Tax Board any tax for which it is liable.

In certain situations, the corporation may take corrective action to avoid a dissolution initiated by the Attorney General.

---

[14]Generally, no provision for the involuntary winding up of a religious corporation is provided in the Nonprofit Corporation Law except that the Attorney General may institute an action, under Section 9230 of the Religious Corporation Law and under the procedural formalities of Section 803 of the Code of Civil Procedure, to seek a judicial determination that the corporation is not properly qualified or classified as a religious corporation.

3. Winding Up Corporate Business and Distribution of Assets

In any voluntary or involuntary dissolution, the corporation must cease transacting business except to the extent necessary to wind up its affairs, pending a distribution of its assets. All corporate debts and liabilities, to the extent of corporate assets, must be paid or provided for. If any corporate assets remain after paying corporate debts, a 501(c)(3) tax-exempt nonprofit corporation must, as we'll see, distribute them to another 501(c)(3) group. Also, if (as is provided for in the forms in this book) the corporation complies with Section 214 of the California Revenue and Taxation Code to obtain personal and real property tax exemptions, it must distribute any such remaining tax-exempt property to the particular type of 501(c)(3) group specified in the "irrevocable dedication" clause of the Articles.

Involuntary and voluntary dissolutions subject to Superior Court supervision must include the publication of a notice to creditors of the corporation. Creditors not filing claims within a specified period of time from such publication are barred from participating in any distribution of the assets of the corporation.

This doesn't mean you can't organize and operate a nonprofit corporation on your own (we obviously believe you can), or that you should suffer mental anguish wondering whether the tax man or Attorney General will be beating down your corporate door. The great majority of small, sensibly run nonprofit corporations will never face any major problems. It does mean that you should use your own judgment as to when and why to pay a financial or legal advisor to answer specific questions related to your individual problems. The fact that you can competently do many things on your own doesn't mean that you will never need to see an accountant or lawyer.

L. Summing Up—More Questions?

Hopefully, this chapter on the basic legal provisions affecting California nonprofit corporations has answered more questions than it has raised. We couldn't (and at this stage you probably wouldn't want us to) include a complete corporate law course here. Our goal is to give you an an appreciation of some of the legalities surrounding nonprofit corporations, as well as an awareness that corporations are closely regulated by statute, subject to scrutiny by courts, and that there are certain problem areas which may require the advice of a tax or legal expert.

Chapter 3

THE FEDERAL 501(C)(3) NONPROFIT INCOME TAX EXEMPTION

CORPORATIONS, LIKE INDIVIDUALS, are subject to federal and state income taxation. One reason for establishing a nonprofit corporation is to be exempt from paying corporate income taxes. Exemption is not automatic—a corporation must apply and show that it is in compliance with nonprofit exemption requirements to receive it. This chapter focuses on the basic federal tax exemption available to nonprofits under Section 501(c)(3) of the Internal Revenue Code. The requirements for an exemption from payment of state corporate income taxes parallel the federal requirements and are discussed in Chapter 7.

A. Special-Purpose Nonprofit Tax Exemptions

Before looking at the IRC §501(c)(3) tax exemption provisions, let's glance at some special tax exemption categories contained in other sections of the Internal Revenue Code. Table 3.1 contains a listing of these special tax exemption categories, with a brief description of each type of organization, the IRS exemption application used to apply for the exemption, the annual information return applicable to each group, and whether or not contributions to each organization are tax deductible.

As you can see, these nonprofits are very narrowly defined and chances are that these categories do not apply to you. If, after scanning over this table, you think that you may wish to form one of these special nonprofit groups rather than a 501(c)(3) corporation, you should consult a nonprofit professional or do your own research. IRS Publication 557 and IRS Form 1024 contain additional information and instructions on forming some of these special-purpose nonprofits.

Humane Societies and Sports Organizations

Groups organized for the prevention of cruelty to children or animals or fostering national or international amateur sports competitions can also claim a 501(c)(3) tax exemption. However, these groups must meet narrowly defined 501(c)(3) requirements, and, for humane societies, special state requirements. See IRS Publication 557 for specifics on each of these special 501(c)(3) groups and contact your state attorney general's office for special incorporation requirements for humane societies.

B. 501(c)(3) Nonprofit Tax Exemption

IRC §501(c)(3) exempts from payment of federal income taxes groups organized and operated exclusively for charitable, religious, scientific, literary, and educational purposes. The Articles of Incorporation of a 501(c)(3) group must limit corporate purposes to one or more allowable 501(c)(3) purposes and must not empower the corporation to engage, other than as an insubstantial part of its activities, in activities not in furtherance of one or more of these tax-exempt purposes. This formal requirement is known as the 501(c)(3) *organizational test*. The tear-out Articles you will prepare as part of Chapter 6 contain language which will assure the IRS that you meet the organizational test of the 501(c)(3) tax exemption.

Multiple 501(c)(3) Purposes Are Permitted: It is common and permissible for a group to engage in more than one 501(c)(3) tax-exempt activity. For example, its activities may be characterized as charitable or educational, or both, such as a school for blind or physically handicapped children.

Cross Purposes Are Not Allowed: It is not permissible to engage simultaneously in 501(c)(3) exempt purpose activities and in activities exempt under other 501(c) subsections. So while you may perform charitable and educational functions together [both are valid 501(c)(3) purposes), you cannot, for example, form a 501(c)(3) for both educational and social or recreational purposes [the latter two purposes are exempt under IRC §501(c)(7)]. This problem rarely occurs, as the non-Section 501(c)(3) subsections are custom-tailored to very specific types of organizations (such as war veterans organizations and cemetery companies).

Nonprofit Purposes—Sometimes Simply a Matter of Definition

You'll notice in going through the material in this section that many IRS tax-exemption criteria are generally stated and seemingly applicable to a wide range of activities, commercial and non-commercial alike. In fact, this is often the case. For instance, many nonprofit scientific organizations perform research that would qualify as 501(c)(3) scientific research in the public interest. Similarly, many commercial publishing houses publish educational materials that could qualify for a 501(c)(3) tax exemption. The dividing line between commercial and tax-exempt activities becomes further blurred by the fact that tax-exempt organizations may charge a reasonable fee for their services and products (and, indeed, may make a profit from pursuing their tax-exempt purposes).

So how does the IRS decide whether a particular organization is tax exempt? The answer lies in the very act of applying for a tax exemption. By defining and organizing your activities as nonprofit, tax-exempt activities, you agree to give up any proprietary interest in the enterprise and irrevocably dedicate organizational assets to tax-exempt purposes. This, in itself, evidences your nonprofit intent and purpose and distinguishes your activities from similar commercial endeavors.

C. 501(c)(3) Tax-Exempt Purposes

Now let's take a closer look at the most common 501(c)(3) purposes and the requirements associated with each.[1]

1. Charitable Purposes

Benefit to the Public: The word "charitable" as used in Section501(c)(3) is broadly defined to mean "providing services beneficial to the public interest." Note that this definition is considerably broader than the traditional meaning of the term, "the relief of poverty or distress." In fact, other 501(c)(3) purpose groups—501(c)(3) educational, religious and scientific groups—are often also considered charitable in nature since their activities usually benefit the public.

Groups which seek to promote the welfare of specific groups of people within the community (e.g., services for handicapped or elderly persons or members of a particular ethnic group) or which seek to advance other exempt activities (e.g., environmental education) will generally be considered to be organized for charitable purposes since these activities can be viewed as benefiting the public at large and are charitable in nature.

Charitable Class: A charitable organization must be set up to benefit an indefinite class of individuals, not particular persons. However, the number of beneficiaries may be relatively small as long as the benefited class is open and the identities of the beneficiaries are not specifically listed.

---

[1]For an in-depth discussion and analysis of the requirements that apply to each type of 501(c)(3) nonprofit, supplemented annually with the latest IRS and court rulings in each area, see *The Law of Tax-Exempt Organizations* by Bruce R. Hopkins, published by John Wiley & Sons, New York, N.Y. (check a nonprofit resource center library).

Table 3.1   Special Nonprofit Tax Exempt Organizations

IRC §	Organization and Description	Application Form	Annual Return	Deductibility of Contributions[1]
501(c)(1)	FEDERAL CORPORATIONS corporations organized under an Act of Congress as federal corporations specifically declared to be exempt from payment of federal income taxes.	No Form	None	Yes, if made for public purposes
501(c)(2)	CORPORATIONS HOLDING TITLE TO PROPERTY FOR EXEMPT ORGANIZATIONS corporations organized for the exclusive purpose of holding title to property, collecting income from property, and turning over this income, less expenses, to an organization which, itself, is exempt from payment of federal income taxes.	1024	990	No
501(c)(4)	CIVIL LEAGUES, SOCIAL WELFARE ORGANIZATIONS OR LOCAL EMPLOYEE ASSOCIATIONS civic leagues or organizations operated exclusively for the promotion of social welfare, or local associations of employees, the membership of which is limited to the employees of a particular employer within a particular municipality, and whose net earnings are devoted exclusively to charitable, educational or recreational purposes. Typical examples of groups which fall under this category are volunteer fire companies, home owners or real estate development associations, or employee associations formed to further charitable community service.	1024	990	Generally, No[2]
501(c)(5)	LABOR, AGRICULTURAL OR HORTICULTURAL ORGANIZATIONS organizations of workers organized to protect their interests in connection with their employment (e.g., labor unions) or groups organized to promote more efficient techniques in production or the betterment of conditions for workers engaged in agricultural or horticultural employment.	1024	990	No
501(c)(6)	BUSINESS LEAGUES, CHAMBERS OF COMMERCE, ETC. business leagues, chambers of commerce, real estate boards or boards-of-trade organized for the purpose of improving business conditions in one or more lines of business.	1024	990	No
501(c)(7)	SOCIAL AND RECREATIONAL CLUBS clubs organized for pleasure, recreation, and other nonprofit purposes, no part of the net earnings of which inure to the benefit of any member. Examples of such organizations are hobby clubs and other special interest social or recreational membership groups.	1024	990	No
501(c)(8)	FRATERNAL BENEFICIARY SOCIETIES groups which operate under the lodge system for the exclusive benefit of their members, which provide benefits such as the payment of life, sick or accident insurance to members.	1024	990	Yes, if for certain 501(c)(3) purposes
501(c)(9)	VOLUNTEER EMPLOYEE BENEFICIARY ASSOCIATIONS associations of employees which provide benefits to their members, enrollment in which is strictly voluntary and none of the earnings of which inure to the benefit of any individual members except in accordance with the association's group benefit plan.	1024	990	No
501(c)(10)	DOMESTIC FRATERNAL SOCIETIES domestic fraternal organizations operating under the lodge system which devote their net earnings to religious, charitable, scientific, literary, educational or fraternal purposes and which do not provide for the payment of insurance or other benefits to members.	1024	990	Yes, if for certain 501(c)(3) purposes
501(c)(11)	LOCAL TEACHER RETIREMENT FUND ASSOCIATIONS associations organized to receive amounts received from public taxation, from assessments on the teaching salaries of members, or income from investments, to devote solely to providing retirement benefits to its members.	No Form[3]	990	No

IRC §	Organization and Description	Application Form	Annual Return	Deductibility of Contributions[1]
501(c)(12)	BENEVOLENT LIFE INSURANCE ASSOCIATIONS, MUTUAL WATER AND TELEPHONE COMPANIES, ETC. organizations organized on a mutual or cooperative basis to provide the above and similar services to members, 85% of whose income is collected from members, and whose income is used solely to cover the expenses and losses of the organization.	1024	990	No
501(c)(13)	CEMETERY COMPANIES companies owned and operated exclusively for the benefit of members solely to provide cemetery services to their members.	1024	990	Generally, Yes
501(c)(14)	CREDIT UNIONS credit unions and other mutual financial organizations organized without capital stock for nonprofit purposes.	No Form[3]	990	No
501(c)(15)	MUTUAL INSURANCE COMPANIES certain mutual insurance companies whose gross receipts are from specific sources and are within certain statutory limits.	1024	990	No
501(c)(16)	FARMERS' COOPERATIVES associations organized and operated on a cooperative basis for the purpose of marketing the products of members or other products.	No Form[3]	990	No
501(c)(19)	WAR VETERAN ORGANIZATIONS posts or organizations whose members are war veterans, formed to provide benefits to their members.	1024	990	Generally, No[4]
501(c)(20)	GROUP LEGAL SERVICE ORGANIZATIONS organizations created for the exclusive function of forming a qualified group legal service plan.	1024	990	No
501(c)(25)	TITLE HOLDING COMPANY a corporation or trust organized to acquire, hold title to and collect income from real property and remit it to tax-exempt organizations that are shareholders or beneficiaries. Participation in the trust is limited to certain qualified plans, government entities and 501(c)(3) organizations.	1024	990	No
501(d)	RELIGIOUS AND APOSTOLIC ORGANIZATIONS religious associations or corporations with a common treasury which engage in business for the common benefit of members. Each member's share of the net income of the corporation is reported on his individual tax return. This is a rarely used section of the Code used by religious groups which are ineligible for 501(c)(3) status because they engage in a communal trade or business.	No Form	1065	No
521(a)	FARMERS' COOPERATIVE ASSOCIATIONS farmers', fruit growers' and like associations organized and operated on a cooperative basis for the purpose of marketing the products of members or other producers, or for the purchase of supplies and equipment for members at cost.	1028	990-C	No

For specific information on the requirements of several of these special-purpose tax exemption categories, see IRS Publication 557, *Tax-Exempt Status for Your Organization.*

1 An organization exempt under a subsection of IRC Section 501 other than (c)(3)—the types listed in this table—may establish a fund exclusively for 501(c)(3) purposes, contributions to which are deductible. Section 501(c)(3) tax-exempt status should be obtained for this separate fund of a non-501(c)(3) group. See IRS Publication 557 for further details.

2 Contributions to volunteer fire companies and similar organizations are deductible, but only if made for exclusively public purposes.

3 Application is made by letter to the key District Director.

4 Contributions are deductible if 90% or more of the members are war veterans.

Examples: A nonprofit corporation established to benefit an impoverished individual, Jeffrey Smith, is not charitable under 501(c)(3). But one whose general charitable purpose is to benefit needy individuals in a particular community is a charitable organization and may select Jeffrey Smith as a beneficiary. A foundation that awards scholarships solely to undergraduate members of a designated fraternity has been held to be a charitable organization even though the number of members in the benefited group or class is small.

Services Need Not Be Free: 501(c)(3) charitable organizations are not required to offer services or products free or at cost. However, doing so, or at least providing services at a substantial discount from the going commercial rate, helps convince the IRS of the group's bona fide charitable intentions. Charging full retail prices for services or products usually demonstrates little benefit to the public.

Examples of Valid Charitable Purposes: Here are examples from IRS regulations of valid 501(c)(3) charitable activities and purposes:

- relief of the poor, distressed or underprivileged;
- advancement of religion;
- advancement of education or science;
- erection or maintenance of public buildings, monuments or works;
- lessening the burdens of government;
- lessening neighborhood tensions;
- elimination of prejudice and discrimination;
- promotion and development of the arts;
- defense of human and civil rights secured by law;
- providing facilities and services to senior citizens;
- maintaining a charitable hospital;

- providing a community fund to support family relief and service agencies in the community;
- providing loans for charitable or educational purposes;
- maintaining a public interest law firm.

The following are specific examples of activities that have been held to be tax-exempt 501(c)(3) charitable activities:

Assistance to Low Income Families: An organization formed to build new housing and to renovate existing housing for sale to low income families on long-term, low payment plans; also, a day care center for children of needy working parents.

Self-Help Programs: A group created to market the cooking and needlework of needy women; a self-help housing program for low income families.

Assistance to the Aged: Homes for the aged where the organization satisfies the special needs of an aged person for housing, health care and financial security. The requirements for housing and health care will be satisfied if the organization is committed to maintaining residents who become unable to pay and if services are provided at the lowest possible cost.

Ministering to the Sick: An organization that takes care of patients' non-medical needs (reading, writing letters, etc.) in a privately-owned hospital.

Rescue and Emergency Services: An organization that provides emergency and rescue services for stranded, injured or lost persons; a drug crisis center and a telephone hotline for persons with drug problems.

Legal Assistance to Low Income Families: A legal aid society offering free legal services to indigent persons.

2. Religious Purposes

Groups falling within this category include general types of religious organizations and more formal institutionalized churches. Let's look at general religious-purpose (non-church) organizations first.

Qualifying as a 501(c)(3) Religious Organization

Traditionally, the IRS and the courts have been reluctant to question the validity or sincerity of religious beliefs or practices. As long as the organization's belief appears to be "truly and sincerely held" and the practice and rituals associated with it are not illegal or against public policy, the IRS generally does not challenge the validity of the religious tenets or practices. However, the IRS will question the nature and extent of religious activities (as opposed to religious beliefs) if they do not appear to foster religious worship or advance a religious purpose, or if they appear commercial in nature.

Examples: A group which holds weekly meetings and publishes material celebrating the divine presence in all natural phenomena should qualify as a religious purpose group. An organization which sells a large volume of literature to the general public, some of which has little or no connection to the religious beliefs held by the organization, may be regarded by the IRS strictly as a regular trade or business, not as a tax-exempt religious organization.

Belief in a Supreme Being Is Not Necessary: A religious group need not profess belief in a Supreme Being to qualify as a religious organization under 501(c)(3). The Supreme Court has stated that serious Constitutional difficulties would result if 501(c)(3) were interpreted to exclude those beliefs that do not encompass a Supreme Being in the conventional sense, such as Taoism, Buddhism and Secular Humanism.[2]

Advancement of Religion: Activities that advance religion are exempt under 501(c)(3)—the IRS is likely to classify these activities as charitable and religious (the advancement of religion is also classified as a charitable purpose). Here are specific examples of activities that have been held to advance religion under 501(c)(3):

Monthly Newspaper: The publication and distribution of a monthly newspaper carrying church news of interdenominational interest accomplishes a charitable purpose by contributing to the advancement of religion.

Coffee House: A nonprofit organization formed by local churches to operate a supervised facility known as a coffee house, in which persons of college age are brought together with church leaders, educators, and leaders from the business community for discussions and counseling on religion, current events, social and vocational problems was held to be advancing religion and thus exempt under 501(c)(3).

Genealogical Research: An organization formed to compile genealogical research data on its family members in order to perform religious observances in accordance with the precepts of their faith was held to be advancing religion.

Missionary Housing: A group established to provide temporary low-cost housing and related services for missionary families on furlough in the

---

[2]Saint Germain Foundation, 26 T.C. 648 (1956).

U.S. from their assignments abroad was held to be operated exclusively for charitable purposes.

Qualifying as a 501(c)(3) Church

You can also qualify under the 501(c)(3) religious-purpose category as a church, but doing so is more difficult to accomplish than qualifying simply as a 501(c)(3) religious organization. One of the advantages of qualifying as a church is that these organizations automatically qualify for 501(c)(3) *public charity status*—a status which all 501(c)(3) groups will want to obtain, as we explain in Chapter 4. [3]

How the IRS Defines a Church: Under IRS rulings, a religious organization should have the following characteristics to qualify as a church (not all are necessary but the more the better):

- a recognized creed or form of worship;

- a definite and distinct ecclesiastical government;

- a formal code of doctrine and discipline;

- a distinct religious history;

- a membership not associated with any other church or denomination;

- a complete organization of ordained ministers;

- a literature of its own;

- established places of worship;

- regular congregations;

- regular religious services.

---

[3] The Internal Revenue Service is developing a guide designed to assist churches and clergy in complying with the requirement of the Internal Revenue Code. The publication is intended to be a "user-friendly" compilation, set forth in question-and-answer format. A draft copy of the guide, tentatively titled *Tax Guide for Churches and Other Religious Organizations*, is available at no charge from the Internal Revenue Service by asking for it by name and sending your request in writing to: Freedom of Information Reading Room, P.O. Box 795, Ben Franklin Station, Washington, DC 20044. Most church and religious-purpose groups will find the information in this material extremely helpful when preparing their federal exemption application (see Chapter 9).

Courts have used similar criteria to determine whether or not a religious organization qualifies as a church. For example, the U.S. Tax Court[4] has looked for the presence of the following "church" factors:

- services held on a regular basis;

- ordained ministers or other representatives;

- a record of the performance of marriage, other ceremonies, and sacraments;

- a place of worship;

- some support required from members;

- formal operations;

- satisfies all other requirements of federal tax law for religious organizations.

All religious-purpose groups claiming church status must complete a special IRS schedule containing specific questions on some of the church characteristics listed above when preparing their federal tax exemption application. We discuss this application and the special church schedule in Chapter 9.

Traditional churches, synagogues, associations or conventions of churches (and religious orders or organizations that are an integral part of a church and engaged in carrying out its functions) may qualify as a 501(c)(3) church without difficulty. Less traditional and less formal religious organizations may have a harder time. Such groups may have to answer additional questions to convince the IRS that they qualify as a tax-exempt church.

Church Audits: Some churches stand a greater chance of being audited by the IRS than others. Not surprisingly, the IRS is more likely to examine and question groups that promise members substantial tax benefits for organizing their households as tax-deductible church organizations.

---

[4] *Pusch v. Commissioner*, 39 T.C.M. 838 (1980), affirmed 628 F. 2d 1353 (5th Cir. 1980).

3. Scientific Purposes

Tax-exempt status is allowed to groups that engage in scientific research carried on in the public interest. Under IRS regulations, research incidental to commercial or industrial operations (such as the normal inspection or testing of materials or products or the design or construction of equipment and buildings) does not qualify under IRC §501(c)(3).

Public Interest Research: Generally, research is considered in the public interest if the results (including any patents, copyrights, processes or formulas) are made available to the public (i.e., if the scientific research is published for others to study and use); if the research is performed for the United States or a state, county or city government; or if the research is conducted to accomplish one of the following purposes:

- aiding in the scientific education of college or university students;

- discovering a cure for a disease;

- aiding a community or region by attracting new industry, or by encouraging the development or retention of an existing industry.

Example: A research organization, operated by a group of physicians specializing in heart defects and investigating the causes and treatment of cardiac and cardiovascular conditions and diseases, was recognized as an exempt 501(c)(3) scientific organization. The physicians practiced medicine apart from the organization's research program; although some of their private patients were accepted for study, they were selected on the same criteria as other patients; the organization's facilities were maintained separately from private practice facilities and were used exclusively for research.

Another Example: Clinical testing of drugs for pharmaceutical companies was held not to be "scientific" under § 501(c)(3) since the clinical testing in question was incidental to a pharmaceutical company's commercial operations.

If you are applying for a scientific exemption under IRC 501(c)(3), your responses to the narrative portions of the federal exemption application (covered in Chapter 9) should show that your organization is conducting public interest research and should provide the following information:

- an explanation of the nature of the research;

- description of past and present research projects;

- how and by whom research projects are determined and selected;

- who will retain ownership of control of any patents, copyrights, processes, or formulas resulting from the research.

This and other specific information required to be submitted to the IRS by scientific groups is listed on page 14 of IRS Publication 557.

4. Literary Purposes

This is a seldom-used 501(c)(3) category, since most literary-purpose nonprofits are classified as educational by the IRS. Nevertheless, valid 501(c)(3) literary purposes include traditional literary efforts such as publishing, distribution, book sales, etc., which are directed toward promoting the public interest rather than engaging in a commercial literary enterprise or specifically serving the interests of particular individuals (such as the proprietors of a publishing house). Generally, this means that literary material must be available to the general public and must pertain to the betterment of the community. Beyond paying reasonable salaries, profits must be put to use for nonprofit purposes.

What distinguishes public interest publishing from a private publishing house? A combination of factors. If you publish materials that are clearly educational and make them available to the public at cost (or at least below standard commercial rates), then you stand a chance of qualifying as a 501(c)(3) organization. However, if your material seems aimed primarily at a commercial market and is sold at standard rates through regular commercial channels, chances are that your literary organization will be viewed by the IRS as a regular business enterprise ineligible for a 501(c)(3) tax exemption.

Example: Publishing of material promoting highway safety or the education of handicapped children qualify as bona fide 501(c)(3) literary purposes. Publishing efforts more private than public in nature—publishing textbooks at standard rates for example—will have difficulty qualifying as tax-exempt literary activities under Section 501(c)(3).

An IRS Literary Organization Ruling: A nonprofit publishing house applied for its 501(c)(3) exemption. It published only books (tracts actually) related to esoteric Eastern philosophical thought. The books were to be sold commercially but at modest prices. The IRS granted the tax exemption after requesting and reviewing the manuscript for the nonprofit's first publication. Apparently, the IRS agreed that the material was sufficiently specialized to render it non-commercial in nature.

5. Educational Purposes

501(c)(3) tax-exempt educational purposes are broad, encompassing instruction for both self-development and for the benefit of the community. The IRS allows advocacy of a particular intellectual position or viewpoint if there "is a sufficiently full and fair exposition of pertinent facts to permit an individual or the public to form an independent opinion or conclusion. However, mere presentation of unsupported opinion is not (considered)

educational." If the group takes political positions, it may not qualify.

Example: If an educational group publishes a newsletter with a balanced analysis of an issue (or at least with some room devoted to debate or presentation of opposing opinions), this should qualify as a 501(c)(3) tax-exempt activity. If its newsletter is simply devoted to espousing one side of a issue, platform or agenda, tax exemption may be denied or revoked.

Educational exempt-purpose activities include:

- publishing public interest educational materials;

- conducting public discussion groups, forums, panels, lectures, workshops, etc.;

- offering a correspondence course or one that uses other media such as television or radio;

- a museum, zoo, planetarium, symphony orchestra, performance groups, etc.;

- serving an educational institution, such as a college bookstore, alumni association or athletic organization;

- publishing educational newsletters, pamphlets, books or other material.

Formal School Not Necessary: To qualify as a 501(c)(3) educational organization a group need not provide instruction in traditional school subjects, nor, for that matter, organize itself as a formal school facility with a regular faculty, established curriculum and a regularly enrolled student body .

501(c)(3) Private School Non-Discrimination Requirements

If you do set up a 501(c)(3) private school, you must include a non-discrimination statement in your Bylaws and must publicize this statement to the community served by the school. [In an 8 to 1 ruling, the U.S. Supreme Court upheld the validity of these private school non-discrimination rules. *Bob Jones v. U.S.*, 433 CCH S.Ct. Bull. B2702 (1983)].

Essentially, this statement must make it clear that the school does not discriminate against students or applicants on the basis of race, color or national or ethnic origin.

For further information on these IRS private school anti-discrimination rules and procedures, see IRS Publication 557.

Additional Federal and State School Requirements: People setting up non-traditional schools should remember that although they do not need a regular faculty, full-time students nor even a fixed curriculum to qualify for a 501(c)(3) educational purpose tax exemption, as a practical matter they may need all of these things to qualify for state or federal support, to participate in federal student loan programs and to obtain accreditation.

Child Care Centers: Providing child care outside the home qualifies as a 501(c)(3) educational purpose under special provisions contained in IRC §501(k) if:

- the care enables parent(s) to be employed; and

- the child care services are available to the general public.

However, a child care facility that gives enrollment preference to children of employees of a specific employer will not be considered a 501(c)(3) educational-purpose organization.

D. Other Tax Exemption Requirements

In addition to being organized for one or more allowable tax-exempt purposes, a 501(c)(3) must meet other requirements.

1. Insubstantial Unrelated Activities Requirement

A 501(c)(3) nonprofit may not substantially engage in activities unrelated to the group's tax-exempt purposes. Or, put affirmatively, this means that your nonprofit corporation may conduct activities not directly related to its exempt purposes as long as they don't represent a substantial portion of total organizational activities. This leeway is granted in recognition of the fact that most nonprofits may need to do unrelated business in order to survive. For example, a nonprofit dance group might rent unused portions of its studio space to an outside group to use for storage. Another nonprofit may invest surplus funds to augment the income of the organization.

Most groups need not be overly concerned with this limitation unless activities unrelated to exempt purposes come to involve a significant amount of the group's energy or time, or if they produce "substantial" income. If these activities are themselves nonprofit, they should be included in the organization's exempt purposes and be classified as related activities. The IRS keeps an eye out for tax-exempt groups that regularly engage in profit-making businesses with little or no connection to their exempt purposes (i.e., a church running a truck company). Business activities necessary to implement the group's exempt purposes, such as hiring and paying employees, and paying rent for space used for the group's exempt purpose or activities, are considered related activities.

Most new nonprofits work full-time simply tending to their exempt purposes and do not explore unrelated money making activities until later, if at all. However, if you plan to engage in unrelated business from the start, be careful. It's hard to pin down exactly when such activities become substantial enough to jeopardize the corporation's tax-exempt status. Also, income derived from unrelated business activities is subject to federal and state corporate income tax, even if it is not substantial enough to affect the group's 501(c)(3) tax-exempt status.

2. Limitation on Private Inurement (Profits and Benefits)

No 501(c)(3) nonprofit corporation may be organized or operated to benefit individuals associated with the corporation (directors, officers, or members) or other persons or entities related to, or controlled by, these individuals (such as another corporation controlled by a director). In tax language, this limitation is known as the "prohibition on private inurement" and means that 501(c)(3) groups can't pay profits to, or otherwise benefit, private as opposed to public interests.

Two specific 501(c)(3) requirements implement this prohibition on self-inurement:

- no part of the net earnings of the corporation may be distributed to individuals associated with the corporation; and

- the assets of a 501(c)(3) group must be irrevocably dedicated to another exempt group.

These requirements are basically the same as the state law requirements that apply to California public benefit and religious corporations. Note that the IRS and the state allow the payment of reasonable salaries by the corporation to directors, officers, employees or agents of the corporation for services rendered the corporation in furtherance of its exempt purposes.

Payment of reasonable salaries to directors, officers, employees or agents for services rendered the corporation in furtherance of its exempt purposes is allowed.

3. Limitation on Political Activities

501(c)(3) tax-exempt nonprofit corporations are absolutely prohibited from participating in political campaigns for or against any candidate for public office.[4] Participation in or contributions to political campaigns can result in the revocation of 501(c)(3) tax-exempt status and the assessment of special excise taxes against the organization and its managers.[5]

Influencing Legislation: Tax-exempt 501(c)(3) nonprofit organizations are also prohibited, "except to an insubstantial degree," from acting to influence legislation.[6] Generally, if a nonprofit corporation contacts, or urges the public to contact, members of a legislative body, or if it advocates the adoption or rejection of legislation, the IRS considers it to be acting to influence legislation.

Also, under IRS regulations, lobbying to influence legislation includes:

- any attempt to affect the opinions of the general public or a segment of it; and

- communication with any member or employee of a legislative body, or with any government official or employee who may participate in the formulation of legislation.

---

[4]Certain voter education activities conducted in a non-partisan manner may be undertaken by 501(c)(3) groups—see IRS Revenue Ruling 78-248 at your local county law library and consult an attorney for recent developments on this issue if you want to engage in this type of political activity. Your organization may request an IRS letter ruling on its voter education activities by writing to the address listed in IRS Publication 557, Chapter 3, section on "Political Activity."

[5]See IRC §§ 4955, 6852 and 7409.

[6]In the past, courts have said that the expenditure of more than 5% of the corporation's budget, time or effort for political activity was "substantial"—more recently, the courts have tended to look at the individual facts of each case.

However, lobbying to influence legislation does not mean:

- making available the results of nonpartisan analysis, study, or research;

- providing technical advice or assistance to a government body, or to its committee or other subdivision, in response to a written request from it, where such advice would otherwise constitute the influencing of legislation;

- appearing before, or communicating with, any legislative body with respect to a possible decision that might affect the organization's existence, powers, tax-exempt status, or the deduction of contributions to it;

- communicating with a government official or employee, other than for the purpose of influencing legislation.

Also excluded from the definition of lobbying efforts are communications between an organization and its members with respect to legislation (or proposed legislation) of direct interest to the organization and the members, unless these communications directly encourage members to influence legislation.

Example: A Housing Information Exchange keeps its members informed of proposed legislation affecting low income renters. This should not be considered legislative lobbying activity unless members are urged to contact their political representatives in support of, or in opposition to, the proposed legislation.

In determining whether a group's legislative activities are substantial in scope, the IRS looks at the amount of time, money or effort expended on legislative lobbying. If they are substantial in relation to other activities, 501(c)(3) tax status may be revoked and, again, special excise taxes can be levied against the organization and its managers.[7]

The Alternative Political Expenditures Test: Since it is impossible to know ahead of time how the IRS will assess the "substantiality" of a group's legislative activity, the IRC allows 501(c)(3) public charities (as you'll see in Chapter 4, we assume you will qualify for public charity classification), to elect an alternative "expenditures test" to measure permissible legislative activity.[8]

Example: If your nonprofit corporation plans to do considerable lobbying activity, carried on primarily by unpaid volunteers, then electing the expenditures test might be a good idea. Why? Because the minimal outlay of money to engage in these activities will probably keep you under the applicable expenditure limits. If you didn't make this election, your 501(c)(3) tax exemption might be placed in jeopardy if the IRS considered your political activities to be a substantial part of your overall purposes and program.

---

[7]See IRC § 4912.

[8]This expenditures test and its provisions for lobbying and grassroots expenditures are not available to churches, an integrated auxiliary of a church, a member of an affiliated group of organizations which includes a church, or to private foundations.

Political Expenditures Test

Under the political expenditures test in IRC § 501(h), limitations are imposed on two types of political activities: lobbying expenditures and grassroots expenditures.

Lobbying expenditures are those made for the purpose of influencing legislation, while grassroots expenditures are those made to influence public opinion.

For examples of activities within these categories, read the section on *Lobbying Expenditures* in IRS Publication 557. The monetary limits are different for each category, and the formulas for computing them are somewhat complicated.

If your 501(c)(3) nonprofit elects the political expenditures test, you must file IRS form 5768, *Election by an Eligible Section 501(c)(3) Organization to Make Expenditures to Influence Legislation*, within the tax year in which you wish the election to be effective. This election is also available under similar rules at the state level.

If you plan to engage in more than a minimum amount of political lobbying or legislative efforts, you need to decide whether it is to your advantage to elect the expenditures test based on the facts of your situation. If you find that these alternative political expenditures rules are still too restrictive,[9] you might consider forming a social welfare organization or civic league[10] under IRC Section 501(c)(4)—this exemption requires a different federal exemption application, IRS Form 1024, and does not carry with it all the attractive benefits of 501(c)(3) status (access to grant funds, tax deductible contributions, etc.). See Table 3.1 above and IRS Publication 557 for further information on 501(c)(4) organizations.

---

[9]Federally funded groups may be subject to even more stringent political expenditure tests than those discussed here (for example, political activity and expenditure restrictions imposed by the federal Office of Management and Budget).

[10]Note that 501(c)(4) social welfare organizations and civic leagues, like 501(c)(3) nonprofits, are considered public benefit corporations under California law.

Political Action Organizations: Another way the IRS can challenge a 501(c)(3) group's political activities is to determine that it is an action organization, one so involved in political activities that *it is not organized exclusively for a 501(c)(3) tax-exempt purpose,* and then revoke its tax-exempt status.[11] Intervention in political campaigns or substantial attempts to influence legislation, as discussed above, are grounds for applying this sanction. In addition, if a group has the following two characteristics, it will be classified as an action organization and lose its 501(c)(3) status:

1. its main or primary objective or objectives—not incidental or secondary objectives—may be attained only by legislation or defeat of proposed legislation; and

2. it advocates or campaigns for the attainment of such objectives rather than engaging in nonpartisan analysis, study, or research and making the results available to the public.

In determining whether a group has these characteristics, the IRS looks at the surrounding facts and circumstances, including the group's Articles and activities, and its organizational and operational structure.

---

[11]Unlike the penalties mentioned earlier for excess political expenditures, a group classified as an action organization may apply for and qualify as a 501(c)(4) social welfare group.

The point here is to be careful not to state your exempt purposes in such a way that they seem only attainable by political action. Even if you indicate that your activities will not be substantially involved with legislative or lobbying efforts, the IRS may decide otherwise and invoke this special classification to deny or rescind 501(c)(3) status.

Example: A group that has a primary purpose of "reforming the judicial system in the United States" will likely sound like a political action organization to the IRS since this sounds like a political goal which must be accomplished mostly by political means. However, if the group rephrases its primary purpose as "educating the public on the efficacy of mediation, arbitration and other alternative non-judicial dispute resolution mechanisms," it stands a better chance of having the IRS approve its application, even if it lists some political activity as incidental to its primary educational purpose.

Chapter 4

501(C)(3) PUBLIC CHARITIES
AND PRIVATE FOUNDATIONS

IN THIS CHAPTER we discuss one of the most difficult areas of nonprofit tax law: qualifying for 501(c)(3) public charity status. You'll see that it is essential to do this to avoid falling into the less favorable tax status of a 501(c)(3) private foundation. Private foundations are subject to special operating rules and restrictions which most nonprofits find unworkable; public charities avoid these limitations.

This chapter covers the most technical and cumbersome part of the nonprofit incorporation process. We wish we could skip this technical area of 501(c)(3) tax law. However, since you will encounter the distinction between public charity and private foundation tax status when you fill out your federal tax exemption application, it's important to come to terms with this material. For now it is enough to read this material through to get a general understanding. Then later, as part of Chapter 9 when you focus on the details of how to prepare your federal tax exemption application, we will ask you to return to this chapter to re-read the sections you'll need.

Why Bother with Internal Revenue Code Sections?

On the federal 501(c)(3) tax exemption application, the different public charity classifications are identified by reference to specific Internal Revenue Code (IRC) sections. We include these IRC sections throughout this chapter to help you understand and fill out the federal form. Don't let the numbers distract you—they're included for reference, not intimidation.

In Chapter 9 we show you how to cross-reference each IRS public charity classification and IRC section to the simple three-part public charity classification used in this chapter.

A. The Importance of Public Charity Status

All 501(c)(3) tax-exempt nonprofit corporations are classified by the IRS as either private foundations or public charities. Initially, and this is the important point, *they are presumed to be private foundations*. This is not in your best interests. Most 501(c)(3) groups would find it impossible to operate under the restrictions imposed on 501(c)(3) private foundations. In short, you must overcome this presumption and show how you qualify as a public charity on your federal 501(c)(3) tax exemption application.[1]

Before looking at how to qualify as a public charity, let's look at the basic characteristics and treatment of private foundations and public charities under Section 501(c)(3).

B. Private Foundations— Background

Broadly speaking, the reason that private foundations are subject to strict operating limitations and special taxes, while public charities are not, is to counter tax abuse schemes by wealthy individuals and families. Before the existence of private foundation restrictions, a person with lots of money could set up his own 501(c)(3) tax-exempt organization (e.g., The William Smith Foundation) with a high-sounding purpose (i.e., to wipe out the potato bug in Northern Louisiana). The potato bugs, though, were never in any danger, because the real purpose of the foundation was to hire all of William Smith's relatives and friends down to the third generation. Instead of leaving the money in a will and paying heavy estate taxes, William Smith neatly

---

[1]A few special groups are not required to apply for public charity status—the same groups that are not required to file a 501(c)(3) tax exemption application. We think it's foolhardy in most cases not to apply for, and obtain, official notification from the IRS that you are a public charity. For a discussion of this issue, see the section entitled "Should You Apply for Tax-Exempt Status?" in Chapter 9A.

transferred money to the next generation tax-free by use of a tax-exempt foundation which just happened to hire all of his relatives.

To prevent schemes such as this, Congress enacted the private foundation operating restrictions, special excise taxes and other private foundation disincentives discussed in the next section.

C. Private Foundation Rules

Let's briefly look at why private foundation restrictions are so burdensome.

1. Operating Restrictions

Here is a summary of the limitations and restrictions that apply to 501(c)(3) private foundations:

- restrictions on self-dealing between private foundations and their substantial contributors and other disqualified persons;

- requirements that the foundation annually distribute its net income for charitable purposes;

- limitations on holdings in private businesses;

- provisions that investments must not jeopardize the carrying out of the group's 501(c)(3) tax-exempt purposes; and

- provisions to assure that expenditures further the group's exempt purposes.

Violations of these provisions result in substantial excise taxes and penalties against the private foundation and, in some cases, against its managers, major contributors and certain related persons. Keeping track of and meeting these restrictions is unworkable for the average 501(c)(3) group, which is the main reason why you'll want to avoid being classified by the IRS as a private foundation.

To learn more about private foundation excise taxes, see IRS Publication 578, *Tax Information for Private Foundations and Foundation Managers.*

2. Limitation on Deductibility of Contributions

Generally, personal income tax deductions for individual contributions to private foundations are limited to 30% of the donor's adjusted gross income, whereas those to public charities are generally deductible to the extent of 50% of adjusted gross income.[2]

Note: Of course, since the overwhelming number of individual contributors do not contribute an amount even close to the 30% limit, this limitation of private foundation status is not very important. The real question of importance to contributors is whether your organization is a qualified 501(c)(3) to which tax deductible charitable contributions may be made at all.

IRS Publication 526, *Charitable Contributions,* discusses in more depth the rules limiting deductions to private foundations (called *30% limit organizations*) and public charities (*50% limit organizations*). 501(c)(3)s (both public charities and private foundations) and other qualified groups eligible to receive tax deductible charitable contributions are listed in IRS Publication 78, *Cumulative List of Organizations.*

D. Special Types of Private Foundations

The IRS recognizes two special types of private foundations that have some of the advantages of public charities: private operating and private non-operating foundations. We mention them briefly

---

[2]Special percentages apply to contributions of securities, real estate and certain types of tangible personal property. See IRS Publication 526.

below since they are included in IRS nonprofit tax publications and forms. Few readers will be interested in forming either of these special organizations.

1. Private Operating Foundations

To qualify as a private operating foundation, the organization generally must distribute most of its income to tax-exempt activities and must meet one of three special tests (an assets, support or endowment test). This special type of 501(c)(3) private foundation is allowed a few benefits not granted to regular private foundations, including the following:

- As with public charities, individual donors can deduct up to 50% of adjusted gross income on contributions to the organization.

- The organization may receive grants from a private foundation without having to distribute the funds received within one year (these funds, moreover, can be treated as "qualifying distributions" by the donating private foundation).

- The private foundation excise tax on net investment income does not apply.

All other private foundation restrictions and excise taxes apply to private operating foundations.

2. Private Non-Operating Foundations

This special type of private foundation is one that either:

- distributes all the contributions it receives to public charities and private operating foundations (discussed just above) each year; or

- pools its contributions into a common trust fund and distributes the income and corpus to public charities.

Individual contributors to private non-operating foundations may deduct 50% of their donations. However, the organization is subject to all excise taxes and operating restrictions applicable to regular private foundations.

E. How to Qualify for 501(c)(3) Public Charity Status

We have no doubt convinced you that, in the nonprofit world, being classified as a private foundation is a fate worse than death. So the burning question becomes how to be sure to qualify for public charity status. There are three basic ways to do this:

1. organize a particular type of nonprofit organization such as a church, school or hospital which automatically qualifies for public charity status (see Section F1 below);

2. receive support primarily from individual contributions, government or other public sources to qualify for public charity status as a publicly supported organization (see Section F2 below);

3. receive most of your revenue from activities related to your tax-exempt purposes to qualify under a special public charity support test that applies to many smaller nonprofits (see Section F3 below).

Here are examples of three different groups using these three different methods to qualify for public charity status.

Automatic Public Charity Status: A church that maintains a facility for religious worship would most easily obtain *automatic* public charity status (Section F1 below). A church qualifies for recognition as a public charity because of the nature of its activities rather than its sources of support.

Publicly Supported Organization: An organization to operate a center for rehabilitation, counseling, or similar services and which plans to carry on a broad-based solicitation program and depend primarily on government grants, corporate contributions and individual donations would most likely seek public charity status as a *publicly supported organization* (Section F2 below).

Support Test: An arts group deriving most of its income from exempt-purpose activities (lessons, performances, renting studio facilities to other arts groups) would probably choose the *support test* discussed in Section F3 below. This public charity test, unlike those that apply to publicly supported organizations, allows groups to count income derived from the performance of their exempt purposes as qualified support.

F. 501(c)(3) Public Charities and Their Requirements

Let's now look at each of the three primary public charity tests together with the IRC sections that apply to each. When reading this material for the first time, simply try and get a sense of which test will most likely apply to your nonprofit organization. You can always return to this material later to refresh yourself on some of the technical details and requirements of each category.

You Can Let the IRS Decide Your Public Charity Classification

For many groups, the most difficult part of applying for a federal 501(c)(3) tax exemption is deciding whether their organization will be a publicly supported public charity as discussed in Section F2 or one which meets the support test discussed in Section F3. To decide this an organization must second-guess future sources of support and tackle quite a few tax technicalities. Fortunately, if you have doubts, the IRS will help. Simply check a box on the federal form and the IRS will decide this question for you based upon the financial and program information submitted with your application.

For the specifics on making this election, see the Chapter 9 instructions to Part III, Line 9(j) of the federal tax exemption application.

1. Automatic Public Charity Status

The IRS automatically recognizes certain 501(c)(3) groups as public charities because they perform particular services or engage in certain activities. Those that can automatically qualify are:

Churches: [IRC Sections 509(a)(1) and 170(b)(1)(A)(i)]: In determining which groups qualify as churches, the IRS uses the criteria discussed in Chapter 3C2 above.

Schools: [IRC Sections 509(a)(1) and 170(b)(1)(A)(ii)]: Certain educational institutions whose main function is formal instruction and that have a regularly enrolled student body qualify as public charities.

School requirements are stricter than those for obtaining an educational purpose tax exemption under Section 501(c)(3) (see Chapter 3C5) and are geared toward primary, secondary preparatory or high schools and colleges and universities. This doesn't mean that less structured educational institutions can't automatically qualify for public charity status as a school, but rather that it's more difficult. However, the farther an educational group is from the "institutional" criteria mentioned, the harder it is to qualify as a public charity under the above IRC sections. Non-traditional groups have a better chance of obtaining public charity status if they have some conventional institutional attributes, such as regional accreditation and a state-approved curriculum.

Hospitals and Medical Research Organizations: [IRC Sections 509(a)(1) and 170(b)(1)(A)(iii)]: Corporations whose main function is providing hospital or medical care, medical education or medical research automatically qualify as public charities under these IRC sections.

Health organizations such as rehabilitation groups, outpatient clinics, community mental health or drug treatment centers should qualify as hospitals if their principal purpose is to provide hospital or medical care.[3] Using consultation services of certified medical personnel such as doctors and nurses helps to establish a group's medical care purpose.

Medical education and research organizations do not qualify under these IRC sections unless they actively provide on-site medical or hospital care to patients as an integral part of their functions. Medical research groups must also be directly and continuously active in medical research with a hospital and this research must be the organization's principal purpose.

Public Safety Organizations: [IRC Section 509(a)(4)]: Groups organized and operated exclusively for public safety testing automatically qualify for public charity status. Generally, these organizations test consumer products to determine their fitness for use by the general public.

Government Organizations: Certain government organizations operated for the benefit of a college or university are automatically classified as public charities [under IRC Sections 509(a)(1) and 170(b)(1)(A)(iv)]. Also, government units described in IRC Section 170(c)(1) that receive gifts or contributions for public purposes qualify as public charities [under IRC Sections 509(a)(1) and 170(b)(1)(A)(v)]. You won't be forming a government corporation, but we mention these organizations because they are included in the list of public charities on the federal tax exemption application form.

Supporting Organizations: [IRC Section 509(a)(3)]: Organizations operated solely for the benefit of, or in connection with, one or more of the above organizations, or those described in sections F2 or F3 below, are also automatically classified as public charities (except those that benefit a public safety organization).

For further information on organizations listed above, see IRS Publication 557, page 16, "Section 509(a)(1) Organizations." For supporting organizations, see page 24 of Publication 557, "Section 509(a)(3) Organizations."

2. Publicly Supported Organizations

Certain publicly supported organizations qualify for 501(c)(3) public charity status [under IRC Sections 509(a)(1) and 170(b)(1)(A)(vi)]—again, don't worry about these code sections for now; they are included as references to help you when you prepare your federal exemption application.

To be classified as a publicly supported public charity, a group must regularly solicit funds from the general community. It must normally[4] receive money from government agencies, and a number of different private contributors or agencies.

---

[3]Convalescent homes, homes for children or the aged, or institutions that provide vocational training for the handicapped are not recognized by the IRS as fitting within this public charity category.

[4]The word "normally" has a special meaning which we discuss below.

Examples: Museums, libraries and community centers to promote the arts that rely on broad based support received from individual members of the community or from various public and private sources should qualify under this public charity test.

Your organization will probably be denied this status if you expect to rely primarily on a few private sources or occasional large grants to fund your operations. Further, this support test is difficult for smaller, grass-roots groups to meet because it does not include as qualifying public support income from the performance of tax-exempt purposes—a source of support commonly relied upon by these groups.

Below we look at the various tests and factors the IRS uses to determine if a 501(c)(3) nonprofit meets the requirements of this public charity category. Because these laws are complex and because many new groups are uncertain about sources of future income, it might be wise to consult a tax advisor or nonprofit lawyer before deciding to pursue this public charity classification. (You can let the IRS decide if this is the best public charity category for you—see the sidebar text.)

For more detailed information on this public charity category, see IRS Publication 557, page 16, "Publicly Supported Organizations."

How Much Public Support Do You Need Under This Test?

Generally, an organization is publicly supported if it:

1. normally receives at least 1/3 of its total support from governmental units, from contributions made directly or indirectly by the general public, or from a combination of the two;[5] or

---

[5]Note that support received from other publicly supported organizations is also counted as qualifying public support.

2. receives at least 1/10 of its support from these sources and meets an "attraction of public support" requirement.

Qualified support (support included in the numerator of the fraction) includes funds from private and public agencies as well as contributions from corporate and individual donors. However, limitations are placed on the amount of qualified support received from one individual or corporation. Also, some membership fees may be included as qualified support. We discuss these areas further below.

Short-Cut for Those with Sufficient Support: If 1/3 of your organization's total support is qualified support, you are the type of group listed under #1 just above and you can skip the following subsection. The attraction of public support requirement discussed below need only be met by the types of groups listed in #2 above where 1/10 or more, but less than 1/3, of the organization's total support is qualified support.

Attraction of Public Support

The IRS considers a number of factors, listed below, in determining whether a tax-exempt nonprofit group meets the attraction of public support requirement. Only Factor 1 absolutely must be met; the rest are not specifically required. Of course, the more you meet, the better your chances are of meeting the attraction of public support requirement.

Factor 1. Continuous Solicitation of Funds Program

Your group must continually attract new public or governmental support. It will meet this requirement if it maintains a continuous program for soliciting money from the general public, community, or membership—or if it solicits support from governmental agencies or churches, schools or hospitals that also qualify as public charities (see section F1 above). Although this mandates broad-based support, the IRS allows new groups to limit initial campaigns to seeking "seed" money from a select number of the most promising agencies or people.

Factor 2. Percentage of Financial Support

At least 10% of your group's total support must come from the public. For this purpose, the greater the percentage of public support, the better; remember that if your public support amounts to 1/3 or more, you do not have to meet the attraction of public support factors listed in this subsection.

Factor 3. Support from a Representative Number of People

If your group gets most of its money from government agencies or from a representative number of people as opposed to getting it from a particular individual or a group with a special interest in its activities, it will more likely meet the attraction of public support requirement.

Factor 4. Representative Governing Body

A nonprofit corporation whose governing body represents broad public interests, rather than the personal interest of a limited number of donors, is considered favorably by the IRS. An organization's governing body is more likely to be treated as representative if it includes:

- public officials;

- people selected by public officials;

- people recognized as experts in the organization's area of operations;

- community leaders or others representing a cross-section of community views and interests (such as members of the clergy, teachers, civic leaders); or

- for membership organizations, people elected under the corporate Articles or Bylaws by a broad-based membership.

Factor 5. Availability of Public Facilities or Services

If an organization continuously provides facilities or services for the general public, this will be considered favorably by the IRS. This would include a museum open to the public; an orchestra that gives public performances; a group that distributes educational literature to the public; or an old age home that provides nursing or other services to low-income members of the community.

Factor 6. Additional Factors

Corporations are also more likely to meet the requirement if:

- members of the public having special knowledge or expertise (such as public officials, or civic or community leaders) participate in or sponsor programs;

- the organization maintains a program to do charitable work in the community (such as job development or slum rehabilitation); or

- the organization gets a significant portion of its funds from another public charity or a governmental agency to which it is, in some way, held accountable as a condition of the grant, contract or contribution.

Factor 7. Additional Factors for Membership Groups Only

A membership organization is more likely to meet the attraction of public support requirement if:

- the solicitation for dues-paying members attempts to enroll a substantial number of people in the community or area, or in a particular profession or field of special interest;

- membership dues are affordable to a broad cross-section of the interested public; or

- the organization's activities are likely to appeal to people with some broad common interest or purpose—such as musical activities in the case of an orchestra, or different forms of dance in the case of a dance studio.

Technical Terms and Requirements for Publicly Supported Organizations

Now we reach a tricky part. We've explained that an organization must normally receive at least 1/3 (or 1/10 if it also meets the attraction of public support requirement discussed above) of its total support from government units, from contributions by the general public, or from a combination of these sources. We call this 1/3 or 1/10 figure "public support." To keep your percentage high enough, you'll want the IRS to:

- classify as much of your income as possible as public support; and

- keep your total support figure as low as possible.

By doing this, your final percentage of public support will be higher. Of course, the IRS has more than a fair number of rules, and exceptions to the rules, to define "public support" and "total support." We provide a guide to the basic technical terms used under this public charity category below. Start by skimming through this material, then go back and read areas that may apply to your organization.

What Does "Normally" Mean?

An organization must "normally" receive either 1/3 or 1/10 of its total support from public support sources. This means that one tax year is not critical. The IRS bases its decision on four year's cumulative receipts. Your organization will meet either the 1/3 or 1/10 support test for both its current and the following tax year if, during the four tax years before

its current tax year, its cumulative public support equals 1/3 or 1/10 of its cumulative total support.

Example: Open Range, Inc. is a nonprofit organization for medical research on the healthful effects of organic cattle ranching. ORI's cumulative total support was $60,000 for 1986 through 1990, and its cumulative public support was $25,000. The organization will, therefore, be considered a publicly supported public charity for 1990 and the following tax year. This remains true even if, for one or more of the previous four years, public support did not equal 1/3 of the total support—it's the cumulative total that counts.

Advance and Definitive Rulings

There are two ways to request public charity status as a publicly supported organization.

If your organization has been operating for one tax year consisting of at least eight months at the time of completion of your federal exemption application, you can ask for a definitive ruling on your public charity status. The IRS will use the past support received by the group to determine if it qualifies as a publicly supported organization.

Existing groups may, and new groups must, request an advance ruling on their public charity status. If your expected sources of support seem likely to qualify you as a publicly supported organization, the IRS will grant you a tentative ruling. Later, at the end of an advance ruling period consisting of the corporation's first five tax years, the IRS will give a definitive ruling. If the group's public support during the advance ruling period satisfies the requirements of this public charity test, the organization will qualify as a publicly supported organization.

In granting advance rulings, the IRS always looks to see if your organization will meet the attraction of public support factors discussed earlier in this section, whether you plan to meet the 1/3 or 1/10 public support test.

For further information on definitive and advance public charity ruling requests, see Chapter 9.

What Is a "Government Unit"?

Money received from a "government unit" is considered public support. Government units include federal or state governmental agencies, county and city agencies, etc. The most common example of governmental support is a federal or state grant.

Limits on Contributions from the General Public

Direct or indirect contributions by the general public are considered public support. Indirect contributions include grants from private trusts or agencies also funded by contributions from the general public, such as grants from Community Chest or the United Fund. However, there is a major restriction. The total contributions of one individual, trust, or corporation made during the preceding four tax years may be counted *only* to the extent that they do not exceed 2% of the corporation's total support for these four years. Money from government units, publicly supported organizations and unusual grants is not subject to this 2% limit. These exceptions are discussed below.

Example: If your total support over the previous four-year period was $60,000, then only $1,200 (2% of $60,000) contributed by any one person, private agency or other source counts as public support.

Why Less Is More, More or Less: Note that the total amount of any one contribution, even if it exceeds this 2%, four-year limitation, is included in the corporation's total support. Paradoxically, therefore, large contributions from an individual or private agency can have a disastrous effect on your status as a publicly supported charity. This is because you only get to include such contributions as public support to the extent of 2% of the previous four years' total income, while at the same time the total income figure is increased by the full amount of the contribution. This makes it more difficult for you to meet the 1/3 or 1/10 public support requirement.

Example: On Your Toes, a ballet troupe, received the following contributions from 1987 through 1990:

1987	$10,000	from individual X
1988	20,000	from individual Y
1989	60,000	from Z Community Chest
1990	<u>10,000</u>	as an additional contribution from individual X

Total Support: $100,000

All support for the four-year period is from contributions, direct or indirect, from the general public. However, in view of the 2% limit, On Your Toes will have trouble maintaining its publicly supported public charity status because while all contributions count toward *total support*, only $2,000 (2% x $100,000) from any one contributor counts as *public support*. Therefore, the troupe's public support for this period is only $6,000 ($2,000 from each contributor, X, Y and Z), which falls $4,000 short of the minimum 1/10 public support requirement.

Now suppose On Your Toes received $2,000 each from 50 contributors over the four-year period. It still has $100,000 total support, but because no one contributor gave more than 2% of the four years' total support, it can count the entire $100,000 as public support.

A Suggestion: To qualify as a publicly supported public charity, solicit smaller contributions through a broad-based fund-raising program and don't rely constantly on the same major sources. This way, you'll beat the 2% limit and have a better chance of qualifying contributions as public support.

Exceptions to the 2% Limit Rule

In a few circumstances, contributions are not subject to the 2% limit:

Money from Government Units or Publicly Supported Organizations: Contributions received from a government unit or other publicly supported organization are not subject to the 2% limit, except those specifically "earmarked" for your organization by the original donor.

Example: Ebeneezer Sax gives one million dollars to National Public Music, a national government foundation that promotes musical arts. NPM then gives your organization the million as a grant. If Sax made the contribution to NPM on the condition that the foundation turn it over to your organization, it's earmarked for you and the 2% limit applies.

Except for earmarked contributions or grants, you can rely on large contributions or grants from specific government agencies or other publicly supported organizations every year, since all such contributions will be counted as public support.

Money from "Unusual Grants": Another major exception to the 2% limit is for "unusual grants" from the private or public sector. A grant is unusual if it:

- is attracted by the publicly supported nature of your organization;

- is unusual—this means you don't regularly rely on the particular grant and it is an unexpectedly large amount; and

- would, because of its large size, adversely affect the publicly supported status of your organization (as we've seen, because of the 2% limit, large grants can cause trouble).

If a grant qualifies as an unusual grant, you can exclude the grant funds from both your public support and total support figures for the year in which they are given.

Example: The National Museum of Computer Memorabilia, Inc. is a nonprofit corporation that operates a museum of computers and artificial intelligence memorabilia. The years 1987 through 1989 are difficult ones and the museum raises very little money. But in 1990 the organization receives an unexpected windfall grant. A look at the receipts for 1987 to 1990 helps illustrate the importance of the unusual grant exception. All amounts are individual contributions from the general public unless indicated otherwise:

1987	$1,000	from A
	1,000	from B
1988	1,000	from C
1989	1,000	from D
	1,000	from E
1990	100,000	from Z, a private grant agency

Total Receipts: $105,000

Assume that the 1990 grant qualifies as an unusual grant. The total support computation for the four year period would be:

1987	$1,000	from A
	1,000	from B
1988	1,000	from C
1989	1,000	from D
	1,000	from E
1990	0	the $100,000 grant drops out from total support

Total Support: $5,000

Since the total support is $5,000, the museum can only count a maximum of 2% times $5,000, or $100, received from any one individual during this period as public support. Therefore, the public support computation for this period looks like this:

1987	$100	from A
	100	from B
1988	100	from C
1989	100	from D
	100	from E
1990	0	the $100,000 contribution also drops out from the public support computation

Total Public Support: $500

The museum meets the 10% support test since total public support of $500 equals 10% of the total support of $5,000 received over the four year period. If the organization also meets the attraction of public support requirement (which must be met by groups whose public support is less than 1/3 of total support), it will qualify as a publicly supported public charity for 1990 and 1991.

If the $100,000 contribution did not qualify as an unusual grant, the nonprofit would not meet the 10% public support test. Total support would equal total receipts of $105,000; a maximum of 2% times $105,000, or $2,100, from each individual and the grant agency would be classified as public support. Public support received over the four year period would consist of $1,000 from individuals A, B, C, D and E and the maximum allowable sum of $2,100 from the grant agency, for a total public support figure of $7,100. The percentage of public support for the four-year period would equal $7,100 divided by $105,000, or less than 7%, and the group would not qualify as a publicly supported public charity in 1990. Again, you can see how a large grant can hurt you if it does not qualify as an unusual grant.

Some Membership Fees as Public Support

Membership fees are considered public support as long as the member does not receive something valuable in return, such as admissions, merchandise, or the use of facilities or services. If a member does receive direct benefits in exchange for fees, the fees are not considered public support. These fees are, however, always included in the total support computation.

What's Not Public Support?

Unrelated Activities and Investments: Net income from activities unrelated to exempt purposes as well as "gross investment income," which include rents, dividends, royalties, and returns on investments, are not considered public support *and are added to the total support figure.*

Selling Assets or Performing Tax Exemption Activity: The following types of receipts are not considered either public support or part of total support (as with unusual grants, they drop out of both computations):

- Gains from selling a capital asset. Generally, capital assets are property held by the corporation to use in its activities, not including any business inventory or resale merchandise, business accounts or notes receivable, or real property used in a trade or business.

- Receipts from performing tax-exempt purposes. Examples include money received from: admissions to performances of a tax-exempt symphony; classes given by a dance studio; tuition or other charges paid for attending seminars, lectures or classes given by an exempt educational organization.

An Exception for Some Exempt-Purpose Receipts: Since we're dealing with tax laws, you'd expect at least one complicating exception. Here it is. If your organization relies primarily on gross receipts from activities related to its exempt purposes, such as an educational nonprofit that receives most of its support from class tuitions, this exempt-purpose income will not be considered public support, *but will be computed in total support*. If your group falls in this category, it will probably not be able to qualify as a publicly supported public charity and should attempt to qualify under the public charity support test discussed in Section F3 below.

3. The Support Test

Don't worry if your Section 501(c)(3) group does not qualify as either an automatic or as a publicly supported public charity. There is another way to qualify as a public charity. Indeed, the support test discussed in this section [under Internal Revenue Code Section 509(a)(2)] is likely to meet your needs if your 501(c)(3) group intends to derive income from performing exempt-purpose activities and services.[6]

How Much Public Support Do You Need Under This Test?

To qualify under this public charity support test, a 501(c)(3) nonprofit organization must meet two requirements:

1. The organization must normally receive more than 1/3 of its total support in each tax year as qualified public support. Qualified public support is support from any of the following sources:

   - gifts, grants, contributions or membership fees; and

   - gross receipts from admissions, selling merchandise, performing services, or providing facilities in an activity related to the exempt purposes of the nonprofit organization; and

2. The organization must normally not receive more than 1/3 of its annual support from unrelated trades or businesses or gross investment income.[7] Gross investment income includes rent from unrelated sources, interest, dividends and royalties—sources of support far removed from the activities of most smaller nonprofit organizations.

Again, the most important aspect of this test, and the one that makes it appropriate for many 501(c)(3) groups, is that it allows the 1/3 qualified public support amount to include the group's receipts from performing its exempt purposes. Hence, this public charity classification is appropriate for many self-sustaining nonprofits that raise income from their tax-exempt activities, such as performing arts groups, schools and other educational purpose organizations, and nonprofit service organizations.

Example: School tuition, admissions to concerts or plays, or payments for classes at a pottery studio count as qualified public support under this public charity test.

---

[6]To make matters even more confusing, IRS publications sometimes refer to groups that meet this IRC 509(a)(2) support test as "publicly supported organizations." We do not follow this practice—for us, publicly supported organizations are only those that qualify under the support test described in section F2 of this chapter.

---

[7]If you pay tax on income from unrelated businesses or activities, the amount of the tax paid will be deducted from this income before it is counted in this 33-1/3% figure.

If Your Nonprofit Sells Services or Information

Under IRC §6711, if a tax-exempt nonprofit (including any 501(c)(3) organization, whether classified as a public charity or private foundation) offers to sell to individuals information or routine services that could be readily obtained free, or for a nominal fee, from the federal government, the nonprofit must include a statement that the information or service can be so obtained. Failure to comply with this disclosure requirement can result in a substantial fine.

If your nonprofit plans to sell services or information, check to see if the same service or information is available from the federal government. If so, you may need to make the required disclosure to clients and customers. For further information on these disclosure requirements, see IRS Publication 557, page 8.

Technical Terms and Requirements of the Support Test

In this subsection we look at specific technical terms, concepts and requirements of this public charity category. Skim through this material and then re-read portions of specific interest or application to your organization.

For more detailed information on this public charity category, see IRS Publication 557, page 21, "509(a)(2) Organizations." Again, if you are unsure whether your organization qualifies for the public charity support test covered below, you can let the IRS decide by checking a box on your federal tax exemption application (see Chapter 9 for further information).

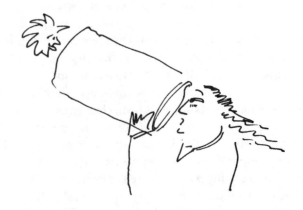

Support Must Be from Permitted Sources

Qualified public support under this test must be from permitted sources including:

- government agencies;
- other 501(c)(3) public charities—generally, those that qualify as public charities under one of the tests described in sections F1 and F2 above.

Permitted sources do not include:

- disqualified persons—people who would be considered disqualified if the organization were classified as a private foundation. These include substantial contributor, the organization's founders, and certain related persons (for a discussion of disqualified persons, see "Who Are Disqualified Persons?" in Chapter 9); or
- groups that qualify for public charity status as Related Organizations or Public Safety Organizations (see these categories in Section F1 above).

Membership Fees and Dues Get Special Treatment

Dues paid to provide support for or to participate in the nonprofit organization, or in return for services or facilities provided only to members, are considered valid membership dues and can be counted as qualified public support. On the other hand, fees or dues paid in return for a discount on products or services provided to the public or in return for some other monetary benefit will not be included as valid membership fees. However, these payments may still be counted as qualified public support if the fee entitles the member to special rates for exempt purpose activities—in this case the payments qualify as receipts related to the group's exempt purposes.

Example: People pay $50 to become members of All Thumbs, a nonprofit group dedicated to rebuilding interest in the unitar, a near-extinct one-stringed guitar-like musical instrument. All Thumbs' members are allowed $50 worth of reduced rate passes to all unitar concerts nationwide. Although these fees can't be counted as valid membership fees since they are paid in return for an equivalent monetary benefit (a $50 discount), they still count as receipts related to the performance of the group's exempt purposes (paid in return for attendance at unitar concerts— putting on these concerts is an exempt purpose and activity of the group). Therefore the fees may be counted by the organization as qualified public support.

Limitation on Large Exempt-Purpose Receipts

There is one major limitation on the amount of income received in return for exempt-purpose activities that can be included in the 1/3 qualified public support figure. Specifically, in any tax year, receipts from the performance of exempt purpose services from individuals or government units which exceed $5,000 or 1% of the organization's total support for the year, whichever is greater, must be excluded from the organization's qualified public support figure. This limitation applies only to exempt-purpose receipts and not to gifts, grants, contributions or membership fees received by the organization.

Example: Van-Go is a visual arts group that makes art available to people around the nation by toting it around in specially marked vans. In 1990, Van-Go derives $30,000 total support from the sale of paintings. The funds are receipts related to the performance of the group's exempt purposes. Any amount over $5,000 paid by any one individual cannot be included in computing its qualified public support for the year, although the full amount is included in total support. Of course, if Van-Go's total support for any year is more than $500,000, then the limitation on individual contributions will be 1% of the year's total support, since this figure exceeds $5,000.

Some Gifts Are Gross Receipts

Generally, when someone pays money or gives property without getting anything of value in return, it is considered a gift or contribution. But gifts made in return for admissions paid, merchandise sold, services performed, or facilities furnished to the contributor are considered gross receipts from exempt-purpose activities and are subject to the $5,000 or 1% limitation.

Example: At its annual fund raising drive, the California Cormorant Preservation League rewards $100 contributors with a book containing color prints of cormorants. The book normally retails for $25. Only $75 of each contribution is considered a gift; the remaining $25 payments are classified as gross receipts from the performance of the group's exempt purposes and are subject to the $5,000 or 1% limitation.

Some Grants are Gross Receipts

The $5,000 or 1% limitation also applies to grants. However, it is sometimes hard to distinguish money received as grants from exempt-purpose gross receipts. The rule used by the IRS is that money paid so that the granting agency gets some economic or physical benefit, such as a service, facility or product, are classified as gross receipts related to the exempt activities of the nonprofit organization. Money contributed to benefit the public will be treated as bona fide grants by the IRS, not as exempt-purpose receipts.

Example: A pharmaceutical company, Amalgamated Mortar & Pestle, provides a research grant to a nonprofit scientific and medical research organization, Safer Sciences, Inc. The company specifies that the nonprofit must use the grant to develop a more reliable child-proof cap for prescription drug containers (the results of the nonprofit research will be shared with the commercial company). The money is treated as receipts received by Safer Sciences in carrying out its exempt purposes and is subject to the $5,000 or 1% limitation.

Another Example: Safer Sciences gets a grant from the federal Center for Disease Control to build a better dish for epidemiological research. Since the money is used to benefit the public, the full amount will be included in the nonprofit organization's qualified public support figure.

Unusual Grants Can Be Excluded from the Support Computations

As with the publicly supported public charities discussed in Section F2 above, IRS rules allow groups seeking public charity status under the public support test discussed in this section to exclude "unusual grants" from their support computations. These are grants and contributions, not regularly relied on and attracted by the publicly supported nature of the organization, which, because of their substantial size, might adversely affect the organization's ability to meet the 1/3 qualified support requirement of this public charity test.

Rents Related to Exempt Purposes Are Not Gross Investment Income

Rents received from people or groups related to the group's exempt purpose are generally not considered gross investment income. Remember: Under this public charity test, the organization must normally not receive more than 1/3 of its annual support from unrelated trades or businesses or from gross investment income.

Example: Good Crafts, Inc., a studio that provides facilities for public education in historic crafts, rents a portion of its premises to an instructor who teaches stained glass classes. Such rent would probably not fall into the negative gross investment income category.

It may be important, therefore, that your group rent to another person or group whose activities are directly related to your exempt purposes. We suggest you consult a nonprofit lawyer or tax advisor if you'll rely on rental income even from related groups. It's a tricky subject.

A Technicality: If, as more and more nonprofits must, you plan to supplement your support with income from activities unrelated to your exempt purposes, check with your tax advisor to make sure this additional income will not exceed 1/3 of your annual support and jeopardize your ability to qualify under this public charity category.

There's That Word "Normally" Again

We've mentioned that the public charities discussed here must normally meet the support requirements of this test. This means that the IRS looks at the total amount of support over the previous four-year period to decide if the organization qualifies as a public charity for the current and the following tax year.

Advance vs. Definitive Public Charity Rulings

Like the publicly supported public charities discussed earlier, the groups discussed here may qualify for public charity status under a definitive or advance ruling.

For further information on advance and definitive rulings, see Section F2 above and Chapter 9.

G. Summing Up

Now that we've looked at the three ways to achieve 501(c)(3) public charity status, we suggest you go back and re-read the three examples given in Section E of this chapter. These summarize the three public charity tests explained in the previous sections and provide typical examples of how these tests are used by 501(c)(3) nonprofit organizations. Again, don't worry if you don't have a thorough command of this material. When you prepare your federal tax exemption application, you can come back to this chapter and re-read the sections that apply to you. And remember: If you are unsure whether the Section F2 or F3 public charity public support test applies to your organization, you can ask the IRS to make this determination for you.

Chapter 5

OTHER NONPROFIT BENEFITS AND REQUIREMENTS

IN THIS CHAPTER we a discuss a few remaining federal tax issues that affect nonprofits. We also cover tax benefits and tax and non-tax requirements that apply to 501(c)(3) nonprofits under California law.

A. Federal Tax Deductions for Contributions

A donor may claim a personal federal income tax deduction for contributions made to a 501(c)(3) tax-exempt organization. These contributions are termed "charitable contributions."

- Corporations may make deductible charitable contributions of up to 10% of their annual taxable income.

- Individuals may deduct up to 50% of adjusted gross income in any year for contributions made to 501(c)(3) public charities and to some types of 501(c)(3) private foundations, as explained in Chapter 4.

What May Be Deducted: The following types of contributions are deductible on the donor's tax return:

- cash;

- property—generally donors may deduct the fair market (resale) value of donated property; special rules apply to gifts of appreciated property (property which has increased in value);

- unreimbursed car expenses, including the cost of gas and oil, paid while performing services for the nonprofit organization; and

- unreimbursed travel expenses incurred while away from home performing services for the nonprofit organization, including the cost of transportation, meals and lodging.

What May Not Be Deducted: Certain types of gifts cannot be deducted as charitable contributions. Nondeductible gifts include:

- the value of volunteer services;

- the right to use property;

- contributions to political parties—these, however, may be taken as a tax credit, subject to dollar and percentage limitations;

- direct contributions to needy individuals;

- tuition—even amounts designated as "donations" that must be paid in addition to tuition as a condition of enrollment are not deductible;

- dues paid to labor unions;

- the cost of raffle, bingo, lottery tickets or other games of chance; and

- child care costs paid while performing services for the nonprofit organization.

What May Be Partially Deducted: Contributions received in return for a service, product or other benefit—such as membership fees paid in return for special membership incentives or promotional products or "donations" charged for attending a performance—are only partially deductible. In these instances, a deduction is allowed only for the portion of the gift that exceeds the fair market value of the service, product or benefit received by the donor.

> **Example:** If a member of a 501(c)(3) organization pays a $30 membership fee and receives a record album that retails for $30, nothing is deductible. But if a $20 product is given in return for the payment, $10 of the fee paid is a bona-fide donation and may be deducted by the member as a charitable contribution.

501(c)(3) nonprofit groups should clearly state the dollar amount that is deductible when receiving contributions, donations, or membership fees in return for providing a service, product, discount or other benefit to the donor.

Reporting Requirements: Deductions for charitable contributions made by individuals are claimed by itemizing the gifts on IRS Schedule A and filing this form with the individual's annual

1040 income tax return. Recent IRS rules require donors to obtain receipts for all charitable contributions claimed on their tax returns. Receipts must describe the contribution and show the value of any goods or services received from the nonprofit by the donor as part of the transaction. See IRS publications for more information on how to prepare donor receipts for your organization and comply with other charitable tax deduction requirements (or see Proposed Treasury Reg. § 1.170A—13T).

The IRS requirements for deducting and reporting charitable contributions change from year to year—for current information see IRS Publication 526, *Charitable Contributions.* For information on valuing gifts, see IRS Publication 561, *Determining the Value of Donated Property.* For additional information, see IRS Publication 1391, *Deductibility of Payments Made to Charities Conducting Fund-Raising Events.*

B. Federal Estate and Gift Tax Exemptions

An important source of contributions for 501(c)(3) nonprofits is gifts made as part of an individual's estate plan (as part of a will or trust document). When the individual dies, these amounts are distributed to the 510(c)(3) organization and are excluded from the taxable estate on the individual's unified estate and gift tax return. The tax savings can be enormous: taxable estates over $600,000[1] are taxed at a rate starting at 37% (and can be taxed as high as 55%).

---

[1]As noted later in the text, this federal estate and gift tax credit amount is lessened by the amount of large taxable gifts made during an individual's life. Specifically, taxable gifts to a non-spouse which exceed $10,000 in a given year are subtracted from the individual's unified estate and gift tax credit of $600,000. Gifts made to 501(c)(3) nonprofits which exceed $10,000 in a year are not taxable (they do not reduce the $600,000 credit).

Even though property which passes to a surviving spouse is not included in an individual's taxable estate, more and more people are realizing that their taxable estate will total more than $600,000. Thus many people are motivated to engage in estate planning, including making charitable gifts to nonprofit organizations.

Traditionally, colleges and universities and larger environmental and health organizations have actively solicited this type of charitable giving by providing information about estate planning and the benefits of charitable bequests to members and donors. Increasingly, smaller nonprofits too are starting to get, and get out, the message and are pursuing similar strategies in their fundraising efforts. You should be familiar with the tax benefits of charitable bequests as an effective way of persuading potential donors to give to your cause.

Gifts: Gifts made during an individual's life are not subject to taxation. However, if made to an individual or non-qualified organization, they reduce the donor's $600,000 unified estate and gift tax credit to the extent they exceed $10,000 in one calendar year. If made to a 501(c)(3) nonprofit they do not reduce this federal and estate gift tax credit.

For further information on federal and state estate and gift taxes and individual estate planning techniques, see *Plan Your Estate* by Clifford (Nolo Press).

C. Federal Unrelated Business Income Tax

All tax-exempt nonprofit corporations, whether private foundations or public charities, may have to pay tax on income derived from activities unrelated to their exempt purposes. The first $1,000 of unrelated business income is not taxed, but after that, the normal federal corporate tax rate applies:

15% on the first $50,000 of taxable corporate income; 25% on the next $25,000; and 34% on taxable income over $75,000 (with a 5% surtax on taxable income between $100,000 and $335,000).

As explained in Chapter 3, Section D1, if unrelated income is substantial, it may jeopardize the organization's 501(c)(3) tax exemption.

1. Activities That Are Taxed

Unrelated business income derives from activities not directly related to a group's exempt purposes. An unrelated trade or business is one that is regularly carried on and not substantially related to a nonprofit group's exempt purposes. It is irrelevant that the organization uses the profits to conduct its exempt-purpose activities.

Example: Enviro-Home Institute is a 501(c)(3) nonprofit organized to educate the public about environmentally sound home design and home construction techniques. Enviro-Home develops a model home kit that applies its ideas of appropriate environmental construction and is very successful in selling the kit. The IRS considers this unrelated business income because it is not directly related to the educational purposes of the organization.

Another Example: A halfway house that offers room, board, therapy and counseling to recently released prison inmates also operates a furniture shop to provide full-time employment for its residents. This has been ruled not to be an unrelated trade or business, since the shop directly benefits the residents (even though it also produces income).

2. Activities That Are Not Taxed

A number of activities are specifically excluded from the definition of "unrelated trades or

businesses."[2] These include the following types of activities:

- those in which nearly all work is done by volunteers;
- those carried on by 501(c)(3) tax-exempt organizations primarily for the benefit of members, students, patients, officers, or employees (such as a hospital gift shop for patients or employees);
- those that sell mostly donated merchandise, such as thrift shops;
- exchanging or renting lists of donors or members;
- distribution of low-cost items, such as stamps or mailing labels worth less than $5, in the course of soliciting funds;
- sponsoring of trade shows by 501(c)(3) groups— this exclusion extends to the exempt organization's suppliers, who may educate trade show attendees on new developments or products related to the organization's exempt activities.

Also excluded from this tax is income not derived from services (termed "gross investment income" in the IRC). Remember: this tax applies to unrelated activities, not necessarily to unrelated income. Examples of nontaxable income include:[3]

- dividends, interest, and royalties;
- rent from land, buildings, furniture and equipment. Some forms of rent are taxed if the rental property was purchased or improved subject to a mortgage or if the rental income is based on the profits earned by the tenant;

---

[2]Some of these exceptions have been hotly contested by commercial business interests at several congressional hearings. The primary objection to these loopholes to the unrelated business income tax is that nonprofits receive an unfair advantage by being allowed to engage in these competing activities tax-free. Expect more hearings and future developments in this volatile area of nonprofit tax law.

[3]See Section 512(b) of the Internal Revenue Code for the complete list of these untaxed sources of income and the exceptions that exist for certain items.

• gains or losses from the sale or exchange of property.

It is often difficult to predict whether the IRS will tax an activity or income as unrelated business. Furthermore, IRS regulations and rulings and U.S. Tax Court decisions contain a number of specific rules classifying specific activities as unrelated businesses that are subject to tax. In short, you should consult a tax specialist if you plan to engage in activities or derive income from sources not directly related to your exempt purposes. Please note, this isn't the same thing as saying you shouldn't engage in an unrelated activity—many nonprofits must engage in commercial businesses unrelated to their exempt purposes to survive. You simply need good tax advice in this situation, so you don't risk jeopardizing your 501(c)(3) tax-exempt status.

D. California 23701(d) Nonprofit Tax Exemption

California corporations are subject to an annual corporate franchise tax of 9.3% on the net income of the corporation (a minimum franchise tax of $800 must, in any case, be paid annually). California nonprofit corporations can apply to be exempt from paying this annual franchise tax.

California tax law exempts the same kinds of groups as are covered by Section 501(c)(3) of the Federal Internal Revenue Code. This means that religious, charitable, scientific, literary and educational organizations—the most common types of nonprofit corporations and the ones with which this book is primarily concerned—can apply for a state exemption from corporate franchise taxes. The California nonprofit corporation tax exemption which parallels the federal 501(c)(3) tax exemption is

contained in Section 23701(d) of the California Revenue and Taxation Code. (Chapter 7 shows you how to apply for and obtain a state corporate tax exemption for your nonprofit organization.)

Political Activities Note: California rules are very similar to federal rules in that California recognizes both the "substantial activities" test and alternative "political expenditures" test. These tests limit the amount of political lobbying and expenditures which can be undertaken by tax-exempt nonprofits.

E. Private Foundation vs. Public Charity Status Under California Law

California does not make a separate determination as to whether your tax-exempt nonprofit corporation is a private foundation or public charity. The state simply follows the determination made by the IRS: if your organization is classified by the IRS as a 501(c)(3) public charity, it will be considered a public charity in California.

F. Deductibility of Contributions on California Tax Returns

Generally, California follows the federal tax deductibility rules for charitable contributions made to nonprofit corporations. For example, individuals who itemize their deductions may deduct contributions made to tax-exempt public charities and to some private foundations to the extent of 50% of their adjusted gross income on their individual income tax returns in a given year. (For the federal rules, see Chapter 4C2.)

G. California Attorney General Reporting Requirements

All charitable corporations and trustees holding property for charitable purposes must also register with the California Attorney General's office, Registry of Charitable Trusts on a one-time basis, and after that must file annual financial disclosure statements about how charitable funds are used. Most public benefit corporations (not just those formed for a specific charitable purpose) are considered charitable corporations for the purpose of these Attorney General registration and annual reporting requirements.

After you incorporate, you will receive a letter from the Attorney General's office. The letter will include a pamphlet describing legal requirements for registration, other statutes affecting charitable organizations, a registration form and instructions. Don't be confused by the legal jargon you'll find here—the registration and annual reporting requirements apply to all 501(c)(3) nonprofit groups, with the exception of religious corporations and certain schools and hospitals. The registration and annual reporting requirements are intended to ensure that the corporate funds are not being misused in any way.

The Attorney General's scrutinization is a formality for most section 501(c)(3) groups since their charitable funds consist mostly of payment for exempt-purpose services (instruction in art forms, admission to lectures or public performances) and the public is getting what they're paying for. However, if your public benefit corporation solicits funds for a specific charitable purpose (such as to provide a free meal program), the Attorney General will want to make sure these earmarked funds are being used for their solicited purpose. For further information on submitting these required forms, see Chapter 10, Step 25.

H. California Unrelated Business Income Tax

California, like the federal government, taxes the unrelated business income of a tax-exempt nonprofit corporation. The rate is 9.3% and applies to the net amount of unrelated business income (gross unrelated business income minus deductions for expenses that are directly connected with carrying on the unrelated business activity). Tax-exempt organizations are allowed a $1,000 deduction before computing their California taxable unrelated business income.

> **Example:** A Section 501(c)(3) traveler's aid society earns $7,000 a year selling baked goods to passers-by. Cost of the ingredients and all expenses related to this profit-making activity totals $3,000. The society pays state unrelated business taxes on the $4,000 net amount ($7,000-$3,000).

1. Activities That Are Taxed

The state's definition of an unrelated trade or business is similar to that of the IRS. It means any trade or business not substantially related to the organization's exempt purposes.

2. Activities That Are Not Taxed

As with the IRS definition, the state does not include a trade or business:

- Where most of the work is performed by volunteers;

- That exists mostly for the convenience of the members, students, patients, officers, or employees; or

- That sells merchandise, most of which was given to the organization as gifts or contributions.

Like the federal law, California also generally excludes specific kinds of passive income (rent, interest income, etc.) from this unrelated business income tax.

I. California Welfare Exemption

Many California tax-exempt nonprofit corporations plan to own or lease property (or portions of property) which will be used exclusively in carrying out their exempt purposes. California law provides a real and personal property tax exemption for these 501(c)(3) groups under the "welfare exemption" contained in Section 214 of the California Revenue and Taxation Code.

Real property (buildings, fixtures, other improvements to land) and personal property (movable property) tax exemptions allow nonprofits to own or lease real and personal property tax-free. This can be quite a savings, especially if, after owning property and paying relatively high taxes, you form a nonprofit tax-exempt corporation, apply for the welfare exemption and receive property tax "bills" from the County Tax Assessor's office showing a zero balance due. Or, if you've been leasing property from another nonprofit group or institution (which, itself, has qualified for the welfare exemption) and, after setting up a nonprofit corporation, you are notified by your landlord that your rent has been cut substantially (as you and the landlord should have previously agreed) because the property tax attributed to your portion of the premises has been dropped from the property tax rolls following the approval of your welfare exemption application.

1. Welfare Exemption Requirements

Many nonprofits qualify for the California welfare exemption. We list the general requirements of this exemption below. For detailed information and special exceptions, call the local Tax Assessor's office (or order the *Assessor's Handbook—Welfare Exemption* as explained in Chapter 10, Step 23).

a. The property must be used exclusively for religious, hospital, scientific or charitable purposes and owned and operated by community chests, funds, foundations, or corporations organized and operated for religious, hospital, scientific or charitable purposes;

b. The owner must be a nonprofit corporation or other organization exempt from taxes under Section 501(c)(3) of the Internal Revenue Code or under Section 23701(d) of the State Revenue and Taxation Code;

c. No part of the net earnings of the owner is allowed to inure to the benefit of any private shareholder or individual;

d. The property must be used for the actual operation of the exempt purposes of the group and it must not exceed the amount of property reasonably necessary to the accomplishment of the group's exempt purposes;

e. The property cannot be used or operated by the owner or by any other person so as to benefit any officer, trustee, director, shareholder, member, employee, contributor, or bondholder of the owner or operator, or any other person, through the distribution of profits, payments of excessive charges or compensation or the more advantageous pursuit of their business or profession;

f. The property cannot be used by the owner or members for fraternal or lodge purposes or for social club purposes except where such use is clearly incidental to a primary religious, hospital, scientific or charitable purpose;

g. The property must be irrevocably dedicated to religious, charitable, scientific or hospital purposes and upon the liquidation, dissolution or abandonment by the owner, will not inure to the benefit of any private person except a fund, foundation or corporation organized and operated for religious, scientific or charitable purposes.

Most 501(c)(3) nonprofit corporations will be able to meet these requirements since they are the same as, or similar to, those which must be met to obtain federal and state income tax exemptions. A few further points about these requirements:

Religious Purposes: Although particular types of property owned and operated for religious purposes are covered by the welfare exemption, religious-purpose groups normally seek property exemptions under the more flexible "church" and "religious" exemptions—see subsection d below.

No Benefit to Individuals: The State Board of Equalization will deny the exemption if the use of the property benefits an individual (requirement e above). The following factors (positive and negative) are taken into account by the Board in making this determination:

(+) A capital investment of the owner or operator for expansion of physical plant is justified by the contemplated return thereon and is required to serve the interests of the community;

(+) The property on which the exemption is claimed is used for the actual operation of an exempt activity (under Section 214) and does not exceed an amount of property necessary to accomplish the exempt purpose.

(-) The services and expenses of the owner or operator are excessive, based upon like services and salaries in comparable public institutions;

(-) The operations of the owner or operator, either directly or indirectly, materially enhance the private gain of any individual or individuals;

Irrevocable Dedication of Property: Requirement g states that the property must be irrevocably dedicated to religious, charitable, scientific or hospital purposes. Since an irrevocable dedication clause of all of the nonprofit corporation's property is required by Section 501(c)(3) of the Internal Revenue Code and by Section 23701(d) of the California Revenue and Taxation Code to obtain the federal and state income tax exemptions, it is customary to satisfy all of these three requirements with one irrevocable dedication clause in the corporate Articles of Incorporation. A specific dedication to a particular group may be made, or, as is more usual, to a designated class of organizations (those which are tax-exempt under federal and state law and satisfy the requirements of Section 214). The tear-out Articles in this book include an irrevocable dedication clause which meets these three requirements.

Dedication Clause for Educational and Scientific Purposes: If property is dedicated to scientific or educational purposes, these purposes must be limited to those which fall within the meaning of the welfare exemption. (We explain this technicality and provide legal language which satisfies this requirement in Chapter 6, Step 2.)

2. How To Apply

To apply for the welfare exemption, call your local County Tax Assessor and ask for a welfare exemption application and materials.

3. Special Rules

Some groups may encounter problems, or face special issues, when attempting to qualify for the welfare exception. Mostly these arise if a group is organized for a purpose other than religious, hospital, scientific or charitable. We discuss these and other special situations below.

a. Special Statutory Categories

A number of special provisions have been enacted specifying that certain purposes are within the scope of the welfare exemption. Here are just a few:

A number of special provisions have been enacted specifying that certain uses of property are within the scope of the welfare exemption. Here are just a few:

Homeless Shelters: Property owned by a qualifying organization which is used wholly or partially to provide temporary shelter for homeless people qualifies for the welfare exemption. The exemption on the property is granted in proportion to the space used for this purpose.

Educational TV and FM Stations: Property used exclusively by a non-commercial educational FM broadcast station, or an educational TV station which is owned and operated by a religious, hospital, scientific or charitable fund, foundation or corporation falls within the meaning of the welfare exemption, if all other requirements are met and if the terms of one or either of the following two provisions are satisfied:

* The educational TV station must be a facility which does not accept paid advertising, which transmits programs by certain conventional means and which receives at least 25% of its operating expense revenues from contributions from the general public or dues from its members.

* The station is a non-commercial educational FM broadcast station licensed and operated under Federal Communications Commission rules (Section 73.501 and following of Title 47 of the Code of Federal Regulations).

Natural Areas: Property used for the preservation of native plants or animals, or geographical formations of scientific or educational interest, or open space land used solely for recreation and for the enjoyment of scientific beauty, and which is open to the general public, subject to reasonable restrictions concerning the needs of the land, and is owned and operated by a scientific or

charitable fund, foundation or corporation and which meets the other requirements of Section 214.

Property Leased to Government Entities: Property which is owned by a nonprofit corporation and leased to, and exclusively used by, a government entity for its interest and benefit is exempt if all the other requirements of Section 214 are met except for the irrevocable dedication requirement. Such dedication will be deemed to exist if the lease provides that the owner's entire interest in the property will pass completely to the government entity upon the liquidation, dissolution or abandonment of the owner, or when the last rental payment is made under the lease, whichever occurs first, and if certain other formal requirements are met.

Property Subject to Revert to a Non-Exempt Group: This provision takes care of a technical problem that can develop if a tax-exempt group gets property on the condition that the title to the property will revert back to the grantor (a tax-exempt group) if the new group ceases to provide certain services. The issue is this: The Revenue and Taxation Code requires that, in order to obtain this tax exemption, the new group must irrevocably dedicate the property to religious, charitable, scientific or hospital purposes. A group that has land subject to a requirement that it revert to the grantor if certain conditions are (or aren't) met can't meet this requirement since it can't irrevocably dedicate property it doesn't irrevocably own. The law states, however, that even if the property is subject to revert, it will still be considered to fall within the welfare exemption if it has been used solely for charitable or hospital purposes for at least 30 years.

Property Under Construction: Facilities under construction, together with the land on which they are located, to be used exclusively for religious, hospital or charitable purposes.

Property Under Demolition: Property which is being demolished with the intent to replace it with facilities to be used exclusively for religious, hospital or charitable purposes.

Volunteer Fire Departments: Property used by volunteer fire departments which meet certain other requirements.

Zoos and Public Gardens: Property used exclusively for the operation of a zoo or for horticultural displays by a zoological society will fall within the provisions of the welfare exemption provided all the other requirements of the exemption are met.

b. Educational Purposes

Educational purposes and activities that benefit the community as a whole (not just a select membership of the nonprofit organization) qualify as charitable purposes under the welfare exemption. Below are examples of the types of educational purposes and activities that meet the requirements of the welfare exemption.

Elementary and High Schools: Property used by elementary and high schools owned and operated by religious, hospital or charitable funds, foundations or corporations fall within the welfare exemption if all of the other requirements of Section 214 are met and the school is an institution of learning with one of the following characteristics:

• Attendance at the school exempts a student from attendance at a public full-time elementary or secondary day school under Section 12154 of the Education Code, or

• A majority of its students have been excused from attending at a full-time elementary or secondary day school under Section 12152 or 12156 of the Education Code.

Basically, this special provision exempts the property of an educational purpose group which sets up a private, institutionalized elementary or high school, with state-approved curriculum and other state-approved institutionalized attributes (such as regular attendance and certified faculty). If you set up a private college in conjunction with a *private* elementary or high school, you can also seek to obtain the welfare exemption under this provision. If, however, your educational purpose is to set up a *private college* by itself, you will usually have to meet the requirements of the separate college exemption to be exempt from personal and real property taxes.[4]

Other Educational-Purpose Groups and Schools of Less than College Grade: The courts have made it clear that many non-institutionalized education groups qualify for the welfare exemption. To qualify, a group need not be a formal school. Groups giving instruction in dance, music or other art forms or groups that publish instructional literature can qualify for the welfare exemption.

---

[4]Special rules extend the welfare exemption to certain property owned by colleges and certain property used for housing facilities for elderly or handicapped persons. Check with the Tax Assessor's office for further information on these special rules.

The courts have said that general educational-purpose groups fall under the welfare exemption, realizing that their educational purposes are charitable in nature and that they should not be subject to the kinds of strict provisions which apply to "diploma mills" and formal schools which grant degrees. The courts and the Assessor's office have set up a number of general guidelines in determining whether an educational-purpose group is eligible for the welfare exemption. These include:

- The organization can't be a formal college, secondary or elementary school.

- The organization can't receive sources of support from public (governmental) agencies.

- The educational program should be available to the community at large and provide a social benefit to the general public—not just a select number of people. In other words, the educational program must have some "charitable" attributes which instruct or benefit those who attend as well as the general public. The fact that admission fees are charged for attendance at performances, or that tuition is charged for instruction, does not negate the charitable nature of the educational activities.

Whether the Tax Assessor's office will consider your educational activities charitable in nature will depend on the particular activities of your group. "Welfare Exemption Case Studies," just below discusses two leading court cases on this issue. If you show the Assessor's Office that your educational-purpose activities (seminars, lectures, publications, courses, performances) benefit the community at large (which most do), you should qualify for the welfare exemption.

Welfare Exemption Case Studies —Educational Purpose Groups

Stockton Civic Theatre (66 Cal. 2d 13 [1967])
A court ruled that a theater group whose primary activities consisted of charging admissions to theatrical performances open to the general public was charitable in nature and its education purpose was one within the meaning of the welfare exemption. In reaching this conclusion, the court took note of the fact that the only real estate owned by the group was a playhouse used for the production of popular plays and musical comedies. The real estate was not used to benefit any officer, trustee, director, shareholder, member, employee, contributor, or bondholder of the corporation. All productions were of amateur standing. Membership in the theater group was unrestricted and was obtained by anyone who purchased a season ticket. In addition, the theater obtained revenue from the sale of tickets to the general public for single performances and from gifts.

The court considered these facts favorably as well as the fact that the theater group was dedicated to providing educational benefits both to those who took part in the productions and to members of the general public (members of the audience). These benefits were found to be beneficial to the community, and therefore "charitable," with the result that the group's educational purposes were found to be within the meaning of the welfare exemption. The group was granted the welfare exemption and the real and personal property owned by the group was held exempt.

California College of Mortuary Science (23 Cal. App. 3d 702 [1972])
In this case an educational-purpose group was denied the welfare exemption. This case involved an educational-purpose mortuary school which was an accredited junior college offering a one-year course in mortuary science leading toward an AA degree. The court found that since the school was a quasi-"diploma mill," it did not qualify for the college exemption and since it was of collegiate grade, it did not meet the welfare exemption's statutory requirements. The court went on to say that the organization was ineligible, in any event, since its educational program (mortuary science) did not benefit the community at large or an ascertainable and indefinite portion of the community. All benefits went to a specific segment of the community (the funeral service industry) by providing it with competently trained personnel.

c. Scientific Purposes

Scientific purposes are narrowly defined for purposes of the welfare exemption. Under Section 214, scientific purposes are limited to medical research whose objects are the encouragement or conduct of scientific investigation, research and discovery for the benefit of the community at large, unless the research is carried on by an institution chartered by the U.S. Government.

d. Religious Purposes

Property owned by religious purpose groups and used for religious purposes is eligible for the welfare exemption. The courts have interpreted the terms "religious" and "religion" broadly under the welfare exemption, as illustrated by this language from a court opinion:

> ...the proper interpretation of the term 'religion' or 'religious' in tax exemption laws should not include any reference to whether the beliefs are theistic or non-theistic. Religion simply includes: (1) a belief, not necessarily referring to supernatural powers; (2) a cult involving a gregarious association openly expressing the belief; (3) a system of moral practice directly resulting from adherence to the belief; (4) an organization within the cult designed to

observe the tenets of the belief. The content of the belief is of no importance.

Property owned and operated for religious worship (such as a church building) and property used for general religious purposes (such as church schools, retreats, summer camps, reading rooms, licensed church nursery schools, etc) qualify for the welfare exemption. Although the welfare exemption applies to a broad range of religious purposes, most religious groups should use California's separate religious exemption. As explained below, it is easier to qualify for and use.

The Religious Exemption: The religious exemption is a separate exemption under Section 207 of the California Revenue and Taxation Code. This exemption provides a streamlined and coordinated procedure which many nonprofit religious groups can use to obtain their real and personal property tax exemptions. (In the past, religious groups applied for both the church exemption—discussed below—and the welfare exemption. The church exemption was used for religious worship property such as a church building; the welfare exemption for religious uses not involving religious worship).

The religious exemption, generally, exempts property owned and used by a nonprofit religious organization for religious purposes (not just religious worship) and involves a simplified application and renewal procedure. This consolidated exemption specifically lists church property used for preschool, nursery school, kindergarten, elementary and secondary school purposes as exempt religious purposes. (As with the welfare exemption, the religious exemption does not exempt college level institutions.) As a result, under this exemption a church need only file a single form to obtain an exemption on property owned by the church and used for religious worship as well as property used for school purposes.

All religious corporations, whether they own and operate church schools, should call their local county Tax Assessor's Office (Exemption Division) and determine if they are eligible to use the religious exemption and its simplified application and reporting requirements.

Note: The religious exemption does not apply to particular uses such as hospitals, educational FM radio or television stations, and certain housing owned by churches. In these cases, the welfare exemption can be used.

The Church Exemption: California law provides certain religious groups with another property tax exemption: the church exemption. Although religious-purpose groups will ordinarily use the religious exemption as explained above, we briefly discuss this third exemption in case you need to rely on it to exempt church property (in case the religious exemption isn't available).

The church exemption applies to personal and real property *used* exclusively by a "church." This includes property owned or leased from another nonprofit or profit-making group. This is a broader exemption than the welfare exemption or religious exemption since under this special religious exemption, it is strictly the use, and not the ownership of the property, which is determinative. As with the term "religious," "property used for church purposes" has been liberally interpreted by the courts. Broadly speaking, the courts define property which qualifies for this separate exemption as "any property or facility which is reasonably necessary for the fulfillment of a generally recognized function of a complete, modern church." This includes not only property used directly for religious worship, but also property used for activities related to the function of churches, such as administrative and business meetings of the church governing body, religious instructional sessions, practice sessions of the choir, and most activities of auxiliary organizations accountable to the local church authority. For further information on the church exemption, call the local Tax Assessor's office.

4. Leasing and the Welfare Exemption

We have looked at some types of ownership, operation and uses of property which will be considered religious, hospital, scientific or charitable under the welfare exemption. The above discussion, for the most part, assumes that the group which is seeking the exemption both uses and owns the property. But what about leasing? How does a tax-exempt group that leases property benefit from the welfare exemption ? What problems are encountered when the tax-exempt group is the landlord?[5]

a. You Are the Renter

Let's first consider the situation in which a group, otherwise qualified as tax-exempt under the welfare exemption, leases the property from another person or group.

Without looking at the characteristics of the lessor (the owner of the building or portion of the premises from whom the group rents the facilities), the group will be exempt from paying any *personal* property taxes[6] on property located on the premises— although the group doesn't own and operate the real property as required by Section 214, it does own and operate the personal property located on the premises.

If the group is renting from another group which, itself, qualifies for and obtains the welfare exemption, then the exemption will apply to both the personal and *real* property taxes associated with the leased property. Groups which lease from such a qualified lessor should have it stated clearly in writing that their rent will be lessened by an amount equal to the real property tax exemption for the

---

[5]Even groups which do not qualify for the welfare exemption may obtain a property tax exemption on leased premises rented to government or charitable organizations and used for public libraries, museums, public schools, colleges, or educational purposes by nonprofit colleges or universities—see Revenue & Taxation Code §§ 251 and 442.

[6]Personal property taxes are levied on equipment, furniture and other movable items located on the premises.

leased premises for each year in which the renter qualifies for the welfare exemption. This is a way of making sure that the benefits of the welfare exemption which apply to the leased premises will be passed on to you.

The only other way to obtain an exemption from payment of both personal and real property taxes on leased premises is for the group to meet the provisions of some exemption other than the welfare exemption (see Section 6, below). Again, if this is true, the lease agreement should clearly state that such a reduction or elimination of real property taxes on the owner's tax bill should be passed on to you for each year in which you qualify for the particular exemption.

b. You Are the Lessor

Now let's look at the situation where a group which qualifies for the welfare exemption leases property or portions of property to another organization. In this case the group need not be concerned at all with the personal property taxes associated with the leased premises—these are levied against the tenant.

- If the property is leased to an organization which meets the welfare exemption requirements, the leased premises will continue to be exempt from real property taxes.

- If the property is leased to a group which meets the requirements of some other real property exemption provided under other provisions of California law, the leased premises will continue to be exempt from real property taxes.

- If the property is leased to a group which cannot meet any of the above three tests, the owner organization (the group which qualifies for the welfare exemption) will not lose its exemption. However, its welfare exemption will only apply to the buildings or portions of buildings which it occupies or uses. The owner will receive a real property tax bill for any portion of the facilities

rented out to non-exempt tenants and will have to pay these taxes as the owner of the property. Of course, in this case, the owner organization will want to ensure that the lease agreement passes these taxes on to non-exempt tenants in the form of rent, if the tenants fail to establish an exemption from real property taxes in a given year.

J. Other California Tax Exemptions

Section 501(c)(3) nonprofits and other groups which do not qualify for the welfare exemption may be eligible for other tax exemptions under different provisions of California law. We've already touched on the separate college, religious and church exemptions above. The following is a partial list of special property tax exemptions which may benefit nonprofit groups.

Note: This is only a partial list and is subject to change—for current information on property tax exemptions which may apply to your nonprofit group, call your local County Tax Assessor's office and the main headquarters of the California State Board of Equalization in Sacramento.

Other Property Tax Exemptions

Type of Owner or Property	Personal Property Exemption	Real Property Exemption
Cemeteries	X	X
Churches	X	X
Colleges	X	X
Exhibitions	X	X
Free Museums	X	X
Religious Organizations	X	X
Veterans' organizations	X	X
Works of art	X	

Chapter 6

ORGANIZING A NONPROFIT CORPORATION

THIS CHAPTER shows you how to form your nonprofit corporation by choosing a name for your corporation and preparing and filing Articles of Incorporation with the California Secretary of State. We also show you how to prepare Bylaws—this document contains the basic legal provisions for operating your corporation in compliance with California law. Later chapters will show you how to complete other organizational forms and obtain your corporate income tax exemptions.

You'll see that these steps are really not complicated and involve, for the most part, simply filling in a small number of blanks on the tear-out forms contained in the Appendix at the end of this book (or on standard state and federal tax forms).[1] Take your time and relax, you'll be surprised at how easy it all is.

Using the Incorporation Checklist: You may wish to use the tear-out Incorporation Checklist in the Appendix to chart your way through the incorporation steps contained in Chapters 6 through 10. One way to use this chart is to browse through each step listed, checking the box labeled "My Group" for each step which applies to your incorporation. Then go back and mark the "Done" box as you complete each of these steps. We think this process will greatly simply your incorporation process.

The process of forming a nonprofit corporation is relatively simple and straight-forward: you become legally recognized as a California corporation by filing Articles of Incorporation with the California Secretary of State. One person may organize and operate a California nonprofit corporation. (However, in practice, most nonprofits are formed by at least a few people.)

---

[1] If you may wish to prepare and print your incorporation forms on your computer (as well as ongoing corporate minute forms for regular and special director and shareholder meetings), see the *How to Form a California Nonprofit Corporation with Corporate Records Binder & Disk*—Computer Version order coupon at the back of this book.

Incorporating a Nonprofit in Another State: If you wish to form a nonprofit corporation in a state other than California, see Nolo's national title, *How to Form a Nonprofit Corporation*. This book provides sample and tear-out forms and instructions to prepare Articles, Bylaws and Minutes and obtain the necessary nonprofit tax exemptions in each of the other 49 states. Incorporation forms are provided on a computer disk included with the book.

Step 1. Choose a Corporate Name

The first step in organizing your corporation is selecting a name for your corporation which you like and which meets the requirements of state law. Your corporate name is approved by the California Secretary of State when you file your Articles of Incorporation.

A. The Importance of Your Corporate Name

Before looking at the legal requirements for choosing a corporate name, let's briefly discuss the importance of choosing the right name for your new corporation. The most significant aspect of choosing a name is that it will, to a large degree, identify the "goodwill" of your nonprofit organization. We don't mean this in any strict legal, accounting or tax sense, but simply that people in the community, grant agencies, other nonprofits, and yes, those you do business with, will identify your nonprofit primarily by your name. For this reason, as well as a number of practical reasons such as not wanting to print new stationery, change promotional literature, create new logos, etc., you will want to pick a name that you will be happy with for a long time. So pay particular attention to your choice of a corporate name. As a practical matter, it's likely to become one of your most important assets.

B. Secretary of State Name Requirements

1. You are not legally required to include a corporate designator in your corporate name such as "Corporation," "Incorporated," "Limited," or an abbreviation of one of these words ("Corp.," "Inc.," or "Ltd.").

   Examples: The Actors' Workshop and The Actors' Workshop, Inc. are both valid corporate names.

2. Your name must not be the same as, or confusingly similar to, a name already on file with the Secretary of State. The Secretary maintains a list of names of:

   • Existing California corporations and out-of-state corporations qualified to do business in California;

   • Names which have been registered with the Secretary of State by out-of-state corporations; and

   • Names which have been reserved for use by other corporations.

   If your name is the same as, or confusingly similar to, any of these, your name will be rejected. We can't give you an exact definition of the phrase, "confusingly similar," but, for practical purposes, this restriction simply means that your proposed name cannot be the same or similar in wording or spelling to that of an existing name already on the Secretary of State's list.

   Example: Your proposed name is "Open Spaces." If another corporation is on file with the Secretary of State with the name "Open Spaces International, Inc.," your name will probably be rejected as too similar.

3. A regular nonprofit corporation (the type you will organize) cannot use certain words in its name which are reserved for special types of corporations. Such restricted words include the following:

Bank	Cooperative	Federal
National	Reserve	Trust
Trustee	United States	

Here are a couple of additional legal points relevant to your choice of a corporate name:

Filing Your Corporate Name With the Secretary of State Does Not Guarantee Your Right to Use It: Having your name approved by the California Secretary of State when you file your Articles of Incorporation does not guarantee that you have the absolute right to use it. (As explained below, an unincorporated organization may already be using it as their name or another nonprofit or profit organization may be using it as a trademark or service mark.) Consequently, you may wish to do some checking on your own to be relatively sure that no one else has a prior claim to your proposed corporate name. We discuss special self-help measures you may wish to take prior to deciding on a corporate name in Section E, below.

Using a Name Different Than Your Formal Corporate Name Is Allowed: If you want to adopt a formal corporate name in your Articles which is different from the one which you have used, or plan to use, locally to identify your nonprofit organization, you can accomplish this by filing a fictitious business name statement with the County Clerk in the counties in which you plan to operate (we explain how to prepare and file this statement in Chapter 10, Step 21).

C. Practical Suggestions When Selecting a Name

Now that we've looked at the basic legal requirements related to your choice of a corporate name, here are some practical suggestions to help you do it.

Use Common Nonprofit Terms In Your Name

There are a number of words that broadly suggest 501(c)(3) nonprofit purposes or activities. Choosing one of these names can simplify the task of finding the right name for your organization and can help alert others to the nonprofit nature of your corporate activities. Here are just a few:

Academy	*House*
Aid	*Human*
American	*Humane*
Appreciation	*Institute*
Assistance	*International*
Association	*Learning*
Benefit	*Literary*
Betterment	*Mission*
Care	*Music*
Center	*Orchestra*
Charitable	*Organization*
Coalition	*Philanthropic*
Community	*Philharmonic*[1]
Congress	*Program*
Conservation	*Project*
Consortium	*Protection*
Council	*Public*
Cultural	*Refuge*
Education	*Relief*
Educational	*Religious*
Environmental	*Research*
Exchange	*Resource*
Fellowship	*Scholarship*
Foundation	*Scientific*
Friends	*Service*
Fund	*Shelter*
Health	*Social*
Help	*Society*
Heritage	*Study*
Home	*Troupe*
Hope	*Voluntary*
Hospice	*Welfare*
Hospital	

Names to Avoid

When selecting a corporate name, we suggest you avoid, or use with caution, the types of words described and listed below. Of course there are exceptions and if one of them relates to your particular nonprofit purposes or activities, it may make sense to use the word in your name.

• **Avoid words that, taken together, signify a profit making business or venture:**

Booksellers Corporation   *Commercial Products Inc.*
Jeff Baxter & Company   *Entrepreneurial Services Corp.*

• **Avoid words that describe or are related to special types of nonprofit organizations [those that are tax exempt under provisions of the IRC other than Section 501(c)(3):**

Business League
Chamber of Commerce
Civic League
Hobby, Recreational or Social Club
Labor, Agricultural or Horticultural Organization
Political Action Organization
Real Estate Board
Trade Group

For a complete listing of these special tax-exempt nonprofit groups, see Table 3.1.

Example: The name Westbrook Social Club, Inc. would clearly identify a social club, tax exempt under IRC §501(c)(7)—you shouldn't use this type of name for your 501(c)(3) nonprofit. However, The Social Consciousness Society might be an appropriate name for a 501(c)(3) educational purpose organization. Also, although The Trade Betterment League of Pottersville would identify a 501(c)(6) business league and The Millbrae Civic Betterment League a 501(c)(4) civic league, The Philanthropic League of Castlemont may be suitable for a 501(c)(3) charitable giving group.

- **Avoid words or abbreviations commonly associated with nationally known nonprofit causes, organizations, programs or trademark:**

You can bet that the well-known group has taken steps to protect its name as a trademark or service mark. Here is a small sampling of some well known nonprofit names and abbreviations:

> *AAA*
> *American Red Cross*
> *American Ballet Theatre or ABT*
> *American Conservatory Theatre or ACT*
> *Audubon*
> *Blue Cross*
> *Blue Shield*
> *Environmental Defense Fund*
> *National Geographic*
> *National Public Radio or NPR*
> *Sierra Club*
> *Public Broadcasting System or PBS*

- **Avoid words using special symbols or punctuation that may confuse the secretary of state's computer name-search software:**

> !@#$%^&*()+?><

Pick a Descriptive Name to Aid Identification

It's often a good idea to pick a name that clearly reflects your purposes or activities (Downtown Ballet Theater, Inc.; Good Health Society, Ltd.; Endangered Fish Protection League, Inc.). Doing this allows potential members, donors, beneficiaries and others to locate and identify you easily. More fanciful names (The Wave Project, Inc., Serendipity Unlimited Inc.) are usually less advisable because it normally takes a while for people to figure out what they stand for, although occasionally their uniqueness may provide better identification over the long term.

Example : Although the name Northern California Feline Shelter, Inc. will alert people at the start to the charitable purposes of the nonprofit group, Cats' Cradle, Inc. may stay with people longer once they are familiar with the activities of the organization.

- **Limit your name geographically or regionally, if necessary, to avoid name conflicts or confusion:**

If you use general or descriptive terms in your name, you may need to further qualify it to avoid conflicts or public confusion.

Example: Your proposed name is The Philharmonic Society, Inc. The secretary of state rejects this name as too close to a number of philharmonic orchestras on file. You refile using the proposed name, The Philharmonic Society of East Creek, and your name is accepted.

Another Example: Suppose you are incorporating the AIDS Support Group, Inc. Even if this name does not conflict with the name of another corporation on file, it is an excellent idea to limit or qualify the name to avoid confusion by the public with other groups in other parts of the state or country that share the same purposes or goals. This could be done by changing the name to the AIDS Support Group of Middleville.

- **Choose a new name rather than limiting your proposed name with a local (or other) identifier if there is still the likelihood of public confusion between your name and the name of another group:**

  Example: Your proposed nonprofit name is The Park School, Inc. If another corporation (specializing in a nationwide network of apprentice training colleges) is already listed with the name Park Training Schools, the secretary of state may reject your name as too similar. You may be able to limit your name and make it acceptable (The Park Street School of Southville, Inc.) but this may not be a good idea for two reasons:

  1. members of the public who have heard of the Park Training Schools may believe that your school is simply a Southville affiliate of the national training program; and

  2. you may be infringing the trademark rights of the national group (they may have registered their name as a state or federal trademark).

- **Use a corporate designator in your name:**

  Even though not legally required in California, you may wish to include a corporate designator in your name to let others know that your organization is a corporation.

  Example: Hopi Archaeological Society, Inc.; The Children's Museum Corporation; Mercy Hospital, Incorporated; The Hadley School Corp.

- **Put an Inc. after your unincorporated name:**

  Of course, if you are incorporating an existing organization, you'll probably wish to use yourcurrent name as your corporate name if it has become associated with your group, its activities, fund raising efforts, products, services, etc. Many new corporations do this by simply adding an "Inc." after their old name (e.g., The

World Betterment Fund decides to incorporate as The World Betterment Fund, Inc.). Using your old name is not an incorporation requirement, however, and if you have been hankering after a new name for your organization, this is your chance to claim it.

Take Your Time When Choosing a Corporate Name

Finding an appropriate and available name for your organization takes time and requires patience. It's usually best not to act on your first impulse—try a few names before making your final choice. Ask others both inside and outside the organization for feedback. And of course, remember: your proposed name may not be available for your use—have one or more alternate names in reserve in case your first choice isn't available.

D. Check to See If Your Proposed Name Is Available

Since your Articles of Incorporation will be rejected if the name you've chosen is not available, you may wish check its availability or reserve it before submitting your Articles to the Secretary of State.

You can check the availability of up to four corporate names by mail by sending a note to the Secretary of State at 1500 11th Street, Sacramento, California, 95814. Provide your name and address, a list of up to four proposed corporate names, and a request that each name be checked to see if it is available for use as a corporate name. The Secretary will respond to your written request within one week or two.

Note: Even if the Secretary indicates by return mail that a corporate name is available, it may not be available when you file your Articles (if someone else actually uses it before you file your papers). To avoid this problem and to save time, you can check and reserve a name for a small fee as explained in the next section.

If the use of your proposed name is crucial to you and you are told that it is unacceptable as being too close to an existing name already on file, there are a few things you can do:

1. Submit a written request for a review of your name's acceptability to the legal counsel's office at the Secretary of State. You should know that the Secretary of State does not publish official guidelines for determining the acceptability of corporate names and maintains a very limited staff to help resolve issues arising from the similarity of proposed corporate names. Further, the questions here are not always easy to resolve: The legal question of whether or not a name is so close to another so as to cause confusion to the public involves looking at a number of criteria contained in a long line of court decisions, including the nature of each trade name user's business (the term "trade name" simply means a name used in conjunction with the operation of a trade or business), the geographical proximity of the two businesses, etc. We cover these issues in more detail below but, for now, we simply note that if you do get into this sort of squabble, you will probably want to see a lawyer who is versed in the complexities of trade name or trademark law or do some additional reading on your own.

2. Obtain the written consent of the other corpo-ration. Often, profit corporations which have registered a name similar to the proposed name of a nonprofit corporation will be willing to allow the nonprofit corporation to use the similar name.

Important: Make sure to call the Secretary of State's office (at 1-916-657-5448) and ask if this written consent procedure will work for you. Even with the consent of the other corporation, the Secretary's office will not allow you to use a similar name if they feel the public is likely to be misled (e.g., if the names are very similar in sound, etc.). If

you get the go-ahead to use this procedure, ask the Secretary for the address of the other corporation and send the corporation a written request for an officer of their corporation to sign, together with an explanatory letter (and/or make a preliminary phone call) indicating why you'd like them to agree to your use of your similar name (e.g., because you will be engaged in nonprofit activities clearly different from their profit-making business in a different locale, etc.).

3. Decide that it's simpler (and less trouble all the way around) to pick another name for your nonprofit corporation. We normally recommend this third approach.

E. Reserve Your Corporate Name

For a small fee, you can check the availability of up to four names at once and reserve the first available name by mail with the Sacramento office of the Secretary of State. We think it makes sense to do this rather than simply checking to see if your name is available as explained above. Besides, good names that are available for use with the Secretary of State are becoming hard to find. Reserving a potential name for your corporation allows you hold on to it while you complete your initial paperwork (and, perhaps, take the additional self-help name search measures discussed in the next section).

To reserve a corporate name, prepare and file the Application for Reservation of Corporate Name included in the Appendix , following the sample form and special instructions below.

√ The parenthetical blanks, i.e., "(_____)," indicate information which you must complete on the tear-out form.

√ Tear out the form in the Appendix and fill in the blanks (using a typewriter with a black ribbon or printing neatly with a blank ink pen) as you follow the sample form and instructions below.

Sample Application for Reservation of Corporate Name

__(Your address)__
__(Date of letter)__

Secretary of State
Corporate Name Availability Section
1500 11th Street
Sacramento, CA 95814-2974

Dear Secretary of State:

Please reserve a corporate name for use of the undersigned for sixty days following the issuance of your certificate of reservation of name. ①

The name desired is one of the following, listed in order of preference: ②

1. __(First Choice for Corporate Name)__
2. __(Second Choice)__
3. __(Third Choice)__
4. __(Fourth Choice)__

I enclose the required fee for the certificate of reservation to be issued. ③

Sincerely,

__(your signature)__   ④
(print or type your name)

SPECIAL INSTRUCTIONS

① The Secretary of State will send you a certificate of reservation which is valid for 60 days from the date it is issued. If you cannot file your Articles within this time, you can re-reserve the name by preparing a new reservation letter. However, the second reservation letter must be received by the Secretary of State at least one day after the first certificate expires. (The law does not allow two consecutive reservations of corporate name—therefore the requests must be separated by at least one day.)

② If you have more than one choice for a corporate name, list your second, third and fourth choices here in case your first choice isn't available for your use.

③ The filing fee for reservation of a corporate name is $10. Make your check payable to the California Secretary of State and mail your check and one copy of the completed form to the Sacramento address of the Secretary of State shown in the letter.

Filing in Person: You can also reserve a corporate name in person at any one of the following offices of the Secretary of State:

SACRAMENTO
1500 11th Street, Room 100
Sacramento, CA 95814

FRESNO
2497 West Shaw, Suite 101
Fresno, CA 93711

LOS ANGELES
107 South Broadway, Room 4001
Los Angeles, CA 90012

SAN DIEGO
1350 Front Street, Suite 2060
San Diego, CA 92101

The fee for reserving a name in person is $20. The clerk will ask for *two* $10 checks. If your proposed name is not available, the clerk will keep $10 and return one $10 check to you.

Warning on Fee Increases: Fees are subject to change. To be sure the above fee amounts are current, call the Secretary of State at 1-916-657-5448.

④ The letter should be signed by one of the persons who will act as your incorporator (one of the persons who will form your corporation by signing the Articles of Incorporation as part of Step 2, below).

F. Perform Your Own Name Search

As we've said, approval by the Secretary of State's office of your corporate name doesn't necessarily mean that you have the legal right to use this name. Acceptance of your corporate name by the Secretary of State's office simply means that your name does not conflict with that of another corporation already on file with the Secretary of State and that you are presumed to have the legal right to the use of this name for your corporation in California. It is important to realize, however, that other organizations (corporate and non-corporate, profit and nonprofit) may already have the right to use this same name (or one similar to it) as a federal or state trademark or service mark used to identify their goods or services. (The Secretary of State does *not* check the state trademark/service mark registration lists maintained in the Secretary of State's office when checking to see if your name is available.) Also, another organization (corporate or non-corporate) may already be presumed to have the legal right to use your name in a particular county if they are using it as trade name (as the name of their business or organization) and have filed a fictitious business name statement with their county clerk.

To underscore the fact that acceptance of a corporate name by the Secretary of State is not determinative of who has this ultimate right, the Secretary's office will send you a notice after you file your Articles which states that the filing of the Articles of Incorporation does not, in itself, authorize the use in California of a corporate name which is in violation of the rights of another person to use the name, including rights in a trade name, rights under state or federal trademark laws or state fictitious business name laws, and rights which arise under principles of common law (the law expressed in court decisions).

Without discussing the intricacies of federal and state trademark, service mark and trade name law, the basic rule is that the ultimate right to use a particular name will usually be decided on the basis of who was first in time to actually use the name in connection with a particular trade, business, activity, service or product. In deciding who has the right to a name, the similarity of the types of businesses or organizations and their geographical proximity are usually taken into account. To avoid problems, we suggest using the name selection techniques discussed in subsection C above and performing the kind of common sense checking described further below.

Of course, disputes involving trade names, trademarks and service marks tend to arise in the private, commercial sector. Further, it is unlikely that your nonprofit will wish to "market" products and services as aggressively as a regular commercial concern and thereby run afoul of another business's trademark or service mark (besides, engaging in a substantial amount of commercial activity of this sort could jeopardize your tax exempt status). Nonetheless, as a matter of common sense, and to avoid legal disputes later on, you should do your best to avoid names already in use by other profit and nonprofit organizations, or in use as trademarks or service marks.

The simplest and most practical solution here is to do a little checking on your own before filing your Articles. Obviously, you will not be able to be 100 percent certain since you can't possibly check all names in use by other groups. However, you can check obvious sources likely to expose similar names which are not listed as corporate names on the Secretary's list. Here are some suggestions:

- Check with the County Clerk in the county or counties in which you plan to operate to see if your name has already been registered by another person, organization or business as a fictitious business name. Most county clerks will require you to come in and check the fictitious business files yourself—it takes just a few minutes to do this.

- Check major metropolitan phone book listings, nonprofit directories, business and trade directories, etc. Larger public libraries have phone directories for many major cities within and outside of California.

  A Likely Resource: One commonly consulted national directory of nonprofit names is the *Encyclopedia of Associations* published by Gale Research Company.

- To check state trademarks and service marks, call the California Secretary of State's trademark and service mark registration section at 1-916-653-4984. They will check up to two names against their list of registered marks over the phone at no charge.

- If you wish to check federal trademarks and service marks, go to a public library or special business and government library in your area which carries the federal Trademark Register, a listing of trademark and service mark names broken into categories of goods and services.

Computer Resource Note: Most of the business name listings mentioned above, including yellow page listings and business directory databases, as well as the federal and state trademark registers, are available as part of several commercial computer databases. For example, the federal and state registers can be accessed through the Trademarkscan® service which is part of the Trademark Research Center forum (Go Traderc) on CompuServe database (call 800-848-8990 for subscription information) or the Dialog database (call 800-462-3411). If you own, or have access to, a computer and a modem and are already signed up on one of these databases, you can check your proposed name against the names in the federal and state registers in just a few minutes time (for an extra charge for your time while using the Trademarkscan service).

Of course, if you wish to go further in your name search, you can pay a private records search company to check various databases and name listings. Alternatively, or in conjunction with your own efforts or search procedures, you can pay a trademark lawyer to oversee or undertake these searches for you. Most smaller nonprofits will not feel the need to do this and will be content to undertake the more modest self-help search procedures mentioned above.

Step 2. Prepare Articles of Incorporation

The next step in organizing your corporation is preparing the tear-out Articles of Incorporation contained in the Appendix. You will file this form with the Secretary of State as explained in later sections. We provide two sets of Articles in the Appendix: one set for California public benefit corporations [those formed for 501(c)(3) educational, charitable, scientific or literary purposes]; and an alternate set for religious corporations [those formed for 501(c)(3) religious purposes]. To prepare the tear-out Articles for a California public benefit nonprofit corporation, follow the instructions in Section A below; to prepare the tear-out Articles for a California religious nonprofit corporation, refer to Section B below.

Note for Unincorporated Associations: If you are incorporating an existing nonprofit organization which was organized and operated as an unincorporated association (with formal Articles of Association, a Charter, or Association Bylaws), then you will need to prepare a special page in addition to the standard Articles shown in Sections A or B below. For a further discussion of unincorporated associations and instructions on preparing this special version of the Articles, see Step 3 below. *Most pre-existing nonprofit organizations are not organized as unincorporated associations and do not need to complete the extra form covered in Step 3.*

Warning: Most groups will wish to use the tear-out form as is. If you wish to modify this form, do so only after making sure your changes conform to the California Nonprofit Corporation Law. (See Chapter 12 for suggestions on doing your own research or finding a lawyer to help you make modifications.)

Computer Users

A special computer version of this book, *How to Form a California Nonprofit Corporation With Corporate Records Binder and Disk*, which contains computer disk files for all incorporation forms (as well as ongoing corporate minute forms for regular and special director and shareholder meetings), is available from Nolo Press. See the special order coupon at the back of this book (together with upgrade discount for prior purchasers of the book).

A. Prepare Articles for a California Public Benefit Corporation

To prepare Articles for your public benefit corporation, fill in the the the tear-out *Articles of Incorporation of California Public Benefit Corporation* in the Appendix, following the sample Articles and special instructions below.

√ The parenthetical blanks, i.e., "(_____)," indicate information which you must complete on the tear-out form.

√ Each circled number (e.g., ①) refers to a special instruction which provides specific information to help you complete an item. The special instructions immediately follow the sample form.

√ Tear out the form in the Appendix and fill in the blanks (using a typewriter with a black ribbon) as you follow the sample form and instructions below.

Sample Articles of Incorporation

ONE: The name of this corporation is ___(name of corporation)___ .①

TWO: This corporation is a nonprofit public benefit corporation and is not organized for the private gain of any person. It is organized under the Nonprofit Public Benefit Corporation Law for charitable② purposes. The specific purposes for which this corporation is organized are ___(include statement of specific purposes in one or two short sentences here)___

_____

_____.③

THREE: The name and address in the State of California of this corporation's initial agent for service of process is ___(indicate name and address of the corporation's agent for service of process)___ .④

FOUR: (a) This corporation is organized and operated exclusively for ___(indicate your 501(c)(3) tax-exempt purposes or purposes; e.g., "charitable," "educational," "scientific," "literary")___ ⑤ purposes within the meaning of Section 501(c)(3) of the Internal Revenue Code.

(b) Notwithstanding any other provision of these Articles, the corporation shall not carry on any other activities not permitted to be carried on (1) by a corporation exempt from federal income tax under Section 501(c)(3) of the Internal Revenue Code or (2) by a corporation contributions to which are deductible under Section 170(c)(2) of the Internal Revenue Code.

(c) No substantial part of the activities of this corporation shall consist of carrying on propaganda, or otherwise attempting to influence legislation, and the corporation shall not participate or intervene in any political campaign (including the publishing or distribution of statements) on behalf of, or in opposition to, any candidate for public office.

FIVE: The names and addresses of the persons appointed to act as the initial Directors of this corporation are:

Name   Address
(show name and business or residence address of initial director(s) on lines below) ⑥

_____   _____

_____   _____

_____   _____

_____   _____

_____   _____

SIX: The property of this corporation is irrevocably dedicated to __(allowable dedication purpose or purposes—see instruction)__ ⑦ and no part of the net income or assets of the organization shall ever inure to the benefit of any director, officer or member thereof or to the benefit of any private person.

On the dissolution or winding up of the corporation, its assets remaining after payment of, or provision for payment of, all debts and liabilities of this corporation, shall be distributed to a nonprofit fund, foundation, or corporation which is organized and operated exclusively for __(allowable dedication purpose or purposes—see instruction)__ ⑦ and which has established its tax-exempt status under Section 501(c)(3) of the Internal Revenue Code.

Date: _____

__(signatures of director(s) listed in Article FIVE)__ ⑧
(typed name) , Director

_____ , Director

_____ , Director

_____ , Director

_____ , Director

We, the above-mentioned initial directors of this corporation, hereby declare that we are the persons who executed the foregoing Articles of Incorporation, which execution is our act and deed.

__(signatures of director(s) listed in Article FIVE)__ ⑧
(typed name) , Director

_____ , Director

_____ , Director

_____ , Director

_____ , Director

Special Instructions

① Type the name of your corporation, remembering the requirements given in Step 1 of this chapter. If you have reserved a corporate name, make sure the name shown here is exactly the same as the name shown on your Certificate of Reservation.

② You'll notice that we indicate in the second sentence of Article TWO that your corporation is organized under the Nonprofit Public Benefit Corporation Law for *charitable* purposes. Don't confuse this purpose with your 501(c)(3) tax-exempt purpose or purposes. This statement is simply meant to satisfy the requirements of the California Corporations Code, not the tax exemption statutes. Public benefit corporations must be organized under state law for a *charitable* or *public* purpose and the accepted practice for non-religious, 501(c)(3) type groups—the type of group you are incorporating—is to indicate a charitable (as opposed to public) purpose in this sentence.[3]

③ Type a short statement of your group's specific purposes here in the blanks at the end of Article TWO. **Important:** Be brief here; one or two short sentences at most—this is a short, formal statement meant only to satisfy state law requirements. (You will provide much more detail on your nonprofit purposes and activities in your tax exemption applications.)

Tips on Preparing a Statement of Specific Purposes: Keep the following in mind when completing this short statement of purposes:

• You should use this statement to succinctly spell out the tax-exempt activities that qualify you for the necessary tax exemptions. Specifically, your statement should make clear that you fall within one or more of the non-religious 501(c)(3) tax exemption categories (charitable, educational, scientific or literary). Make sure you use the key words associated with one or more of these categories (e.g., "charitable" or "educational"). If necessary, describe the kinds of activities you pursue in any one or more of these categories with language that will clearly identify them as ones which the IRS considers to be tax-exempt.

• Remember, although you may qualify as tax-exempt under one or more categories of Section 501(c)(3) (e.g., a charitable and educational organization), you may not fall under a 501(c)(3) category and another category associated with another tax-exempt section of the Internal Revenue Code.

Example: An educational and social welfare organization would not be eligible for tax exemptions since social welfare groups are exempt under the provisions of a different Internal Revenue Code section.

Therefore, be careful to avoid using key words associated with these other tax-exempt sections—such as "social," "fraternal" and "recreational."

Examples of Specific Purpose Statements: These examples are illustrations, not boiler-plate clauses which will necessarily apply to your group. Since the purposes and activities of each group differ, there is no simple custom-tailored clause that will fit every one. First, take a look at the examples to get a feel for the kind of information you should provide in your statement. Then, look again at the considerations listed above and refer back to the discussions of each tax exemption category in Chapter 3. Now find a pencil (with a good eraser) and prepare a few sentences describing your specific purposes. Finally, reduce these few sentences to two short sentences summarizing your tax-exempt purposes and type the final version on the tear-out form. You'll see that it is not too difficult.

---

[3]In contrast, social welfare groups, tax-exempt under a different section of the Internal Revenue Code, are expected to use the alternate word "public" in this sentence.

Educational: Publishing and Lectures: Here is a sample clause for a group that wishes to publish books and give public lectures. Notice that these activities are clearly earmarked as educational and that, although the purposes refer to an educational institution, no mention need be made of any institutional attributes such as a full-time faculty, standard curriculum or regularly enrolled student body. **Note:** All examples start with the beginning of the last sentence of Article TWO: "The specific purposes for which this corporation is organized are…" Remember, your wording will be inserted in the blanks on the tear-out form and will complete this sentence.

The specific purposes for which this corporation is organized are to develop an institution to teach and disseminate educational material to the public, including, but not limited to, material relating to __(the areas of instruction are mentioned here)__, through publications, lectures, or otherwise.

Educational: Dance Group: This sample clause is for a group that wants to set up studios where it can teach dance and hold dance performances. As you will notice, this group leaves itself open to teaching and promoting other art forms. This paves the way for the future. Revenue taken in for cultural activities other than dance will be considered to be related to the group's specific purposes and, therefore, will be treated as tax-exempt income. Again, the term education is clearly identified and the general public is specified as the recipient of these tax-exempt services.

The specific and primary purposes for which this corporation is organized are to educate the general public in dance and other art forms. The means of providing such education includes, but is not limited to, maintaining facilities for instruction and public performances of dance and other art forms.

Charitable and Educational: Housing Improvement: Here is a sample clause for a group planning to get grants and tax exemptions for improving housing conditions for low and moderate income people by organizing a housing information and research exchange. Note that this activity is characterized as both educational and charitable. Also note that the following example simply restates the group's specific purposes, characterizing them as charitable and educational purposes in the interests of the general public.

The specific purposes for which this corporation is organized are to provide education and charitable assistance to the general public by organizing a housing information and research exchange.

Charitable: Medical Clinic: This sample clause is for a community health care clinic for low-income people.

The specific purposes for which this corporation is organized are to establish and maintain a comprehensive system of family-oriented health care aimed primarily at the medically underserved areas of __(city and county)__.

④ Type the name and residence or business address of the corporation's initial agent for service of process—this is the person to whom legal documents in any future lawsuit against the corporation must be sent. Normally, the name of one of the initial directors (see special instruction ⑤) will be given here along with the address of the corporation. You cannot use a post office box number in this address.

⑤ Indicate your 501(c)(3) tax-exempt purpose or purposes in this blank: type the word "charitable," "educational," "scientific," "literary," or a combination of these words ("charitable and educational").

⑥ Indicate the names and addresses of the initial directors of the corporation. You may organize a public benefit corporation with just one, but will probably want to provide for more. You may give the business address—usually the address of the corporation—or the residence address of each initial director.

Remember: Public benefit corporations must have two unpaid directors for each paid director—see Chapter 2E).

⑦ The blanks in Article SIX serve a few basic purposes:

- They irrevocably dedicate the property of the corporation to specific tax-exempt purposes to fulfill state corporation law requirements and allow qualifying nonprofit groups to obtain personal and real property tax exemptions under California's welfare exemption;

- They fulfill the requirements of the state and federal tax exemptions by specifying that the assets and income of the corporation will not inure to the benefit of any individual and that any assets remaining after paying off corporate debts will be distributed to another 501(c)(3) tax-exempt nonprofit organization.

Both blanks should state the same purpose or purposes—ones that meets both the requirements of 501(c)(3) of the Internal Revenue Code and the California welfare exemption. Since the allowable purposes of these sections are different, you should irrevocably dedicate property and assets to a group organized only for purposes allowed by both sections.

Checklist for filling in these blanks: The following summary explains the choices available for these blanks and shows you how easy it is to fill them in.

√ Both blanks should indicate the same purpose or purposes.

√ The basic purposes allowed by both Section 214 of the State Revenue and Taxation Code and Section 501(c)(3) are charitable, religious, educational or scientific purposes. As a public benefit corporation, you will not normally wish to dedicate property or assets to religious purpose groups—this leaves you with charitable, educational or scientific purposes as choices for filling in these blanks. If you indicate an educational or scientific purpose, you must not only state the purpose, but include additional words, as follows: "...scientific [and/or educational] purposes meeting the requirements of Section 214 of the California Revenue and Taxation Code." Consequently, you should use one of the following three phrases to fill in both of these blanks:

1. "charitable purposes";

2. "educational purposes meeting the requirements of Section 214 of the California Revenue and Taxation Code"; or

3. "scientific purposes meeting the requirements of Section 214 of the California Revenue and Taxation Code."

√ All groups may simply show "charitable purposes" in these two blanks—*this is the simplest approach and is our recommendation*. If you wish, you can indicate the same purpose as your 501(c)(3) tax-exempt purpose (Special Instruction 5, above) in both blanks, provided they are charitable, educational or scientific. You can also indicate a purpose that is different from the tax-exempt purpose of your group, but it must be one or more of the three purposes permitted for these blanks. You must include the additional language for educational or scientific purpose dedication clauses set out just above if you indicate either or both of these purposes.

√ Make sure to type the complete phrase in both blanks—the word "purposes" is not included after each blank in the tear-out form so you must include this word in each response. See the three examples listed above for the exact wording to use.

⑧ Date the Articles and have each person named as a directors in Article FIVE sign on the signature lines at the bottom of the Articles. Note that there are two sets of signature lines—each director signs twice. Type the director's name under each signature line.

B. Prepare Articles for a California Religious Corporation

To prepare Articles for your religious corporation, fill in the the tear-out *Articles of Incorporation of California Religious Corporation* in the Appendix, following the sample Articles and special instructions below. This form contains few blanks since the term "religious purposes" has already been inserted in the appropriate sections in the tear-out form.

√ The parenthetical blanks, i.e., "(_____)," indicate information which you must complete on the tear-out form.

√ Each circled number (e.g., ①) refers to a special instruction which provides specific information to help you complete an item. The special instructions immediately follow the sample form.

√ Tear out the form in the Appendix and fill in the blanks (using a typewriter with a black ribbon) as you follow the sample form and instructions below.

Sample Articles of Incorporation

ONE: The name of this corporation is ___(name of corporation)___.①

TWO: This corporation is a nonprofit religious corporation and is not organized for the private gain of any person. It is organized under the Nonprofit Religious Corporation Law primarily for religious purposes. The specific purposes for which this corporation is organized are ___(include statement of specific purposes in one or two short sentences here)___

_____

_____.②

THREE: The name and address in the State of California of this corporation's initial agent for service of process is ___(indicate name and address of the corporation's agent for service of process)___.③

FOUR: (a) This corporation is organized and operated exclusively for religious purposes within the meaning of Section 501(c)(3) of the Internal Revenue Code.

(b) Notwithstanding any other provision of these Articles, the corporation shall not carry on any other activities not permitted to be carried on (1) by a corporation exempt from federal income tax under Section 501(c)(3) of the Internal Revenue Code or (2) by a corporation contributions to which are deductible under Section 170(c)(2) of the Internal Revenue Code.

(c) No substantial part of the activities of this corporation shall consist of carrying on propaganda, or otherwise attempting to influence legislation, and the corporation shall not participate or intervene in any political campaign (including the publishing or distribution of statements) on behalf of, or in opposition to, any candidate for public office.

FIVE: The names and addresses of the persons appointed to act as the initial directors of this corporation are:

Name   Address
(show name and business or residence address of initial director(s) on lines below) ④

_____   _____

_____   _____

_____   _____

_____   _____

SIX: The property of this corporation is irrevocably dedicated to religious purposes and no part of the net income or assets of the organization shall ever inure to the benefit of any director, officer or member thereof or to the benefit of any private person.

On the dissolution or winding up of the corporation, its assets remaining after payment of, or provision for payment of, all debts and liabilities of this corporation, shall be distributed to a nonprofit fund, foundation, or corporation which is organized and operated exclusively for religious purposes and which has established its tax-exempt status under Section 501(c)(3) of the Internal Revenue Code.

Date: _____

(signatures of director(s) listed in Article FIVE) Ⓢ
(typed name) , Director

_____ , Director

_____ , Director

_____ , Director

_____ , Director

We, the above-mentioned initial directors of this corporation, hereby declare that we are the persons who executed the foregoing Articles of Incorporation, which execution is our act and deed.

(signatures of director(s) listed in Article FIVE) Ⓢ
(typed name) , Director

_____ , Director

_____ , Director

_____ , Director

_____ , Director

Special Instructions

① Type the name of your corporation, remembering the requirements given in Step 1 of this chapter. If you have reserved a corporate name, make sure the name shown here is exactly the same as the name shown on your Certificate of Reservation.

② First refer back to special instruction ③ for the Articles of Public Benefit Corporation in Section A above to get a general idea of what this specific purpose statement is meant to accomplish and how it should be written. Complete the sentence at the end of Article TWO using one or two short sentences.

Example: A religious corporation which plans to establish a formal church might simply state its specific purposes this way:

The specific purposes for which this corporation is organized are to establish and maintain a church for religious worship.

③ Type the name and residence or business address of the corporation's initial agent for service of process—this is the person to whom legal documents in any future lawsuit against the corporation must be sent. Normally, the name of one of the initial directors (see special instruction ④) will be given here along with the address of the corporation. You cannot use a post office box number in this address.

④ Type the names and addresses of the initial directors of the corporation. You may organize a religious corporation with just one director. However, most religious groups will name three or more directors here. You may give the business address—usually the address of the corporation—or the residence address of each initial director.

⑤ Date the Articles and have each person named as a directors in Article FIVE sign on the signature lines at the bottom of the Articles. Note that there are two sets of signature lines—each director signs twice. Type the director's name under each signature line.

Step 3. Prepare Articles for Unincorporated Association

This section only concerns you if you are incorporating an unincorporated association: a group of people who have operated a collective organization according to a formal set of ground rules (such as Articles of Association, a Charter, Association Bylaws, etc.) under the supervision of a governing board (consisting of directors or officers or similar officials). A typical example of an unincorporated association would be an unincorporated church organized and operated under a formal Church Charter and governed by a board of directors, elders, etc.

Note: Most existing nonprofit organizations are not organized as unincorporated associations and do not need to follow the special procedures explained below (skip to Step 4 below if this section does not apply to you).

If you are incorporating a formal unincorporated association of the type described above, you need to prepare a special last page for your Articles of Incorporation (first prepare the basic tear-out Articles as explained in Section A or B above; then transfer the information in the tear-out version to special retyped Articles as explained below).

Here is a checklist to follow when preparing special Articles when incorporating an unincorporated association:

√ Prepare one of the sets of tear-out Articles according to the instructions in Section A or B above.

√ Retype the completed tear-out Articles, up to and including the last Article (Article SIX) on the tear-out form.

√ Add a new Article SEVEN to your retyped
Articles, which reads as follows:

> SEVEN: The name of the existing unincorporated association, now being incorporated by the
> filing of these Articles of Incorporation, is ___**(type name of unincorporated association here)**___ .

√ Then add the two sets of signature lines
(including the declaration paragraph that falls
between the two sets of signature lines) that
appear after Article SIX in the original Articles, as
follows:

Date: _____

___**(signatures of director(s) listed in Article FIVE)**___
(typed name)   , Director

_____
                                                    , Director

_____
                                                    , Director

_____
                                                    , Director

_____
                                                    , Director

We, the above-mentioned initial directors of this corporation, hereby declare that we are the persons who
executed the foregoing Articles of Incorporation, which execution is our act and deed.

_____
                , Director

_____
                , Director

_____
                , Director

_____
                , Director

_____
                , Director

√ Then type and fill in the following declaration at
the end of your retyped Articles (after the second
set of signature lines):

DECLARATION

__(Name of association board member or officer)__ and __(name of association board member or officer)__ declare under penalty of perjury that they are the __(titles of association board members or officer)__ of __(name of unincorporated association)__, the unincorporated association referred to in the Articles of Incorporation to which this declaration is attached, and that said association has duly authorized its incorporation by means of said Articles of Incorporation.

Date: __(date of signing)__

__(signature of association board member or officer)__
(typed name)

__(signature of association board member or officer)__
(typed name)

Instructions for Declaration: Any two officers (e.g., President, Vice President, Secretary, Treasurer) or any two members of the governing board (e.g., directors, trustees) of the unincorporated association can prepare and sign the above declaration. Indicate their names and positions in the blanks provided and have the two association officers or two association governing members sign below the declaration.

Special Rules When Incorporating an Unincorporated Association

- The incorporation of the association must be approved by the association in accordance with its rules and procedures (usually at least a majority vote of association members is required). A failure to obtain proper association approval of its incorporation could result in legal action being taken against the new corporation.

- Upon the change of status by an unincorporated association to a corporation, the property of the association becomes the property of the corporation. Also, if association members had any voting rights of the type which entitle members of a corporation to be "formal members" (e.g., right to vote for directors or to vote for dissolution, etc.), then these association members become formal members of the corporation (you must organize as a membership corporation). See Chapter 1 for a further discussion of the rules and consequences of formal membership in a corporation.

- All rights of association creditors and all liens on the property of the association remain intact after the incorporation. This means that creditors can still look to property transferred to the new corporation to satisfy creditor claims. If legal action is pending against the association at the time of its incorporation, any judgment in the legal action will bind the corporation, and creditors can satisfy their judgments by going after the assets of the new corporation.

Retyping Requirements

Note the following Secretary of State requirements when retyping your Articles:

- Use 8 1/2" x 11" letter-size or 8-1/2" x 14" legal paper;

- Type on one side of the page only;

- Leave a 3" x 3" blank square in the upper right of the first page of your Articles (for the Secretary's file stamp);

- Use black ink ribbon—copies must be legible and of sufficient contrast for photocopying.

Step 4. File Articles Early (Optional)

This step is optional and applies only to those who need to file their Articles and form their nonprofit corporation early, before they obtain their California tax exemption. **Note:** The normal sequence is to file your Articles *after* obtaining your California franchise tax exemption (to avoid paying the California franchise tax)—most groups will wish to skip this step and go ahead to Step 5 below.

Your corporate existence begins on the date your Articles are filed with the California Secretary of State. Some groups may wish to form their corporation immediately after preparing their Articles (because they want to be incorporated prior to applying for a grant or holding an upcoming special event). When you file your Articles this way, before obtaining your state tax exemption, you are subject to regular California corporate franchise tax reporting and payments. Specifically, you must make a minimum annual franchise tax payment[3] when you file your Articles; and you may be

required to file regular corporate tax returns at the end of the tax year, paying corporate taxes on any taxable income derived during the year. Further, filing your Articles this way can be risky: if your application for a state tax exemption is denied later, you will be stuck with a nonprofit, non-tax exempt California corporation (which you will probably wish to dissolve). Obviously it's best to follow the standard procedure and wait to file your Articles until you have obtained your state tax exemption.

For specific instructions on making copies of your Articles, preparing a cover letter and filing your Articles by mail or in person with the Secretary of State, see Steps 8 and 9 below. (Make sure to increase the amount of your check and the fee amount shown in your cover letter by the amount of minimum franchise tax payment.)

Filing Your State Tax Exemption Separately: When you're ready to apply for your state tax exemption, follow the instructions in Chapter 8. In this case, however, mail your state exemption package (which will include a copy of your file-endorsed Articles) directly to the Exempt Organizations Unit, Franchise Tax Board, P.O. Box 942857, Sacramento, CA 94257-4041.

Step 5. Prepare Bylaws

Preparing the Bylaws for a nonprofit corporation is not difficult. It simply involves filling in several blanks in the tear-out Bylaws contained in the Appendix. We have included several Bylaw forms in the Appendix as follows:

Basic Bylaws for Public Benefit Corporation

Membership Provisions for Public Benefit Corporation

Basic Bylaws for Religious Corporation

Membership Provisions for Religious Corporation

---

[3]The minimum franchise tax amount payable when filing profit corporation Articles is $800 (and the profit corporation filing fee is $100). Note: If you do obtain your state tax exemption later, the minimum franchise tax amount paid for the current tax year should be refunded to you within approximately two months of obtaining the exemption.

The Importance of Bylaws: The tear-out Bylaws have been written to serve several important purposes:

- They contain specific information central to the organization and operation of your particular corporation (dates of meetings, quorum requirements, etc.);

- They restate the most significant legal and tax provisions applicable to tax-exempt nonprofit corporations, useful for your own reference and necessary to assure the IRS and the state that you are eligible for these tax exemptions;

- They provide a practical, yet formal, set of rules for the orderly operation of your corporation, to resolve disputes, to provide certainty regarding procedures, and to ensure at least minimum control over corporate operations.

Important: Please read through the bylaws to understand the purpose and effect of the different provisions included in the tear-out forms.

Making Modifications to the Bylaws

Some groups may wish to add language or make other modifications to the tear-out Bylaws. Here are just two examples:

Schools: If your nonprofit activities will consist of operating a formal "school," you will need to add an article to the sample Bylaws below consisting of a "nondiscriminatory policy statement." For information on the applicability of this statement to your group and how to prepare it, see Chapter 9, instructions to Part III, Line 15.

Participants in Federal Programs: If your nonprofit corporation plans to receive federal or other public grants, these funding sources (particularly federal agencies) often require that you include a "conflict of interest" article in your Bylaws, which states that no member of the board, officer or other person exercising supervisory power in the corporation or any of their close relatives can be individually benefited from the receipt of grant funds. Generally, this means that board members, officers (President, Vice President, Secretary, Treasurer) or

members of their families can't be hired as part of the salaried staff of the corporation and that the corporation can't make decisions that would benefit any of these people in their private capacities at least unless there is full disclosure of the potential benefit and the interested director does not vote on the transaction.[4]

Publicly-funded corporations usually have both a volunteer (unpaid) board of directors and volunteer officers who serve the corporation on a part-time basis, attending board and committee meetings, but delegating the day-to-day management of the corporation to a salaried executive director and paid staff members. If you plan to receive grant funds from government or other public sources, check with the particular funding agency to determine the exact language of any conflict of interest provisions or other language that you should include in your Bylaws. In many cases, you won't want to provide for payment of directors or officers and should delete or modify ARTICLE 3, Sections 5 and 6; ARTICLE 4, Section 10; and ARTICLE 11, Section 1 of the tear-out Bylaws, below.

Important: Matters of this sort (such as the payment of salaries, duties of officers, composition of advisory or standing committees) are usually left to the discretion of the nonprofit corporation—you can usually make administrative changes of this type to your Bylaws without researching the law. However, if you wish to change the basic legal provisions in your Bylaws (such as notice or call of meeting rules, voting or quorum provisions, etc.) you should check the Nonprofit Corporation Law prior to approving these changes.

---

[4]Conflict of interest provisions of this type are usually more restrictive than the Public Benefit Corporation Law provision which prohibits more than 49% of the directors of a public benefit corporation being paid salaries for serving in some other capacity for the corporation (e.g., a director who is also a salaried officer of the corporation).

Computer Users

A special computer version of this book, *How to Form a California Nonprofit Corporation With Corporate Records Binder and Disk*, which contains computer disk files for all incorporation forms (as well as ongoing corporate minute forms for regular and special director and shareholder meetings), is available from Nolo Press. See the special order coupon at the back of this book (together with upgrade discount for prior purchasers of the book).

The following sections show you how to choose among and fill in these Bylaw forms.

A. Choose a Membership or Non-Membership Structure

Your first step in preparing Bylaws is to decide whether you wish your nonprofit corporation to be a membership or non-membership corporation. Please re-read Chapter 2G for a discussion of the legal consequences of setting up a membership structure.

Remember: A non-membership nonprofit corporation is one that has no "legal" members—members that are entitled to vote for the election of the board of directors, to vote on a merger or dissolution, to approve a sale of substantially all of the corporation's assets, or to approve changes to the Articles or Bylaws of the corporation. Most groups will probably wish to form a non-membership corporation. Why? Because a non-membership corporation is simpler to establish and operate and does not result in the loss of any significant advantages (non-legal members can always be admitted).

Some groups will conclude that the nature of their activities requires a membership structure. This is a reasonable decision in circumstances where membership participation in the affairs of the non-profit corporation is essential or desirable (to in-crease member involvement, raise dues, help attract broad-based support, etc.).

Here are some reasons why you may prefer a non-membership corporation:

- Setting up a formal membership structure dilutes directorship control over corporate operations since voting members are allowed, under law, to participate in certain major corporate decisions (e.g., of directors, amendment of Articles).

- The termination of membership rights in the corporation can often be a complicated, and sometimes risky, affair. The courts usually require that a member only be expelled for good cause after being afforded due process (e.g., notice and opportunity to respond via a formal hearing).

- The fact that you provide for formal membership in your corporation does not, necessarily, result in any advantage in obtaining public charity status before the IRS. Many "membership" dues are paid in return for reduced rates and other discounts for corporate services or events and are, therefore, not considered valid membership dues, but rather simply income derived from the performance of services.

- Deciding not to adopt a formal membership structure doesn't prevent you from receiving tax-exempt revenue from outsiders [who may be called subscribers, sponsors, or even (non-voting) members, if you like]. In other words, you can offer discounts or other benefits to outsiders who participate in the activities and programs of the corporation without giving them a legal right to participate in the management of the corporation. This is usually the preferable means of attracting public support.

B. Prepare Basic Bylaws for a Public Benefit Nonprofit Corporation

Who Should Use This Form? The Appendix contains a tear-out multi-page form entitled *Bylaws for Public Benefit Corporation*. This form should be used by all groups formed for 501(c)(3) charitable, educational, scientific, or literary purposes which have decided to form a California public benefit corporation. California religious corporations will need to prepare Religious Corporation Bylaws instead—see Section D, below.

If You Have a Formal Membership Structure:
All public benefit corporations should start by preparing these basic public benefit corporation bylaws. Groups with a formal membership structure should then prepare the separate tear-out membership provisions as explained in Section C below.

Note: There are certain provisions in these basic public benefit corporation bylaws which refer to "the members, if any," of the corporation or use other language making certain provisions applicable to the corporation only if the corporation has members. These provisions have no practical effect for non-membership corporations using these bylaws: since these corporations have no members, the directors may simply approve matters which would otherwise be subject to membership approval by normal board approval. These references to the members, if any, allow public benefit membership corporations to use these basic bylaw provisions in their final membership bylaws. Also, this format allows non-membership corporations to later amend their basic bylaws and add the specific membership provisions included in Section B below, if and when they decide to adopt a membership structure.

Prepare the public benefit corporation Bylaws by filling in the tear-out form according to the sample Bylaws and special instructions below. **Note:** The sample Bylaws below are an abbreviated version of the complete tear-out form—we only provide sample language and instructions of the few sections which contain blanks.

√ The parenthetical blanks, i.e., "(_____)," indicate information which you must complete on the tear-out form.

√ Each circled number (e.g., ①) refers to a special instruction which provides specific information to help you complete an item. The special instructions immediately follow the sample form.

√ We suggest you tear out the form in the Appendix and fill in the blanks as you follow the sample form and instructions.

√ A vertical series of dots in the sample form below indicates a gap where we have skipped over language in the tear-out form.

Sample Bylaws

of

_____ ①

a California Public Benefit Corporation

ARTICLE 1
OFFICES

SECTION 1. PRINCIPAL OFFICE

The principal office of the corporation for the transaction of its business is located in
__(name of county)__ County, California. ②

SECTION 2. CHANGE OF ADDRESS

The county of the corporation's principal office can be changed only by amendment of these Bylaws and not otherwise. The Board of Directors may, however, change the principal office from one location to another within the named county by noting the changed address and effective date below, and such changes of address shall not be deemed an amendment of these Bylaws:

(Fill lines in below later, if and when address changes) ③

_____ Dated: _____, 19__

_____ Dated: _____, 19__

_____ Dated: _____, 19__

SECTION 3. OTHER OFFICES

The corporation may also have offices at such other places, within or without the State of California, where it is qualified to do business, as its business may require and as the board of directors may, from time to time, designate.

ARTICLE 2
PURPOSES

SECTION 1. OBJECTIVES AND PURPOSES

The primary objectives and purposes of this corporation shall be: ④
__(provide specific statement of your group's nonprofit purposes and activities)__

_____

_____

_____

_____

_____

ARTICLE 3
DIRECTORS

SECTION 1. NUMBER

The corporation shall have __(number of directors)__ ⑤ directors and collectively they shall be known as the Board of Directors. The number may be changed by amendment of this Bylaw, or by repeal of this Bylaw and adoption of a new Bylaw, as provided in these Bylaws.

.

.

.

SECTION 5. COMPENSATION

Directors shall serve without compensation except that they shall be allowed and paid __("their actual and necessary expenses incurred in attending Directors meetings" or state other provisions allowing reasonable compensation for attending meetings)__ .⑥ In addition, they shall be allowed reasonable advancement or reimbursement of expenses incurred in the performance of their regular duties as specified in Section 3 of this Article. Directors may not be compensated for rendering services to the corporation in any capacity other than director unless such other compensation is reasonable and is allowable under the provisions of Section 6 of this Article.

.

.

.

SECTION 8. REGULAR AND ANNUAL MEETINGS

Regular meetings of Directors shall be held on __(date)__ ⑦ at __(time)__ _M, ⑦ unless such day falls on a legal holiday, in which event the regular meeting shall be held at the same hour and place on the next business day.

If this corporation makes no provision for members, then, at the annual meeting of directors held on __(date)__, ⑦ directors shall be elected by the Board of Directors in accordance with this section. Cumulative voting by directors for the election of directors shall not be permitted. The candidates receiving the highest number of votes up to the number of directors to be elected shall be elected. Each director shall cast one vote, with voting being by ballot only.

.

.

.

SECTION 13. QUORUM FOR MEETINGS

A quorum shall consist of __(state number of percentage, e.g., "a majority of the Board of")__ ⑧ Directors.

.

.

.

SECTION 15. CONDUCT OF MEETINGS

Meetings of the Board of Directors shall be presided over by the Chairperson of the Board, or, if no such person has been so designated or, in his or her absence, the President of the corporation or, in his or her absence, by the Vice President of the corporation or, in the absence of each of these persons, by a Chairperson chosen by a majority of the directors present at the meeting. The Secretary of the corporation shall act as secretary of all meetings of the board, provided that, in his or her absence, the presiding officer shall appoint another person to act as Secretary of the meeting.

Meetings shall be governed by ___**("Roberts' Rules of Order" or state other rules or procedures for conduct of directors' meeting)**___,⑨ as such rules may be revised from time to time, insofar as such rules are not inconsistent with or in conflict with these Bylaws, with the Articles of Incorporation of this corporation, or with provisions of law.

.

.

.

ARTICLE 5
COMMITTEES

SECTION 1. EXECUTIVE COMMITTEE

The Board of Directors may, by a majority vote of directors, designate two (2) or more of its members (who may also be serving as officers of this corporation) to constitute an Executive Committee and delegate to such Committee any of the powers and authority of the board in the management of the business and affairs of the corporation, except with respect to:

(a) The approval of any action which, under law or the provisions of these Bylaws, requires the approval of the members or of a majority of all of the members.

(b) The filling of vacancies on the board or on any committee which has the authority of the board.

(c) The fixing of compensation of the directors for serving on the board or on any committee.

(d) The amendment or repeal of Bylaws or the adoption of new Bylaws.

(e) The amendment or repeal or any resolution of the board which by its express terms is not so amendable or repealable.

(f) The appointment of committees of the board or the members thereof.

(g) The expenditure of corporate funds to support a nominee for director after there are more people nominated for director than can be elected.

(h) The approval of any transaction to which this corporation is a party and in which one or more of the directors has a material financial interest, except as expressly provided in Section 5233(d)(3) of the California Nonprofit Public Benefit Corporation Law.

By a majority vote of its members then in office, the board may at any time revoke or modify any or all of the authority so delegated, increase or decrease but not below two (2) the number of its members, and fill vacancies therein from the members of the board. The Committee shall keep regular minutes of its proceedings, cause them to be filed with the corporate records, and report the same to the board from time to time as the board may require. ⑩

.

.

.

ARTICLE 8
FISCAL YEAR

SECTION 1. FISCAL YEAR OF THE CORPORATION

The fiscal year of the corporation shall begin on the __(day and month, e.g., "first day of January")__ ⑪ and end on the __(day and month, e.g., "last day of December")__ ⑪ in each year.

.

.

.

ARTICLE 12 ⑫
MEMBERS

SECTION 1. DETERMINATION OF MEMBERS⑬

If this corporation makes no provision for members, then, pursuant to Section 5310(b) of the Nonprofit Public Benefit Corporation Law of the State of California, any action which would otherwise, under law or the provisions of the Articles of Incorporation or Bylaws of this corporation, require approval by a majority of all members or approval by the members, shall only require the approval of the Board of Directors.

WRITTEN CONSENT OF DIRECTORS ADOPTING BYLAWS⑭

We, the undersigned, are all of the persons named as the initial directors in the Articles of Incorporation of ___(name of corporation)___,⑭ a California nonprofit corporation, and, pursuant to the authority granted to the directors by these Bylaws to take action by unanimous written consent without a meeting, consent to, and hereby do, adopt the foregoing Bylaws, consisting of ___(number of pages)___ ⑭ pages, as the Bylaws of this corporation.

Dated: ___(date)___   ___(signature of Director)_____ ⑭
                             (typed name)   , Director

                             _____
                             (typed name)   , Director

                             _____
                             (typed name)   , Director

                             _____
                             (typed name)   , Director

                             _____
                             (typed name)   , Director

CERTIFICATE

This is to certify that the foregoing is a true and correct copy of the Bylaws of the corporation named in the title thereto and that such Bylaws were duly adopted by the Board of Directors of said corporation.

(Fill in Certificate date and signature of Secretary later, after first board meeting)⑮

Dated: ___(date)___   ___(signature of Secretary)_____
                             (typed name)   , Secretary

Special Instructions

① Type the name of your corporation in the heading of the Bylaws.

② Type the name of the county where the corporation's principal office is located. The principal office is the legal address of the corporation and, generally, fixes the county where legal action must be brought against the corporation.

③ The blanks in this section should not be filled in at this time. Use these blanks later to change the principal office of the corporation to another location, within the same county, by showing the new address and date of the address change.

④ This section allows you to state in more detail the primary objectives and purposes of your nonprofit corporation. (Remember, your statement of specific purposes in your Articles of Incorporation should have been brief.) Here you can go into as much detail as you want, describing the specific purposes and activities of your corporation. You can be brief here as well if you wish. We suggest, however, that you go into more detail here, listing the major purposes and activities in which you plan to engage. Doing this will give "insiders" a sense of certainty regarding the specific goals you intend to achieve and the means by which you plan to achieve them. A more detailed statement here will also serve to provide the State Franchise Board and the IRS with additional information in order for them to determine if the specific activities you plan to engage in entitle you to the necessary tax exemptions.

In all cases, you should refer back to Step 2, special instruction 3 of this chapter and re-read the considerations listed there which you should take into account in preparing a statement of purposes— they apply here as well, although you don't need (and as we've said, probably won't want) to be brief.

Example: Here's an example of an expanded list of objectives and purposes which might be used here for the same Educational-Dance Group we used as an example in preparing a short statement of specific purposes for this group's Articles.[1] If you compare this more detailed statement with the Educational-Dance Group example given above in Step 2, special instruction 3, we think you'll get the idea of what this Bylaw provision is meant to accomplish and how to prepare it.

Sample Response for an Educational Group

ARTICLE 2
PURPOSES

SECTION 1. OBJECTIVES AND PURPOSES

The primary objectives and purposes of this corporation shall be:

(a) to provide instruction in dance forms such as jazz, ballet, tap, and modern dance;

(b) to provide instruction in body movement and relaxation art forms such as tumbling, tai-chi and yoga;

(c) to give public performances in dance forms and creative dramatics;

(d) to sponsor special events involving the public performance of any or all of the above art forms as well as other performing arts by the corporation's performing troupe as well as by other community performing arts groups; and

(e) to directly engage in and to provide facilities for others to engage in the promotion of the arts, generally.

---

[1] We'll be using this hypothetical dance group in other sections of this book since it is illustrative of a large number of public benefit corporations which will derive tax-exempt revenue primarily from the performance of services related to their exempt purposes (rather than from grants, contributions, etc.).

⑤ Indicate the total number of persons authorized to serve on your board. Generally, this number should be the same as the number of people you've already indicated as the first directors of the corporation in Article FIVE of the Articles of Incorporation. However, you may at this time state a greater number to allow for additional directors to be elected at a future meeting of the board.

Important Reminder: A majority of the board of a nonprofit public benefit corporation must be disinterested—generally, this means that a majority of the board must not be paid by the corporation or related to another person who is paid by the corporation.

Example: If, as is often the case, three "active" directors also wish to work full-time as salaried officers, you will need to provide for a seven-person board here, electing four additional directors who will not be paid (they can be paid only as directors, usually on a per meeting or other reasonable basis) and who are not related to any paid persons.

Variable Number of Board Members: A few groups may wish to change this section to provide for a range of numbers of directors, with the exact number to be later fixed by resolution of the board of directors.

Example: For example, you may wish to retype this section to provide:

SECTION 1. NUMBER

The corporation shall have not less than two (2) nor more than five (5) directors, with the exact number to be fixed within these limits by approval of the Board of Directors or the members, if any, in the manner provided in these Bylaws.

⑥ Indicate in this blank any specific payments which will be allowed to board members for attending meetings of the board (note that reasonable advancement and reimbursement of expenses for performing other director duties is

allowed by this section). You may indicate a specific per-meeting amount (or you may use the sample language shown in the blank on the sample form above to authorize payment of "actual and necessary" expenses incurred by directors in attending board meetings). If, as is often the case, you do not wish to pay directors for attending meetings, simply type "no payments authorized" in this blank.

Remember: Paying a director (a small amount) solely for attending board meetings does not make a director an "interested person" for purposes of Section 5227 of the Corporations Code.

Sample Responses:

Directors shall serve without compensation except that they shall be allowed and paid **$50 for attending each meeting of the board of directors**.

Directors shall serve without compensation except that they shall be allowed and paid **no payment authorized**.

⑦ In the blanks in the first paragraph, indicate the date and time when regular meetings of the board will be held. Many nonprofits hold regular board meetings while others simply schedule regular meetings once each year and call special meetings during the year when required. In any case, make sure to indicate that you will hold a regular board meeting at least annually in the blanks.

Sample Responses:

Regular meetings of Directors shall be held on **the first Friday of each month** at **9 o'clock** AM...

Regular meetings of Directors shall be held on **the second Monday of December** at **1 o'clock PM**...

Regular meetings of Directors shall be held on **July 1st and February 20th** at **9 o'clock A**M...

In the second paragraph of this section, fill in the blank to indicate which one of your regular board meetings will be specified as the annual regular meeting of the board to elect (or re-elect) directors of your corporation. Note that in a non-membership corporation, the directors vote for their own re-election or replacements, with each director casting one written vote. Of course, if a corporation has provided for only one regular meeting each year in the first paragraph of this section, then the date of this regular meeting will be repeated in this blank as the date of the annual meeting of directors.

Sample Responses:

If this corporation makes no provision for members, then, at the annual meeting of directors held on **January 1st**, directors shall be elected…

If this corporation makes no provision for members, then, at the annual meeting of directors held on **the first Friday of July**, directors shall be elected…

Membership Note: The provisions in the second paragraph of this section only take effect for non-membership corporations—membership corporations can leave this line blank since they will add provisions to their bylaws which specify that the members, not the directors, elect directors of the corporation.

⑧ Indicate the number of directors who must be present at a director meeting to constitute a quorum so that business can be conducted. Although the usual practice is to provide for a majority, a nonprofit public benefit corporation may provide for a larger or smaller number. However, there is a limit on how small a quorum you can provide for. Specifically, the Bylaws cannot provide for a quorum of less than one-fifth of the authorized number of directors (the number given in special instruction 5, above), or two, whichever is larger. Of course, one-director corporations may and will provide for a quorum of one director. For example, a 7-director corporation can't provide for a quorum of

less than 2 directors, while a 15-director corporation must have at least a 3-director quorum.

Whatever number or percentage you decide on, you should realize that this section of the Bylaws concerns a quorum, not a vote requirement. A meeting can only be held if at least a quorum of directors is present, but a vote on any matter before the board must, generally, be passed by the vote of a majority of those present at the meeting.

Example: If a public benefit corporation with seven directors provides for a minimum quorum of two, and just two directors hold a meeting, action can be taken by the unanimous vote of these two directors. However, if all seven directors attend the meeting, action must be approved by at least four directors (a majority of those present at the meeting).

Many public benefit corporations may wish a less-than-majority quorum rule. One primary reason relates to the fact that these corporations must have a majority of "disinterested" directors on their board. Because of the presence of such disinterested persons on the board, many nonprofit public benefit corporations may wish a lower quorum requirement to ensure that meetings of directors can be held on a regular basis in case the corporation occasionally has difficulty in getting these non-salaried directors to attend board meetings on a regular basis.

⑨ In this blank indicate the rules of order which will be used at directors' meetings. Most nonprofits specify Roberts' Rules of Order here but you may indicate any set of procedures for proposing, approving, and tabling motions that you wish (or, if you will have a small board, you can leave this line blank if you see no need to specify formal procedures for introducing and discussing items of business at your board meetings).

⑩ This section of the bylaws applies to the establishment of an executive committee consisting of board members only—the Nonprofit Corporation Law allows an executive committee of this sort much of the management power of the full board (as specified in this section of the bylaws). Although at least two board members must serve on this committee, in practice, most nonprofit corporations establish an executive committee of from three to five board members. Of course, you can set up other types of committees with or without board members (see Section 2 of this Article in the tear-out Bylaws)

⑪ Indicate the beginning and ending dates of the fiscal year of the corporation. The fiscal year of the corporation is the period for which the corporation keeps its books (its accounting period) and will determine the corporation's tax year for purposes of filing certain tax returns and reports. It may be the calendar year from January 1 to December 31 (this is the usual case for nonprofits), or it may be what the IRS considers a true fiscal year consisting of a 12-month period ending on the last day of any month other than December, e.g., from July 1 to June 30.

⑫ **Last Page of Basic Public Benefit Bylaws.** The last page of the basic bylaws (consisting of Article 12, Written Consent of Directors and the Certificate section) is only intended for *non-membership groups.* Membership public benefit corporations do not need to fill in and use this last tear-out page—we provide a separate last page for membership public benefit corporations as part of the tear-out membership provisions (see Section C below).

⑬ Section 1 of Article 12 makes it clear that the directors of non-membership corporations can take the place of members in taking any action which, under law, otherwise requires membership approval (in other words, the directors can act in place of the members in non-membership corporations).

⑭ Fill in the Written Consent of Directors paragraph, showing the name of the corporation and the number of pages in your final bylaws. All of the initial directors of the corporation (the directors named in your Articles) should sign their names on the lines following this paragraph. Fill in the date and type each director's name below each signature line.

⑮ The blanks following the Certificate at bottom of the bylaws should not be filled in at this time. Your corporate Secretary will complete these blanks after the holding of the first meeting of your board.

C. Prepare Membership Provisions for a Public Benefit Nonprofit Corporation (Optional)

This section applies to public benefit membership corporations only and shows them how to add membership provisions to the basic public benefit corporation bylaws.

Note: If you have decided to form a non-membership public benefit corporation, this section does not apply to you and you should skip ahead to Chapter 7, Step 6.

To add membership provisions to your public benefit corporation bylaws, prepare the tear-out *Membership Provisions for Public Benefit Corporations* in the Appendix following the sample form and instructions below.

Important: As with the other Bylaw provisions, read the provisions in the tear-out form carefully to make sure you understand their purpose and effect. If you wish to modify the tear-out form to include your own language, you should make sure your changes conform to the Nonprofit Corporation Law (or have an attorney check over your changes).

Prepare the *Membership Provisions for Public Benefit Corporation* by filling in the tear-out form according to the sample Bylaws and special instructions below.

Note: The sample form below is an abbreviated version of the complete tear-out form—we only provide sample language and instructions of the sections which contain blanks.

√ The parenthetical blanks, i.e., "(＿＿＿)," indicate information which you must complete on the tear-out form.

√ Each circled number (e.g., ①) refers to a special instruction which provides specific information to help you complete an item. The special instructions immediately follow the sample form.

√ We suggest you tear out the form in the Appendix and fill in the blanks as you follow the sample form and instructions.

√ A vertical series of dots in the sample form below indicates a gap where we have skipped over language in the tear-out form.

Sample Membership Provisions

of

_____(name of corporation)_____ ①

a California Public Benefit Corporation

ARTICLE 12 ①
MEMBERS

SECTION 1. DETERMINATION AND RIGHTS OF MEMBERS

The corporation shall have only one class of members. No member shall hold more than one membership in the corporation. Except as expressly provided in or authorized by the Articles of Incorporation or Bylaws of this corporation, all memberships shall have the same rights, privileges, restrictions and conditions.

SECTION 2. QUALIFICATIONS OF MEMBERS

The qualifications for membership in this corporation are as follows: _(specify qualifications or, if none, type "Any person is qualified to become a member of this corporation")_ .②

SECTION 3. ADMISSION OF MEMBERS

Applicants shall be admitted to membership _(state procedure, e.g., "on making application therefor in writing" and indicate if payment will be required, e.g., " and upon payment of the application fee and/or first annual dues, as specified in the following sections of this Bylaw")_ . ③

SECTION 4. FEES, DUES AND ASSESSMENTS

(a) The following fee shall be charged for making application for membership in the corporation: _(state specific admission fee or leave to discretion of board, e.g., "in such amount as may be specified from time to time by resolution of the Board of Directors charged for, and payable with, the application for membership," or, if no fee, type "None")_ . ④

(b) The annual dues payable to the corporation by members shall be _(state amount of annual dues, leave to discretion of board, e.g., "in such amount as may be determined from time to time by resolution of the Board of Directors," or type "None")_ . ④

(c) Memberships shall be nonassessable.

.
.
.

ARTICLE 13
MEETINGS OF MEMBERS

SECTION 1. PLACE OF MEETINGS

Meetings of members shall be held at the principal office of the corporation or at such other place or places within or without the State of California as may be designated from time to time by resolution of the Board of Directors.

SECTION 2. ANNUAL AND OTHER REGULAR MEETINGS

The members shall meet annually on **(date, e.g., " the first Monday of July, September 30th)"** ⑤ in each year, at ___**(time)**___ _M,⑤ for the purpose of electing directors and transacting other business as may come before the meeting. Cumulative voting for the election of directors shall not be permitted. The candidates receiving the highest number of votes up to the number of directors to be elected shall be elected. Each voting member shall cast one vote, with voting being by ballot only. The annual meeting of members for the purpose of electing directors shall be deemed a regular meeting and any reference in these Bylaws to regular meetings of members refers to this annual meeting.

Other regular meetings of the members shall be held on ___**(date)**___ ⑥ at ___**(time)**___ M.⑥

If the day fixed for the annual meeting or other regular meetings falls on a legal holiday, such meeting shall be held at the same hour and place on the next business day.

.

.

.

SECTION 5. QUORUM FOR MEETINGS

A quorum shall consist of ___**(state percentage, which may be more or less than a majority)**___ ⑦ of the voting members of the corporation.

The members present at a duly called and held meeting at which a quorum is initially present may continue to do business notwithstanding the loss of a quorum at the meeting due to a withdrawal of members from the meeting provided that any action taken after the loss of a quorum must be approved by at least a majority of the members required to constitute a quorum.

In the absence of a quorum, any meeting of the members may be adjourned from time to time by the vote of a majority of the votes represented in person or by proxy at the meeting, but no other business shall be transacted at such meeting.

When a meeting is adjourned for lack of a sufficient number of members at the meeting or otherwise, it shall not be necessary to give any notice of the time and place of the adjourned meeting or of the business to be transacted at such meeting other than by announcement at the meeting at which the adjournment is taken of the time and place of the adjourned meeting. However, if after the adjournment a new record date is fixed for notice or voting, a notice of the adjourned meeting shall be given to each member who, on the record date for notice of the meeting, is entitled to vote at the meeting. A meeting shall not be adjourned for more than forty-five (45) days.

Notwithstanding any other provision of this Article, if this corporation authorizes members to conduct a meeting with a quorum of less than one-third (1/3) of the voting power, then, if less than one-third (1/3) of the voting power actually attends a regular meeting, in person or by proxy, then no action may be taken on a matter unless the general nature of the matter was stated in the notice of the regular meeting.

·

·

·

SECTION 8. PROXY VOTING

Members entitled to vote ___(type "shall" or "shall not")___ ⑧ be permitted to vote or act by proxy. If membership voting by proxy is not allowed by the preceding sentence, no provision in this or other sections of these Bylaws referring to proxy voting shall be construed to permit any member to vote or act by proxy.

If membership voting by proxy is allowed, members entitled to vote shall have the right to vote either in person or by a written proxy executed by such person or by his or her duly authorized agent and filed with the Secretary of the corporation, provided, however, that no proxy shall be valid after eleven (11) months from the date of its execution unless otherwise provided in the proxy. In any case, however, the maximum term of any proxy shall be three (3) years from the date of its execution. No proxy shall be irrevocable and may be revoked following the procedures given in Section 5613 of the California Nonprofit Public Benefit Corporation Law.

If membership voting by proxy is allowed, all proxies shall state the general nature of the matter to be voted on and, in the case of a proxy given to vote for the election of directors, shall list those persons who were nominees at the time the notice of the vote for election of directors was given to the members. In any election of directors, any proxy which is marked by a member "withhold" or otherwise marked in a manner indicating that the authority to vote for the election of directors is withheld shall not be voted either for or against the election of a director.

If membership voting by proxy is allowed, proxies shall afford an opportunity for the member to specify a choice between approval and disapproval for each matter or group of related matters intended, at the time the proxy is distributed, to be acted upon at the meeting for which the proxy is solicited. The proxy shall also provide that when the person solicited specifies a choice with respect to any such matter, the vote shall be cast in accordance therewith.

SECTION 9. CONDUCT OF MEETINGS

Meetings of members shall be presided over by the Chair of the Board, or, if there is no Chairperson, by the President of the corporation or, in his or her absence, by the Vice President of the corporation or, in the absence of all of these persons, by a Chair chosen by a majority of the voting members, present in person or by proxy. The Secretary of the corporation shall act as

Secretary of all meetings of members, provided that, in his or her absence, the presiding officer shall appoint another person to act as Secretary of the Meeting.

Meetings shall be governed by __(type "Roberts' Rules of Order" or indicate other rules or procedures)__ ,⑨ as such rules may be revised from time to time, insofar as such rules are not inconsistent with or in conflict with these Bylaws, with the Articles of Incorporation of this corporation, or with any provision of law.

.

.

.

WRITTEN CONSENT OF DIRECTORS ADOPTING BYLAWS

We, the undersigned, are all of the persons named as the initial directors in the Articles of Incorporation of __(name of corporation)__ ⑩ a California nonprofit corporation, and, pursuant to the authority granted to the directors by these Bylaws to take action by unanimous written consent without a meeting, consent to, and hereby do, adopt the foregoing Bylaws, consisting of __(number of pages)__ ⑩ pages, as the Bylaws of this corporation.

Dated: __(date)__   __(signature of Director)__   ⑩
                                          (typed name)   , Director

.

.

.

CERTIFICATE

This is to certify that the foregoing is a true and correct copy of the Bylaws of the corporation named in the title thereto and that such Bylaws were duly adopted by the Board of Directors of said corporation.

(Fill in Certificate date and signature of Secretary later, after first board meeting) ⑪

Dated: __(date)__   __(signature of Secretary)__
                                          (typed name)   , Secretary

Special Instructions

① You should include these membership provision pages at the end of the basic bylaws prepared as part of Section B above (place this page following the page of the basic bylaws which ends with Article 11). Remember, don't include the last page of the basic bylaws (containing an Article 12 for non-membership corporations) in your membership bylaws (these membership provisions start with Article 12 and end with a special last page for your membership bylaws).

② Use this blank to indicate any special qualifications required for members (e.g., over the age of 16, currently enrolled students in a school's curriculum, etc.). Please realize, however, that the IRS likes to see 501(c)(3) tax-exempt corporations with an open-admissions policy for members with membership in the corporation being open to the general public. Consequently, most public benefit corporations will not specify any qualifications for membership (see the suggested wording in the blank on the sample form).

③ Most public benefit corporations do not require formal application for membership in the corporation. However, some will indicate that members must pay an admission fee and/or annual dues prior to acceptance as a member in the corporation (see the suggested wording in the blank on the sample form).

④ Indicate the manner of determining, or the amount of, admission fees and/or annual dues for members in the appropriate blanks (see the suggested wording in the blanks on the sample form).

⑤ Indicate the date and time of the annual meeting of members (the members elect directors at this annual meeting). You may wish to coordinate this date with your annual directors' meeting (e.g., slightly before the annual directors' meeting).

⑥ Type the date and time of any regular meetings of members. Many nonprofits will leave this line blank and decide only to provide for the annual meeting of members in their bylaws (in the previous paragraph). Some with a more active membership will indicate monthly or semi-annual regular meetings of members here.

⑦ As indicated, you can set the quorum requirement for members' meetings at any number, whether greater or less than a majority. However, as indicated in the last paragraph of this section, if your public benefit corporation sets a quorum at less than one-third of the voting power and less than one-third of the members actually attend a meeting, then no action may be taken at the meeting unless the notice of the meeting stated the general nature of the proposals to be acted upon. Fixing a quorum at less than one-third of the voting power, therefore, can make matters more complicated— the normal rule is that any action may be taken at a regular members' meeting, whether or not it was stated in the notice of the meeting [see subsection (c) of this Article in the tear-out form]. In any case, it's a good idea to have at least a one-third quorum to help make members' meetings more representative of the entire membership.

⑧ Indicate whether the corporation will or will not allow proxy voting by members (a proxy is simply a written authorization by a member allowing another person to vote for the member). Many small membership corporations will indicate that proxy voting "shall not" be permitted to avoid problems and complications that can arise in times of controversy or difficult decisions (such as proxy wars—solicitations of proxies by outside or competing interests, etc.).

If you do decide to allow proxies, the restrictions relating to proxies contained in the next sections of this Article will apply.

⑨ Indicate, if you wish, the sets of rules which will govern the proposing and taking of action at your membership meetings. Roberts' Rules of Order is the standard, of course, but you may specify another set of procedures if you wish.

⑩ Fill in the Written Consent of Directors paragraph, showing the name of the corporation and the number of pages in your final bylaws. All of the initial directors of the corporation (the directors named in your Articles) should sign their names on the lines following this paragraph. Fill in the date and type each director's name below each signature line.

⑪ The blanks following the Certificate at bottom of the bylaws should not be filled in at this time. Your corporate Secretary will complete these blanks after the holding of the first meeting of your board.

D. Prepare Basic Bylaws for a Religious Nonprofit Corporation

If you are forming a religious corporation—a nonprofit corporation formed primarily or exclusively for religious purposes as discussed in previous sections of this book—and have prepared Articles of Incorporation for your religious corporation, you need to prepare special religious corporation Bylaws or a similar document setting forth the ground rules for your corporation. The reason we say "a similar document" is that the law which governs religious corporations, the Nonprofit Religious Corporation Law (this is a separate part of the entire Nonprofit Corporation Law), defines the Bylaws of such corporations as "the code or code of rules used, adopted, or recognized for the regulation or management of the affairs of the corporation irrespective of the name or names by which such rules are designated." What this means, in the words of the Assembly Select Committee for the Revision of the Nonprofit Corporations Code, is that the state "recognizes that certain religions are governed in part by 'canons' or other ecclesiastical documents or doctrines not contained in a document labeled 'Bylaws.'" Moreover, as we have mentioned earlier, the provisions of law which apply to religious corporations, and which would customarily be included in a corporation's Bylaws, are also considerably more flexible than those which apply to other nonprofit corporations. Specifically, while they do state certain fundamental rules regarding the operations of religious corporations, many of these apply only if the corporation's Bylaws, canons, etc., do not provide otherwise.

As you can see, religious corporations are treated quite liberally by the Nonprofit Corporation Law, particularly with respect to the form and content of their "Bylaws." This was done, according to the Assembly Committee, "in recognition of the wide diversity of religious activity, the inappropriateness of state intrusion in most religious disputes and the constitutional protection afforded religions."

We've already provided you with some general information as to the flexibility afforded religious corporations in Chapter 1; we provide further specifics on "Special Religious Corporation Rules," below.

Customizing the Basic Tear-Out Religious Corporation Bylaws: The tear-out Bylaws for a Religious Corporation in the Appendix are basic, non-membership religious corporation Bylaws and contain the standard default provisions of the Religious Corporation Law. These bylaws can be used "as is" by non-membership religious corporations (membership groups should add membership provisions as explained in Section E below).

Special Religious Corporation Rules

They may set up their own rules regarding the terms of office, election, selection, designation, removal and resignation of directors. Only in the absence of Bylaw provisions dealing with these subjects will specific provisions of the Nonprofit Religious Corporation Law apply. Also, the restriction that applies to public benefit corporations which requires that at least 51% of the board must be "disinterested" (not paid for performing services other than as directors or not related to any paid persons) does not apply to religious corporations. All of their directors may, if they wish, serve also as salaried officers, employees, independent contractors, etc.

Subject to a few exceptions, religious corporations may set up their own reasonable rules as to the calling, noticing and holding of meetings of members or obtaining the approval of members. As in (a) above, if the corporation doesn't provide these rules, then the provisions of the Religious Corporation Law will apply. The reason for this wide latitude relating to membership meetings is that the Assembly Committee felt that questions involving meetings and voting of the members in a religious context might involve doctrinal matters and First Amendment rights. For similar reasons, the Religious Corporation Law does not have any special provisions which govern the procedures for election of directors of religious corporations by members.

The general standard of conduct ("duty of care") for directors of religious corporations is similar to that which applies to public benefit corporation directors (see Chapter 2, Section E), except that religious corporation directors can take into account the religious purposes of the corporation and its religious tenets, canons, laws, policies and authority when making decisions. These directors are also allowed to rely on information provided by religious authorities, ministers, priests, rabbis, or other people whose positions or duties in the religious organization the directors believe justify reliance and confidence. This more lenient general duty of care for religious corporations also applies to decisions relating to compensation for directors, loans to directors and guaranties of obligations of directors (generally, for public benefit corporations such loans or guaranties must be approved by the Attorney General) and to purchasing and managing corporate investments (public benefit

corporations must follow strict ["trustee"] investment standards).

The rules regarding the approval of self-dealing transactions (ones in which a director has a material financial interest and which haven't been properly approved by the board or a committee) are generally the same as those which apply to public benefit corporations, except for loans and guaranties to directors as mentioned above. However, directors of religious corporations can take into account the religious purposes of the corporation when considering approval of a self-dealing transaction.

Membership inspection rights (to inspect the corporation's membership list, financial books, records of members' and board meetings, etc.) may be limited or totally eliminated by the Bylaws of a religious corporation. This is due to the fact that the Assembly Committee felt it inappropriate or, perhaps, unconstitutional, to require broad inspection rights or financial disclosure of corporate affairs to members. In the absence of any limitation on such inspection rights, members of religious corporations have basically the same right to inspect the records and reports of the corporation as do members of public benefit corporations.

The Attorney General is given less authority to oversee and intervene in the affairs of religious corporations. More specifically, the Religious Corporation Law mandates a "hands off" policy by the Attorney General towards religious corporations except as the Attorney General is empowered to act in the enforcement of the criminal laws of the state. However, a few exceptions were provided whereby the Attorney General may step in based on the authority of the Religious Corporation Law.

The California Attorney General's traditional role of enforcing the "charitable trust" theory has, since 1980, been severely curtailed. A charitable trust, under Section 9142 of the Religious Corporation Law, is deemed to exist only under certain narrowly defined conditions. Moreover, the Attorney General's office is, for the most part, prohibited from enforcing the terms of any implied or express trust (except with respect to certain property received by the corporation for a specific purpose from the general public, again subject to further restrictions, Section 9230). Expect future legislation action in the church vs. state arena.

Many non-membership nonprofit religious groups will wish to add customized provisions to these basic bylaws to take advantage of the flexibility allowed under the Nonprofit Corporation Law and to tailor the bylaws to the specific operating procedures of their organization. If you do this, make sure your changes conform to law. You can do this by reviewing the legal provisions of the Religious Corporation Law (Sections 9110 through 9690 of the Nonprofit Corporation Law) at a local county law library or by having a lawyer do this for you (it shouldn't take the lawyer more than one or two hours to check the bylaws).

Prepare the Religious Corporation Bylaws by filling in the tear-out form according to the sample form and special instructions below.

Note: The sample Bylaws below are an abbreviated version of the complete tear-out form—we only provide sample language and instructions of the few sections which contain blanks. Also: the provisions of these bylaws are based upon the provisions which we drafted for public benefit corporations. However, a number of technical changes were made to conform these bylaws to the specific provisions of the California Religious Corporation Law.

√ The parenthetical blanks, i.e., "(_____)," indicate information which you must complete on the tear-out form.

√ Each circled number (e.g., ①) refers to a special instruction which provides specific information to help you complete an item. The special instructions immediately follow the sample form.

√ We suggest you tear out the form in the Appendix and fill in the blanks as you follow the sample form and instructions.

√ A vertical series of dots in the sample form below indicates a gap where we have skipped over language in the tear-out form.

Sample Bylaws

of

_____ ①

a California Religious Corporation

ARTICLE 1
OFFICES

SECTION 1. PRINCIPAL OFFICE

The principal office of the corporation for the transaction of its business is located in
____**(name of county)**____ County, California.②

SECTION 2. CHANGE OF ADDRESS

The county of the corporation's principal office can be changed only by amendment of these
Bylaws and not otherwise. The Board of Directors may, however, change the principal office from
one location to another within the named county by noting the changed address and effective date
below, and such changes of address shall not be deemed an amendment of these Bylaws:

(Fill lines in below later, if and when address changes)③

_____   Dated: _____, 19__

_____   Dated: _____, 19__

_____   Dated: _____, 19__

SECTION 3. OTHER OFFICES

The corporation may also have offices at such other places, within or without the State of
California, where it is qualified to do business, as its business may require and as the Board of
Directors may, from time to time, designate.

ARTICLE 2
PURPOSES

SECTION 1. OBJECTIVES AND PURPOSES

The primary objectives and purposes of this corporation shall be: ④

_____**(provide specific statement of your group's nonprofit purposes and activities)**_____

_____

_____

_____

**ARTICLE 3
DIRECTORS**

SECTION 1. NUMBER

The corporation shall have __(number of directors)__ ⑤ directors and collectively they shall be known as the Board of Directors. The number may be changed by amendment of this Bylaw, or by repeal of this Bylaw and adoption of a new Bylaw, as provided in these Bylaws.

.
.
.

SECTION 5. COMPENSATION

Directors shall serve without compensation except that they shall be allowed and paid __("their actual and necessary expenses incurred in attending Directors meetings" or state other provisions allowing reasonable compensation for attending meetings)__ . ⑥ In addition, they shall be allowed reasonable advancement or reimbursement of expenses incurred in the performance of their regular duties as specified in Section 3 of this Article.

.
.
.

SECTION 7. REGULAR AND ANNUAL MEETINGS

Regular meetings of Directors shall be held on __(date)__ ⑦ at __(time)__ M, ⑦ unless such day falls on a legal holiday, in which event the regular meeting shall be held at the same hour and place on the next business day.

If this corporation makes no provision for members, then, at the annual meeting of directors held on __(date)__, ⑦ directors shall be elected by the Board of Directors in accordance with this section. Cumulative voting by directors for the election of directors shall not be permitted. The candidates receiving the highest number of votes up to the number of directors to be elected shall be elected. Each director shall cast one vote, with voting being by ballot only.

.
.
.

SECTION 12. QUORUM FOR MEETINGS

A quorum shall consist of __(state number of percentage, e.g., "a majority of the Board of")__ ⑧ Directors.

.
.
.

SECTION 14. CONDUCT OF MEETINGS

Meetings of the Board of Directors shall be presided over by the Chairperson of the Board, or, if no such person has been so designated or, in his or her absence, the President of the corporation or, in his or her absence, by the Vice President of the corporation or, in the absence of each of these persons, by a Chairperson chosen by a majority of the directors present at the meeting. The Secretary of the corporation shall act as secretary of all meetings of the Board, provided that, in his or her absence, the presiding officer shall appoint another person to act as Secretary of the Meeting.

Meetings shall be governed by __("Roberts' Rules of Order" or state other rules or procedures for conduct of directors' meeting)__ ,⑨ as such rules may be revised from time to time, insofar as such rules are not inconsistent with or in conflict with these Bylaws, with the Articles of Incorporation of this corporation, or with provisions of law.

.
.
.

ARTICLE 5
COMMITTEES

SECTION 1. EXECUTIVE COMMITTEE

The Board of Directors may, by a majority vote of directors, designate two (2) or more of its members (who may also be serving as officers of this corporation) to constitute an Executive Committee and delegate to such Committee any of the powers and authority of the Board in the management of the business and affairs of the corporation, except with respect to:

(a) The approval of any action which, under law or the provisions of these Bylaws, requires the approval of the members or of a majority of all of the members.

(b) The filling of vacancies on the Board or on any committee which has the authority of the Board.

(c) The fixing of compensation of the directors for serving on the Board or on any committee.

(d) The amendment or repeal of Bylaws or the adoption of new Bylaws.

(e) The amendment or repeal or any resolution of the Board which by its express terms is not so amendable or repealable.

(f) The appointment of committees of the Board or the members thereof.

By a majority vote of its members then in office, the Board may at any time revoke or modify any or all of the authority so delegated, increase or decrease but not below two (2) the number of its members, and fill vacancies therein from the members of the Board. The Committee shall keep regular minutes of its proceedings, cause them to be filed with the corporate records, and report the same to the Board from time to time as the Board may require.⑩

.
.
.

ARTICLE 8

FISCAL YEAR

SECTION 1. FISCAL YEAR OF THE CORPORATION

The fiscal year of the corporation shall begin on the ___(day and month, e.g., "first day of January")___ ⑪ and end on the ___(day and month, e.g., "last day of December")___ ⑪ in each year.

. . .

ARTICLE 12 ⑫

MEMBERS

SECTION 1. DETERMINATION OF MEMBERS ⑬

If this corporation makes no provision for members, then, pursuant to Section 9310(b) of the Nonprofit Religious Corporation Law of the State of California, any action which would otherwise, under law or the provisions of the Articles of Incorporation or Bylaws of this corporation, require approval by a majority of all members or approval by the members, shall only require the approval of the Board of Directors.

WRITTEN CONSENT OF DIRECTORS ADOPTING BYLAWS

We, the undersigned, are all of the persons named as the initial directors in the Articles of Incorporation of ___(name of corporation)___,⑭ a California nonprofit corporation, and, pursuant to the authority granted to the directors by these Bylaws to take action by unanimous written consent without a meeting, consent to, and hereby do, adopt the foregoing Bylaws, consisting of ___(number of pages)___ ⑭ pages, as the Bylaws of this corporation.

Dated: ___(date)___   ___(signature of Director)___ ⑭
                                        (typed name)   , Director

. . .

CERTIFICATE

This is to certify that the foregoing is a true and correct copy of the Bylaws of the corporation named in the title thereto and that such Bylaws were duly adopted by the Board of Directors of said corporation.

(Fill in Certificate date and signature of Secretary later, after first Board meeting) ⑮

Dated: ___(date)___   ___(signature of Secretary)___
                                        (typed name)   , Secretary

Special Instructions

① Type the name of your corporation in the heading of the Bylaws.

② Type the name of the county where the corporation's principal office is located. The principal office is the legal address of the corporation and, generally, fixes the county where legal action must be brought against the corporation.

③ The blanks in this section should not be filled in at this time. Use these blanks later to change the principal office of the corporation to another location, within the same county, by showing the new address and date of the address change.

④ This section allows you to state in more detail the primary objectives and purposes of your religious corporation (remember, your statement of specific purposes in your Articles of Incorporation should have been brief). Here you can go into as much detail as you want, describing the specific religious purposes and activities of your corporation. You can be brief here as well if you wish. Remember, however—a more detailed statement here will also serve to provide the State Franchise Board and the IRS with additional information in order for them to determine if the specific activities you plan to engage in entitle you to the necessary tax exemptions. (See Step 2A, above, for examples of sample responses by non-religious groups).

⑤ Indicate the total number of persons authorized to serve on your board. Generally, this number should be the same as the number of people you've already indicated as the first directors of the corporation in Article FIVE of the Articles of Incorporation. However, you may at this time state a greater number to allow for additional directors to be elected at a future meeting of the board.

For information on providing for a variable number of directors, see Step 5, special instruction 5.

⑥ Indicate in this blank any specific payments which will be allowed to board members for attending meetings of the board. (Note that reasonable advancement and reimbursement of expenses for performing other director duties is allowed by this section.) You may indicate a specific per-meeting amount (or you may use the sample language shown in the blank on the sample form above to authorize payment of "actual and necessary" expenses incurred by directors in attending board meetings). If, as is often the case, you do not wish to pay directors for attending meetings, simply type "no payments authorized" in this blank.

⑦ In the blanks in the first paragraph, indicate the date when regular meetings of the board will be held. Many nonprofits hold regular board meetings while others simply schedule regular meetings once each year and call special meetings during the year when required. In any case, make sure to indicate that you will hold a regular board meeting at least annually in the blanks.

Sample Responses:

Regular meetings of Directors shall be held on the first Friday of each month at 9 o'clock AM…

Regular meetings of Directors shall be held on the second Monday of December at 1 o'clock PM…

Regular meetings of Directors shall be held on July 1st and February 20th at 9 o'clock AM…

In the second paragraph of this section, fill in the blank to indicate which one of your regular board meetings will be specified as the annual regular meeting of the board to elect (or re-elect) directors of your corporation. Note that in a non-membership corporation, the directors vote for their own re-election or replacements, with each director casting one written vote. Of course, if a corporation has provided for only one regular meeting each year in the first paragraph of this section, then the date of this regular meeting will be repeated in this blank as the date of the annual meeting of directors.

Sample Responses:

If this corporation makes no provision for members, then, at the annual meeting of directors held on <u>January 1st</u>, directors shall be elected…

If this corporation makes no provision for members, then, at the annual meeting of directors held on <u>the first Friday of July</u>, directors shall be elected…

Membership Note: The provisions in the second paragraph of this section only take effect for non-membership corporations—membership corporations can leave this line blank. Membership religious corporations will wish to add membership provisions to their bylaws indicating the procedure for the election of directors by the members.

⑧ Indicate the number of directors who must be present at a directors' meeting to constitute a quorum so that business can be conducted. Although the usual practice is to provide for a majority, a nonprofit religious corporation may provide for a larger or smaller number.

Whatever number or percentage you decide on, you should realize that this section of the Bylaws concerns a quorum, not a vote requirement. A meeting can only be held if at least a quorum of directors is present, but a vote on any matter before the board must, generally, be passed by the vote of a majority of those present at the meeting.

Example: If a religious corporation with five directors provides for a majority quorum, then a quorum of at least three directors must be present to hold a meeting of directors. If three directors actually attend, then action can be taken at the meeting by the vote of two of the directors present (the majority vote of those present at the meeting).

⑨ In this blank indicate the rules of order which will be used at directors' meetings. Although many nonprofits specify Roberts' Rules of Order here, religious groups may wish to refer to special rules established by their organization for the conduct of business at directors' meetings. Alternatively, you

may wish to leave this item blank if you see no need to specify formal procedures for introducing and discussing items of business at your board meetings.

⑩ This section of the bylaws applies to the establishment of an executive committee consisting of board members only—the Nonprofit Corporation Law allows an executive committee of this sort much of the management power of the full board (as specified in this section of the bylaws). Although at least two board members must serve on this committee, in practice, most nonprofit corporations establish an executive committee of from three to five board members. Of course, you can set up other types of committees with or without board members (see Section 2 of this Article in the tear-out Bylaws).

⑪ Indicate the beginning and ending dates of the fiscal year of the corporation. The fiscal year of the corporation is the period for which the corporation keeps its books (its accounting period) and will determine the corporation's tax year for purposes of filing certain tax returns and reports. It may be the calendar year from January 1 to December 31 (this is the usual case for nonprofits), or it may be what the IRS considers a true fiscal year consisting of a 12-month period ending on the last day of any month other than December, e.g., from July 1 to June 30.

⑫ **Last Page of Basic Religious Corporation Bylaws:** The last page of the basic bylaws (consisting of Article 12, Written Consent of Directors and Certificate sections) is only intended for *non-membership groups*. Membership religious corporations do not need to fill in and use this last tear-out page—we provide a separate last page for membership corporations as part of the tear-out religious corporation membership provisions (see Section E below).

⑬ Section 1 of Article 12 makes it clear that the directors of non-membership corporations can take the place of members in taking any action which, under law, otherwise requires membership approval (in other words, the directors can act in place of the members in non-membership corporations).

⑭ Fill in the Written Consent of Directors paragraph, showing the name of the corporation and the number of pages in your final bylaws. All of the initial directors of the corporation (the directors named in your Articles) should sign their names on the lines following this paragraph. Fill in the date and type each director's name below each signature line.

⑮ The blanks following the Certificate at bottom of the bylaws should not be filled in at this time. Your corporate Secretary will complete these blanks after the holding of the first meeting of your board.

E. Prepare Membership Provisions for a Religious Corporation (Optional)

This section applies to religious membership corporations only. If you have decided to form a non-membership religious corporation, this section does not apply to you and you should skip ahead to Chapter 7, Step 6.

As we've said, most religious groups will not wish to have formal or "legal" members due to the active role such members assume in the affairs of the corporation (see Section A of this step and Chapter 2G). Of course, you can establish a *non-formal* membership, a congregation or other non-legal structure to allow individuals to contribute financially to, or participate directly in, the religious purposes of your organization.[2]

If you do wish to set up a formal membership structure, prepare the *Membership Provisions for Religious Corporation* by filling in the tear-out form according to the sample Bylaws and special instructions below. **Note:** The sample form below is an abbreviated version of the complete tear-out form—we only provide sample language and instructions of the sections which contain blanks.

Making Modifications: The membership provisions contained in the Religious Corporation law are, in many cases, quite generalized, allowing religious groups considerable flexibility in fashioning their own specific provisions. In preparing the tear-out form, therefore, we have included a number of specific membership provisions taken from the public benefit corporation law and the public benefit corporation bylaws discussed earlier. These specific provisions will, we think, make sense for the majority of smaller membership religious organizations. However, you may wish to customize these provisions to take advantage of the flexibility allowed under law. If you do make modifications, make sure to check your work against the Religious Corporation Law (or have an attorney check your work).[3]

√ The parenthetical blanks, i.e., "(_____)," indicate information which you must complete on the tear-out form.

√ Each circled number (e.g., ①) refers to a special instruction which provides specific information to help you complete an item. The special instructions immediately follow the sample form.

√ We suggest you tear out the form in the Appendix and fill in the blanks as you follow the sample form and instructions.

√ A vertical series of dots in the sample form below indicates a gap where we have skipped over language in the tear-out form.

---

[2]Non-formal members (individuals who are not given the technical legal status of "members" in the Bylaws) can still be called members and participate in the programs, services, and events of the corporation. In fact, this is exactly what most churches and other religious groups do.

---

[3]Most of the statutory religious corporation membership provisions are contained in Sections 9310 through 9420 of the California Corporations Code.

Membership Provisions

of

_____(name of corporation)_____ ①

a California Religious Corporation

ARTICLE 12 ①
MEMBERS

SECTION 1. DETERMINATION AND RIGHTS OF MEMBERS

The corporation shall have only one class of members. No member shall hold more than one membership in the corporation. Except as expressly provided in or authorized by the Articles of Incorporation or Bylaws of this corporation, all members shall have the same rights, privileges, restrictions and conditions.

SECTION 2. QUALIFICATIONS OF MEMBERS

The qualifications for membership in this corporation are as follows __**(specify qualifications or, if none, type "Any person is qualified to become a member of this corporation")**__ .②

SECTION 3. ADMISSION OF MEMBERS

Applicants shall be admitted to membership __**(state procedure, e.g., "on making application therefor in writing" and indicate if payment will be required, e.g., " and upon payment of the application fee and/or first annual dues, as specified in the following sections of this Bylaw")**__ . ③

SECTION 4. FEES, DUES AND ASSESSMENTS

(a) The following fee shall be charged for making application for membership in the corporation: __**(state specific admission fee or leave to discretion of board, e.g., "in such amount as may be specified from time to time by resolution of the Board of Directors charged for, and payable with, the application for membership," or, if no fee, type "None")**__ . ④

(b) The annual dues payable to the corporation by members shall be __**(state amount of annual dues, leave to discretion of board, e.g., "in such amount as may be determined from time to time by resolution of the Board of Directors," or type "None")**__ . ④

(c) Memberships shall be nonassessable.

.
.
.

SECTION 9. TERMINATION OF MEMBERSHIP ⑤

(a) Grounds for Termination. The membership of a member shall terminate upon the occurrence of any of the following events:

(1) Upon his or her notice of such termination delivered to the President of Secretary of the corporation personally or by mail, such membership to terminate upon the date of delivery of the notice or date of deposit in the mail.

(2) Upon a determination by the Board of Directors that the member has engaged in conduct materially and seriously prejudicial to the interests or purposes of the corporation.

(3) If this corporation has provided for the payment of dues by members, upon a failure to renew his or her membership by paying dues on or before their due date, such termination to be effective thirty (30) days after a written notification of delinquency is given personally or mailed to such member by the Secretary of the corporation. A member may avoid such termination by paying the amount of delinquent dues within a thirty (30)-day period following the member's receipt of the written notification of delinquency.

(b) Procedure for Expulsion. Following the determination that a member should be expelled under subparagraph (a)(2) of this section, the following procedure shall be implemented:

(1) A notice shall be sent by first-class or registered mail to the last address of the member as shown on the corporation's records, setting forth the expulsion and the reasons therefor. Such notice shall be sent at least fifteen (15) days before the proposed effective date of the expulsion.

(2) The member being expelled shall be given an opportunity to be heard, either orally or in writing, at a hearing to be held not less than five (5) days before the effective date of the proposed expulsion. The hearing will be held by the Board of Directors in accordance with the quorum and voting rules set forth in these Bylaws applicable to the meetings of the Board. The notice to the member of his or her proposed expulsion shall state the date, time, and place of the hearing on his or her proposed expulsion.

(3) Following the hearing, the Board of Directors shall decide whether or not the member should in fact be expelled, suspended, or sanctioned in some other way. The decision of the Board shall be final.

(4) If this corporation has provided for the payment of dues by members, any person expelled from the corporation shall receive a refund of dues already paid. The refund shall be pro-rated to return only the unaccrued balance remaining for the period of the dues payment.

SECTION 10. RIGHTS ON TERMINATION OF MEMBERSHIP

All rights of a member in the corporation shall cease on termination of membership as herein provided.

ARTICLE 13
MEETINGS OF MEMBERS ⑥

SECTION 1. PLACE OF MEETINGS

Meetings of members shall be held at the principal office of the corporation or at such other place or places within or without the State of California as may be designated from time to time by resolution of the Board of Directors.

SECTION 2. ANNUAL AND OTHER REGULAR MEETINGS

The members shall meet annually on ___(date, e.g., " the first Monday of July, September 30th)"___ ⑦ in each year, at ___(time)___ M,⑦ for the purpose of electing directors and transacting other business as may come before the meeting. Cumulative voting for the election of directors shall not be permitted. The candidates receiving the highest number of votes up to the number of directors to be elected shall be elected. Each voting member shall cast one vote, with voting being by ballot only. The annual meeting of members for the purpose of electing directors shall be deemed a regular meeting and any reference in these Bylaws to regular meetings of members refers to this annual meeting.

Other regular meetings of the members shall be held on ___(date)___,⑧ at ___(time)___ M.⑧

If the day fixed for the annual meeting or other regular meetings falls on a legal holiday, such meeting shall be held at the same hour and place on the next business day.

.

.

.

SECTION 8. PROXY VOTING

Members entitled to vote ___("shall" or "shall not")___ ⑨ be permitted to vote or act by proxy. If membership voting by proxy is not allowed by the preceding sentence, no provision in this or other sections of these Bylaws referring to proxy voting shall be construed to permit any member to vote or act by proxy.

If membership voting by proxy is allowed, members entitled to vote shall have the right to vote either in person or by a written proxy executed by such person or by his or her duly authorized agent and filed with the Secretary of the corporation, provided, however, that no proxy shall be valid after eleven (11) months from the date of its execution unless otherwise provided in the proxy. In any case, however, the maximum term of any proxy shall be three (3) years from the date of its execution. No proxy shall be irrevocable and may be revoked following the procedures given in Section 9417 of the California Nonprofit Religious Corporation Law.

If membership voting by proxy is allowed, all proxies shall state the general nature of the matter to be voted on and, in the case of a proxy given to vote for the election of directors, shall list those persons who were nominees at the time the notice of the vote for election of directors was given to the members. In any election of directors, any proxy which is marked by a member "withhold" or otherwise marked in a manner indicating that the authority to vote for the election of directors is withheld shall not be voted either for or against the election of a director.

If membership voting by proxy is allowed, proxies shall afford an opportunity for the member to specify a choice between approval and disapproval for each matter or group of related matters intended, at the time the proxy is distributed, to be acted upon at the meeting for which the proxy is solicited. The proxy shall also provide that when the person solicited specifies a choice with respect to any such matter, the vote shall be cast in accordance therewith.

SECTION 9. CONDUCT OF MEETINGS

Meetings of members shall be presided over by the Chairperson of the Board, or, if there is no Chairperson, by the President of the corporation or, in his or her absence, by the Vice President of the corporation or, in the absence of all of these persons, by a Chairperson chosen by a majority of the voting members, present in person or by proxy. The Secretary of the corporation shall act as Secretary of all meetings of members, provided that, in his or her absence, the presiding officer shall appoint another person to act as Secretary of the Meeting.

Meetings shall be governed by __("Roberts' Rules of Order" or indicate other rules or procedures)__,⑩ as such rules may be revised from time to time, insofar as such rules are not inconsistent with or in conflict with these Bylaws, with the Articles of Incorporation of this corporation, or with any provision of law.

.
.
.

WRITTEN CONSENT OF DIRECTORS ADOPTING BYLAWS

We, the undersigned, are all of the persons named as the initial directors in the Articles of Incorporation of __(name of corporation)__,⑪ a California nonprofit corporation, and, pursuant to the authority granted to the directors by these Bylaws to take action by unanimous written consent without a meeting, consent to, and hereby do, adopt the foregoing Bylaws, consisting of __(number of pages)__ ⑪ pages, as the Bylaws of this corporation.

Dated: __(date)__   __(signature of Director)__   ⑪
                        (typed name)   , Director
                              .
                              .
                              .

CERTIFICATE

This is to certify that the foregoing is a true and correct copy of the Bylaws of the corporation named in the title thereto and that such Bylaws were duly adopted by the Board of Directors of said corporation.

Dated: __(date)__   __(signature of Secretary)__   ⑫
                        (typed name)   , Secretary

Special Instructions

① You should include these membership provision pages at the end of the basic religious corporation bylaws prepared as part of Section D above (place this page following the page of the basic bylaws which ends with Article 11). Remember, don't include the last page of the basic religious corporation bylaws (containing an Article 12 for non-membership corporations) in your membership bylaws (these membership provisions start with Article 12 and end with a new special page for your membership bylaws).

② Use this blank to indicate any special qualifications required for members. Please realize, however, that the IRS likes to see 501(c)(3) tax-exempt corporations with membership in the corporation being open to the general public. Consequently, most religious corporations will not specify any qualifications for membership (see the suggested wording in the blank on the sample form).

③ Most religious corporations do not require formal application for membership in the corporation. However, a few wish to indicate that members must pay an admission fee and/or annual dues prior to acceptance as a member in the corporation (see the suggested wording in the blank on the sample form).

④ Indicate the manner of determining, or the specific amount of, admission fees and/or annual dues for members in the appropriate blanks (see the suggested wording in the blanks on the sample form). If, as is the usual case, no application or admission fees will be charged, type "None" in both blanks.

⑤ The termination of membership provisions on Section 9 of this Article are taken from the public benefit corporation law. Essentially, they provide due process to members, allowing them notice and an opportunity to be heard prior to a final determination by the Board on whether a member shall be expelled. Although we think these provisions reflect a sensible set of specific rules, religious corporations are free to fashion their own specific procedures.[4] If you wish to do so, replace the language of Section 9 with your own termination of membership rules.

⑥ Under Section 9410(a) of the Corporations Code, religious corporations can provide any reasonable method of calling, noticing and holding regular or special meetings of members. Therefore, you may wish to replace the procedures for calling, noticing and holding meetings contained in the various sections of this Article with your own rules (e.g., you may wish to allow directors to call special meetings of members upon two day's telephone notice, etc.).

Exceptions: In special cases, the Religious Corporation Law requires that members receive notice of the general nature of the proposal in a written notice or waiver of notice (if the proposal is passed by less than the unanimous approval of all members)—you cannot vary these special notice rules.[5] Special notice rules also apply to certain proxies (if you authorize proxies). We won't list all the special cases here.[6] If you wish to change the notice rules and wish to check these special cases, see Section 9410(b) of the California Corporations Code. (If you have a lawyer review your changes, ask the lawyer to make sure your changes conform to this section of the Code.)

⑦ Indicate the date and time of the annual meeting of members. The members elect directors at this annual meeting. You may wish to coordinate

---

[4]Section 9340(d) of the Corporations Code states: "A membership may be terminated as provided in the articles or bylaws of the corporation."

[5]These special circumstances are listed in Section 4(b) of Article 13 of the tear-out religious corporation membership provisions.

[6]Special provisions of the Code relating to a judicial determination of the validity of an election cannot be varied.

this date with your annual directors' meeting (e.g., slightly before the annual directors' meeting).

⑧ Type the date of any regular meetings of members. Many nonprofits will leave this line blank and decide only to provide for the annual meeting of members in their bylaws (in the previous paragraph). Some with a more active membership will indicate monthly or semi-annual regular meetings of members here.

⑨ Indicate whether the corporation will or will not allow proxy voting by members. (A proxy is simply a written authorization by a member allowing another person to vote for the member.) Many small membership corporations will indicate that proxy voting "shall not" be permitted to avoid problems and complications that can arise in times of controversy or difficult decisions (such as proxy wars—solicitations of proxies by outside or competing interests, etc.).

If you do decide to allow proxies, the restrictions relating to proxies contained in the next sections of this Article will apply.

⑩ Indicate, if you wish, the sets of rules which will govern the proposing and taking of action at your membership meetings. Roberts' Rules of Order is the standard, of course, but you may specify another set of procedures if you wish.

⑪ Fill in the Written Consent of Directors paragraph, showing the name of the corporation and the number of pages in your final bylaws. All of the initial directors of the corporation (the directors named in your Articles) should sign their names on the lines following this paragraph. Fill in the date and type each director's name below each signature line.

⑫ The blanks following the Certificate at bottom of the bylaws should not be filled in at this time. Your corporate Secretary will complete these blanks after the holding of the first meeting of your board.

Chapter 7

PREPARE YOUR CALIFORNIA TAX EXEMPTION APPLICATION

AFTER YOU HAVE PREPARED your Articles and Bylaws, the next step in forming your nonprofit corporation is preparing the California Application for Exemption from State Corporate Franchise Tax. There are a number of details here that require your attention but if you approach this task with fresh energy and a little determination, you will complete this step easily.

Step 6. Prepare State Tax Exemption Application

First obtain two copies of the California Franchise Tax Board Form, FTB 3500, *Exemption Application,* and separate *Instructions for Form FTB 3500,* from your local California Franchise Tax Board Office. This office is listed under "Franchise Tax Board" in the State Government Offices section of your telephone directory. If you don't mind waiting a week or so, simply call the toll-free Franchise Tax Board telephone number to obtain your forms.

A. First Things First

We assume here that your nonprofit corporation will be able to meet the requirements of exemption from corporate income taxes under Section 23701(d) of the California Revenue and Taxation Code—this state tax exemption parallels the federal corporate income tax exemption under Section 501(c)(3) of the Internal Revenue Code.

Before preparing the state exemption application you should read the specific Instructions for Form FTB 3500 and review the material relating to obtaining tax-exempt status covered in Chapters 2 through 4. Three key points:

1. The state exemption categories, for the most part, parallel federal IRS exemption categories so that the same general considerations and requirements apply at the state and federal level, and

2. The state doesn't attempt to determine whether your organization is a private foundation or public charity. This distinction will become important later when you fill out your Federal Application for Recognition of Exemption.

3. The information provided in the state form is similar to the information needed for the federal tax exemption application. Many incorporators find it convenient to prepare both the state and federal tax applications at the same time (see Chapter 9 for instructions on preparing the federal form).

B. Filling in the Blanks on Form FTB 3500

In the following section, we go through each line of the state exemption application, indicating the appropriate response or kind of information you should provide. Each reference to a particular blank below corresponds to the same blank on the state exemption application.[1]

If you experience any difficulty in understanding the content or significance of certain responses, reread the previous chapters of this book. Some of you will wish to turn parts of this work over to a tax advisor or lawyer.

Top of Form: Indicate the full name of your corporation exactly as given in the heading of your Articles of Incorporation. Indicate the street address of the principal office of the corporation and its telephone number. The Franchise Tax Board will use it as a mailing address to send forms to your organization. Under "Federal Employer Identification

---

[1]We are basing these references to blanks on the most current state exemption application (1995 version of Form FTB 3500) at the time of printing of this edition. Forms do change, and future revisions may contain a few extra blanks. However, revisions usually contain only minor format changes and these slight differences, if they occur, should not present significant problems for you in filling out your exemption application. Call the Franchise Tax Board as discussed earlier in this step if you encounter any new material not covered by our instructions.

Number," type: "Number not yet assigned. Will indicate on first annual report." Of course, if you have applied for and received a federal employer number (see Chapter 9, Section C, Part 1, instructions for Line 2), you will show it here.

Then fill in the name, address and telephone number of a "representative" who will be responsible for receiving communications from the Franchise Tax Board regarding your application (one of the initial directors will usually be shown here).

Blank 1(a): Type "23701(d)" in the blank provided at the end of this line. This is the section of the California Revenue and Taxation Code which provides a state exemption for 501(c)(3) charitable, educational, religious, scientific or literary groups.

Special Exemption Categories: If you fall under another category as listed in the Instructions for Form FTB 3500 (and are using this book to form a non-501(c)(3) tax exempt organization), indicate the appropriate subsection of Section 23701 which corresponds with the type of nonprofit corporation you are organizing. (For a further discussion of these special organizations, see the parallel federal tax exemption categories listed in Table 3.1.)

Blank 1(b): Enter on this line the primary activity of your organization, using the keywords associated with your group's 501(c)(3) tax-exempt purposes. Use one or more of the following words to describe your activities: " charitable," "educational," "religious," "scientific," or "literary."

Sample Responses:

Primary Activity of Organization:
Charitable Activities or
Charitable and Educational Activities or
Religious Activities

Blanks 2(a) - (b):

2(a): Groups that have not yet filed their Articles should check "Currently being incorporated" and type "Upon filing of Articles with Secretary of State" as the "Date organized" in 2(a)1.

If You Filed Your Articles Early: If you filed your Articles before applying for tax-exempt status as explained in Chapter 6, Step 4, check "Incorporated" and show the date you were incorporated as the "Date organized" in 2(a)1. This is the date the Articles of Incorporation were endorsed-filed by the Secretary of State. This date appears in the upper right-hand corner of the first page of the copies of the certified Articles as part of the Secretary of State's "endorsed-filed" stamp. It is not necessarily the date of certification indicated on the facing certification page (containing the gold seal of California) attached to the front of each of the certified copies of the filed Articles.

2(b): Groups which have not yet filed their Articles should ignore this item. Groups which have already incorporated should show the date of incorporation again in 2(b)1 and their corporate number in 2(b)2. This is the number appearing above or to the left of the endorsed-filed stamp of the Secretary of State in the upper right-hand corner of the first page of the Articles. Ignore blank 2(b)3.

Blanks 3(a) - 3(d): Most groups should be able to indicate "No" to question 3(a) and can skip the remaining question under this item (to be thorough, we suggest you type "N/A" in blank 3(c) to show that you do not have a filing number with the FTB). However, if you are incorporating a pre-existing nonprofit association that was granted a tax exemption for prior years, check "Yes" to 3(a) and provide the information requested under 3(b) through 3(d), attaching copies of the determination letter(s) received by the nonprofit association.

Note: Unincorporated associations that were granted tax-exempt status must file a new FTB 3500 to reapply for a tax exemption for their newly-formed corporation.

Also Note: If your nonprofit association or other type of pre-existing organization was previously denied an exemption, then your situation is more complex than anticipated here and you should consult an attorney or tax specialist before preparing and filing your exemption application.

Blanks 4(a) - 4(b): Check "No" to 4(a). If you've formed and operated a nonprofit corporation before obtaining your tax exemptions and filed federal income tax returns, indicate "Yes" and provide the additional information requested in 4(b).

Blank 5: Indicate your annual accounting period. This is the same period as the fiscal year specified in Article 8 of the tear-out Bylaws (e.g., "January 1 to December 31").

Blank 6(a): Indicate "Yes" unless you are incorporating an already existing organization. Generally a "No" response is only appropriate for predecessor organizations whose activities you will continue or whose property and other assets will be transferred to the new nonprofit corporation. Generally, only those groups that have adopted special articles of incorporation for an unincorporated association as explained in Chapter 6, Step 3 will answer "No" here.

If you check "No," attach a statement providing the information requested. As the reason for termination of the predecessor organization you can simply state: "To incorporate the predecessor organization." If your pre-existing nonprofit organization did not file tax returns with the Franchise Tax Board and therefore was not assigned a tax filing number by the FTB, don't worry about it; this is normal. Besides, the FTB is not interested in the tax filing history of smaller nonprofits, realizing that such groups rarely have profits to be reported and taxed. Rather, they appreciate the fact that you are now making your group "legal" by filing a tax-exemption application for your new corporation.

Exception: In the unlikely event that you are incorporating a pre-existing profit making business, then the FTB may be interested in seeing the prior year returns for the unincorporated commercial business. Again, this is indeed a rare circumstance.

Preparing Attachment Pages: A "No" answer to this question or a "Yes" response to the following questions under number 6 of the application will require answers on an attachment page (you can type one or more answers on your attachment page). Simply follow the instructions for preparing attachments given for question 7 below when providing additional information required by any response under this question.

Blank 6(b): If you have adopted non-membership Bylaws, check "No." If you have included membership provisions in your Bylaws, check the "Yes" box and provide the information requested on an attachment page to your application. Indicate the qualifications for members contained in Article 12, Section 1 of the tear-out membership provisions. Most organizations will have used our suggested language for this provision and will show that "Any person is qualified to become a member of this corporation." If you have not modified the membership provisions in the tear-out form, you should indicate on the attachment that: "The corporation shall have only one class of members and all memberships have the same rights, privileges, restrictions and conditions." Also indicate that "each member of the corporation is entitled to one vote on each matter submitted to a vote of the members and has no other rights or interest with respect to the assets or affairs of the corporation except as expressly provided by law." Unless you know the actual number of members who will be admitted to the corporation (which is unlikely), indicate that: "the number of members of the general public who will be admitted to the corporation is undetermined."

Blank 6(c): Check "No." If your proposed operations require a "Yes" response, you probably won't meet the requirements for obtaining nonprofit corporate status or receiving your tax exemptions since the applicable statutes, as previously discussed, require that no part of the net earnings of the corporation be distributed to members.

Blank 6(d): Mark "No." If your corporation plans to share space with any of the incorporators (e.g., a room in a director's house is used, in the beginning, as a corporate office with the house given as the principal place of business of the corporation), mark "Yes" and provide the details of the arrangement on an attachment page. The above arrangement will, generally, be permitted if no rent or reasonable rent is charged by the director for the corporation to use part of his or her house (a "no rent" situation is preferable). If an incorporator is being unreasonably benefited by such a shared-facilities arrangement, this most likely will jeopardize your tax exemption.

Blank 6(e): Mark "No." If a "Yes" response is appropriate, you should provide the details on an attachment page. The example and discussion in 6(d) above applies to this blank also.

Blank 6(f): If, as is often the case, you plan to hire a promoter, incorporator (initial director), founder or member as a salaried or compensated employee of the nonprofit corporation, indicate "Yes." Provide the information requested as to the employee's duties, responsibilities, qualifications and compensation on the attachment page. At this point in the formation of your corporation, you may have decided that certain directors are to be employed as salaried officers (e.g., President, Treasurer, Secretary), or that these people will be salaried employees whose exact duties as employees and compensation have not yet been determined. In such cases, give as much information as you can and indicate the manner of determining their employee duties and the amount of compensation.

Sample Response: Assume that a nonprofit corporation with ten directors wishes to employ three of its initial directors as salaried officers and also possibly as salaried employees for other services, and that the rate of compensation to be paid has not yet been determined. An appropriate response to this question on the attachment page might read as follows:

Blank 6(f): Three of the Incorporators and first directors, __**(names of directors)**__ , will be employed in the following officer capacities:

__(name of director)__	President
__(name of director)__	Vice President
__(name of director)__	Secretary/Treasurer, Vice President

They may also be employed as regular employees. Their titled positions, job functions, and compensation for such regular employee status, as well as compensation for their officer positions, is, at present, undetermined, although total proposed budget figures have been determined for director and employee salaries (see attached Exhibit).[2] Compensation will be reasonable and be paid in return for services rendered the nonprofit corporation in furtherance of its exempt purposes as required by the Bylaws of the corporation and shall be fixed from time to time by resolution of the board of directors.

Blank 6(g): If any of your directors will be paid (other than as directors, e.g., for attending board meetings), check the "Yes" box. You'll need to provide the requested information on an attachment page. Essentially, the Franchise Tax Board is trying to determine if public benefit corporations meet the "disinterested director" rule contained in Section 5227 of the Nonprofit Corporation Law. You should realize, in describing the relationship, if any, of unpaid board members to paid board members, that the Franchise Tax Board considers any relationship by blood or marriage to a paid director to constitute an "interested" relationship—this is a broader class of related people than the Code refers to. Consequently, any person on the board related by

---

[2]As you'll see, you will have to attach a proposed budget to your application which should indicate proposed total expenditures for salaries.

blood or marriage to a paid director will be considered an interested director. Therefore, if your response to this question does not show that a majority of your public benefit corporation board is disinterested, the Franchise Tax Board may deny (or at least question) your state tax exemption.

Item 7: Item 7 requires information concerning the organization and operation of your nonprofit corporation. Most groups will be able to prepare the material themselves. However, if your operations will be financially complex, or if you are incorporating a predecessor organization, you may need to consult a tax specialist to assist you in preparing the financial data requested here.

Preparing Attachments: Submit the information required under question 7 on attachment pages to your application. Simply use 8-1/2" x 11" paper and type the information needed. At the top of the attachment page(s) indicate that the material is an attachment to your exemption application, giving the name of the corporation, the date of preparation, and the material included in each attachment. (Any information required under question 6 above should be included on the attachment page preceding the responses to question 7.) Use the following format:

ATTACHMENT TO EXEMPTION APPLICATION OF

_____ **(name of corporation)** _____

Items: 6 and 7   Dated _____ (page number)

Preparing Exhibits: Particular sections of question 7 require you to submit copies of documents. These documents should be labeled as Exhibits and lettered in alphabetical order. The first page of each exhibit should state the name of the corporation and the nature of the material contained in the exhibit. For example:

EXHIBIT __**(letter)**__,   ____**(name of corporation)**____

Proposed Budget for __**(year)**__

Item 7(a): This item requires that you attach a copy of your Articles of Incorporation, prepared in Chapter 6, Step 3. Respond to this item on the attachment page to your application for Blanks 6 and 7 by typing the following:

7(a): Copy of proposed Articles of Incorporation attached, Exhibit A.

Make a copy of your original Articles and mark it as explained above. Don't make the copy now, since other copies of corporate documents will also be needed. Make copies of this and other documents required by the exemption application when you get to Chapter 7, Step 10.

Item 7(b): Type the following on the attachment page in response to this item:

> 7(b): Copy of proposed Bylaws attached, Exhibit ___(letter, i.e., "B")___ .

You will need to make a copy of your Bylaws and mark it as an exhibit. Again, make the copy when you get to Chapter 8, Step 8.

Item 7(c):

New Corporations: If you are a new organization, just now incorporating and not yet doing business (engaging in activities) as a nonprofit corporation (most groups using this book will fall within this category), respond to this question as follows:

> 7(c): ___(Name of corporation)___ is a new organization, just now incorporating, and has not yet commenced operations. See 7(d) below for a proposed budget for the new organization.

New groups do not need to prepare the statements of assets, liabilities, receipts and expenditures requested in this blank of the exemption application and can go on to 7(d).

Corporations in Existence Less Than One Year: If you filed your Articles before submitting your exemption application, and your corporation has been in existence for less than one year, you do not have to submit the financial statements requested by this item. Remember, the date on which your corporation comes into existence and begins operations is the date of the Secretary of State's endorsed-filed stamp on the first page of your certified Articles. By the way, it won't hurt, and may help, to include these statements for your initial operations if you've acquired assets, incurred liabilities, or can show receipts or expenditures for this less-than-one-year period. (Also, all corporations will have to prepare these financial

statements for the current year when preparing their federal exemption application—see Chapter 9, instruction for Part V). If you do not wish to prepare these financial statements, simply respond as follows:

> 7(c): ___(name of corporation)___ is a newly-formed nonprofit corporation and has been operating for less than one year. See Item 7(d) for a proposed budget.

Corporations in Existence One Year or More: If you filed your Articles before seeking your state exemption and have been in existence for one year or more, provide the financial statements for the periods for which you have been in existence and for which you wish to obtain tax exempt status.

Example: GoodWorks, Inc, a California nonprofit corporation, filed it s Articles on May 15th, 1989. The group has a fiscal year and accounting period ending on December 31st of each year and is submitting its exemption application at the end of September, 1991. Like other groups, it wishes to claim an exemption going back to the date the organization was formed. Therefore, GoodWorks submits three sets of financial statements for the following full or partial tax periods of the corporation (remember, you must submit financial statements for the periods for which you wish an exemption):

1. May 15, 1989 to December 31, 1989 [this is the first (short) tax year of the corporation]

2. January 1, 1990 to December 31, 1990 (the organization's second tax year)

3. January 1, 1991 to September 30, 1991 (the past portion of the current tax year)

Pre-Existing Nonprofit Associations: If you indicated "No" to item 6(a) because you are incorporating a pre-existing nonprofit association, and if the association was not previously granted a tax-exemption by the FTB (as reported in item 3a), you can, if you wish, seek to have your exemption effective as well for the prior years operation of the association. Normally this is not necessary since most nonprofit associations do not make a profit in their early years and therefore rarely owe taxes for this period. Nonetheless, if you or your tax advisor decide you do have a reason to do this, you must submit financial statements for the prior years during which the unincorporated association was in operation.

If you are required to prepare financial statements under this part of your exemption application, here's what to do:

Prepare a balance sheet (a statement of assets and liabilities) and an income statement (a statement of receipts and expenditures) for each full or partial accounting period of your corporation. You may need to take your books to an accountant or bookkeeper to prepare these statements unless someone in your organization is familiar with these bookkeeping chores. Respond to this item as follows:

> 7(c): Statement of assets and liabilities, Exhibit __(letter)__, and statement of receipts and expenditures, Exhibit __(letter)__, of __(name of corporation)__, are attached, for the following accounting periods that the corporation has been in existence and for which the exemption is claimed:
>
> __(beginning and ending dates of accounting period)__
> __(beginning and ending dates of accounting period)__
> __(etc.)__

Sample Response:

Here is the completed response to this item submitted by GoodWorks, Inc:

> 7(c): Statement of assets and liabilities, Exhibits __C-E__, and statement of receipts and expenditures, Exhibits __F-H__, of __GoodWorks, Inc.__, are attached, for the following accounting periods that the corporation has been in existence and for which the exemption is claimed:
>
> __May 15, 1989 - December 31, 1989__
>
> __January 1, 1990 to December 31, 1990__
>
> __January 1, 1991 to September 30, 1991__

After preparing the financial statements, make copies, and attach the originals, marked as exhibits, to your exemption application. Sample statements are provided below to use as guides when preparing your financial statements.

A typical (simple) statement of assets and liabilities, in the form of a balance sheet, would be prepared as follows:

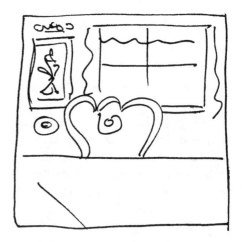

Sample Balance Sheet

EXHIBIT __(letter)__   ____(name of corporation)____

Balance Sheet as of ___(date of end of previous tax year or present date)___

Assets:
Cash	$_____
Equipment	$_____
Furniture and Fixtures	$_____
Accounts Receivable	$_____
Total Assets	$_____

Liabilities:
Accounts Payable	$_____
Loans Outstanding	$_____
Total Liabilities	$_____

Net Worth or Fund Balances:

Net Worth: $_____
  (Total Assets - Total Liabilities)

Total Liabilities and Net Worth $_____
  (Total Liabilities + Net Worth)

A typical (simple) statement of receipts and expenditures, in the form of an income statement, might look like this:[3]

---

[3]Note that this statement is broken down into specific receipt and expenditure categories, without using "lump sum" amounts. This is known as a "classified" financial statement. All financial statements submitted with your tax exemption application should be classified (broken down as much as possible).

Sample Income Statement

EXHIBIT __(letter)__   ___(name of corporation)___

Income Statement for period ending: __(date of end of previous tax year or present date)__

Receipts:

Membership Dues	$_____
Donations	$_____
Student Fees	$_____
Admissions to Performances	$_____
Total Receipts	$_____

Expenditures:

Rent	$_____
Salaries	$_____
Maintenance	$_____
Advertising	$_____
Telephone	$_____
Office Supplies	$_____
Utilities	$_____
Postage	$_____
Miscellaneous	$_____
Total Expenditures	$_____

Net Income
(Total Receipts - Total Expenditures) $_____

Item 7(d): Groups which have not yet incorporated and those which filed their Articles early and have been in existence for less than one year should prepare a proposed budget for their first year of operation. Respond to this question on the attachment page as follows:

> Proposed budget for nonprofit corporation, __(name of corporation)__, for first year of operation from __(beginning date)__ to __(ending date)__ attached, Exhibit __(letter)__.

Prepare, or have a bookkeeper or accountant prepare, a proposed budget, showing proposed sources of income and expenditures, based, as stated in the application, upon "the most reasonable expectations." Make copies and attach one as an exhibit to your application.

Note: Sources of income and expenditures should be related to your exempt purposes and should reflect reasonable amounts. As before, this statement should be classified—items should be broken down as best as possible; avoid lump sum figures.

Item 7(e): This item requires a detailed statement on your attachment page regarding the specific purposes of your corporation. You shouldn't quote from the "specific purpose" clause contained in your Articles of Incorporation. The concise statement in your Articles is meant to entitle you, under the letter of law, to your tax exemptions under a particular category or categories of the tax exemption statutes (public benefit corporations, see Chapter 6, Step 2, Section A, special instruction 3; religious corporations, see Chapter 6, Step 2, Section B, special instruction 2). The statement to be furnished here should give the Franchise Tax Board a down-to-earth and more extensive summary of the specific purposes of your corporation in terms of the major goals and primary activities of your group.

If you've already provided a detailed list of your primary objectives and purposes in Article 2, Section 1 of your Bylaws, you've already done your homework. Generally, even though the application states that you shouldn't quote from your Bylaws, this detailed list of purposes can be used directly in responses to this item in your application if it is thorough. All you need to do is change the introductory clause to conform to the language of this item in the application. Specifically, respond to this item by stating:

> The specific purposes for which this nonprofit corporation is being formed are __(list your primary objectives and purposes from Article 2 of your Bylaws)__.

If, in drafting your primary purposes and objectives for your Bylaws, you didn't provide a thorough and detailed list of your purposes, you'll have to do it now. Simply follow the instructions given in Chapter 6, Step 5, Section B, special instruction 4 [religious corporations should first refer to Chapter 6, Step 5, Section D, special instruction 4] and prepare a thorough list of your specific purposes to use in response to this item.

Sample Budget

EXHIBIT __(letter)__   ____(name of corporation)____

Proposed Budget for Year __(beginning and ending dates of first year of operation)__

Expenses:

Dance Studio:

Teachers' Fees	$_____
Administrative Salaries	$_____
Rent	$_____
Utilities	$_____
Janitorial Service	$_____
Office Supplies	$_____
Repairs & Maintenance	$_____
Advertising	$_____
Printing of	
Promotional Literature	$_____
Postage	$_____
Telephone	$_____
Insurance	$_____
Fees & Licenses	$_____
Total Studio Expenses	$_____

Productions:

Equipment	$_____
Costumes	$_____
Technicians' Fees	$_____
Dancers' Fees	$_____
Choreographers' Fees	$_____
Posters	$_____
Graphics	$_____
Printing	$_____
Distribution	$_____
Flyers	$_____
Mailings	$_____
Advertising	$_____
Total Production Expenses	$_____
Total Expenses	$_____

Receipts:

Student Fees	$_____
Special Events	$_____
Performances	$_____
Donations	$_____
Total Receipts	$_____

Item 7(f): The information requested in this item is self-explanatory; the Franchise Tax Board wants you to list the specific activities which you will conduct (or, for corporations which have filed their Articles early and have been operating, those activities which they have been conducting) to achieve the specific charitable, educational, literary, scientific or religious purposes indicated in response to item 7(e).

For example, if you've indicated that one of your purposes is to educate the public on environmental issues, you might respond here that one of the methods you will use to accomplish this goal will be the dissemination of brochures and other literature explaining how to implement solar energy heating systems as an alternative to traditional energy sources.

Many groups will have already given a complete, or partial, indication of the activities they will engage in to perform their specific purposes in item 7(e). For example, groups often couch their purposes in language which is descriptive of the activities they will carry on—for instance, an educational group may have stated in 7(e) that one of its purposes is to operate a school or provide classes for members of the general public in subjects relevant to their educational purposes. These groups may respond to this item by simply referring to some or all of their responses to previous items as follows:

Refer to item 7(e) for further information as to the programs and activities which will be carried on by the nonprofit corporation in order to accomplish the specific purposes of the organization.

As usual, you provide the response to this item on the attachment page to your exemption application for questions 6 and 7.

Item 7(g): Indicate the specific fundraising activities and business enterprises you plan to engage in on the attachment page. They, of course, should be related to your tax-exempt purposes. These activities may include, as we've mentioned in

previous portions of this book, performing services for a fee as long as the services are related to the tax-exempt purposes of the organization. Also include as exhibits copies of any agreements with outside groups relating to the production of income for the corporation.

Example: Our hypothetical dance group might respond to this question as follows:

Proposed fundraising activities [we suggest you don't include the phrase "and business enterprises" unless you include in your list revenue raising activities that are unrelated to your exempt purposes] of the corporation consist of:

1. The maintenance of a dance studio which will produce income derived from enrollment by the public in dance classes and other body movement art forms such as tumbling, yoga, etc., taught by the corporation's faculty;

2. Revenues received from public performances by the corporation's resident dance troupe as indicated in response to item 7(e);

3. Revenues received from sponsoring special events related to body movement (e.g., dance performances) and other art forms (e.g., musical concerts) as indicated in response to item 7(e).

Note: References are made to information already furnished by the group in its response to item 7(e) above.

Also refer to and attach any copies of agreements your organization has entered into to conduct any of the listed activities. For example, an organization sponsoring an annual book festival may attach a copy of an agreement for the lease of festival space and copies of agreements that will be signed by bookstores who exhibit at the festival.

Item 7(h): For new groups, simply respond to this question on the attachment page by stating, ___(name of corporation)___ is a newly-formed organization, not yet incorporated, with no discontinued activities.

If you're seeking a state tax exemption for a corporation which has already filed its Articles or if you are incorporating a pre-existing nonprofit organization, and have discontinued activities previously engaged in, provide the information requested in response to this question.

Item 7(i): This item will not apply to most newly-formed nonprofit corporations. It's not a good idea to enter into pre-incorporation agreements with respect to property (e.g., a lease) or other pre-incorporation contractual arrangements. If you have not entered into a lease or made other agreements for the development or use of property, respond on the attachment page as follows:

___(name of corporation)___ has not entered into a lease, nor does it own an interest in property, and has not entered into any agreement with other parties for the development of property.

If your organization has entered into a lease or an agreement relating to the development of property, you should so indicate in your response to this question and attach a copy of the lease to your application as an exhibit.

Sample Response:

Copy of lease, entered into between ___(name of corporation)___ and ___(name of lessor)___ with respect to the premises located at ___(address of leased property)___ attached, Exhibit ___(letter of exhibit)___.

Of course, the leased premises should be used by your group in carrying out its exempt purposes and the use of the leased premises for these purposes should already have been indicated as one of your activities under item 7(e), 7(f) or 7(g), above.

If you are incorporating a pre-existing nonprofit organization which currently leases property and your new corporation will continue to use the leased premises, you should indicate that the lease is currently held in the name of the predecessor organization. You will also need to assign this lease to the new corporation or negotiate a new lease with the owner once the corporation is formed (see Chapter 10, Step 18). If you plan to assign the lease to the corporation, you should indicate the following in this response:

The lease will be assigned to the corporation upon its incorporation and obtaining of federal and state corporate income tax exemptions.

You may, as an alternative, prepare an assignment of the lease by the predecessor organization to the proposed corporation at this time and attach it to your lease as an exhibit. This assignment should state that it is contingent upon the proposed corporation attaining nonprofit corporate status and its federal and state tax exemptions. It should be given without "consideration" (the payment of any money for the assignment) and will, under the terms of most standard leases, require the written approval of the lessor to be effective. A sample Assignment of Lease which might be used for this purpose is shown below.

Item 7(j): If you have copies or samples of literature which the corporation will sell or distribute (publications, advertising copy or promotional literature which you plan to distribute to solicit contributions, obtain student enrollment in classes, etc.), include copies with your exemption application and indicate that this material is being submitted with your exemption application in response to this item.

If, like other newly-formed nonprofits, you do not have copies of promotional literature prepared, simply respond here as follows:

The proposed corporation has not yet prepared promotional literature [or, does not plan to distribute promotional literature] or advertising.

You should be aware that the state and federal government like to see you taking an active role in soliciting public participation in the activities of your nonprofit corporation by distributing promotional literature or by arranging for space in newspapers, time on radio, etc.

Items 8, 9 & 10: Skip these items. They relate to other types of tax-exempt groups.

Assignment of Lease

__(name of original lessee, e.g., the predecessor nonprofit organization)__, Lessee of those premises commonly known as __(address of leased property)__, hereby assigns the attached Lease relating to the above premises, executed __(date original lease was signed)__, and all rights, liabilities and obligations thereunder to a proposed California corporation, __(name of corporation)__. This Assignment is given without consideration and no consideration will be required to effectuate this Assignment. This Assignment is, however, contingent upon said proposed California corporation, __(name of corporation)__, obtaining nonprofit corporate status from the California Secretary of State, exemption from payment of California corporate franchise taxes from the California Franchise Tax Board, and exemption from payment of federal corporate income taxes from the Internal Revenue Service within one year from the date of execution of this Assignment of Lease.

Dated: _____

__(name of predecessor organization)__

By: __(signature of representative of above organization)__
   (typed name of representative)

The undersigned Lessor of the above premises hereby assents to this Assignment of Lease.

Dated: _____

__(signature of Lessor)__
(typed name of Lessor), Lessor

Item 11: All 501(c)(3) type groups (religious, charitable, scientific, literary or educational organizations) should answer questions 11(a) through 11(d). Religious groups claiming an exemption as a church must also respond to the questions under 11(e) on an attachment page.

Special-Purpose Groups: Special purpose groups (which do not plan to be exempt under 501(c)(3) of the Internal Revenue Code) will have to circle and complete a different item on the exemption application and should consult an attorney for help in forming their nonprofit corporation and obtaining the necessary tax exemptions.

Blanks 11(a)-(e): If your organization will receive 10% or more of its assets from any one individual, or from members of a family (brothers, sisters, spouses, grandparents, children or grandchildren[4]), check "Yes" in blank 11(a) and explain on an attachment page. There is nothing wrong with arrangements of this sort and it does sometimes happen that one person or family will provide substantial assets (such as a major cash contribution) to a newly-formed nonprofit. The state will scrutinize your application more closely in this case to make sure the organization is not set up and operated to serve the interests of these individuals or family members.

If you check "Yes" in this blank because your group will receive 10% or more of its assets from another group, or "Yes" in blank 11(d) because your group will own or hold a 10% voting interest in another corporation, you may be considered a member of an affiliated group of organizations or may encounter other problems—please consult a lawyer or tax advisor.

If you answer "Yes" to 11(b), be prepared to show that your legislative activities will be "insubstantial" or that your lobbying and grassroots political activities will fall under and meet the requirements of the political expenditures election. Look ahead to Chapter 8, Part III, Blank 11 if you indicate "Yes."

If you answer "Yes" to 13(c), you will not be able to obtain your state exemption under Section 23701(d) and will not be eligible for your federal tax exemption under Section 501(c)(3) of the Internal Revenue Code (remember, 501(c)(3) type groups cannot participate in political campaigns of this sort).

If you are setting up a church, provide the information requested in 11(e), keeping in mind the general guidelines and information contained in Chapter 3, Section C2. Also refer to the church guidelines contained IRS Publication 557.

Items 12, 13,14, 15, 16, 17, 18, 19, 20, 21, 22 and 23: Skip these items. They relate to other types of tax-exempt groups.

C. Sign Your Exemption Application

After filling in all the blanks and completing your attachment pages and exhibits, make sure to sign the application at the bottom of the first page. Indicate the date and place of signing and have one of the people who have signed the Articles (one of the initial directors) sign as a representative, indicating his or her title as an "Incorporator"—officially, your organization doesn't have directors until your Articles are filed with the California Secretary of State.

Congratulations! You've finished completing your state exemption application and are just a few steps away from completing the organization of your nonprofit corporation! Your next step is to file your Articles, Bylaws and state tax exemption as explained in the next two chapters.

---

[4]The application refers to "lineal descendants." These are people in a direct line of descent from another person, i.e., a person's children, grandchildren, great-grandchildren, etc.

Chapter 8

FILE YOUR INCORPORATION PAPERS

THIS CHAPTER CONSISTS mostly of housekeeping details—what to file, where to file it and when. Filing the right form in the wrong place or even the wrong number of copies of the right form in the right place may result in needless delay. So pay close attention to these instructions and make a copy of each original document for safekeeping.

Step 7. Consolidate Your Papers

By now you've accumulated quite a few documents and are about to create more. This is a good time to establish a convenient means of keeping track of your papers by setting up a corporate records system. One easy way to do this is to get a sturdy three-ring, loose-leaf notebook with a series of dividers to use as a corporate records book.[1] We explain the details of setting up your corporate records book in Chapter 10, Step 12, so jump ahead if you wish to set up your corporate records book now. If you prefer to do this after preparing all of your papers, make sure to consolidate your incorporation forms, together with the copies you will make as explained below, and place them in one safe place.

Step 8. Make Copies of Documents

By now you have completed preparing your Articles, Bylaws, state tax exemption application and the attachments and exhibits associated with the exemption application. Your next step is to make copies of these documents for filing with state and federal offices, and for your corporate records book as follows:

---

[1] If you wish to order a fancier nonprofit corporate records book, see the order page at the back of this book for one of the Nolo Press corporate kits.

Articles of Incorporation

Make four copies [five copies if you are forming a public benefit corporation] for the following purposes:

- One file copy to place in your corporate records book.

- One copy to be attached to your state exemption application as an exhibit.

- Two copies to be sent to, and certified by, the Secretary of State. These two copies will be certified at no charge by the Secretary of State and returned to you. You will send one of these certified copies to the I.R.S. when you apply for your federal tax exemption; the other certified copy will be placed in your Corporate Records Book as a permanent copy.

- **For public benefit corporations only:** One copy to be submitted to the Secretary of State and forwarded by that office to the Attorney General, Registry of Charitable Trusts (see Chapter 10, Step 25).

Note: Later on you will need to make your own copies of the certified copy of your Articles returned by the Secretary of State for the following purposes:

- One copy to be filed with the post office to obtain a nonprofit mailing permit (see Chapter 10, Step 22);

- Two copies to be filed with the local Tax Assessor's office if you wish to obtain an exemption from payment of local personal and real property taxes (see Chapter 10, Step 23); and

- Additional copies to be filed in connection with any licenses or permits you wish to obtain (see Chapter 11, Section G).

- If you are incorporating an unincorporated association (see Chapter 5, Step 3) one copy to be filed with the County Recorder of *each* county in which the unincorporated association owns property (see Chapter 10, Step 27);

Bylaws

Make at least three copies [four copies if you are forming a public benefit corporation] for the following purposes:

- One copy to be attached to your state exemption application as an exhibit (proposed Bylaws);

- One copy to be attached to your federal exemption application;

- One copy to be kept in your Corporate Records Book.

- **For public benefit corporations only:** One copy to be filed with the Registry of Charitable Trusts (Chapter 10, Step 25); and

   If applicable, make the following additional copy:

- One copy to be filed with the post office to obtain a nonprofit mailing permit, if you wish to obtain one (Chapter 10, Step 22).

State Tax Exemption Application (including attachment pages and exhibits)

- Make one copy of the completed state tax exemption application (Form FTB 3500) and one copy of each attachment page and exhibit for your Corporate Records Book.

Step 9. Apply For Your State Tax Exemption and File Your Articles of Incorporation

To apply for your state tax exemption and file your Articles of Incorporation, take the following steps:

1. First organize your state tax exemption application "package." Staple together your completed original exemption application, original attachment pages containing responses to questions 6 and 7, and all exhibits (including a copy of your Articles and Bylaws). Staple a check made payable to the Franchise Tax Board in the amount of $25 (the application fee) to the front of the exemption application.

2. Then gather up the *original* Articles of Incorporation and the copies of your Articles made in Step 8 above to submit to the Secretary of State's office (two copies to be certified for free and returned to you; one copy to be forwarded to the Registry of Charitable Trusts if you are forming a public benefit corporation). Include these copies in your papers to send to the Secretary of State's office.

3. Next prepare the tear-out cover letter to the California Secretary of State included in the Appendix. This cover letter requests the Secretary to forward your exemption application and attachments to the Franchise Tax Board and to file the original Articles and certify the two copies of the Articles *after* your exemption application has been approved.

Prepare the tear-out cover letter, following the sample form and special instructions below.

√ The parenthetical blanks, i.e., "(_____)," indicate information which you must complete on the tear-out form.

√ Each circled number (e.g., ①) refers to a special instruction which provides specific information to help you complete an item. The special instructions immediately follow the sample form.

√ We suggest you tear out the form in the Appendix and fill in the blanks (using a typewriter with a black ribbon or printing neatly with a blank ink pen) as you follow the sample form and instructions below.

Sample Cover Letter to Secretary of State

(address of incorporator)   ①
(date)

Secretary of State
Corporate Filing Division
1500 11th Street
Sacramento, California 95814-2974

Dear Secretary of State:

I enclose an original and __(number)__ ② copies of the proposed Articles of
Incorporation of __(name of corporation)__, a proposed California nonprofit __("public
benefit" or "religious")__ ③ corporation, together with the California Franchise Tax
Board Exemption Application, application fee and its attachments, fastened separately.

Please forward the exemption application materials to the Franchise Tax Board and, upon
exemption approval, file the enclosed original Articles of Incorporation. After filing,
please return to me, at the above address, two of the enclosed copies of the Articles,
compared and certified by your office. A check in the amount of $30, ④ made payable to
your office, for filing Articles for the above nonprofit corporation is also enclosed.

Optional: ["Please note that above corporate name has been reserved for use by the
undersigned pursuant to Reservation Certificate No. __(number)__, issued __(date)__."⑤

Sincerely,

__(signature of incorporator)__ ⑥
(typed name), Incorporator

SPECIAL INSTRUCTIONS

① One of the initial directors named in your
Articles should prepare and sign this letter as the
incorporator of your organization. **Note:** If you have
reserved a corporate name, the person who reserved
the corporate name should prepare and sign this
cover letter.

② Public benefit corporations should show three
copies here: one to be forwarded to the Attorney
General's office; two to be certified for free and
returned to the incorporator. Religious corporations
should submit two copies.

Note: You can submit extra (more than two) copies for certification by the Secretary of State if you wish. The fee for comparing and certifying each additional copy is $8 per copy. Make sure to change the amount of your check to the Secretary of State and the language of the cover letter if you submit extra copies for certification.

③ In this blank, indicate whether you are filing Articles for a public benefit or a religious corporation.

④ The fee for filing Articles of Incorporation for a nonprofit corporation is $30. Staple a check made payable to the *California Secretary of State* for this amount to your cover letter.

Warning on Fee Increases: This fee amount (and other fees, such as the charge for comparing and certifying extra copies of the Articles) increases periodically. Call the Secretary of State at 1-916-657-5448 to make sure these fee amounts are current before filing your papers.

⑤ If you have reserved the corporate name shown in your Articles and are filing your Articles within sixty days of the effective date of your Certificate of Reservation, type this optional paragraph at the bottom of your cover letter, supplying the number and date of your Certificate of Reservation.

⑥ The incorporator should sign at the bottom of the letter, with the incorporator's name typed under the signature line). Make sure to place a copy of the completed cover letter in your corporate records book.

4. After completing the tear-out cover letter to the Secretary of State, mail the following papers to the Corporate Filing Division of the Secretary of State's office at the address indicated in the cover letter:

- California exemption application package;

- Original and copies of the Articles; and

- Cover letter with check made payable to Secretary of State.

Your next step is to wait. The Secretary of State will make sure your corporate name is available for use and that your Articles conform to law. If there are no problems, the Secretary of State will send you a letter within a week or two indicating that your Articles are acceptable for filing and that your exemption application has been forwarded to the Franchise Tax Board. The Franchise Tax Board will process your application and, if your exemption is granted, will mail you a determination letter indicating you are exempt from payment of state corporate income taxes. This letter will also contain information concerning the annual returns you must file with the state (see Chapter 11).

The state tax exemption will normally be contingent upon your obtaining your federal tax exemption. Expect to wait approximately 30 to 60 days before receiving your State Exemption Determination letter. The Franchise Tax Board will send a copy of this exemption approval letter to the Secretary of State, at which time the Secretary will file your Articles, compare and certify the copies, and send these certified copies to you. Once your Articles have been filed, you are a California nonprofit corporation, exempt from payment of state corporate income taxes.

Special Considerations When Filing Your Articles

If you have retyped the tear-out Articles, make sure you comply with the following requirements:

- Use 8 1/2" x 11" letter-size or 8 1/2" x 14" legal paper;

- Type on one side of the page only;

- Leave a 3" x 3" blank square in the upper right of the first page of your Articles for the Secretary's file stamp;

- Use black ink ribbon—copies must be legible and of sufficient contrast for photocopying.

If You File Your Articles Early: If you plan to file your Articles early, before obtaining your state tax exemption, read and follow the special procedure contained in Chapter 6, Step 4.

In Case of Difficulty: If there are any problems with your Articles or state exemption application, you can expect to wait longer. If the Secretary of State finds a problem, this office will return your Articles, indicating the items that need correction. You should then call the Franchise Tax Board (ask for the Exempt Organization Unit) and speak to an auditor for Exempt Organizations to try to determine if the problem with your Articles will have an effect on obtaining your tax exemption. If you can't get a definite answer, wait until you receive a response from the Franchise Tax Board (the Secretary of State forwards your exemption application even though your Articles are faulty). If you are told over the telephone, or by way of an exemption approval letter from the Franchise Tax Board, that your exemption application is OK, you may be able to correct your Articles and refile them with the Secretary of State using the information given in the Secretary's correction letter (and by reviewing the information in this book on preparing your Articles). When you have made the necessary changes, refile your corrected Articles.

If You Get Stuck: If you don't understand how to fix your Articles or the Franchise Tax Board requests further information or denies your exemption, you may be able to correct your documents or furnish any additional information requested after studying the instructions in this book. If you need help, consult an attorney who specializes in nonprofit corporations (see Chapter 12).

If You Are In a Rush: If you have a bona fide emergency on your hands and need to obtain your exemption in a hurry (for example, you have to meet a funding agency's grant disbursal deadline and can't afford to wait up thirty to sixty days before receiving your state exemption by mail), you can try to obtain the approval of the Sacramento Franchise

Tax Board to bring your exemption application package to the Sacramento office. You'll need to do some articulate convincing to be able to accomplish this, but grant deadlines and upcoming charitable events have occasionally been recognized as valid emergencies by the Franchise Tax Board.

To do this, call the Franchise Tax Board in Sacramento and ask for the Exempt Organization Unit. Ask the exempt organization auditor for approval to have your exemption application processed in person. If your request is granted, make a note of the auditor's name, the date of your conversation and the address and office number where you should bring your exemption application.

Once in Sacramento, you will need to follow three steps:

- Go to the Secretary of State's office at 1500 11th Street. Show the filing clerk your Articles and have them officially approved for filing.

- Go to the Franchise Tax Board and obtain your state tax exemption determination letter (if your application is in order, this should only take an hour or so).

- Go back to the Secretary of State's office with your exemption determination letter and the original and copies of your Articles. Give the clerk your exemption determination letter, original Articles and copies to be certified, together with your check for the total fees made out to the Secretary of State. You will need to pay an extra $15 as an over-the-counter filing fee. Ask the clerk to file your original Articles and compare and certify the copies. The clerk will file your original Articles and return the copies, "endorsed-filed" and certified with a facing certification page on each copy containing the seal of the State of California. The clerk will also return your exemption determination letter. If not, ask for it to be copied and the original returned to you.

Chapter 9

APPLY FOR YOUR FEDERAL 501(C)(3) TAX EXEMPTION

NOW THAT YOU'VE obtained your state tax exemption and formed a California nonprofit corporation by filing your Articles with the California Secretary of State, it's time to prepare your federal exemption application.

This is a critical step in the formation of your nonprofit organization since most of the real benefits of being a nonprofit flow from 501(c)(3) tax-exempt status. The time and effort devoted to this task will be well worth it.

Remember: We assume that your organization is a nonprofit corporation formed for a Section 501(c)(3) religious, educational, charitable, scientific or literary purpose that will qualify for 501(c)(3) public charity status as explained in Chapters 3 and 4.[1]

How Much Time and Effort?

The IRS estimates that it takes the average person 4 hours + to learn about the form and 8 hours + to prepare and send it to the IRS. Hopefully, by reading and following our line-by-line instructions below, you will accomplish this task in substantially less time.

How to Handle the Technicalities

This is not an easy form, particularly for nonprofit corporations that have been in existence for eight months or more—for these groups, a number of questions are quite technical and require attention to the fine print in the specific instructions. So, a suggestion: If you get stuck on a difficult question or run low on energy, take a break and return to this task when you feel better able to follow and absorb this material.

---

[1]Special purpose nonprofit groups, exempt under other subsections of Section 501(c), must use IRS Form 1024 to apply for their federal tax exemption. Technical Exception: Certain cooperative hospital service organizations and cooperative educational service organizations can use Form 1023 (see the General Instructions to Form 1023, Section A3).

Step 10. Prepare and File Your Federal Tax Exemption Application

Call your local IRS forms request telephone number (or the national IRS forms and publications request number 1-800-TAX-FORM) or stop by your local IRS office in person to obtain the following federal tax forms and publications (latest form version dates as of this book printing are shown in parenthesis):

Form 8718   User Fee for Exempt Organization Determination Letter Request (version: 1-96)

Package 1023   Application for Recognition of Exemption with official instructions (version: July 1993)

Form SS-4   Application for Employer Identification Number (12-95)

Form 5768   Election by an Eligible Section 501(c)(3) Organization to Make Expenditures to Influence Legislation (1-94)

Note: Nolo Nonprofit Corporate Kits include IRS Package 1023 plus Forms SS-4 and 8718 (see kit order page at the back of this book).

√   To make sure that each tear-out form is the most current version at the time of your incorporation, call your local IRS tax information number. If you wish to be absolutely safe here, order one copy of each of the above forms when you place your order for the additional IRS forms and publications listed below. You can work with the tear-out form while you wait for your IRS forms order to arrive. If the ordered forms are more current than the tear-out versions, simply transfer your responses from the tear-out form to the current version. In most cases, revisions to the forms result in only minor, non-substantive changes and you should be able to follow the format of the new form without difficulty.[2]

---

[2]Remember, if you are using an older edition of this book, you can call Nolo Press to order the latest edition which may contain newer forms and instructions.

√ Make at least one copy of the tear-out form and use this copy for your first draft, following the line-by-line instructions below. After making corrections to the draft form, copy your final responses to the original tear-out form.

√ Call your local IRS forms request telephone number (or the national IRS forms and publications request number 1-800-TAX-FORM) or stop by your local IRS office in person to obtain the following additional federal tax forms and publications:

Publication 557	Tax-Exempt Status for Your Organization
Publication 578	Tax Information for Private Foundations and Foundation Managers

Preliminary Reading

As a first step in preparing your federal tax exemption application, read the General and Specific Instructions to Package 1023 [again, this is the federal 501(c)(3) tax exemption application package]. Also read through the information in IRS Publication 557 before filling out your federal exemption application.

Don't get bogged down in this technical material. The information in this book relating to the requirements for obtaining your federal tax exemption and achieving public charity status, together with the line-by-line instructions below should be enough to get you through. If you need to, you can always refer to the IRS publications and instructions later in responding to particular questions, or to fill out specific schedules.

1023 Schedules and Attachments

Form 1023 contains several schedules designed to be used only by certain types of nonprofit corporations (schools, hospitals, etc.). Don't include any schedule with your application unless it specifically applies to you. Some items will require the preparation of an attachment page or pages. Use letter-sized (8 1/2" x 11") paper and make sure each attachment page contains the following information:

- a description of the information on the attachment (specify Form 1023 and identify the part and line item number); and

- the name and address of your corporation.

Example

GoodWorks, Inc.
1220 Buena Vista Avenue
Glendora, California 94567
EIN _____

Attachment To Form 1023
Continuation of Response To Part II, Line 1
Page 1

Public Inspection Requirements

Your federal 1023 tax exemption application, any papers submitted with the application, and your tax exemption determination letter from the IRS must be made available for public inspection during regular business hours at your organization's principal office (any information that has been approved as confidential need not be disclosed). If your organization regularly maintains one or more regional or district offices having three or more employees, copies of these documents also must be made available for public inspection at each of these offices.

Copies of your organization's three most recent annual information returns also must be available for public inspection at your principal office (and, if applicable, your regional or district office).

The names and addresses of contributors do not have to be disclosed.

Members of the public also can obtain copies of these documents at any IRS office by paying a small fee. These public inspection requirements apply to 501(c)(3) public charities, not to 501(c)(3) private foundations—again, we expect most incorporators to qualify as public charities.

Failure to permit public inspection carries a $10 per day penalty. An automatic $1,000 additional penalty is imposed if any failure to comply is willful. These penalties are not imposed on the organization—they are applied against "the person failing to meet [these] requirements." See IRS Publication 557 and IRC §§ 6104(e), 5562(c)(1)(C) and (D). and 6685 for further information on these rules.

A. Do You Need to Apply for Your 501(c)(3) Tax Exemption?

Form 1023 serves two purposes:

1. It is used by nonprofit organizations to apply for 501(c)(3) tax-exempt status; and

2. It serves as your notice to the IRS that your organization is a public charity, not a private foundation. Remember, as discussed earlier, 501(c)(3) nonprofit groups are presumed to be private foundations unless they notify the IRS that they qualify for public charity status.

A few groups, technically, are not required to file Form 1023:

- a group that qualifies for public charity status and that normally has gross receipts of not more than $5,000 in each tax year;[3]

- a church, interchurch organization, local unit of a church, convention or association of churches, or an integrated auxiliary of a church; or

- a subordinate organization covered by a group exemption letter (if the parent organization timely submits a notice covering the subordinate organization—see the group exemption letter requirements in IRS Publication 557).

Even if one of the above exception applies to you, we recommend filing Form 1023 anyway. Why? First, because it's risky to second guess the IRS. If you're wrong and the IRS denies your claim to 501(c)(3) tax status several years from now, your organization may have to pay substantial back taxes and penalties. Second, because the only way, on a practical and legal level, to assure others that you are a bona-fide 501(c)(3) group is to apply for an exemption. If the IRS agrees and grants your tax exemption, then, and only then, can you assure contributors, grant agencies, and others that you are a qualified 501(c)(3) tax exempt, tax-deductible organization listed with the IRS.

---

[3]A special formula is used to determine if a group "normally" has annual gross receipts of not more than $5,000. For specifics, see IRS Publication 557, page 9, "Gross Receipts Test."

What if You File Late?

In our experience, the single most common problem faced by nonprofits is a failure to file their Form 1023 on time. Your 1023 application is timely filed if it is postmarked within 15 months after the end of the month in which your Articles were filed. Note that you can request an extension of time to file your 1023 package if you submit your request within this 15 month period—see IRS Publication 557. If you file on time (or within the extension period approved by the IRS), the tax exemption is effective retroactively to the date on which your Articles were filed. If you file late, it is effective from its postmark date.

If you're just now getting around to filing your 1023 Form several years after the initial organization of your nonprofit, don't despair; you've got plenty of good company. The important point here is to persevere, complete your application and mail it to the IRS as soon as possible.

How to Keep Form 1023 Information Confidential

Generally, any information submitted with your 1023 is open to public inspection. However, if any attachment or response to your application contains information regarding trade secrets, patents or other information that would adversely affect your organization if released to the public, you should clearly indicate "NOT SUBJECT TO PUBLIC INSPECTION" next to the material and include your reasons for requesting secrecy. If the IRS agrees, the information will not be open to public inspection

B. Prepare User Fee Form 8718

Form 8718, User Fee for Exempt Organization Determination Letter Request, must be completed and submitted with your tax exemption application. This form is used to compute and pay the fees due for applying for your tax exemption. Fill in the 8718 Form as you follow these instructions:

Line 1: Type the name of your corporation.

Line 2: Insert your Federal Employer ID Number or, if you haven't received it yet, state "Applied for

[date of mailing IRS SS-4 form]" (see Section C, Part 1, Line 2 instruction in this chapter).

Line 3: Groups that qualify for a reduced user fee of $150 check box a. Your organization qualifies for this reduced fee if it is submitting its initial exemption application and:

1. it is a new organization (not in operation for four years) and it anticipates gross receipts of not more than $10,000 during each of its first four tax years; or

2. it has been in operation for four tax years or more and has had annual gross receipts averaging not more than $10,000 during the preceding four years.[4]

If you check box a to qualify for the lower $150 fee, complete the Certification section in the middle of item 3. Type the name of your corporation in the blank and have the person who signs your exemption application sign on the line below the certification, showing this person's title in the blank to the right.[5]

Other nonprofit groups (except those seeking a group exemption letter) should check box b—the user fee in this case is $465 (don't complete the certification section if you check this box).

Box c only applies to special organizations seeking an exemption for a group of nonprofits (such as an association of churches—see Publication 557 and check with a nonprofit advisor for more help; you can't use Form 1023).

How to Pay: Write a check made payable to the Internal Revenue Service for the amount of the user

---

[4]For the full text of the regulations which explain these user fees, see Revenue Procedure 88-8.

[5]What if you incorrectly guess that gross receipts will be no more than $10,000 during each of your first four tax years and actual gross receipts during this period exceed this amount in one or more years? We don't know the answer although it seems reasonable to assume that the IRS may monitor your annual information returns and ask you to pay the remaining balance on the full Form 8718 fee if you make more than this threshold amount. Of course, if the financial information submitted with your 1023 exemption application shows that your group has, or expects to have, average gross receipts exceeding $10,000 for its first four years and you check the wrong box here, expect the IRS to return your exemption application due to insufficient payment.

fee and staple your check to the 8718 form (place the check in the box at the bottom of the form). The check does not have to be an organizational check. The person preparing the application or any other incorporator may write a personal check in payment of this fee.

What to Send: After completing your 1023 application, attach Form 8718 together with your user fee check to the front page.

Where to File: Mail your completed exemption application package to the appropriate IRS District office listed on the User Fee Form. These addresses are the most current and supersede the IRS addresses listed in the 1023 application package and in other IRS forms and publications.

C. Prepare Your Tax Exemption Application

Now it's time to get your pencil out and go through Form 1023, line by line. The IRS 1023 package includes two copies of the form. Use one as a draft. When you are satisfied with your draft responses, type or neatly print your final answers on the second copy of the form. Keep your completed state exemption papers handy. Since much of the information requested is the same or similar to the information submitted with your state exemption application, we occasionally refer to previous material on filling out your state application.

Part I. Identification of Applicant

Lines 1a-d: Show the name of your corporation exactly as it appears in your Articles of Incorporation. If you have operated (or plan to operate) your corporation under a fictitious corporate name, show this name in parenthesis after your formal name in item 1(a).

Provide the address of the corporation in blanks 1(c)-(d). If you have designated one person to receive tax information and forms from the IRS (usually your corporate Treasurer), show this person's name as the "c/o name" in item 1(b).

Line 2: All nonprofit corporations (with or without employees) must obtain a federal Employer Identification Number (EIN)—you will use this identification number on all your federal tax returns and reports. Even if your organization held an EIN prior to incorporation, it must obtain a new one for the corporate entity. Most new groups will not have obtained their EIN yet and should do so now.

The easy way is to complete the SS-4 form, "Application for Employer Identification Number," then to call the IRS Tele-TIN number for your state listed in the SS-4 instructions. Type in the EIN number assigned to your organization over the phone in Line 2 of your 1023 form, then mail or fax a copy of your completed SS-4 form to the IRS as explained in the SS-4 instructions.

Note: You can get an EIN the slow way by mailing your SS-4 form to the IRS without calling. Expect to wait at least four weeks. In this case, type the following in Line 2: "Applied for: __[insert date of mailing of SS-4 form]__."

Complete the SS-4 Form Prior to Calling the IRS Tele-TIN number

The date you started your business is the date your Articles were filed with the secretary of state. Use the file-stamped date on the copy of your Articles returned by the secretary of state's office. You can indicate that the date you will pay wages is "unknown." Have an incorporator or initial director sign the form, indicating his or her title as incorporator or director.

Line 3: Provide the name and telephone number of a director or other person to be contacted regarding your application and the phone number where this person can be reached during business hours. We suggest you show the name and telephone number of the person who is preparing your tax exemption in this blank.

Line 4: Specify the month your accounting period will end in this item. The accounting period must be the same as the tax year selected for your corporation. Most nonprofits use a calendar year as their accounting period and tax year and specify December here.

If you anticipate special seasonal cycles for your activities or non-calendar year record keeping or grant accountability procedures, you may wish to select a non-calendar accounting period for your corporation. For example, a federally funded school may wish to specify June in this blank to indicate an accounting period of July 1 to June 30th.

If you have any questions regarding the best accounting period and tax year for your group, check with your (probable) funding sources and consult your accountant or bookkeeper for further guidance.

Line 5: Show the date your Articles were filed by the secretary of state.

Line 6: Indicate up to three IRS activity codes, obtained from the list of codes printed on the back of the 1023 Schedule I form that best describe your tax-exempt primary purposes, activities or type of organization. Enter these codes in order of importance. For example, a non-institutional educational group that plans to provide seminars and lectures, publish materials, and engage in non-scientific research would indicate numbers 123 (discussion groups, forums, panels, lectures), 120 (publishing activities), and 124 (study and research—non-scientific), in order of importance. If you don't find three codes that apply to you, list only one or two.

Line 7: The boxes that appear here will not apply to most incorporators and should be ignored by most groups:

- 501(e) applies to organizations that perform cooperative services for hospitals;

- 501(f) applies to groups that perform collective investment services for educational organizations;

- 501(k) applies to child care organizations. Certain child care groups will be treated as 501(c)(3) educational organizations if they meet special requirements contained in this IRC section—see Chapter 3C5, "Child Care Centers," and IRS Publication 557, page 8, "Child Care Organizations."

Line 8: Naturally, we assume this is your first application for your federal tax exemption and that you will check "No" here. If your organization has previously applied for its federal tax exemption (perhaps because it incorrectly applied under another section of the code), check "Yes" and attach a letter explaining the status or determination of the previous application.

Line 9: Some nonprofits using this box will be exempt from filing IRS Form 990, the annual information return for nonprofits or the shorter 990EZ form for smaller groups—see Chapter 11, Section A1. If you expect to be exempt—the most common exemptions apply if you are forming a church or plan to have gross receipts of less than $25,000 per year—mark "No" and state the reason why you are exempt. All other nonprofits using this book should mark "Yes" here. Only 501(c)(3) private foundations can check the not applicable ("N/A") box—as explained in Chapter 4, we're sure most incorporators will not want to form a private foundation.

Note: For more information on the specific exemptions from the annual information return filing requirements, see Publication 557 and obtain and look at the instructions to the 990 form (call 1-800-TAX-FORM for a copy of this and the 990EZ tax form).

Line 10: If your corporation has previously filed regular income tax returns or tax-exempt information returns, check "Yes" and provide the information requested. Most groups should be able to indicate "No" to this question. If you indicate "Yes" to either of these questions, you're probably converting a profit corporation to a nonprofit corporation or are late in submitting your exemption application—in this case, be sure to specify the form number of each return filed, the year covered by the return, and the IRS office where it was filed.

Important Note: If the deadline for filing the annual information return for a tax-exempt organization (IRS Form 990 and Form 990 Schedule A) occurs while your federal exemption is pending, you are required to file the return. Indicate that your 1023 is pending on the return.

Line 11: Check box (a) to indicate that your group is a corporation and attach copies of your Articles and completed Bylaws to your application. Make sure your Articles are a *conformed copy* of the original Articles (a copy received from the Secretary of State with the Secretary's file-date stamped on the top of the first page). Make sure you have filled in all the blanks in your printed Bylaws. Although not required, you can have the person who will be designated to serve as corporate secretary sign and date the Certificate section at the end of the bylaws if you wish. Since you are enclosing your Bylaws, do not check the box at the right of the last line of this item on the application.

Submitting a Conformed Copy of Your Articles to the IRS

An important technical IRS requirement is that you submit with your exemption application a *conformed copy* of your Articles. A conformed copy is one that agrees with the original, shows the signatures of your initial directors or incorporators and the acceptance of your secretary of state. Therefore make sure to submit a copy of your Articles that bears the California Secretary of State's file stamp. Don't submit a copy of unfiled Articles with your 1023 application—the IRS wants proof that your organization has been officially incorporated.

Part II. Activities and Operational Information

Note: The answers to the next series of questions will require a thorough familiarity with the material in Chapters 3 and 4. Here is where terms such as "public charity" and "private foundation" start to become important. We will make specific cross-references as we go along, but it would be wise to look over Chapters 3 and 4 again before you proceed.

Line 1: Provide a narrative description of *all* your organization's activities—past, present and those you plan to conduct in the future—in their order of importance. For each activity note in detail:

- its purpose;
- when it was initiated (or, if it hasn't yet begun, when it will);
- where and by whom it will be conducted.

Many new groups will be describing proposed activities that are not yet operational, but you must still be very thorough in providing information about the activities that will be engaged in. [Much of this information may often be obtained from your responses to Blanks 7(e) and 7(f) on your state exemption application.]

If appropriate, include a description of any unrelated business you plan to engage in. At this point of course, most nonprofits will not have formulated specific plans for unrelated business activities. If they have, they will not want to stress the importance or scope of these incidental unrelated activities—see Chapter 3D1 for further information.

Using Purpose Clause Language: The IRS does not want to see language repeated here that has been taken from the purpose clause in your Articles. If you wish, you may include a reference or repeat the language of the more expanded statement of specific objectives and purposes included in Article 2, Section 1 of your Bylaws. However, unless your bylaw language includes a detailed narrative of both your activities and purposes, we suggest you use it only as a starting point for a fuller response here. Generally, we recommend starting over with a fresh, straightforward statement of your group's nonprofit activities in this response.

Example: A response by an environmental organization might read in part as follows:

The organization's purpose is to educate the public on a variety of environmental issues with special attention to educating the public on how to use less energy. Since January, 1992, the organization has published informational brochures explaining how to implement solar energy heating systems as an alternative to traditional energy sources. Publications are provided to the public at a fee slightly above cost— see copies of educational material enclosed, Attachments A-D.The brochures are published in- house at (address of principal office). Both paid and volunteer staff actively contribute to the research, writing, editing and production process. In addition to publishing, the organization's other activities include the following [list in order of importance other current, past or planned activities]:

Another Example: A nonprofit organization plans to sponsor special activities for the purpose of supporting other nonprofit charities. It should describe both its activities to obtain revenue at special events and the manner in which this money will be spent to support other groups.

If you are forming an organization that automatically qualifies for public charity status (a church, school, hospital or medical research organization) or has special tax exemption requirements, you will want to show that your organization meets the criteria that apply to your type of organization (see Chapter 4, Section F1 and the instructions to the appropriate schedule in the 1023 package).

Type of Organization	See Schedule
Church	A
School, College or University	B
Hospital and Medical Research Organization	C
Home for the Aged or Handicapped	F
Child Care Organization	G
Student Aid or Scholarship Benefit Organization	H

Line 2: Briefly indicate the anticipated sources of financial support of your organization in the order of their magnitude (most money to least money). [This information can often be copied from your response to Blanks 7(f), 7(g) and, possibly, from Blank 7(d), of your completed state tax exemption application.] Here are a few additional points to help you complete your response to this item:

• Your sources of support should be related to your exempt purposes, particularly if you plan to be classified as a public charity under the support test described in Chapter 4, Section F3, where the group's primary support is derived from the performance of tax-exempt activities.

• If you plan to qualify as a publicly supported public charity described in Chapter 4, Section F2, your responses here should show significant support from various governmental grants, private agency funding or individual contributions.

• If you expect your principal sources of support to fluctuate substantially, attach a statement describing and explaining anticipated changes— see the specific instructions to Part II, Line 2 in the 1023 package.

There is not much room in this item to list your anticipated sources of financial support. Although your response should be as brief as possible, if it won't fit in the allotted space, continue it on an attachment page.

Line 3: This question asks how the corporation will go about obtaining revenues from the sources of expected support that you have just set out in your answer to the preceding question. If you've provided the details of your fundraising activities in the previous response, simply indicate "Fundraising activities are described in Part II, No. 2, above." [Your response to Blanks 7(d) and 7(f) of your state exemption application also may be of help here.]

Otherwise, indicate how you will go about implementing your fundraising activities. For example, if you will give classes to obtain revenue, indicate how instructors will be recruited and students attracted; or if you will rely on grants, how grant funds will be solicited and the particular or general categories of grant agencies you plan to approach. The question also requests information regarding the extent to which these fundraising activities have been implemented. For newly-incorporated groups, most fundraising activities will not yet be operative and you should so indicate, perhaps including a general indication of what set-up work and initial operations will be entered into during your first year.

Include any literature you plan to distribute to solicit support and indicate that this material is attached in your response to this item. [See response 7(j) of your California tax exemption application.]

Unrelated Business Activities: As explained in the 1023 instructions for this line, fundraising activities include unrelated business activities that will supply cash to fund your nonprofit. If you have concrete plans to engage in unrelated activities (which, of course, will be clearly characterized as an insubstantial part of your overall activities), include the details here.

Reality Note: At this point, most nonprofits will not have formulated specific plans for unrelated business activities. If they have, they will not want to stress the importance or scope of these incidental commercial activities—see Chapter 3, Section D1 for further information.

Lines 4(a) and 4(b): Provide the names and addresses of the initial directors named in your Articles. Show the residence or business address of

each director—do not show the address of the corporation for any person listed here. Since directors will not be paid a salary, you may wish to reply: "Pursuant to Article 3, Section 5 of the corporation's Bylaws, directors will not be paid a salary but may be paid a reasonable fee for attending meetings of the board and may be allowed reasonable reimbursement or advancement for expenses incurred in the performance of their duties."

Since you will formally elect officers (President, Vice-President, Secretary, and Treasurer) and provide for any officer salaries later as part your first board meeting, you may wish to insert the following in your response to this item: "The persons who will serve as officers, and the compensation they will receive, if any, has not been determined as yet by the board of directors. Any such compensation will be reasonable and will be paid in return for the performance of services related to the tax-exempt purposes of the corporation."

Alternatively, if you have decided who will be elected to serve as officers (and the amounts of any salaries to be paid), you can provide the details of these officer arrangements. [Your response to Blank 6(f) on your state exemption application may be used here.]

Line 4(c): Check "Yes" or "No." Although not necessary, the IRS likes to see public officials, or people appointed by public officials, on your board when they consider whether or not you have a representative governing body, particularly if you are seeking public charity status as a publicly-supported organization (as discussed in Chapter 4, Section F2). If you check "Yes," provide the information requested.

Line 4(d): Before answering this question, read the definition of disqualified persons in the sidebar (a shortened explanation is contained in the 1023 specific instruction for this line). Basically, the IRS is trying to determine whether your directors are disqualified persons for any reason other than the fact that they are directors (directors are disqualified persons, by definition, as foundation managers), or are related to, or have a business relationship with, disqualified persons.

The answer to this question is not critical to most groups planning to qualify as 501(c)(3) public charities. Receiving money from disqualified persons only serves as a minor limitation if you seek public charity status under the support test described in Chapter 4, Section F3, in that money received from disqualified persons can't be included as public support. Since these groups will be relying primarily on payments from outsiders (not directors) in return for services as their primary source of qualifying public support, there should be little problem.[6]

Of course, the IRS would like to see people on the board who are not disqualified persons since they are likely to have less personal and self-interested motives in carrying out the public purposes of the organization. Don't worry, though—it's quite common for directors or officers to be disqualified in a tax sense either because they are members of the family of a disqualified person (e.g., directors related to each other or to officers) or for some other reason.[7]

So, indicate whether any of the directors are disqualified persons (other than by virtue of the fact of being directors), or are related to or have a business relationship with disqualified persons. If so, describe how each director is disqualified in the space indicated.

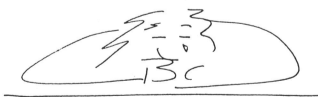

---

[6]Of course, if your 501(c)(3) nonprofit is classified as a private foundation (a classification you will try to avoid), the significance of being a disqualified person becomes more substantial.

[7]Don't forget that putting people on the payroll who are related to directors may create a conflict of interest problem for government-funded organizations (and cause you to run afoul of California's disinterested director rule—see Chapter 2E).

Who Are Disqualified Persons?

The concept of disqualified person is an important one for 501(c)(3) private foundations and public charities alike.

The IRS uses the word "disqualified" only in a tax sense, which does not necessarily mean that these persons are disqualified from participating in the operation of the 501(c)(3) nonprofit corporation. If the corporation is classified as a 501(c)(3) private foundation, the corporation and the individual can be held liable for certain private foundation excise taxes. If the corporation is classified as a 501(c)(3) public charity (we assume yours will be), it is prevented in some cases from counting contributions received from disqualified persons as public support.

Disqualified persons include:

1. Substantial contributors: donors of more than $5,000 if the amount contributed is more than 2% of the total contributions and bequests received by the organization from the date it was created up to the end of the year in which the donation was made by the individual.

2. All foundation managers: directors, trustees and officers (or people with similar powers or responsibilities), or any employee with final authority or responsibility to act on the matter in question. Officers include persons specifically designated as such in the Articles, Bylaws or Minutes and persons who regularly exercise general authority to make administrative and policy decisions. Officers do not include independent contractors such as accountants, lawyers, financial and investment advisors and managers, nor, generally, any person who simply makes recommendations for action, but who cannot implement these recommendations.

3. An owner of more than 20% of either the total combined voting power of a corporation, the profits' interests of a partnership, or the beneficial interest of a trust or unincorporated enterprise, if any of these entities is a substantial contributor to the foundation.

4. A member of the family—this includes ancestors, spouse, lineal descendants such as children and grandchildren, but not brothers and sisters—of any of the individuals described in 1, 2 or 3 above.

5. Other business entities (e.g., corporations, partnerships, trusts, etc.) in which the persons described in 1-4 above have at least a 35% ownership interest.

For example, Ms. X makes a gift of $20,000 to your nonprofit corporation. If this gift exceeds 2% of all contributions and bequests made to your organization from the time it was created until the end of the corporate tax year in which Ms. X made the contribution, Ms. X is a substantial contributor.

For purposes of this test, gifts and bequests made by an individual include all contributions and bequests made by the individual's spouse. Once a person is classified as a substantial contributor, he generally remains classified as one (regardless of future contributions made, or not made, by the individual or future support received by the organization). However, if other conditions are met, a person will lose his status as a substantial contributor if he makes no contribution to the organization for ten years.

For further information on disqualified persons, see Chapter V of IRS Publication 578.

Line 5: Indicate "Yes" or "No" as appropriate to these two questions. If you answer "Yes" to the first question because your nonprofit controls, or is controlled by, another organization, your operations are more complex than usual and you should consult a lawyer before applying for your federal exemption.

Check "Yes" to the second question if you have incorporated a pre-existing organization such as an unincorporated association [see the discussion to Item 6(a) on the state exemption application, Chapter 7B] and provide a short statement to this effect in your response.

Sample Response:

"The Better Living Center, Inc." is an outgrowth of, and successor to, the operations of an unincorporated association, "The Better Living Association."

If you check "Yes" to the second question because of shared directors, officers, employees or office space (or other special relationships) with another group, the IRS will wish additional information on the purposes and activities of the other group. Again, consult a lawyer for help with this complex incorporation scheme.

Line 6: You should be able to answer "No" to this item. Only unique groups, such as those that will set up, share facilities with, or support another politically active affiliate organization, will answer "Yes" here. A "Yes" response means that you should be applying for your tax exemption with the help of an experienced nonprofit professional.

Line 7: You should be able to indicate "No" to this question unless you are financially accountable to another organization (if you must report income and expenses to another tax-exempt, or taxable, organization). If so, you will need to provide the information requested and should check with a tax advisor or lawyer to make sure you will qualify for your 501(c)(3) tax exemption.

Line 8: Indicate what assets you have obtained since your incorporation, or at the time of your incorporation from a pre-existing unincorporated organization (such as land, buildings, equipment and publications—don't include cash and income producing property). [Generally, for corporations that have been in operation for one year or more, operational assets will be those listed in the balance sheet prepared in response to Item 7(c) on the state exemption application.] Indicate if your assets are not fully operational, as would be the case if a building is under construction.

Most newly formed nonprofit corporations will have few, if any, operational assets unless they have incorporated an existing organization. Some may have made arrangements for acquiring assets or putting them into use. If so, you should provide this information.

If you have not acquired assets or made arrangements for the acquisition of assets, you need only indicate that the question is not applicable.

Sample Response:

The corporation has the following operational assets: Brand Name Computer System consisting of 1 file server and 4 workstations. Once the main system hub is connected to the 4 workstations in approximately 1 month, system will be fully operational and will be used to maintain organizational mailing lists, keep corporate books, generate organizational invoices and purchase orders, make and record payroll transactions and pay ongoing bills.

Line 9: Frankly, we're not sure why the IRS is asking this question, but most groups will check "No" here anyway. If you answer "Yes" because your organization expects to receive tax-exempt bond financing in the next two years, the IRS may have a few extra questions about this item when it responds to your tax exemption application.

Line 10(a): Indicate if any of your facilities will be managed by another organization or individual under the terms of a contract, explaining the relationship of the parties involved. What the IRS is looking for here is whether some person or organization closely associated with your nonprofit corporation will be unduly benefited by this type of managerial contract. If, for instance, a day care center plans to hire a director, officer or other person who is closely associated with the corporation to manage the center, the IRS will want to make sure that the corporation is not paying more than fair value for these services (of course, it helps if some portion of these services is volunteered by the director or officer). If you have reduced the terms of this type of management agreement to writing, include a copy of the contract as an attachment.

Line 10(b): If your nonprofit corporation leases property (as the landlord or tenant), check "Yes" here, attach a copy of the lease or rental agreement and explain the relationship of the parties to the

lease in your response. [See instructions to Item 7(i) of the state exemption application in Chapter 7B for a discussion of leases together with a sample assignment of lease; also see Chapter 10, Step 18.]

Mostly, the IRS is looking here for lopsided or special-interest rental agreements, as would be the case where a director leases space in his home to the nonprofit for an excessive rent payment. Although not required in situations of this sort, it helps if the director or officer donates the use of a portion of the space or rents the premises to the nonprofit at a substantial discount so that it's clear that no self-dealing is involved.

Line 11: Indicate whether or not you are a membership organization. If you have adopted a formal membership structure by including the tear-out membership provisions provided in the appendix in your Bylaws, you should check "Yes" and answer questions 11(a), (b) and (c). If you have not formed a formal membership organization, check "No" and go on to question 12.

Line 11(a): Indicate any membership qualifications you've decided on and attach a schedule of fees and dues to be charged to members (see Article 12, Sections 2 through 4 of your membership bylaws). If the amount for such fees hasn't been determined, you should so indicate and state that "the amounts shall be reasonable and as specified from time to time by resolution of the Board of Directors."

Line 11(b): In all cases, the IRS likes to see you actively solicit the general public to become members of the corporation, so describe your present and proposed efforts to attract members. If you have final or draft copies of literature for soliciting members, indicate that they are enclosed and include them as attachments. If you haven't prepared (but plan to distribute) such literature, indicate that "promotional literature to attract members of the general public to become members of the corporation is not yet prepared, but will be prepared and distributed to members of the general public" (or of the "community served by the corporation").

Line 11(c): Certain membership groups solicit the general public to become members and give them exclusive rights to participate in the activities and events of the corporation in exchange for payment of dues. This is acceptable in most cases provided you allow members of the general public, or a broad cross-section of the community, to become members and actively solicit public or community membership in your corporation.

If corporate programs, activities and benefits are available to members and non-members alike, indicate this in your response. If members are given special discounts or preferences, list these differences in your answer. Use an attachment page to continue your response if you run out of room on the application form.

Line 12(a): It's a common (and completely permissible) practice to charge members of the public for services related to your exempt functions. (Of course it helps overall with your tax exemption application if you charge less than commercial enterprises for goods or services, but this is not a tax requirement.) Many groups will derive income primarily from these services. This might be the case for a performing arts group, a dance studio, a health clinic or a nonprofit school. If your group is in this category, indicate "Yes," also stating, if appropriate, that benefits, services and products will be available to the "general public." A "Yes" response requires a statement as to what specific services you will charge for, and the amount of such charges. Usually, at this point, groups have not fully determined the amount of payment to be charged for services. If this is the case, first list the services and benefits that will be provided to the public and explain how the fees for them will be determined. Indicate that "charges for the above benefits, products or services, although at present undetermined, will be reasonable and related to the cost of the service to be provided." If you already know what the charges are, attach a copy of your fee schedule as requested.

Line 12(b): Most groups will indicate "No" to this question since the IRS frowns upon the limitation of benefits or services to a specific class of individuals. However, if the class of people benefited by the corporation is broad, not limited to specific individuals, and related to the exempt purposes of the nonprofit group, the IRS should have no objection.

Example: A nonprofit musical heritage organization plans to provide programs and benefits to needy musicians residing in the community. If the overall tax-exempt purpose of the organization is allowed, this limitation of benefits will be permitted by the IRS.

Line 13: Most groups will indicate "No" to this question. If you plan to engage in efforts to influence legislation, check "Yes" and read the discussion in Chapter 3, Section D3. You should indicate in your response here that you will engage in efforts to influence legislation either "to an insubstantial degree" or, if you plan to elect to fall under the political expenditures test, "within the limits allowed under Section 501(h) of the Internal Revenue Code." Be sure to provide an estimate of the percentage of your organization's time and funds that will go into activities to influence legislation. Keep in mind that if the IRS considers the percentages "substantial," you risk putting your 501(c)(3) status in jeopardy (see Chapter 3, footnote 6).

Line 14: A 501(c)(3) nonprofit organization may not participate in political campaigns. Participation in or donations to a campaign can result in denial or revocation of tax-exempt status. Most groups should answer "No" here.

If you must answer "Yes" to this question, your activities should be strictly limited to nonpartisan voter education work and statements—see Chapter 3, footnote 4, and check with a nonprofit lawyer or tax consultant to make sure you are on safe ground before proceeding with your exemption application

Part III. Technical Requirements

Line 1: Most new groups will be able to answer "Yes" to indicate that they are mailing their exemption application within 15 months from the end of the first month in which their Articles of Incorporation were filed. If you answer "Yes," skip Lines 2-7 and go on to Line 8.

Lines 2 (a)-(c): If you are filing your application late (you answered "No, " to Line 1), you may qualify for one of the three exceptions to the 15-month filing deadline listed here (other extensions to the normal filing deadline are covered in later Lines of this part). These are the groups not required to file Form 1023: churches; public charities that normally have gross receipts of not more than $5,000 in each year; and subordinate organizations exempt under a group exemption letter. If you are mailing your exemption application late (after 15 months from the end of the month of incorporation) and feel that you are one of these groups, check the box that applies to you and go on to line 8 (if you are filing within 27 months of your incorporation date, you may prefer to ask for one of the other automatic late-filing extensions available under Lines 3 or 4 instead—see below). If the IRS agrees that you qualify under one of the three special tests listed here, your federal exemption will be effective retroactively from the date of your incorporation.

A Common Exception to the 15-month Deadline Under Line 2: The 2(b) exception is often applicable to new nonprofits.[8] This applies to your group if: (a) Your organization is a public charity (not a private foundation—since one of the purposes of completing your 1023 application is to establish that you are eligible for public charity status, we assume you meet this requirement); and (b) Your organization "normally" has gross receipts of not more than $5,000 in each tax year. For groups that have been in existence for two tax years, under the regulations this means gross receipts of $12,000 or less during the first two years (we assume you are into your second tax year at this point since you missed the 15 month filing deadline). Many new groups without outside sources of support can meet this gross receipts test during their beginning tax years.[9]

Line 3: If you will not mail Form 1023 within the 15-month limit and you are unable—or don't wish—to qualify under the exceptions discussed in Lines 2 (a)—(c) above, you automatically qualify for an extension of time to file as long as you submit a completed 1023 application to the IRS within 12 months from the end of the normal 15-month period—in other words, before the end of the 27th month following the date of your incorporation. This is a handy extension and allows you to apply within two years plus from your date of incorporation—ample time for most groups (just don't miss this extended 27-month deadline—finish your application and mail it to the IRS pronto). This means your tax exemption, if granted, will apply retroactively to the date of your incorporation. If you are filing your application late and qualify for this extension, check "Yes" and go on to Line 8. If you

---

[8]Again, a safer way to qualify for an exception to the normal filing deadline is to ask for the automatic extension available under Line 3 of this part. If you submit your application within 27 months of the end of the month of your incorporation, you will qualify for late filing without having to take your organization's gross receipts or activities into account.

[9]Even if your group files its 1023 application late and cannot meet this gross receipts test for all initial tax years, it may still be eligible for this exception if gross receipts did not exceed these amounts. See IRS Publication 557, Chapter 3, "Gross Receipts Test," for further information on this point.

don't qualify for this automatic extension, check "No" and go on to Line 4.

Line 4: This line asks you if the IRS has contacted you about your failure to file your 1023 application within 27 months of your incorporation. If they haven't, check "No" and go on to Line 8. You qualify for another extension to the normal 15-month filing deadline.[10] If the Service has contacted you, you must check "Yes," then go on to Line 5.

5. Here is where you end up if your group is filing the 1023 application more than 27 months from the date of your incorporation, and the IRS has contacted you about your failure to complete your application within 27 months of incorporating. This doesn't happen too often—most groups are not notified unless they fail to respond to questions posed by the IRS in response to the filing of a prior 1023 application.

To qualify for late filing under these circumstances, check "Yes" and attach a statement giving the reasons why you failed to complete the 1023 application process within 27 months of your incorporation. Revenue Ruling 92—85 contains a list of the reasons that are normally acceptable to the IRS, as well as ones that aren't. This ruling is summarized in the 1023 instructions for this Line. If you want more information, you can look this ruling up at the law library—see the 1992—2nd volume of the IRS Cumulative Bulletin, starting at page 490—or check with your tax advisor. After attaching your statement, go on to Line 8.

If you don't think you can qualify for an extension under this Revenue Ruling (or if you decide not to bother—see the sidebar), check "No" and go on to Line 6.

If You End Up On Line 5, Should You Ask for Relief?

Most groups will not end up on Line 5 in Part III because even those that file late (beyond 27 months of incorporation) qualify for an automatic extension of time to file unless they have been contacted by the IRS—see the Line 4 instructions in the text. If your group does end up here, you may decide not to bother with seeking an extension to file and simply check "No" here. This means that your 501(c)(3) exemption, if granted, will only be effective from the date of its receipt by the IRS, not from the date of your incorporation. Is this so terrible? Often, it isn't. Here's why: many nonprofits will not have any taxable income and will not have received contributions from donors during these early startup months (the 27 plus months of operation prior to filing their 1023 application). Consequently, obtaining a tax exemption for these early months will not normally provide a tax benefit. However, if your group is facing tax liability for early operations, needs to provide donors with tax deductions for gifts contributed during the first 27-plus months, or needs to obtain 501(c)(3) tax-exempt status from the date of its creation for some other pressing reason, then it makes sense to prepare a special statement under Line 5 as explained in the text. If you are unsure, check with your tax advisor.

Line 6: If you checked "No" to Line 5 (you don't want to qualify for an extension under revenue Ruling 92—85, you end up here and should check "Yes," then go on to Line 7. This means that you agree that your 501(c)(3) exemption can only be recognized from the date of its receipt by the IRS, not retroactively to the date of your incorporation. By the way, we don't know what happens if you check "No" here—literally, this response means that you are not asking for an extension to file your application late, but don't agree that it should be treated as late. Such stubbornness is to be commended, but the Service probably will not be impressed and probably will hold up the processing of your application until you give in and answer "Yes" to this question in later correspondence with

---

[10]Although we call this another "automatic" extension, it really isn't: technically, you are qualifying for an extension under grounds listed in Revenue Ruling 92—85.

the IRS (or the Service may deny your exemption outright[11]).

Line 7: If you end up here (your application for 501(c)(3) status will only be considered from the date of its receipt by the IRS), you may wish to check the box in this question. If you do, you are asking the IRS to grant your group tax-exempt status as a 501(c)(4) organization—a social welfare group or a civic league—during your late filing period. This is the 27-month plus period from the date your Articles were filed up to the date your 1023 application is received by the IRS. What does this do for you? If your request for 501(c)(4) status is approved, your organization will be exempt from paying federal corporate income taxes (as a 501(c)(4) organization) from the date of its formation until the date of approval of your 501(c)(3) tax-exempt status. For most newly-formed groups without taxable income during this initial period, obtaining this extra tax exemption will not be necessary and this box can be ignored.

However, if you or your tax advisor determine that your organization is subject to tax liability for this initial period, check this box and call 1-800-TAX-FORM to order IRS Publication 1024. Fill in the first page of Form 1024 and submit it with your exemption application. If you qualify as a 501(c)(4) social welfare group (as many 501(c)(3)'s do—see the sidebar), your 501(c)(3) tax determination letter will indicate that you qualify as a 501(c)(4) organization during your initial late filing [your pre-501(c)(3)] period.

501(c)(4) Organizations

IRC Section 501(c)(4) provides a federal corporate income tax exemption for nonprofit social welfare groups and civic leagues (see Table 3.1 in Chapter 3). Since the promotion of public welfare is defined as "promoting the common good and general welfare of the people of the community," many 501(c)(3) nonprofits also qualify as 501(c)(4) social welfare organizations. Although 501(c)(4) nonprofits are exempt from federal corporate income taxation, they are not eligible to receive tax deductible contributions from donors and do not enjoy many of the other advantages associated with 501(c)(3) tax-exempt status, such as eligibility to receive public and private grant funds, to participate in local, state and federal nonprofit programs, to obtain county real and personal property tax exemptions, etc. But 501(c)(4) organizations do enjoy one advantage not available to 501(c)(3) groups: they may engage in substantial legislative activities and may support or oppose candidates to public office. For further information on 501(c)(4) tax-exempt status, see IRS Publication 557.

Line 8: Lines 8 though 15 relate to whether or not you are seeking to be classified as a 501(c)(3) public charity or as a 501(c)(3) private foundation. In Chapter 4, we discussed the distinction between these two classifications and why you should wish to meet one of the three primary tests for being classified as a public charity.

The 1023 instructions for Line 8 provide a brief explanation of the differences between public charity and private foundation status and the types of organizations that qualify as public charities. The table below shows how the organizations listed under the IRS instructions to line 8 fit in with our organizational scheme in Chapter 4:

---

[11] It's also possible that a "No" response here simply makes you ineligible to move ask for 501(c)(4) tax status during your late-filing period. Not such a terrible fate, really, but we've speculated enough on these technical niceties—let's get back to more important questions.

Check "Yes" or "No" on Line 8 to indicate whether or not you are a private foundation. Hopefully, as we've said, you will expect to qualify as a public charity and will mark "No " to this question. If your response is "No," go on to line 10. If you are forming a 501(c)(3) private foundation, check "Yes" and go on to line 9.

Line 9: If you've checked "Yes" to Line 8 indicating that you are a private foundation and you believe you can obtain the benefits of being a private operating foundation as explained in Chapter 4, Section D1 (also see the heading "Private Operating Foundations" in IRS Publication 557 and IRS Publication 578), check this box and complete Schedule E of the application. To understand the technical requirements of this special classification, you will need to refer to various subsections of Federal Income Tax Regulation 53.4942 and will probably wish to consult a tax advisor for help in preparing this schedule.

If you are forming a 501(c)(3) private foundation but do not seek to be classified as a private operating foundation, check "No" here and go on to Part IV.

Line 10: Check the box [letters (a)-(j)] that corresponds to the basis of your claim to public charity status. First, absorb what you can of the technical material given in the 1023 Line 10 instructions. Then reread Chapter 4, Sections F1, F2 and F3—these sections provide the names of these public charity organizations, the requirements they must meet, and the Internal Revenue Code sections that apply to them. Note that Letter (j) is a special case that allows certain groups to have the IRS determine which public charity support test best suits their activities and sources of revenue—more on this special choice later in this discussion.

After checking the appropriate public charity classification box for your organization under Line 10, make sure to go on to the next question on the 1023 that applies to your organization.

The table below shows how the different types of groups listed in this part of the application fit within the three different categories of public charity status discussed in Section F of Chapter 4. If you concentrate on our basic division of these different groups into the three public charity categories rather than focusing on the individual Internal Revenue Code sections, we think this part will go smoothly.

Let's look a little more closely at each of the lettered boxes in Line 10:

Box (a): If you are seeking to qualify automatically for public charity status as a church, also see the instructions to Schedule A in the 1023 package and our discussion of this schedule in the Line 15 instructions below. Go on to Part III, Line 15.

Box (b): Groups seeking to qualify as private schools should refer to the IRS instructions to Schedule B and see our discussion of this schedule under the Line 15 instructions below. Go on to Part III, Line 15.

Boxes (c)-(g): Few groups will choose one of these boxes since each applies to a special type of organization such as a hospital, public safety organization or government agency.

Box (c) hospitals and medical research groups will need to complete Schedule C and should refer to the 1023 instructions for this schedule before checking this box.

Box (e) organizations operated solely for the benefit of, or in connection with, any of the other public charity organizations (except one testing for public safety) must complete Schedule D. This information helps the IRS determine whether this type of organization supports other qualified public charities. For further information, refer to the 1023 instructions and Publication 557, "Section 509(a)(3) Organizations."

Groups checking boxes (c) through (f) go on to Part III, Line 15. Governmental organizations checking box (g) go on to answer questions 12 and 13 in Part III.

For More Help: If you do check one of the (c)-(g) boxes, the lawyer, accountant or other advisor who is helping you organize one of these special corporations should help you with your application. Again, we don't expect many nonprofit groups to be seeking public charity status under these IRC provisions.

Box (h) This box is for organizations that receive a substantial part of their support from government agencies or from the general public. These are the publicly supported groups discussed in Chapter 4, Section F2. If you believe this is the public charity best suited to your organization's sources of support, check the box on this line. If you are unsure whether this is the best support test to use for your group (if you think that the public charity support test listed in box (i) also may apply to your organization), you may wish to let the IRS make this decision for you as explained in the box (j) instructions below.

As discussed in Chapter 4, Section F2, many groups will not want to fall under this public charity test since it does not allow receipts from the performance of services related to the corporation's exempt purposes to be included as "qualified public support."

Groups checking box (h) go on to Part III, Line 11.

Box (i) This box is for organizations that normally receive 1/3 of their support from contributions, membership fees and gross receipts from activities related to the exempt functions of the organization (subject to certain exceptions) but not more than 1/3 from unrelated trades and businesses or gross investment income. The support test applicable to this means of achieving public charity status is discussed in Chapter 4, Section F3—this is the most common and often the easiest way of qualifying a new nonprofit organization as a public charity. So reread the requirements of this test and the definition of terms associated with it in Chapter 4. If you believe this public charity test best suits your expected sources of support, check this box. If you are unsure, see the instructions to box (j) just below.

Groups checking box (i) go on to Part III, Line 11.

Box (j): If you feel that your group may qualify as a public charity either under box (h) or box (i) but aren't sure which, then you can check this box. The IRS will decide which of these two public charity classifications best suits your organization based upon the financial data and other financial support information included in your 1023 application. For many new groups, box (j) is the best way to go. Rather than work through the math and technical definitions necessary to approximate whether you will qualify as a public charity under box (h) or box (i), checking this box lets the IRS do the work for you.

Groups checking box (j) go on to Part III, Line 11.

Sample Responses to Line 10

The First Fellowship Church, a religious organization that plans to maintain a space to provide weekly religious services to its congregation, checks box (a) to request automatic public charity status as a church.

The Workshop for Social Change, an educational group that plans to receive support from public and private grant funds and from individual and corporate contributions checks box (h) to request public charity status as a publicly supported organization.

Everybody's Dance Studio and Dinner Theater, a group that expects to derive most of its operating revenue from student tuitions, special workshops, and ticket sales (as well as from other exempt purpose activities), selects box (i) to be classified as a group that meets the public charity public support test discussed in Chapter 4, Section F3.

The School for Alternative Social Studies, an accredited private post-graduate school with a formal curriculum, full-time faculty and regularly enrolled student body, checks box (b) to request automatic public charity status as a formal private school.

The Elder Citizens Collective and Information Exchange, which plans to derive support from contributions and grants as well as subscriptions to its weekly newsletter (and other exempt-purpose services and products made available to members and the public at large), checks box (j) to have the IRS decide whether box (h) or box (i) is the appropriate public charity classification.

Line 11: Groups that checked Line 10 boxes (h), (i) or (j) must answer this question (we refer to these groups as "Line 11 groups"). All other groups should ignore this question and should go on to Line 15.

Your responses in Line 11 will indicate whether your group is requesting an advance or definitive IRS ruling as to its public charity status and whether you must go on to answer additional questions 12 through 14 in Part III. Note that the IRS automatically makes a definitive ruling as to the public charity status of groups that are not required to fill in Line 11. In other words, the only groups allowed to request an advance ruling on their public charity status are some Line 11 groups.

Advance vs. Definitive Rulings: We've already discussed the basic differences between advance and definitive public charity rulings in Chapter 4, Sections F2 and F3. Here we discuss these differences in more detail.

If your group has not been in existence for one tax year consisting of at least eight months, it *must* request an advance public charity ruling by checking the fourth Line 11 box (the "No" box). Your group must complete two copies of Form 872-C and attach

them to your application (see the instructions for this form below). Go on to Question 15—you do not have to answer Lines 12 through 14.[12]

Example: The Nonprofit Center, Inc. filed its Articles with the secretary of state on September 1st and closed its first tax year on December 31st (it specified December as the ending month of its accounting period in Part I, Line 4 of the 1023 application). The corporation is a Line 11 group and is preparing its tax 1023 exemption application during October of the following year. The group must check the "No" box here and request an advance ruling period since it has completed one tax year consisting of less than eight months. Its first and only completed tax year was a "short year" running from September 1st to December 31st of the previous calendar year. For further tax year examples, see the back of IRS Form 872-C.

If your group has been in existence for one tax year consisting of at least eight months, check the first Line 11 box (the "Yes" box). Your group has the option of requesting a definitive or an advance ruling by checking the second or the third Line 11 box respectively.

Which Type of Ruling Should Your Line 11 Group Request? Most nonprofits given a choice opt for an advance public charity ruling. If you request a definitive ruling on your public charity status, the IRS will look at the actual support received to-date by your group. If this support is not sufficient to qualify your group under the applicable public charity category, your public charity status will be denied or the IRS will issue an advance, not a definitive, public charity ruling anyway. Further, requesting a definitive ruling may take extra time and could involve responding to additional IRS questions before your tax exemption is approved.

---

[12]As often happens with technical tax forms, explicit instructions to guide some groups (in this case, Line 11 "No" groups) to the next question are missing. Our directions here (to skip lines 12, 13 and 14 and go on to Line 15) are based on our interpretation of the questions and instructions on this form and a comparison of this material with similar material on previous 1023 application forms.

Obtaining an advance public charity ruling is easier. The IRS will approve an advance ruling if it appears from the financial statements and other information contained in and submitted with the 1023 application that the group's anticipated sources of support will qualify the organization for public charity status. At the end of a five-year advance ruling period, the IRS will look at the annual information returns of the organization. If actual support meets the requirements of the selected public charity category, the group will then receive final approval of its 501(c)(3) public charity status. If the group does not qualify for public charity status at the end of this period, it will be classified as a 501(c)(3) private foundation during succeeding tax years.

Two related points:

- If the organization does not qualify as a public charity at the end of its advance ruling period, it is subject to excise taxes on investment income (only if it has not met the private foundation investment income rules during this period). The group is not, however, retroactively liable for other private foundation excise taxes during its advance ruling period.

- Even if public charity status is denied at the end of the advance ruling period, contributions made during the advance ruling period by individual donors will still be treated as having been made to a valid public charity.

In our opinion, it is usually best to request an advance ruling period for your public charity status. Of course, if your group is the exception and you can reasonably predict that its past support qualifies it for public charity status, go ahead and request a definitive ruling.

- Remember to check the second or third Line 11 box to specify the type of public charity ruling you are requesting. Check the second box to request a definitive ruling (and go on to answer lines 12 through 15). To request an advance ruling, check the third box, then go on to answer questions 12 and 15 (skip questions 13 and 14), and make sure to attach two completed 872-C forms to your application.

Sample Responses to Line 11

Remember the Workshop for Social Change from the earlier example? This is a group that plans to qualify for public charity status as a Line 10 box (h) publicly supported organization. If the group has not completed one tax year of at least 8 months, it must request an advance ruling by checking the Line 11 "No" box and going on to Line 15.

Everybody's Dance Studio and Dinner Theater is seeking public charity status as a Line 10 box (i) group. It has completed its first tax year consisting of 11 months and checks the Line 11 "Yes" box. It decides to check the third Line 11 box to request an advance ruling of its public charity status and goes on to Line 12.

If You're Feeling Woozy

We know completing the Part III Technical Requirements section of the federal tax exemption application can be tricky. If you are feeling lost, overwhelmed, or just plain disgusted, take a break. After coming back and reading our instructions to this part one or two more times, most groups will be able to tackle successfully this material and move on to the next (and last!) part of this federal form. If you do get stuck choosing the proper public charity classification or responding to special questions that apply to your group, ask a board member, friend, or friend of a friend with some legal or tax background to give you a hand getting over this incorporation hurdle.

Line 12: This line applies only to Line 11 groups that have checked the first Line 11 box (the "Yes" box) indicating that they have completed a tax year consisting of at least eight months.

Government Groups Note: Government groups that have checked Line 10 box (g) must also complete Line 12. Again, few readers will be applying on behalf of this special sort of group.

Complete the Financial Data in Part IV-A First: To answer this question, you must first supply the financial data (statement of revenue and expenses) requested in Part IV-A. If you have listed any unusual grants on Line 12 of any of the financial statements prepared in Part IV-A, list them here along with the donor's name, date and amount and the nature of the grant (was it general, restricted to a specific use, etc.).

Have You Received Sums Large Enough to Need Classification as Unusual Grants?

Unusual grants are large contributions, bequests, or grants received by the organization that are attracted by the publicly supported nature of the organization. The benefit of having a large grant qualify as an unusual grant is that it does not jeopardize the group's public charity status (as do other large sums received from a single source). It is unlikely that your beginning nonprofit has received sums that need classification as unusual grants. For further information on this technical area, see the 1023 instructions to Line 12 of Part IV-A; the discussions and examples of unusual grants in Chapter 4, Sections F2 and F3; and the specific rules on unusual grants contained in IRS Publication 557.

Line 13: This item should be filled out only if *both* the following conditions apply:

1. Your group checked Line 10, box (g) or (h); and

2. You checked the first and second Line 11 boxes indicating that your organization has completed a tax year consisting of at least eight months and you wish to obtain a definitive ruling as to its public charity status.

If both conditions apply, check the box in Line 13 and answer sections 13(a) and 13(b) following the instructions below after completing Part IV-A (statement of revenue and expenses) of the exemption application.

What About Line 10, Box (j) Groups? If condition 2 applies to you [you have completed one tax year of at least eight months and you are requesting a definitive ruling, but you checked Line 10, box (j)], does Line 13 apply to you? This is a good question, not covered by the current 1023 instructions. Remember: Line 10, box (j) groups have asked the IRS to decide whether they are a Line 10 box (h) or box (i) public charity. If the IRS decides that the group is a box (h) public charity, it may request that Line 13 be answered before the 501(c)(3) tax exemption is approved. So a suggestion: If condition 2 above applies to you and you checked Line 10, box (j), try to answer this question. If this seems too much trouble just now, fine—the IRS will ask for this information later if it is determined that this question does apply to your group.

Line 13(a): Enter 2% of the amount shown in Part IV-A, Line 8, column (e)—this is 2% of your organization's total support received over the tax years shown in Part IV.

Line 13(b): If any individual or organization—other than a government unit or another 501(c)(3) public charity described in Line 10, boxes (h) or (i)—has contributed more than the amount shown in Line 13(a) during the tax years covered in Part IV-A of your application, supply the name(s) of the contributor(s) and the amount(s) contributed on an attachment page.

Why the IRS Wants This Information: For Line 10(h) public charities, amounts that exceed 2% of the group's total support generally are not counted as qualified public support (see Chapter 4, Section F2 and IRS Publication 557, "Support from the General Public").

Line 14: This line should be filled out only if both the following conditions apply:

1. Your group checked Line 10, box (i); and

2. You checked the first and second Line 11 boxes indicating that your organization has completed a tax year consisting of at least eight months and wishes to obtain a definitive ruling as to its public charity status;

If both conditions apply to you, check the box in Line 14 and answer sections 14(a) and 14(b) following the instructions below after completing Part IV-A (statement of revenue and expenses) of the exemption application. Again, if condition 2 above applies to you, but you checked Line 10 box (j), we suggest you act as though this line applies to your organization. By doing this, you'll avoid a delay later if the IRS concludes you are a Line 10, box (i) public charity and must answer this question.

Why the IRS Wants This Information: Both questions here are intended to get you to disclose sources of support that are not considered qualified public support for groups in this public charity category: contributions from disqualified persons or gross receipts from other individuals that exceed $5,000 in any tax year.

Line 14(a): For a definition of disqualified persons, see the earlier sidebar above titled "Who Are Disqualified Persons?" If a disqualified person provided gifts, grants or contributions; membership fees; or payments for admissions or other exempt-purpose services or products (these are the categories listed in Lines 1, 2 and 9 of Part IV-A) during any tax year shown in Part IV-A, provide the names of the disqualified persons and amounts contributed or paid on an attachment page.

Line 14(b): If any person (other than a disqualified person), has paid more than $5,000 to your organization for admissions or other exempt-purpose services or products (these payments are reported in Part IV-A, Line 9) during any tax year shown in Part IV-A, provide the information requested on an attachment page. Payments by government agencies and other public charities described in Line 10, boxes (a)-(c), (d) and (g) must also be disclosed here.

A Reminder: Coming to terms with these (and other Part III) questions can be a trying experience. So relax and take your time. If you get stuck on these technical questions, seek out a nonprofit legal or tax person to help you get through this material, or come back to this material in a day or two when you're not feeling so overwhelmed.

Line 15: All groups seeking 501(c)(3) public charity status should answer "Yes" or "No" to each question listed here. If you answer "Yes" to any question, fill out the schedule indicated. The following information is furnished to help you determine whether or not you need to fill out a particular schedule and, if you do, to help you do it. For the most part, these schedules are required to ensure that particular types of organizations are "charitable" in nature, meet special 501(c)(3) exemption requirements applicable to their activities, or meet special requirements associated with the Part III, Line 10 public charity classification they are seeking. For further help in following this material, see the 1023 instructions to Line 15 and any specific instructions included on the schedules.

Churches: If you if you checked Line 10, box (a) to seek automatic public charity status as a church or an association of churches, check this "Yes" box and complete Schedule A. We've already discussed requirements for churches in Chapter 3, Section C2. Questions 1 through 15 seek to determine if your organization possesses conventional, institutional church attributes. Questions 16 through 19 relate to whether your organization unduly benefits, or was created to serve the personal needs of, your pastor or the pastor's family and relatives. You can use the information completed for Line 11(e) of your California tax exemption application (see Chapter 7) in your response here

Schools: Check the "Yes" box and fill in Schedule B if you checked Line 10, box (b) to seek automatic public charity classification as a formal private school. Make sure to check "No" to Line 2 on Schedule B—only state schools answer "Yes" to this question. A school is defined as an educational organization that has the primary function of presenting formal instruction, normally maintains a regular faculty and curriculum, normally has a regularly enrolled body of students and has a place where its educational activities are carried on (e.g., private primary or secondary schools, colleges, etc.). Your responses to this schedule should show that your operations are nondiscriminatory and in accordance with a statement to this effect included in your Bylaws that has been published in the community that you serve (you must attach this bylaw resolution to Schedule B). For information on drafting and publishing this statement of nondiscrimination, see IRS Publication 557, "Private Schools."

Hospitals and Medical Research Organizations: If your activities will consist of operating a hospital or medical research organization [and you checked Line 10, box (c)], check the "Yes" box and complete Schedule C. Make sure to check the appropriate boxes at the top of the schedule and to fill out the appropriate section of the form. Generally this schedule seeks to determine two things: (1) whether the hospital is charitable in nature and qualifies for 501(c)(3) tax-exempt status (see IRS Publication 557, "Hospitals"); and (2) whether the hospital or medical research organization qualifies for automatic public charity status (see the Schedule C instructions and IRS Publication 557, "Hospitals and Medical Research Organizations.")

If you are submitting your 1023 on behalf of a cooperative hospital service organization under IRC Section 501(e)—you checked the box in Part I, Line 7a—do not complete Schedule C. Your tax advisor can help you obtain an exemption for this special type of organization.

A 501(c)(3) charitable hospital normally has many of the following characteristics:

- doctors as part of its courtesy staff who are selected from the community at large;

- a community-oriented board of directors;

- emergency room facilities open on a community-access basis;

- admission of at least some patients without charge (on a charity basis);

- nondiscrimination with respect to all admissions and particularly Medicare or Medicaid patients;

- a medical training and research program that benefits the community.

The IRS frowns upon nonprofit hospitals that rent office space to individual physicians to allow them to engage in their individual practices, unrelated to the community service programs of the hospital, particularly if such physicians are prior tenants and present members of the board of the nonprofit hospital whose rent is below fair market value. Question 6 of Schedule C addresses this issue.

Supporting Organizations: If you have checked Line 10, box (e), complete Schedule D. This is a complicated schedule and a number of special tests must be met. Your nonprofit legal or tax advisor can help you qualify this special type of 501(c)(3) public charity classification.

Private Operating Foundations: See our instructions to Part III, Line 9 and complete Schedule E if you are applying for a tax exemption for a private foundation that qualifies as a "private operating foundation." Again, we expect your organization to qualify as a 501(c)(3) public charity, not as this special type of 501(c)(3) private foundation.

Homes for the Aged or Handicapped: If you are forming a 501(c)(3) charitable organization that is a home for the aged or handicapped, check "Yes" and fill in Schedule F. This schedule attempts to determine whether or not the home is charitable in nature, looking to see if the facilities are available to members of the public or the particular community at reasonable rates, whether provision is made for indigent residents, whether health care is adequate, and whether facilities are adequate to house a sufficient number of residents. For further information on IRS Guidelines, see Chapter 3, Section C1, "Assistance to the Aged," and IRS Publication 557, "Home for the Aged."

Child Care Organizations: If you are forming a child care organization—you have checked the box under Part I, Line 7c—check "Yes" and complete Schedule G. This schedule is used by the IRS to see if you qualify as a 501(c)(3) educational organization providing child care under IRC Section 501(k). See our instructions to Part 1, Line 7 above for further information. If your child care center also may qualify under 501(c)(3) as a private school, complete Schedule B—see our instructions for schools above.

Scholarship Benefits Organizations: Whether you are a formal "school" or not, if you provide or administer scholarship benefits, student aid, etc., check "Yes" to this question and fill out Schedule H. Of course, it's unlikely that you will be able to administer any private or public student aid funds unless you have set up a school with institutional attributes. The basic intent of Schedule H is to ensure that you administer or provide financial aid on a nondiscriminatory basis to recipients. For further information on IRS guidelines, see IRS Publication 557, "Charitable Organization Supporting Education" and "Organization Providing Loans."

Lines 1(b)-(c) allow your 501(c)(3) organization to apply for approval of your grant procedures in the event that your organization is classified as a private foundation (in the event that your request for public charity classification under Part III, line 10 is denied). If you wish to plan for this contingency, consult your tax advisor to help you select the appropriate IRC section on Line 1(c).

Successors to Profit-Making Organizations: If you are incorporating a pre-existing profit organization (for instance one that has been doing business and filed tax returns for prior tax years) check the "Yes" box and fill in Schedule I. If you have incorporated an unincorporated association or similar nonprofit organization in which no person was allowed a propriety (monetary or property) interest, this question does not apply to you.

The IRS intent behind Schedule I is to see if the activities, principals or policies of the pre-existing group and the newly-formed nonprofit corporation are the same or different. The IRS wants to know whether the former profit-making enterprise that served the needs of a few individuals is now truly directed by, and serving the interests of, the community or general public. Yes, you may engage

in the same activities as those of the pre-existing organization and still obtain your tax exemption (if the activities qualify for tax-exempt status), but the more differences, the better. You should not, of course, still be serving the interests of, or providing special benefits to, the major figures of the former for-profit business.

You'll notice that question 4(a) on the schedule asks that you attach a copy of an agreement of sale or other contract relating to the transfer of the assets of the predecessor organization to the corporation. We provide instructions for preparing an Offer for the transfer of assets to the nonprofit corporation in Chapter 10, Step 13. You may, at this time, prepare this Offer and attach it to your application or, in the alternative, state that no agreement has been formalized, stating, if applicable, the general nature of the terms of the agreement you will prepare later for the sale of the assets of the predecessor organization to the nonprofit corporation.

Question 4(b) of this schedule requests that you have an independent qualified expert attach an appraisal of the facilities or property interest sold, showing the fair market value at the time of sale. Have an accountant prepare this statement. At the same time, seek the accountant's advice with respect to the preparation of the Offer of Sale, if appropriate.

If your nonprofit corporation will lease property or equipment used by the predecessor organization, include an explanation and copies of any leases as required by question 5. The IRS will scrutinize a lease to ensure that it does not provide for excessive rent payments to the principals of the former business. It's usually best, if possible, simply to assign such leases to the nonprofit corporation without payment and have the corporation deal with the landlord directly (or have the corporation renegotiate the lease with the landlord), rather than have the former business owners retain the lease and require rent payments from the nonprofit corporation. See Chapter 7, instructions to Item 7(i) for a sample assignment of lease form and further information.

Part IV. Financial Data

All groups should complete the financial data sheets (Statement of Revenue and Expenses and the Balance Sheet) contained in Sections A and B in this part. [Financial data shown on the income statements, balance sheets and proposed budgets submitted under Items 7(c) and 7(d) of the California tax exemption application also may be used here in filling in the financial statements included in this part of the federal form.]

Statement of Revenue and Expenses

The number of columns you use in Section A depends on how long your group has been in existence. Use column (a) to show revenues and expenses for the current tax year. The ending date for this period must be within 60 days of the mailing date of the application.

If your group has been in existence in prior tax years, use the remaining (b)-(d) columns to show revenues and expenditures for the corporation's previous tax years. In other words, go back three tax years if your corporation has been in existence that long.

If your group has not been in existence for any prior tax year, use column (b) and (c) to show proposed revenues and expenditures for your next

two years (indicate the future year each column applies to in the blank at the top of each column).

Remember, your corporation's first tax year begins on the date your Articles of Incorporation were filed with the secretary of state.

New Corporations: If you are a new group applying for your tax exemption during the corporation's first tax year, the beginning date of the period shown at the top of column (a) is the date when your Articles were filed. The ending date for this period must be within 60 days of the date you expect to mail your application to the IRS. Use columns (b) and (c) to show projected figures for your next two tax years. Many new groups will repeat much of the information from their first tax year for the next two proposed tax years unless they anticipate a major change in operations or sources of support.

The IRS will use this financial data for a few purposes:

- to make sure your group's receipts and expenses correspond to the exempt purpose activities and operational information you've supplied in Part II of the application;

- to make sure you do not plan to engage substantially in unrelated business activities;

- to make sure you meet the appropriate public charity support test if you checked Part III, Line 10, box (h), (i), or (j).

How to Fill in the Items: Read the 1023 instructions describing the various items included on the Section A statement. Don't expect to fill in all the items. The IRS knows you've just commenced operations and expects to see a few blank lines. In fact, the bulk of the revenues and expenses shown by many new groups for their first tax year and the two proposed tax years do not neatly fit the categories shown in section A. Rather, this information is often attached as schedules in response to revenue item 7 (other income) and expense item 22 (other expenses). If you do attach these schedules of other income and expenses, make sure to break down the amounts as much as possible—the IRS does not like to see large lump-sum amounts.

Balance Sheet

Prepare the balance sheet to show assets and liabilities of your corporation as of the last date of the tax year period covered by column (a) of your statement of revenues and expenses in Part IV-A.

Example: You have organized a new nonprofit corporation, formed on April 1. You are preparing your 1023 application in November. The current tax year period covered by column (a) of your Statement of Revenue and Expenses is April 1, 19_ to October 31, 19_. Your balance sheet ending date will be October 31, 19_. This date should appear in the blank at the top-right of the balance sheet page.

Its not uncommon for a small starting nonprofit without liabilities and accounts receivable simply to show a little cash as its only reportable balance sheet item. The other most common items reported are Line 8 depreciable assets—equipment owned by the corporation and used to conduct its exempt activities.

If you experience any difficulty in preparing the financial information under this part, get the help of a tax or legal advisor.

Form 872-C

If you request an advance ruling of your public charity status by checking the first and third—or just the fourth—box of Part III, Line 11, you must complete and file *two* copies of Form 872-C with your 1023 application The 1023 package from the IRS, contains three copies of this form.

By completing and filing this form, you allow the IRS one year longer than normal to assess the excise taxes on investment income if your group is not granted public charity status at the end of its advance ruling period. By signing this form you're not signing your life away. You are letting the IRS collect one excise tax from you for a limited, but

longer than usual, period of time, only if you are determined not to be a public charity at the end of the extended advance ruling period and only if you are then liable for this particular excise tax because of your operations during the extended advance ruling period. The IRS can assess this tax for any of the five years in the advance ruling period any time up to 8 years, 4 months and 15 days after the end of the first tax year in the advance ruling period.

If this form applies to you, complete it by typing the name of the corporation and the address of its principal office in the items at the top of the form. Show the ending date of your first tax year in the last paragraph (the month when your accounting period and tax year ends is given in Part I, Line 4 of Form 1023). Finally, fill in the bottom portion of the form. Type in the name of the corporation and the name of one of your directors, indicating this person's title as Director. Have the director sign and date the form. This person should sign your exemption application and User Fee form (Form 8718) as well. Do not fill in the items under "For IRS use only" at the bottom of the form.

Sign Your Federal Exemption Application

The final step in preparing your federal exemption application is to have a director sign and date the application at the bottom of the first page. Show the person's title as director in the blank provided.

D. Mail Your Tax Exemption Application to the IRS

Now, gather up your application papers and do the following:

√ Organize your federal tax exemption materials. These will include your original Form 1023 application papers as well as any necessary attachments (copies of your Articles and Bylaws, etc.). All groups should submit pages 1 through 9 of the form. Also submit any schedules (A-I) you may have prepared under Part III, Line 15 of the application. Don't include blank schedules that do not apply to your organization. Also include two completed Form 872-C Consent forms if you have requested an advance public charity ruling period. Make sure to include a completed 8718 User Fee form.

√ Make sure you have dated and signed your 1023 application, 8718 User Fee form and, if applicable, the two completed copies of the 872-C Consent form.

√ Make out a check payable to the IRS in the amount of the user fee.

√ Make one photocopy of all pages and attachments to your application and file them in your corporate records book.

√ Staple the pages of your completed original 1023 application together. Remember to staple your check to the space provided at the bottom of the completed User Fee form and staple this form to the front of your exemption application.

√ Mail your exemption application papers to the IRS District office for your area shown on the 8718 User Fee form. These addresses are the most current and supersede the addresses shown in the 1023 package. If you're not sure which address applies to you, call your local IRS office.

Your next step is to wait. Although the IRS turnaround time is often two months, you may have to wait three to six months before receiving a response to your exemption application.

File Your Annual Information Returns

Make sure to file annual federal and state information returns for your organization while your federal tax exemption application is pending (see Chapter 11). Indicate on your annual returns that your federal 1023 application is pending approval by the IRS.

E. What to Expect from the IRS

The IRS will respond to your application in one of the following ways:

- grant your federal tax exemption;
- request further information; or
- issue a proposed adverse determination—this is a denial of tax exemption that becomes effective 30 days from the date of issuance.

If the IRS asks for more information and you feel the issues are too complex or are not sure what the IRS is getting at, you may wish to consult a nonprofit attorney or tax advisor. If you receive a proposed denial and you wish to appeal, see a lawyer *immediately*. For further information on appeal procedures, see the general instructions to the 1023 package and IRS Publication 892, *Exempt Organization Appeal Procedures for Unagreed Issues*—this publication should be mailed to you with the denial letter.

The Federal Determination Letter

When you receive a favorable determination letter from the IRS indicating that you are exempt from federal corporate income taxes, read it carefully. It contains important information regarding the basis for your exemption and the requirements for maintaining it.

Briefly, the information in the determination letter will state that you are tax exempt under Section 501(c)(3) of the Code and will indicate under what section of the Internal Revenue Code you qualify as a 501(c)(3) public charity. Check to make sure that the section listed by the IRS corresponds to the kind of public charity status you have sought for your nonprofit corporation. You will find the various public charity code sections listed in Part III,

Line 10 of your copy of the 1023 form. Remember: Some groups will have checked Part III, Line 10(j) to let the IRS determine the proper public charity category support test for the organization.

The determination letter will indicate if you are required to file a federal annual information return, IRS Form 990. Most 501(c)(3) groups must file this form (see Chapter 11). Unless you filed your application late and were not entitled to an extension, your tax exemption and public charity status should be effective retroactively to the date when your Articles were filed with the secretary of state.

The determination letter also should state that you are not liable for excise taxes under Chapter 42 of the Internal Revenue Code. These are the taxes applicable to private foundations. With the exceptions noted below for groups that have requested an advance public charity ruling, these excise taxes do not apply to you. The letter also refers to other excise taxes for which you may be liable. These are the regular excise taxes applicable to all businesses that engage in certain activities, such as the sale of liquor, the manufacturing of certain products, etc. For further information, see IRS Publication 510, *Excise Taxes*.

Your letter also will provide information on the deductibility of charitable contributions made to your organization and will provide technical IRC section references as to the deductibility of such donations. It also should indicate (for most groups) that you are exempt from Federal Unemployment (FUTA) taxes and that you are subject to filing nonprofit unrelated business income tax returns (Form 990-T).

Remember: 501(c)(3)s and their employees are subject to Social Security (FICA) taxes—see Chapter 11, Section C1.

If you have requested an advance ruling period for determining your public charity status, the letter will indicate that a final determination of your status will be made 90 days after the end of your advance ruling period. Check to make sure that the IRS has the correct ending date of your annual accounting period. At the end of this period, the IRS will review your past annual information returns and determine whether you have, in fact, met the public charity support requirements during the advance ruling period. Although the determination letter indicates that you must submit information to the IRS, this is not normally necessary. You need submit additional information only if you want to, or are asked to do so later, to help the IRS determine that you have qualified as a public charity during the advance ruling period.

The determination letter also may refer to IRC Sections 507(d) and 4940—these sections will apply to you if you are found to be a private foundation, not a public charity, at the end of your advance ruling period. We have already mentioned the Section 4940 tax on investment income that may apply to you in such a case. Section 570(d) refers to an extra tax imposed on private foundations if they repeatedly engage in activities that give rise to the private foundation excise taxes discussed in Chapter 4.

If the IRS determines that you are not a public charity, but rather a private foundation, both your current and previous corporate activities will be scrutinized and may be subject to private foundation excise taxes. Don't be alarmed by this. These taxes don't normally apply to newly-formed nonprofits. Again, your organization should be able to meet the support requirements of its public charity category during the advance ruling period.

Congratulations! You've just finished the most complicated, and indeed most crucial, part of your nonprofit incorporation process. The remaining formal incorporation steps are explained in the next chapter.

Chapter 10

FINAL STEPS IN ORGANIZING YOUR NONPROFIT CORPORATION

MOST OF THE HARD WORK is over, but there are still a few important details to attend to. Don't be overwhelmed by the number of steps which follow—many will not apply to your particular nonprofit corporation and others are very simple.

How to Follow the Steps: If a step is optional or only applies to certain groups, a parenthetical notation is included in the heading for the step. For example, many steps apply only to groups which have incorporated an existing organization—in this case, the headings indicate "(Existing Organizations)." Similarly, for steps which only apply to existing corporations *and* which are optional even for these groups, the headings show "(Existing Organizations—Optional)."

Again, we recommend you use the Incorporation Checklist included in the Appendix to chart your way through these steps. First mark each step which applies to you by checking the appropriate boxes in the "My Group" column. Then check off the box in the "Done" column for each step you complete.

Step 11. Mail IRS Letter to Franchise Tax Board

Usually, your state determination of exemption letter will indicate that your state tax exemption is contingent upon your obtaining a federal tax exemption and that you must file a copy of the federal determination letter with the Franchise Tax Board. If this is the case, mail a copy of your federal determination letter to the Franchise Tax Board address shown on your state determination of exemption letter. Attach a brief cover letter indicating that you are submitting the copy per the instructions on your state exemption letter and show the date of the federal determination letter and the name of your corporation. Also show your California corporate number in the heading of your letter. This is the 6-digit number stamped at the top of the first page of each of the certified copies of your Articles.

Step 12. Set Up a Corporate Records Book

A. Corporate Records Book

You will need a corporate records book to keep all your papers in an orderly fashion. These documents include Articles of Incorporation, Bylaws, Minutes of your first board meeting and ongoing director and shareholder meetings, tax exemption applications and determination letters, membership certificates, etc. You should keep your corporate records book at the principal office of your corporation at all times.

To set up a corporate records book, you can simply place all your incorporation documents in a three-ring binder. If you prefer, however, you can order a custom designed corporate records book as part of one of the Nolo corporate kits described below.

B. Nolo Corporate Kits

If you wish to order a Nolo nonprofit corporate kit, you can do so by completing the order form contained at the back of this book. Nolo nonprofit corporate kits include:

- a corporate records book with minute paper and index dividers for Articles of Incorporation, Bylaws, Minutes and Corporate Certificates;

- a metal corporate seal designed to emboss your corporate name and year of incorporation on important corporate documents;

- IRS nonprofit tax forms: IRS Package 1023—the 501(c)(3) tax exemption application—plus IRS Forms 8718 and SS-4;

- 20 Director Certificates are included with each kit acknowledging the services of members of the board of directors. Additionally, you may order 20 Sponsor Certificates which recognize the contributions made by these individuals to your nonprofit corporation's program and purposes;

- an option to order a membership materials is also included: a Membership Index and Roll Sheets to keep a consolidated record of the names and addresses of your corporation's members plus 40 printed Membership Certificates.

Here are brief descriptions of each kit:[1]

The Ex Libris®

features a higher quality brown vinyl binder with an integrated slipcase with your corporate name embossed on the spine.

The Centennial®

features a handcrafted, simulated red and black leather binder with your corporate name embossed in gold on the spine. If you are willing to pay for a fancier binder, this kit is definitely worth it.

C. Corporate Seals

A corporation is not legally required to have or use a corporate seal, but many find it handy to do so. A corporate seal is a formal way of indicating that a given document is the duly authorized act of the corporation. It is not normally used on everyday business papers (invoices, purchase orders, etc.) but is commonly employed for more formal documents such as leases, membership certificates, deeds of trust, certifications of board resolutions, and the like. As indicated above, a good quality, reasonably-priced metal pocket seal is available as part of the Nolo corporate kits described above. Embossed and stamped seals are also available separately through legal stationers (for approximately $40). Most seals are circular in form and contain the name of the corporation, the state, and year of incorporation.

---

[1]"Ex Libris" and "Centennial" are registered trademarks of Julius Blumberg, Inc.

D. Corporate Certificates

Each Nolo corporate kit includes 20 Director Certificates to distribute to your board members. You may also wish to order 20 Sponsor Certificates. These contain language recognizing the contributions of benefactors, patrons, volunteers and friends of your nonprofit. We also include an option on the order form at the back of the book for you to order membership materials including 40 printed Membership Certificates, a Membership Roll and Index. If you have set up a formal membership corporation by including the tear-out membership provisions in your Bylaws, you may wish to order these membership materials.

Note: Unlike stock certificates in profit corporations, membership certificates in nonprofit 501(c)(3) corporations do not represent an ownership interest in the assets of the corporation and serve only as a formal reminder of membership status.

Step 13. Prepare Offer to Transfer Assets (Existing Organizations—Optional)

If your nonprofit corporation does not involve the incorporation of a pre-existing business or activity, you should skip this step. If you have incorporated a pre-exiting *profit business*, you may wish to prepare an offer to transfer the assets and liabilities of the predecessor organization to your nonprofit corporation after the corporation has obtained its federal tax exemption. (You may prepare this offer, as we've indicated in Chapter 9, when preparing Schedule I included with the federal tax exemption application—in this case refer to special instruction 8 below.)

Note: Some pre-existing nonprofit groups may also wish to prepare this form—see "Note for Existing Nonprofit Groups" below.

The reason for preparing an offer is to formalize the transfer of assets and liabilities of the prior business, providing documentation of the transfer. It is also a valuable device to protect the interests of the people associated with the pre-existing profit organization who are transferring its assets and liabilities to the nonprofit corporation. Of course, where the people connected with the pre-existing business and the newly-formed nonprofit corporation are the same, or where the assets are donated without payment, protection becomes less important, but we recommend that you still prepare this offer to document the transaction. If no assets or liabilities are to be transferred from a pre-existing profit business to the nonprofit corporation, this transfer form isn't appropriate and you probably should not characterize your incorporation as one involving a pre-existing profit business. Why? Because incorporating a pre-existing business or activity, by definition, almost always involves such an exchange of assets and liabilities.

Note for Existing Nonprofit Groups: If you are simply incorporating a pre-existing nonprofit association or other less formal type of nonprofit group, preparing this form may also make sense to document the details of your incorporation. Documentation of this type (who is transferring or contributing what to the new nonprofit) can avoid disputes or misunderstandings later on. In this case, you will need to modify the form to show that it is being prepared by the trustees, officers, members, organizers, etc. of the pre-existing nonprofit organization or group.

A few additional points regarding the preparation of your offer (although these points apply primarily to the incorporation of a regular profit-making business, some apply to the incorporation of a pre-existing nonprofit organization as well):

- This is a preliminary agreement which will later be accepted by the board of directors at the first meeting of the board and finally formalized by a Bill of Sale after the first meeting.

- You may wish to consult an accountant regarding what assets are to be transferred to, and liabilities assumed by, the corporation. You will want to consider that the pre-existing business will wish to retain sufficient assets to pay liabilities not assumed by the corporation; real property might be more properly retained by the prior business owners and leased under fair terms to the corporation; payment by the prior business owners of liabilities not assumed by the corporation allows them a current, and sometimes necessary, tax deduction for the prior business; and the transfer should be made on the date (the "closing date" referred to below) most advantageous for the prior owners of the profit business.

- The new nonprofit corporation is not normally liable for the debts or liabilities of the prior business unless it assumes them. If the debts aren't assumed by the nonprofit corporation, the prior business assets it acquires will not be subject to these debts or liabilities unless the transaction was fraudulent (e.g., with intent to frustrate and deceive the prior business creditors), or not in compliance with the Bulk Sales Law (this Act normally doesn't apply to nonprofit incorporations—see Step 16, below).

- The former business owners remain personally liable for debts or liabilities of the prior business (even if they are assumed by the corporation) which were incurred prior to the transfer of assets to the corporation. They may also be held personally liable for debts incurred after the transfer, if credit is extended to the corporation by a creditor who believes and relies on the fact that she is still dealing with the prior profit business and hasn't been notified of the incorporation (see Step 20, below, for notification procedures).

To prepare an offer, retype the sample offer below, filling in the blanks by referring to the instructions in the sample form and the special instructions which follow the sample form.

√ The parenthetical blanks, i.e., "(_____)," indicate information which you must complete on the sample form.

√ Optional information is enclosed in brackets, i.e.,"[**optional information**]"

√ Each circled number (e.g., ①) refers to a special instruction which provides specific information to help you complete an item. The special instructions immediately follow the sample form.

Sample Offer

TO: __(name of corporation)__ , a California nonprofit __(public benefit [or] religious)__ corporation.

1. The undersigned is [are] the sole proprietor [partners] known as __"(name of prior business)"__ , located at __(street address)__ , __(city)__ , __(county)__ , California.

2. A true and correct statement of the assets and liabilities of this business as of the close of business on __(date of statement)__ , __, is attached to this offer.①

3. On the terms and conditions herein set forth, I [we] offer to sell and transfer to you at the close of business on __(closing date)__ , 19__,② subject to such changes as may occur therein in the ordinary course of business between the date of this offer and the close of business on __(closing date)__ , 19__ :②

   (a) All stock in trade, merchandise, fixtures, equipment and other tangible assets of the business as shown on the financial statement attached to this offer [except ... __(indicate here any exceptions, e.g., real property to be leased to the corporation, retained cash, etc.)__ ;]

   (b) The trade, business, name, goodwill and other intangible assets of the business [free and clear of all debts and liabilities of the business as shown on the financial statement attached to this offer, and all such additional liabilities as may be incurred by me (us) between the date of the financial statement and the close of business on the __(closing date)__ , 19__].③

4. As consideration for the sale and transfer, you agree:

   [(a) To assume and pay all debts and liabilities of the business as shown on the financial statement attached to this offer, and all such additional liabilities as may be reasonably incurred by me (us) between the date of the financial statement and the close of business on __(closing date)__ , 19__, except ... (indicate any unassumed debts or liabilities).]④

   (b) To pay an amount of $_ [which represents the fair market value of the business as transferred to the above Corporation per the terms prescribed above], to be paid as follows: __(state terms of payment)__ .⑤

[or]

(b) To execute a note in the amount of $____, [which amount represents the fair market value of the business as transferred to the above Corporation], incorporating the following provisions regarding payment under the note: __(state terms of loan)__ .⑥

5. If this offer is accepted by you and upon payment of $____, per the terms of paragraph 4(b), above [or "upon execution of a note per the terms of paragraph 4(b), above"],⑦ I [we] shall:

(a) Deliver possession of the business and assets described in paragraph 3 of this offer to you at the close of business on __(closing date)__, 19__.

(b) Execute and deliver to you such instruments of transfer and other documents as may be required to fully perform my [our] obligations hereunder or as may be required for the convenient operation of said business thereafter by you.

[NOTE: It is clearly understood that this offer is contingent upon the above nonprofit corporation obtaining tax-exempt status with the State of California under Section 23701(d) of the Revenue and Taxation Code and with the IRS under Section 501(c)(3) of the Internal Revenue Code and that failure to obtain either or both of these exemptions within __(number)__ months shall allow me (us) to rescind this offer at any time thereafter, notwithstanding any of the other provisions of this offer, contained above.]⑧

Dated:_____, 19__ ⑨
__(signature of prior business owner[s])__

[The blanks below are to be filled in later, after the first board meeting, Step 14 below].

The above Offer was accepted by the board of directors on __(date of board meeting)__, 19__, on behalf of __(name of corporation)__, a California nonprofit __(public benefit [or] religious)__ corporation.

By:_____
, President

_____
, Secretary

[When you have completed the form, you will wish to make several attachments as indicated in special instruction ⑩.]

SPECIAL INSTRUCTIONS

① Attach a statement of the assets and liabilities of the prior business. You should attach a copy of an Assets and Liabilities Statement (Balance Sheet) for the last accounting period of the prior business. For an example, see the general format of the balance sheet provided in Part V of your federal exemption application. The bookkeeper or accountant of the prior business can help you prepare this statement.

② The closing date is the date on which you plan to formally transfer the assets of the prior business to the nonprofit corporation after the first meeting of the board by executing a Bill of Sale (Step 17, below). As indicated earlier, this date should be determined with the help of your accountant so as to be as advantageous as possible to the prior business owners. If you are preparing this Offer at the same time that you prepare your federal exemption application, keep in mind the three- to six-month time lag which usually occurs before your exemption is approved. Also, in the unlikely event that the Bulk Sales law applies to you, make sure this date allows you enough time to comply with the appropriate pre-scale notice requirements.

③ If the nonprofit corporation is not to assume any debts or liabilities of the pre-existing business, include these bracketed provisions in paragraph 3(b) and omit the bracketed provisions of paragraph 4(a).

④ If the corporation is going to assume the debts and liabilities of the business, include the bracketed provisions of paragraph 4(a) and omit the bracketed provisions in paragraph 3(b) as explained above. If the corporation is to assume some, but not all, debts and liabilities, indicate any exceptions in paragraph 4(a).

⑤ Use this paragraph 4(b) if you are transferring the business for a lump sum of cash to be paid by the corporation. If the assets are to be donated, state $1.00 as the amount. Normally there must be some consideration (e.g., money) for a contract to be valid, although the law doesn't usually concern itself with the actual amount. If you are transferring the business for its "fair market value," you should indicate this dollar amount here. In most cases, you should be able to use the figure determined by the qualified expert in response to question 4(b) of Schedule I of your federal tax exemption application unless this figure has changed since the preparation of your application. If the transfer of the assets is for fair market value, include the language in brackets in this paragraph. State the terms of the cash payment at the end of this paragraph (date of payment, etc.).

⑥ Use this paragraph 4(b) instead of the preceding paragraph 4(b) if the corporation will not pay cash for the business assets immediately, but instead sign a loan note and pay the amount specified in installments at some future date. The discussion above concerning fair market value applies here as well. Specify the terms of the loan. This includes the amount and date of installment payments, the rate of interest and maturity date, whether it's an interest-only loan with the principal amount paid at some future date, whether it's a non-interest note for the principal amount only, payable on demand, etc. **Warning:** The loan terms should be no better than they would be between disinterested people. This will avoid the possibility of the IRS determining that the prior business owners (who are now directors or officers of the corporation) are receiving some monetary advantage from the corporation. Again, the more generous the terms, the less likely are your chances of having your exemption application denied or having problems with the IRS later upon an audit of your organization.

⑦ Use the unbracketed sentence of paragraph 5 if the corporation is to pay the full sum of money at the time of transfer of the business to the corporation, or use the bracketed phrase if the amount will be paid off over time per the terms of a loan note.

⑧ Type this bracketed NOTE paragraph if you are making out the Offer at the time of preparation of your federal exemption application, indicating how much time the corporation has to obtain its exemption before the prior business owner(s) can cancel the Offer.

⑨ Have the prior business owner(s) sign and date the Offer. Don't fill in the blanks at the bottom of the Offer—you should fill in these blanks after the first meeting of your board of directors (Step 14, below). If you are preparing the Offer for submission with your federal exemption application, you should indicate in response to Schedule I, question 4(a) of the application form (on a facing attachment page to the Offer), that "the Offer is contingent upon the nonprofit corporation obtaining its federal tax exemption, at which time the Offer will be submitted to the the board of directors and, upon approved by the board, will be signed by the appropriate officers of the corporation."

⑩ Attach a copy of the prepared financial statement to the Offer and, if the lump sum or loan amount for the transfer of assets is the fair market value of the business, a copy of the appraisal which you prepared in response to Schedule I, question 4(b) of your federal exemption application. You don't need to attach the appraisal statement to your Offer if you are preparing the Offer for submission with your federal application (the appraisal schedule should be submitted separately as required by Schedule I).

Note: If you are submitting this Offer with your federal exemption application, make a copy of this form and all attachments and submit these copies with your federal application. All groups should place the originals of these papers in their corporate record books.

Step 14. Prepare Minutes of First Board Meeting

Now that you've prepared your Articles and Bylaws, obtained your state exemption, filed your Articles with the Secretary of State, and obtained your federal tax exemption, your next step is to prepare minutes of your first board of directors meeting. The purpose of this meeting is to transact the initial business of the corporation (elect officers, fix the legal address of the corporation, etc.) and to authorize the newly elected officers to take actions necessary to get your nonprofit corporation going (set up bank accounts, admit members, if appropriate, etc.). Although this meeting can simply be, and often is, a "paper meeting," not requiring that directors actually sit down and talk business, we suggest that you take this opportunity to do so, and, in addition to discussing matters covered by these paper minutes, talk about other steps you'll need to take to get your nonprofit corporation off the ground.

Prepare the minutes by filling in the blanks in the tear-out form contained in the Appendix as you follow the sample form and special instructions below. **Note:** Optional resolutions have been printed on separate tear-out pages in the Appendix. If an optional resolution does not apply to you, simply leave it out of your final minutes.

Computer Users

A special computer version of this book, *How to Form a California Nonprofit Corporation With Corporate records Binder and Disk*, which contains computer disk files for all incorporation forms (as well as ongoing corporate minute forms for regular and special director and shareholder meetings), is available from Nolo Press. See the special order coupon at the back of this book (together with upgrade discount for prior purchasers of the regular book edition).

√ The parenthetical blanks, i.e., "(_____)," indicate information which you must complete on the tear-out form.

√ Each circled number (e.g., ①) refers to a special instruction which provides specific information to help you complete an item. The special

instructions immediately follow the sample form.

√ We suggest you tear out the form in the Appendix and fill in the blanks (using a typewriter with a black ribbon or printing neatly with a blank ink pen) as you follow the sample form and instructions below.

Sample Minutes of First Meeting of Board of Directors

of

_____ **(name of corporation)** _____

WAIVER OF NOTICE AND CONSENT TO HOLDING ¿
OF FIRST MEETING OF BOARD OF DIRECTORS

OF
__ **(NAME OF CORPORATION)** __

a California Nonprofit __ **(Public Benefit [or] Religious)** __ Corporation

We, the undersigned, being all the directors of __ **(name of corporation)** __, a California nonprofit __ **(public Benefit [or] religious)** __ corporation, hereby waive notice of the first meeting of the Board of Directors of the corporation and consent to the holding of said meeting at __ **(principal place of business)** __, California, on __ **(date)** __, 19__, at __ **(time)** __ M., and consent to the transaction of any and all business by the directors at the meeting, including, without limitation, the adoption of Bylaws, the election of officers and the selection of the place where the corporation's bank account will be maintained.

Dated: _____

_____, Director

_____, Director

_____, Director

_____, Director

_____, Director

MINUTES OF FIRST MEETING OF BOARD OF DIRECTORS ②
OF
(NAME OF CORPORATION)

a California Nonprofit __(Public Benefit [or] Religious)__ Corporation

The Board of Directors of __(name of corporation)__ held its first meeting on __(date)__, 19__ at __(principal office address)__, California. Written waiver of notice was signed by all of the directors.

The following directors, constituting a quorum of the full board, were present at the meeting:

__(names of directors present at meeting)__

_____

_____

_____

There were absent:

__(names of absent directors, if any)__

_____

_____

_____

On motion and by unanimous vote, __(name of director)__ was elected temporary Chairperson and then presided over the meeting. __(name of director)__ was elected temporary Secretary of the meeting.

The Chairperson announced that the meeting was held pursuant to written waiver of notice signed by each of the directors. Upon a motion duly made, seconded and unanimously carried, the waiver was made a part of the records of the meeting; it now precedes the minutes of this meeting in the Corporate Records Book.

BYLAWS ③

There was then presented to the meeting for adoption a proposed sets of Bylaws of the corporation. The Bylaws were considered and discussed and, on motion duly made and seconded, it was unanimously

RESOLVED, that the Bylaws presented to this meeting be and hereby are adopted as the Bylaws of the corporation;

RESOLVED FURTHER, that the Secretary insert a copy of the Bylaws in the Corporate Records Book and see that a copy of the Bylaws is kept at the corporation's principal office as required by law.

CALIFORNIA AND FEDERAL TAX EXEMPTIONS ④

The Chairperson announced that, upon application previously submitted to the California Franchise Tax Board, the corporation was determined to be exempt from payment of state corporate franchise taxes as a/n __(tax-exempt classification, e.g., "educational," "charitable," "religious," etc.)__ organization under Section 23701(d) of the California Revenue and Taxation Code per Franchise Tax Board determination letter dated __(date of state determination letter)__, 19__. The Chairperson also announced that, upon application previously submitted to the Internal Revenue Service, the corporation was determined to be exempt from payment of federal corporate income taxes as a/n __(tax-exempt classification, e.g., "educational," "charitable," "religious," etc.)__ organization under Section 501(c)(3) of the Internal Revenue Code per Internal Revenue Service determination letter dated __(date of federal determination letter)__, 19__ and, further, that the corporation has been classified as a public charity under Section __(IRC section or sections under which the corporation qualifies as a public charity)__ of the Internal Revenue Code.

☐ The corporation has obtained an advance ruling of its federal public charity classification. The advance ruling period ends __(ending date of five year advance ruling period)__.

The Chairperson then presented the originals of both state and federal tax exemption determination letters, and the Secretary was instructed to insert these documents in the Corporate Records Book.

ELECTION OF OFFICERS ⑤

The Chairperson then announced that the next item of business was the election of officers. Upon motion, the following persons were unanimously elected to the offices shown after their names:

_____(names of officers)_____	President
_____	Vice President
_____	Secretary
_____	Treasurer

Each officer who was present accepted his or her office. Thereafter, the President presided at the meeting as Chairperson, and the Secretary acted as Secretary.

COMPENSATION OF OFFICERS ⑥

There followed a discussion concerning the compensation to be paid by the corporation to its officers. Upon motion duly made and seconded, it was unanimously

RESOLVED, that the following annual salaries be paid to the officers of this corporation:

President $_____

Vice President $_____

Secretary $_____

Treasurer $_____

CORPORATE SEAL ⑦

The Secretary presented to the meeting for adoption a proposed form of seal of the corporation. Upon motion duly made and seconded, it was:

RESOLVED, that the form of corporate seal presented to this meeting be and hereby is adopted as the seal of this corporation, and the Secretary of the corporation is directed to place an impression thereof in the space next to this resolution.

(Impress seal here)

PRINCIPAL OFFICE ⑧

After discussion as to the exact location of the corporation's principal office for the transaction of business in the county named in the Bylaws, upon motion duly made and seconded, it was

RESOLVED, that the principal office for the transaction of business of the corporation shall be at __(street address)__ , in __(city)__ , California.

BANK ACCOUNT ⑨

Upon motion duly made and seconded, it was

RESOLVED, that the funds of this corporation shall be deposited with __(name of bank)__ .

RESOLVED FURTHER, that the Treasurer of this corporation be and hereby is authorized and directed to establish an account with said bank and to deposit the funds of this corporation therein.

RESOLVED FURTHER, that any officer, employee or agent of this corporation be and is authorized to endorse checks, drafts or other evidences of indebtedness made payable to this corporation, but only for the purpose of deposit.

RESOLVED FURTHER, that all checks, drafts and other instruments obligating this corporation to pay money shall be signed on behalf of this corporation by any __(number)__ of the following:
              __(names of directors, officers and/or staff)__

              _____

              _____

RESOLVED FURTHER, that said bank be and hereby is authorized to honor and pay all checks and drafts of this corporation signed as provided herein.

RESOLVED FURTHER, that the authority hereby conferred shall remain in force until revoked by the Board of Directors of this corporation and until written notice of such revocation shall have been received by said bank.

RESOLVED FURTHER, that the Secretary of this corporation be and hereby is authorized to certify as to the continuing authority of these resolutions, the persons authorized to sign on behalf of this corporation and the adoption of said bank's standard form of resolution, provided that said form does not vary materially from the terms of the foregoing resolutions.

....

CORPORATE CERTIFICATES (Optional) ⑩

The Secretary then presented to the meeting proposed director, sponsor, membership or other forms of corporate certificates for approval by the board. Upon motion duly made and seconded, it was

RESOLVED, that the form of certificates presented to this meeting are hereby adopted for use by this corporation and the Secretary is directed to attach a copy of each form of certificate to the minutes of this meeting.

....

ISSUANCE OF MEMBERSHIPS (Optional) ⑪

The board next took up the matter of issuance of memberships in the corporation.

Upon motion duly made and seconded, it was unanimously

RESOLVED, that upon __["making application therefor in writing" (or state other procedure as specified in the membership provisions in your Bylaws]__   __["and upon payment of an application fee" (and/or) "first annual dues in the amount(s) of $,"]__ members shall be admitted to the corporation and shall be entitled to all rights and privileges and subject to all the obligations, restrictions and limitations applicable to such membership in the corporation as set forth in the Articles of Incorporation and Bylaws of the corporation and subsequent amendments and changes thereto, and subject to any further limitations as resolved from time to time by the board of directors.

RESOLVED FURTHER, that the Secretary of the corporation shall record the name and address of each member in the membership book of the corporation and, upon the termination of any membership in accordance with the termination procedures specified in the Bylaws of the corporation, the Secretary shall record the date of termination of such membership in the membership book.

[RESOLVED FURTHER, that each person admitted to membership in the corporation shall be given a Membership Certificate, signed by the President and Secretary of the corporation, and the Secretary shall record the date of issuance of said Certificate in the corporate membership book.]

....

ACCEPTANCE OF OFFER TO TRANSFER ASSETS AND ⑫
LIABILITIES OF PREDECESSOR ORGANIZATION (Optional)

Upon motion duly made and seconded, it was unanimously

RESOLVED, that the corporation accept the written offer dated _____, 19__ to transfer the
assets and liabilities of the predecessor organization,   (name of predecessor organization) , in
accordance with the terms of said offer, a copy of which precedes the minutes of this meeting in
the Corporate Records Book.

RESOLVED FURTHER, that the appropriate officers of this corporation are authorized and
directed to take such actions and execute such documents as they deem necessary or appropriate
to effect the transfer of said business to this corporation.

....

Since there was no further business to come before the meeting, on motion duly made and
seconded, the meeting was adjourned.

Dated:_____

_____⑬
           , Secretary

Special Instructions

① This Waiver of Notice form allows you to
dispense with the formal notice requirements which
apply to special meetings (the first meeting of the
board is a special meeting). Fill in this form as
indicated, giving the time, date and place of the
meeting. Have all the directors sign the form and
type the director's name under the signature line. It
may be signed and dated before the actual meeting
of the board.

② This is the first page of your minute form. Fill
in the blanks as indicated, showing the names of
directors present at and, if applicable, absent from,
the meeting (a quorum of the board, as specified in
the Bylaws, must be shown in attendance). Name
one of the directors Chairperson, and another
Secretary of the meeting.

③ This resolution shows acceptance of the
contents of the Bylaws by your directors.

④ Fill in the blanks in this resolution, as
indicated, using information contained in your state
and federal tax exemption determination letters.
Indicate your tax-exempt classification with the

state. This is the "Form of Organization" shown at the top of your state exemption letter, e.g., educational, religious, charitable, etc., and the date of your state determination letter. Provide the same information from your federal tax determination letter. Also show the Code section or sections under which you have obtained federal public charity status status (as shown in your IRS exemption letter, e.g., "a publicly-supported organization of the type described in Section 509(a)(2)"]. If you have requested and obtained an advance ruling period for your federal public charity status, check the box preceding the next to last paragraph in this resolution and type the date your advance ruling period ends (as specified in the heading of your IRS determination letter).

⑤ Type the names of the persons you elect as officers of your corporation. Remember, directors may be officers and any one person may hold more than one officer position with the exception that the person(s) who serve(s) as the Secretary and/or Treasurer cannot also serve as the President (or Chairperson of the Board).

⑥ If you decide to provide for officers' salaries, indicate each officer's salary in the blanks in this resolution. Of course, you may decide to omit one or more officer salary here—if so, simply type a zero in the appropriate blank.

Important: Remember, a majority of the directors of California public benefit corporations may not be paid (other than as directors of the corporation). See Chapter 2E for further information on this disinterested director rule for public benefit corporations.

⑦ If you've ordered a corporate seal (see Step 12, above) impress your corporate seal in the space indicated on the tear-out form.

⑧ So far, your formal documents have indicated only the county of the principal place of business of your corporation. Here you should provide the street address and city of this office. You should not show a post office box.

⑨ It is important to keep corporate funds separate from any personal funds by depositing corporate funds into, and writing corporate checks out of, at least one corporate checking account. Indicate the bank and branch office where you will maintain corporate accounts. In the fifth paragraph, indicate how many people must co-sign corporate checks, giving the names of individuals allowed to co-sign checks on the lines below this paragraph. Normally, officers or supervisory staff of the corporation are designated. The names of the President and Treasurer are often listed among those who can sign corporate checks.

⑩ This is an optional resolution on a separate tear-out page in the Appendix. Include this page in your Minutes if you have ordered director, sponsor, membership or other certificates for your corporation and attach a sample of each certificate to your completed Minutes. Director, sponsor, and membership certificates may be ordered as part of each of the Nolo corporate kits as explained in Step 12D above.

⑪ This is an optional resolution on a separate tear-out page in the Appendix. If you have established a membership corporation, include this resolution in your minutes. State your procedure for admitting members into the corporation in the first bracketed phrase according to the membership provisions in your Bylaws. If you have provided for application fees and/or annual dues in your Bylaws, use the second bracketed phrase to indicate the amount of such fees and/or dues provided for in your Bylaws. If your membership corporation has neither qualification requirements, annual fees nor dues, you can use this paragraph without filling in the blanks or retype this paragraph to read: "RESOLVED that members shall be admitted to the corporation and shall be entitled to all rights and privileges and subject to all the obligations..." If you have ordered membership certificates, type the optional bracketed paragraph shown on the sample form above on the tear-out page in the Appendix.

⑫ This is an optional resolution on a separate tear-out page in the Appendix. If you have incorporated a pre-existing profit making business or other organization and have prepared an Offer to Transfer Assets (see Step 13, above), include this tear-out resolution in your final minutes, indicating the date of the Offer and the name of the predecessor organization.

⑬ Your Secretary should date and sign the last page to the tear-out minutes. Typing the officer's name below the signature line.

Step 15. Place Minutes and Attachments in Corporate Records Book

You are now through with the preparation of your Minutes. Place your minutes and all attachments in your corporate records book. Your attachments may include the following forms or documents:

- Waiver of Notice and Consent to Holding of the First Meeting;

- Written Offer (fill in the blanks at the end of the form and have your President and Secretary sign the offer);

- A certified copy of your Articles;

- Copy of your Bylaws, certified by the Secretary of the corporation;

- Original state and federal tax exemption determination letters;

- Membership Certificate marked as a "Sample."

Note: To certify your Bylaws, have the corporate Secretary date and sign the Certificate section at the end of all copies of your Bylaws.

Remember: You should continue to place an original or copy of all formal corporate documents in your corporate records book and keep this book at your principal office. For example, if you have prepared Membership Certificates and Stubs, make sure to place them in the Membership Certificate section of your records book.

Short Cut: The following Steps 16 through 20 apply only to groups incorporating a prior (pre-existing) organization. If you are a new organization, just now commencing operations as a nonprofit corporation, skip these steps and go on to Step 21.

Step 16. Comply with Bulk Sales Law (A Few Existing Organizations)

A few nonprofits may find that they have to comply with California's Bulk Sales Law. [1] The provisions of this law only apply to you if:

1. The business being incorporated is a restaurant or is engaged in the principal business of selling inventory from stock (such as a retail or wholesale business including a business that manufactures what it sells); and

2. You are transferring more than half the value of the inventory and equipment of an

---

[1] See Division 6 of the California Commercial Code, starting with Section 6101.

unincorporated business located in California to your new corporation; and

3. The value of the business assets being transferred is $10,000 or more.[2]

If, as is usually the case for nonprofits, all of the above conditions do not apply to your incorporation, you can ignore this step and go on to Step 17 below.

Even if you are incorporating the type of business covered by this law (a pre-existing retail or wholesale business that is incorporating to obtain nonprofit corporate status, such as a charitable thrift shop) and you meet the other two conditions listed above, you may still be eligible for an exemption from most of the provisions of this law.

The most important exemption available to incorporators covered by the Bulk Sales Law is the following:[3]

You are exempt from further compliance with the bulk sales act if your corporation:

• Assumes the debts of the unincorporated business;

• Is not insolvent after the assumption of these debts; and

• Publishes and files a notice to creditors within 30 days of the transfer of assets.

To comply with this exemption to the bulk sales law, call a local legal newspaper. The paper will send you a notice of bulk transfer form to prepare and will publish and file this form with the county recorder's and tax collector's offices for a small fee.

Note: There are various notice forms that fit specific provisions of the bulk sales law. To rely on the exemption above, prepare and have the

newspaper publish and file a Notice to Creditors under Section 6013(c)(10) of the Uniform Commercial Code. This notice will usually include a heading indicating that it is a Bulk Sale and Assumption form. In any case, it must include a clause stating, or to the effect that, "the buyer has assumed or will assume in full the debts that were incurred in the seller's business before the date of the bulk sale."

Step 17. Prepare Bill of Sale for Assets (Existing Organizations—Optional)

If you are incorporating a pre-existing business or organization, you may wish to prepare a Bill of Sale to formally transfer the assets of the organization to the nonprofit corporation according to the terms of the written offer. (The Offer was accepted by the board at the first meeting and signed by the officers on behalf of the corporation after the meeting.)

Prepare the bill of sale by typing the sample form shown below as you follow the instructions included in the sample form and the special instructions which immediately follow it.

---

[2]Note: An exemption from the provisions of the bulk sales law also applies if the value of the assets being transferred is more than $5 million.

[3]Other exemptions to full compliance with the bulk sales act law exist. Again, see Division 6 of the California Commercial Code for specifics.

Sample Bill of Sale

This is an agreement by __(names of prior business owners)__ , herein called "transferor(s)," and __(name of corporation)__ , herein called "the corporation."

1. In return for __["payment of $_____ which represents the fair market value of the business transferred" (or state other amount to be paid per the terms of the written Offer)]__ ① (or) __["execution of a promissory note in the principal amount of $_____, with the terms as contained in said note, a copy of which is attached to this agreement"]__ ② by __(name of corporation)__ , a California nonprofit corporation, I [we] hereby sell, assign and transfer to the corporation all my [our] right, title and interest in the following property:

   All the tangible assets listed on the inventory attached to this Bill of Sale, and all stock in trade, trade, goodwill, leasehold interests, trade names, and other intangible assets ["except … __(show non-transferred assets)__) of __(name of prior business)__ , located at __(street address)__ , __(city)__ , __(county)__ , California"]. ③

2. [In return for the transfer of the above property to it, the corporation hereby agrees to assume, pay and discharge all debts, duties and obligations that appear on the date of this agreement, on the books and owed on account of said business ["except … __(list any unassumed debts or liabilities)__ "]. The corporation agrees to indemnify and hold the transferor(s) of said business and their property free from any liability for any such debt, duty or obligation and from any suits, actions, or legal proceedings brought to enforce or collect any such debt, duty or obligation.] ④

3. [The transferor(s) hereby appoint(s) the corporation as his (her, their) representative to demand, receive and collect for itself, all debts and obligations now owing to said business ["except __(list any exceptions)__ "]. The transferor(s) further authorize(s) the corporation to do all things allowed by law to recover and collect such debts and obligations and to use the transferor's(s') name(s) in such manner as it considers necessary for the collection and recovery of such debts and obligations, provided, however, without cost, expense, or damage to the transferor(s).] ⑤

Dated:_____ , 19__

_____ ⑥
                    , Transferor

_____
                    , Transferor

_____ __(name of corporation)__ _____
By:

_____
                    , President

_____
                    , Secretary

Special Instructions

① Include this first bracketed phrase if your written Offer specified an amount of money to be paid upon the transfer of the business. If appropriate, indicate, as shown, that this amount represents the fair market value of the business.

② Include this second bracketed phrase (instead of the first bracketed phrase referred to above) if the business is to be transferred in return for a promissory note. A sample promissory note is provided below. You may need to modify it to conform to the terms contained in your Offer. In all cases your note should state the date and place of its execution, the due date, amount to be paid, and rate of interest, if any.

③ Attach an inventory to the Offer showing all tangible assets of the business—this can be copied

from the schedule of assets and liabilities you've attached to your written Offer. Indicate, in the blank provided, any non-transferred assets according to the terms of your Offer.

④ Include this paragraph if the corporation is to assume liabilities of the prior business, indicating any exceptions.

⑤ Include this paragraph if accounts receivable of the business are to be transferred to the corporation, indicating any exceptions.

⑥ Fill in the bottom portion of the Bill of Sale and have it signed by the prior business owners (the "transferors") and the President and Secretary of the corporation. Place the completed form, together with the attachments (inventory, promissory note), in your corporate records book. Copies should be given to the prior business owners. The business is now officially transferred.

Sample Promissory Note

For value received, the undersigned California nonprofit corporation promises to pay to __(names of prior business owners)__ the principal amount of $_____, together with interest at the rate of __% per annum with a total amount due under this note of $__(principal + interest)__, to be paid in full by __(due date)__, with payment to be made in __(number)__ equal monthly installments of $_____ each payable on the ____ day of each month, with the first installment being due on __(date)__ [or state other provisions per the terms of the written Offer regarding rate of interest, if any, due date, and manner of payment].

Executed this _____ day of _____, 19__ at _____, _____, County of _____, California.

_____(name of corporation)_____

By:

_____
, President

_____
, Secretary

Step 18. Prepare Assignments of Leases and Deeds (Existing Organizations—Optional)

If you have transferred a prior business or organization to your corporation, the prior owners may wish to prepare Assignments of Leases or deeds if they are transferring real property interests to the corporation. For an example of an Assignment of Lease form, see Chapter 6, Instructions to Item 7(D). (You won't want to include the clause making the Assignment of Lease contingent on the corporation's obtaining its federal tax exemption since you've already obtained it.)

Reality Note: Of course, assignments can be dispensed with if rental agreements or leases are simply renegotiated between the landlord and the new corporation. Even if you do prepare an assignment, the terms of the lease itself will normally require you to get the landlord's consent. It is particularly important to communicate with the landlord if the nonprofit corporation expects to obtain an exemption from local real property taxes on the leased premises from the County Tax Assessor (see Chapter 10, Step 23). Nonprofit groups in this situation will want to insert a clause in their new lease allowing them a credit against rent payments for the amount of the decrease in the landlord's property tax bill as a result of their real property tax exemption.

A real estate broker can help you obtain and prepare forms to transfer property in which the prior owners have an ownership interest.[4] If a mortgage or deed of trust is involved, you may well need the permission of the lender.

---

[4]An excellent sourcebook for California deeds is *The Deeds Book* by Mary Randolph (published by Nolo Press).

Step 19. File Final Papers for Prior Organization (Existing Organizations—Optional)

If you have incorporated a prior business or other organization, you may need to final final sales tax and other returns for the pre-existing organization. You will also want to cancel any permits or licenses issued to the prior business and/or the prior business owners. If new licenses are necessary, they should be obtained in the name of the corporation (see Chapter 11).

Step 20. Notify Creditors of Prior Organization (Existing Organizations)

If a pre-existing group has been incorporated, notify creditors and other interested parties, in writing, of the termination and dissolution of the prior organization and of its transfer to the new corporation. This is advisable as a legal precaution and as a courtesy to those who have dealt with the prior organization.

To notify past creditors, suppliers, organizations and businesses of your incorporation, send a friendly letter which shows the date of your incorporation, your corporate name and its principal office address. Retain a copy of each letter for inclusion in your corporate records book.

Note for Prior Partnerships Although not common, if the prior group was organized as a partnership, have a local legal newspaper publish a *Notice of Dissolution of Partnership* in the county where the partnership office or property was located. Then file the form with the local county clerk's office according to the instructions on the form or have the newspaper make this filing for you for an extra fee.

Step 21. File Fictitious Business Name Statement (Optional)

If your nonprofit corporation is to do engage in activities (advertise, sell goods or services, etc.) under a name other than the exact corporate name given in the Articles of Incorporation, it may wish to file and publish a Fictitious Business Name Statement. Although nonprofit corporations are exempt from California's fictitious business name statutes, your nonprofit may wish to file this statement with the county as a safeguard to let others know that you are using a fictitious name.[6]

Example: If the name stated in your Articles is "ART WORKS" and the corporation plans to continue using the name of the pre-existing organization which was incorporated, "THE ART STUDIO, " (or chooses another name different from the one set out in the Articles), you may wish to file and publish a Fictitious Business Name Statement. Here's how to do it:

---

[6]Note: The filing of a fictitious business name statement does not authorize the use of a name which is already in use by another business or organization as a trademark, service mark or trade name. To help make sure your name is truly your own, see Chapter 6, Step 1E.

1. Obtain a *Fictitious Business Name Statement* and instructions from the local County Clerk's office.

2. Prepare the Statement, following the instructions.

3. File the original Statement with the County Clerk of the county in which the principal place of business of the corporation is located (a small filing fee must be paid). Place an endorsed-filed copy of the statement in your corporate records book.

4. Mail a copy of the Statement to a legal newspaper for publication in the county in which the principal office of the corporation is located. Also request that the newspaper file an affidavit of publication with the County Clerk of that county. Include appropriate fees. The newspaper will publish the Statement once a week for four successive weeks and file the affidavit with the County Clerk.

Step 22. Apply for Nonprofit Mailing Permit (Optional)

Most 501(c)(3) tax-exempt nonprofit corporations will qualify for and wish to obtain a third-class nonprofit mailing permit from the U.S. Post Office. This permit entitles you to lower rates on mailings, an important advantage for many groups since the nonprofit rate is considerably lower than the regular third-class rate.

To obtain your permit, bring the following papers to your local or main post office branch:

• file-stamped or certified copy of your Articles;

• a copy of your Bylaws;

• a copy of your federal and state tax exemption determination letters; and

• copies of program literature, newsletters, bulletins and any other promotional materials.

The post office clerk will ask you to fill out a short application and take your papers. If your local post

time fee and an annual permit fee. The clerk will take your papers and forward them to the regional post office classification office for a determination. In about a week or so you will receive notice of the post office's determination.

Once you have your permit, you can mail letters, parcels, etc., at the reduced rate by affixing stamps to your mail; taking the mail to your post office and filling out a special mailing form; or by using the simpler methods of either stamping your mail with an imprint stamp (made by a stampmaker) or leasing a mail stamping machine that shows your imprint information. Ask the classifications clerk for further information.

Note: You may be able to obtain your nonprofit mailing permit before obtaining your federal tax exemption letter—the regional office sometimes issues a nonprofit mailing permit if the state exemption has been granted.

Step 23. Apply for Property Tax Exemption (Optional)

We've already discussed in some detail the requirements for obtaining an exemption from local (county) property taxes on personal and real property owned or leased by nonprofit groups which have obtained their income tax exemptions. So re-read this section before deciding whether or not to apply for the welfare exemption from these taxes.[6]

A few points to keep in mind:

• If you meet the tests for this exemption, most groups will want to prepare and submit the

---

[6]If the requirements for qualifying, or the procedure for obtaining, the welfare exemption are unclear, or you simply want more information, these items are covered in detail in a pamphlet (actually, a small book) put out by the State Board of Equalization for use by the local Assessor's office which anyone can obtain free. Call or write the State Board of Equalization, Assessment Standards Division, Property Tax Department, P.O. Box 1799, Sacramento CA 95808, and request a copy of the Assessor's Handbook—Welfare Exemption, publication number AH-267.

application in order to be exempt from personal property taxes.

• If you lease from an organization that, itself, is exempt under the welfare exemption, you should prepare and submit the application to be exempt from real property taxes.

• You do not have to have your federal or state tax exemption to apply for the welfare exemption. Even if you have not yet filed your Articles with the Secretary of State (but are sure that you will do so), go ahead and file if the March 15 property tax assessment deadline is approaching. Simply indicate what stage you are at in your incorporation process on the claim form (e.g., "nonprofit corporation, preparing to apply for state corporate franchise tax exemption;" "proposed nonprofit corporation to be exempt from corporate taxation under Section 23701(d) of the California Revenue and Taxation Code and Section 501(c)(3) of the Internal Revenue Code") in the appropriate blanks, submitting whatever information you can on the form and whatever attachments you can prepare, or already have prepared (filed or unfiled Articles, proposed financial statements, etc.). Also indicate that you will supply the appropriate documents (filed Articles, exemption letters, financial data, description of real and/or personal property) during the fiscal year, when available.

The reason to apply early is as follows: If you file a timely, although sketchy, claim, when you do become a tax-exempt nonprofit corporation during the year and submit the required additional information, you will be able to obtain a complete, partial or prorated refund on any applicable real or personal property taxes associated with real property you buy or rent or personal property you acquire during the following fiscal year.

The procedure for applying for the welfare exemption is as follows:

1. Call the local County Assessor's office and request three complete sets of the welfare exemption claim forms.

2. Complete the claim form per the instruction sheet and submit the copies of your certified Articles, federal and state exemption determination letters, and the financial statements requested (operating statement and balance sheet—you should be able to use the financial information submitted with your federal exemption application), as well as any other appropriate attachments (e.g., copy of lease) to the County Assessor. Fill in all of the blanks on the form. If a particular item doesn't apply, mark it as "Not Applicable." If your area has a separate City Assessor, copies of this material should also be submitted to this office. You should submit your claim and attachments before March 15 of the fiscal year (which goes from July 1 to June 30) for which you are seeking the exemption. If you submit it after this date and before March 1 of the following year, you will only be allowed a 90% exemption if your claim is approved. If you file even later than this during the fiscal year, you will be allowed an 85% exemption, except that the maximum amount in taxes you will have to pay is $250.00.

   Note: If you are seeking an exemption for real property owned by the nonprofit corporation, the grant deed for the property should be filed in the County Recorder's office before March 1 (15 days before you file your claim). If you are seeking an exemption on leased property, your lease or assignment of lease should be dated before March 1.

3. The Assessor will make a field inspection of your property to determine if the uses to which it is being put meet the requirements of the welfare exemption. A field inspection report is then prepared and forwarded, together with one copy of your claim and attachments, to the State Board of Equalization in Sacramento. The Board reviews the documents and makes a finding, sending a copy of the finding to you and one copy to the local Assessor. If you've been granted the exemption, the local assessment roll will be updated and a tax "bill" showing your exemption will be sent to you. If you are renting, the updated tax bill will go to your landlord.

Reminder for Religious Corporations: Religious corporations may be able to avail themselves of the streamlined application and renewal procedures of the religious exemption under Section 207 of the Revenue and Taxation Code—call your local County Tax Assessor's office (Exemption Division).

Step 24. File Domestic Corporation Statement

Shortly after your Articles of Incorporation are filed, you will receive a Domestic Nonprofit Corporation Statement from the Secretary of State's office. This form requests basic organizational information (which will be a matter of public record and can be obtained by anyone for a small fee) including the address of your principal office, the names and addresses of your officers and agent for service of process, etc. This form must be filled out and sent back to the Secretary of State within 90 days of the date your Articles were filed. You may wish to retain some anonymity for your officers by listing the principal office of the corporation as their business address. Generally, you can't indicate post office boxes as addresses on this form.

Every year thereafter you should receive a new statement to prepare and file if any of the original information has changed. Failure to file this statement when required can result in penalties and can, eventually, lead to suspension of corporate powers by the Secretary of State.

Step 25. Register with Attorney General (Public Benefit Corporations)

As discussed in Chapter 4, all 501(c)(3) tax-exempt groups, except religious corporations, must register and file annual reports with the California Office of Attorney General, Registry of Charitable Trusts.[8] The following special groups, however, are exempt from these registration requirements:

Schools: Educational organizations set up as formal schools with the institutional attributes (regular faculty and curriculum, enrolled body of students, established place of instruction, etc.). Notice that this definition is more restrictive than the one used for qualifying for your federal tax exemption and is basically the same as that which applies to "schools" for purposes of obtaining public charity status.

Hospitals: The Registry has a restrictive definition of "hospitals." In addition to being the kind of charitable hospital eligible for your federal tax exemption and public charity status, the hospital must be operated on a 24-hour-a-day basis and have

a round-the-clock medical staff. Day or outpatient clinics or those which don't have licensed practitioners regularly working at the clinic will not, in most cases, qualify for the exemption.

Note: If you do fall under one of the above exemptions, don't fill in the Registration Form. Instead, simply write a letter to the Registry at the address on top of the Registration Form, indicating why you feel you are exempt, and request an exemption determination letter. Religious corporations are not sent a Registration Form and do not, therefore, have to send an explanatory letter to the Registry requesting an exemption ruling—they are automatically exempt from registration and reporting.

Registration: Shortly after obtaining your state tax exemption, you'll receive a Notice to Register, two Registration Forms (CT-1), and a copy of the Uniform Supervision of Trustees for Charitable Purposes Act from the Registry's office. All California public benefit corporations exempt from taxes under Section 23701(d) of the California Revenue and Taxation Code and Section 501(c)(3) of the Internal Revenue Code must complete this registration form except the types of organizations mentioned above. Provide the information on the form, referring to the specific instructions on the back. Make two copies, keeping one for your corporate records book.

Annual Reporting: Each year public benefit corporations are required to submit an Annual Periodic Report (Form CT-2) to the Registry. This form should be mailed to you before the deadline. It requests information regarding revenues and expenditures, assets and liabilities, fund balances and fundraising activities associated with each year's activities. For information on submitting this annual report, see Chapter 11, Section B4.

---

[8]The Attorney General's *Guide for Charities* is a helpful guide for California nonprofits as well as a source of specific information on the AGs reporting and filing requirements. Call the Attorney General's office in Sacramento to order this excellent sourcebook.

Step 26. Issue Membership Certificates (Membership Corporations—Optional)

If you have set up a membership corporation and have ordered membership certificates, issue them to members after they have applied for membership in the corporation and paid any fees required by the membership provisions in your Bylaws. The corporate President and Secretary should sign each certificate before it is distributed to the member. Enter each member's name and address, together with the number of the certificate, in the membership roll in your corporate records book.

Step 27. File Articles with County Recorders (Certain Existing Unincorporated Associations)

Unincorporated associations which have just incorporated (see Chapter 6, Step 3) and which owned real property prior to incorporating should file a certified copy of their Articles of Incorporation with the County Recorder of the county or counties in which the previous unincorporated association owned property. This is done to show legal ownership by the new nonprofit corporation of the pre-existing unincorporated association's real property.

When filing these copies of your Articles, send the County Recorder two copies together with the required fee. Request that one copy, "file-stamped" by the County Recorder, be returned to you. Place this copy in the Articles section of your corporate records book.

Step 28. Register with Fair Political Practices Commission (Political Groups)

As we've already indicated in Chapter 3, Section 3D, some 501(c)(3) tax-exempt nonprofit corporations may engage, to an insubstantial degree, in lobbying efforts to influence legislation or influence the public's attitude regarding political issues. Also, some nonprofits will decide to elect to fall under the state and federal "political expenditures" test to avoid jeopardizing their tax-exempt status.

If you decide to retain a lobbyist, be employed as a lobbyist, or simply support or oppose state, county or city measures to be voted on by the public, you must comply with registration and reporting requirements for lobbying activity administered by the California Fair Political Practices Commission. Call this office in Sacramento for further information if you think these registration and reporting requirements may apply to the activities of your nonprofit corporation. (Request a copy of the *Information Manual for Lobbying Disclosure Provisions of the Political Reform Act* or read this manual at your county law library.)

Check Local Solicitation Ordinances

If you plan to solicit contributions locally (for example, as part of a door-to-door fundraising drive), make sure to comply with all local solicitation ordinances and regulations. Some counties and cities enforce local registration and reporting requirements. Other localities require the furnishing of specific statements and disclosure information to persons solicited by the nonprofit corporation. The AG's *Guide for Charities* (see footnote) lists sources of information on local solicitation regulations in effect in California.

Chapter 11

AFTER YOUR CORPORATION IS ORGANIZED

THE ORGANIZATION and initial business details of your nonprofit corporation are now complete. But before you close this book, read just a little more. You must become familiar with the formalities of corporate life. These include preparing minutes of formal corporate meetings, filing tax returns and paying employment taxes.[1] The information presented here is not meant to tell you everything you will need to know about these subjects but simply to provide the basics and indicate some of the major areas which you (or your tax advisor) will need to go over in more detail.

A. Piercing the Corporate Veil (or, If You Want to Be Treated Like a Corporation, It's Best to Act Like One)

After you've set up a corporation of any kind, you should act like one. Although filing your Articles with the Secretary of State brings the corporation into existence and makes it a legal entity, this is not enough to ensure that a court or the IRS will treat your organization as a corporation. What we are referring to here is not simply maintaining your various tax exemptions or even your nonprofit corporate status—we are talking about being treated as a valid corporation in court and for tax purposes. Remember, it's your general corporate status which allows your corporation to be treated as an entity apart from its directors, officers and employees and allows it to be taxed (or not taxed), sue or be sued, on its own. It is the corporate entity that insulates the people behind the corporation from taxes and lawsuits.

For More Information

We suggest all nonprofits obtain IRS Publication 509, *Tax Calendars*, prior to the beginning of each year. This pamphlet contains tax calendars showing the dates for corporate and employer filings during the year.

Further information on withholding, depositing, reporting and paying federal employment taxes can be found in IRS Publication 15, *Circular E, Employer's Tax Guide* and the Publication 15 Supplement, as well as IRS Publication 937, *Employment Taxes*. Further federal tax information can be found in IRS Publication 542, *Tax Information on Corporations* and Publication 334, *Tax Guide for Small Business*.

Helpful information on accounting methods and book-keeping procedures is contained in IRS Publication 538, *Accounting Period and Methods* and Publication 583, *Information for Business Taxpayers*.

These publications can be picked up at your local IRS office (or ordered by phone—call your local IRS office or try the toll-free IRS forms and publications request telephone number 1-800-TAX-FORM).

For information on withholding, contributing, paying, and reporting California employment taxes, obtain the *California Employer's Tax Guide* (Publication DE 44) and *Employer's Guide* (Publication DE 4525—for unemployment and disability tax information) from your local California Employment Tax District Office.

Small Time Operator by Kamoroff (Bell Springs Publishing—see order information at back of book): An extremely useful source of information for employer tax matters and recordkeeping details, generally. Specifically applicable to starting a non-corporate business (contains general business ledgers, worksheets, etc.), but helpful to nonprofit enterprises too.

Courts and the IRS do, on occasion, scrutinize the organization and operation of a corporation, particularly if it is directed and operated by a small number of people who wear more than one hat (fill director and officer positions, etc.). If the corporation doesn't have adequate money to start with (making it likely

---

[1] The information regarding taxes (return deadlines, tax rates, penalties, etc.) is subject to change. Make sure it's current when you attend to your taxes.

that creditors or people who have claims against the corporation won't be able to be paid); if corporate and personal funds are commingled; if the corporation doesn't keep adequate corporate records (e.g., minutes of meetings); or generally doesn't pay much attention to the theory and practice of corporate life, a court may disregard the corporate entity and hold the principals (directors, officers, etc.) personally liable for corporate debts. Also, the IRS may assess taxes and penalties personally against those connected with managing the affairs of the corporation if they conclude that the corporation is not a valid legal or tax entity. In legal jargon, this is called "piercing the corporate veil."

To avoid problems of this type, be careful to operate your corporation as a separate legal entity. This includes holding regular and special meetings of your board and membership as required by your Bylaws and as necessary to take formal corporate action. It is critical that you document formal corporate meetings with neat and thorough minutes. Also, it is wise to have enough money in your corporate account to pay foreseeable debts and liabilities which may arise in the course of carrying out your activities. Above all, keep corporate funds separate from the personal funds of the individuals who manage or work for the corporation.

B. Federal Corporate Tax Returns

1. Annual Exempt Organization Returns for Public Charities

Nonprofit corporations exempt from federal corporate income tax under Section 501(c)(3) and qualified (under an advance or definitive ruling) as public charities must file IRS Form 990, annual Return of Organization Exempt From Income Tax (together with Form 990, Schedule A), on or before the 15th day of the fifth month (within four and a half months) following the close of their accounting period (tax year). This return should be filed even if your 1023 federal application for exemption is still pending.

IRS Form 990-EZ: This is a short form annual return which can be used in place of Form 990 by smaller tax exempt public charities—those with gross receipts of less than $100,000 and total assets of less than $250,000.

Note: Your first 990 return deadline may come upon you sooner than you expect if your first tax year is a "short year"—a tax year of less than 12 months.

Example: If your accounting period as specified in your Bylaws runs from January 1 to December 31 and your Articles were filed on December 1, your first tax year consists of one month, from December 1 to December 31. In this situation, your first Form 990 would have to be filed within four and a half months of December 31 (by May 15th), only five and a half months after your Articles were filed. It is likely that your federal tax exemption application would be pending at this time.

Exemptions: The Internal Revenue Code exempts certain public charities from filing this return, including the following: certain churches, schools, mission societies, religious activity groups, state institutions, corporations organized under an Act of Congress, tax-exempt private foundations, certain trusts, religious and apostolic organizations and public charities, generally, whose gross receipts are "normally" not more than $25,000 in each taxable year.[2]

Your federal exemption determination letter should indicate whether you must file Form 990. Most public charities will be publicly supported organizations (see Chapter 4F2) or receive a major of their support from exempt-purpose revenue (see Chapter 4F3). Since these groups are not institutional

---

[2]See IRS Form 990 for the details of these exemptions.

public charities falling under one of the exemptions to filing listed above, they will have to file Form 990 unless they meet the "normally" not more than $25,000 gross receipts exemption. To rely on this exemption, fill in the top portion of the 990 form and check the box which indicates you are eligible for this exemption.

Important Note: If you are required to file a Form 990 and don't, or if the information given on the return is incomplete, you are subject to substantial penalties (see the 990 instructions). In addition, if the IRS notifies you of a delinquent return and you don't file it by the date shown on the demand letter, the person responsible for filing or overseeing the filing of corporate returns is personally subject to these penalties.

The Moral: Make sure to file your 990 form on time. If you are entitled to an exemption, file the form anyway, indicating why you are exempt from the filing requirements on the 990 form.

IRC § 501(h) Political Expenditures Test: If your nonprofit corporation has made the political expenditures election discussed in Chapter 3, Section D3 by filing the Federal Election Form 5768, indicate on Form 990, Schedule A that you have made this election and fill in the appropriate part of this schedule showing actual lobbying expenditures made during the year.

2. Annual Exempt Organization Return for Private Foundations

Although we don't expect many nonprofit 501(c)(3) tax-exempt corporations to be classified as private foundations, if this is the case, or, if you fall within the special category of a private operating foundation, you must file a Federal Annual Return of Private Foundation Exempt From Income Tax, Form 990-PF, instead of the 990 discussed above, within four and half months of the close of your tax year. This return requests specific information relevant to determining whether you are liable for

the private foundation excise taxes mentioned in Chapter 4C, as well as the usual information on receipts and expenditures, etc. This form and separate instructions for completing it should be mailed to you close to the end of your accounting period. Again, watch out for a first short year and an early deadline for filing your 990-PF.

The foundation manager(s) must publish a notice of availability of public inspection of this Annual Report form in a local county newspaper by the filing date for the 990-PF. This notice must indicate that the annual report is available for public inspection, at the principal office of the corporation, within 180 days after the publication of notice of availability. A copy of the published notice must be attached to the 990-PF.

Note: The IRS and the California Attorney General require that you submit a copy of your completed 990-PF to the California Attorney General with your annual CT-2 (Periodic Report to the Attorney General—see Section C4 of this chapter).

As with the 990, the 990-PF form carries with it substantial late filing penalties. Make sure you file it on time.

An Important Warning

The IRS and the state are notoriously efficient in assessing and collecting late filing and other penalties. So, while it's generally true that your nonprofit corporation normally does not have to worry about paying taxes, you should worry a little about filing your annual information returns (and employment tax returns and payments). Too many nonprofit corporations have had to liquidate when forced to pay late filing penalties for a few years' worth of simple informational returns that they inadvertently forgot to file.[3]

Another important aspect associated with the assessment of late filing penalties and delinquent employment taxes is that the IRS (and state) can, and often do, try to collect these often substantial amounts from individuals associated with the corporation if the corporation doesn't have sufficient cash to pay them. Remember, one of the exceptions to the concept of limited liability is liability for unpaid taxes and tax penalties. The IRS and state can go after the person (or persons) associated with the corporation who are responsible for reporting and/or paying taxes—particularly those who look most likely to be able to pay the taxes or penalties.

3. Annual Exempt Organization Unrelated Business Income Tax Return

Section 501(c)(3) federal tax-exempt corporations, with a few minor exceptions, having gross incomes of $1,000 or more for the year from an unrelated trade or business must file an Exempt Organization Business Income Tax Return (Form 990-T), within two and a half months after the close of their annual accounting period. For a definition and discussion of unrelated trades and businesses, see Chapter 3,

---

[3]Although the IRS regulations state that late filing penalties won't be assessed if you can show "reasonable cause" for the delay, don't count on this provision. The IRS can be quite unreasonable here.

Section D1 and obtain Federal Publication 598, *Tax on Business Income of Exempt Organizations*. Use booklet 598 and the separate instructions to Form 990-T in preparing this form.

The taxes imposed on any taxable unrelated business income are the same as the normal federal corporate income tax rates. Remember: Too much unrelated business income may indicate to the IRS that you are engaging in non-exempt activities to a "substantial" degree and may jeopardize your tax exemption.

C. California Corporate Tax Returns and Reports

1. Annual Exempt Organization Returns for Public Charities

Nonprofit corporations exempt from tax under 23701(d) of the California Revenue and Taxation Code [the state parallel exemption to the federal 501(c)(3) exemption] and classified by the IRS as public charities must file a California annual Exempt Organization Annual Information Return, Form 199, within four and a half months of the close of their tax year. Some groups are allowed to file Form 199-B.

The state exemptions from the filing requirements for this form are similar to the IRS exemptions from filing Form 990. **Note:** Even if you are exempt from filing state annual returns, you may have to file an annual statement indicating the name and address of your corporation, its major activities, its sources of income and the section of the Internal Revenue Code under which you are exempt (plus, in some cases, information concerning gross receipts and assets). Check the instructions to Form 199 for further information on these rules.

If you've made a political expenditures election with the state (by submitting a copy of your federal

5768 election form to the Franchise Tax Board within the year, attach Form FTB-3509, Political or Legislative Activities by Section 23701(d) Organizations, to your 199 or 199-B annual state return.

Penalties apply for failure to file Form 199 on time. A failure to file Form 199 or 199-B can result in a suspension of corporate rights, powers and privileges, or a revocation of the corporation's state tax exemption.

2. Annual Exempt Organization Return for Private Foundations

California corporations exempt under Section 23701(d) of the Revenue and Taxation Code and classified as private foundations must file the 199 form. The preparation of their 199 requires providing additional information which isn't required of public charities which must file a 199. As an alternative to filling out Part II of this form, they may (and should, to avoid extra paperwork) provide a copy of their annual report to the Attorney General if they are required to file this report (Form CT-2—see Section C4 of this chapter) or furnish a copy of IRS Form 990-PF and its associated schedules instead (see Section A2 above) .

3. Annual Exempt Organization Unrelated Business Income Tax Return and Quarterly Estimated Tax Payments

Nonprofit corporations, tax-exempt under state law, are subject to payment of a 9.3% state tax (the normal corporate tax rate) on their taxable unrelated business income. Specifically, all corporations (except those formed to carry out a state function) exempt from state corporate franchise taxes under Section 23701(d) must file an annual Exempt Organization Business Income Tax Return, Form 109, if gross income during the year from an unrelated trade or business is $1,000 or more. This

return must be filed within four and a half months of the end of the tax year. Payment of the tax, unlike payment of federal unrelated business income tax, must be estimated and paid during the year for which the tax is due, with any unpaid amount being submitted with the annual return.

The estimated tax is computed on the corporation's expected income from unrelated trade or business activities during the current year. Twenty-five percent of the estimated tax must be paid within three and a half months of the beginning of the tax year. The balance of the tax is payable in three equal installments on or before the 15th day of the sixth, ninth and twelfth months of the tax year.

The state normally doesn't send out forms and instructions for paying estimated tax to nonprofit corporations during their first year, or for later years, unless a prior annual information return indicates that the nonprofit corporation is likely to have unrelated business income. If a form is mailed, Form 100-ES will be sent—this is the form used by regular profit corporations. You should realize that the normal minimum franchise tax which profit corporations must pay with their first annual estimated tax payment does not apply to tax-exempt nonprofits. Nonprofits pay a simple 9.3% rate on their estimated taxable unrelated business income. Since you must make estimated unrelated business tax payments if this tax applies to you whether or not the Franchise Tax Board sends you the forms, make sure you pay attention to this often overlooked aspect of nonprofit corporate taxation, particularly since penalties apply to underpayment of this estimated tax and to late filing of the return referred to above.

4. Annual Periodic Report to Attorney General by Public Benefit Corporations

Subject to a few exceptions, 501(c)(3) and 23701(d) tax-exempt public benefit nonprofit corporations must file an annual report to the California Attorney

General (Form CT-2). This form should be mailed to you. It must be filed within four and one-half months after the end of your tax year. You must attach to the CT-2 your Federal 990 or 990-PF, and the schedules and attachments associated with either of these forms. Failure to file this form with the Attorney General on time can result in a disallowance of your state tax exemption and the assessment of late filing penalties.

5. Annual Corporate Report to Directors (and Members, If Any) of Public Benefit Corporations

Non-membership public benefit corporations must furnish all directors with the annual report required by Article 7, Section 6 of their Bylaws, containing financial information (including a statement of assets, liabilities, receipts and expenditures) within 120 days after the close of the fiscal year. Membership public benefit corporations must also submit this annual report within the same time period to all members who request the report. Also, public benefit corporations must include information in their annual report, or provide a separate statement which must be sent to all directors and members, disclosing the details of certain indemnification or self-dealing transactions according to the provisions of their Bylaws (see Article 7, Section 7 of the public benefit corporation Bylaws).

Most of this financial information to directors and, if applicable, to members, will already have been prepared by the corporation in complying with the state and federal annual tax return requirements discussed above and should not be too difficult to compile for purposes of this annual report. Keep in mind that most of the annual state and federal tax returns must be submitted within four and one-half months of the close of the tax year while this annual public benefit corporate report to "insiders" must be furnished to the appropriate corporate people a little

sooner (within approximately four months—120 days—after the close of the fiscal year).

D. Federal and State Corporate Employment Taxes

Employment taxes must be paid on behalf of the people who work for the nonprofit corporation. Independent contractors (e.g., consultants) who are not subject to the control of the corporation (both as to what shall be done and how the work is to be performed) are generally not considered employees.[4] Wages paid to these outsiders are not subject to the employment taxes discussed below.[5] Also, nonprofit tax-exempt corporations are often exempt from having to pay certain employment taxes for their employees (e.g., Federal Unemployment Insurance). We look at these unemployment taxes with respect to 501(c)(3) tax-exempt corporations in this section. In addition to reading this material, obtain the publications listed in the introduction to this chapter for more detailed and current information and for help in computing your withholding and employer contribution payments.

---

[4]Directors, with certain exceptions, are not considered employees if they are paid only for attending board meetings. However, if they are paid for other services or are salaried employees of the corporation, they will be considered employees whose wages are subject to the employment taxes discussed in this section—check with the IRS and your local state Employment Tax district office for further information.

[5]Be careful of trying to avoid the payment of employment taxes by classifying people as "independent contractors." The law in this area is fuzzy, and the IRS (and the California Employment Development Department which oversees state unemployment taxes) are often obstinate. For more information, see IRS Publication 937.

1. Federal Employment Taxes and Forms

a. Employee's Withholding Certificate

Each employee of the corporation must fill out and furnish the corporation with an Employee's Withholding Allowance Certificate (IRS Form W-4), on or before commencing employment. This form indicates the marital status and number of allowances claimed by the employee and is used in determining the amount of income taxes withheld from the employee's wages.

b. Income Tax Withholding

The corporation must withhold federal income tax from wages paid to employees based upon the wage level, marital status and number of allowances claimed on the employee's W-4. These, as well as other employment taxes, are withheld and reported on a calendar year basis (January 1 to December 30), regardless of the tax year of the corporation, with returns being submitted on a quarterly basis and deposits of withheld tax made in an authorized bank on a quarterly or more frequent basis or paid with the quarterly return—see IRS Publication 15.

c. Social Security Tax Withholding

Employment in a nonprofit corporation exempt under 501(c)(3) of the Internal Revenue Code is subject to Social Security (FICA) tax withholding. FICA taxes must be withheld from the employee's wages, and matching contributions must be made by the corporation. The taxes are reported quarterly and paid either with the quarterly return or deposited in an authorized bank—see subsection d below and IRS Publication 15 for specifics.

d. Quarterly Withholding Returns and Deposits

On or before the last day of the month immediately following the end of each calendar quarter the corporation must file an Employer's Quarterly Federal Tax Return, Form 941. This return consolidates a report of both withheld income taxes and Social Security taxes, and carries with it specific payment and deposit rules.

Deposits of income and Social Security taxes must be made on a quarterly, monthly, or more frequent basis. You will want to pay careful attention to withholding, depositing, paying, and reporting these taxes to avoid costly penalties—again, consult IRS Publication 15 for the details.

e. Federal Unemployment Tax

Generally, your 501(c)(3) tax-exempt nonprofit corporation is exempt from payment of Federal Unemployment (FUTA) taxes. Your federal exemption letter should indicate that you are exempt from these taxes.

f. Annual Wage and Tax Statement

Your nonprofit corporation is required to furnish two copies of the Wage and Tax Statement (IRS Form W-2) to each employee from whom income tax has been withheld or would have been withheld if the employee had claimed no more than one withholding allowance on his W-4. This form must show total wages paid and amounts deducted for income and Social Security taxes. A special six-part W-2 should be used in California to show state income tax and disability insurance contributions in addition to the required federal withholding information. W-2s must be furnished employees no later than January 21 following the close of the calendar year.

The corporation must submit each employee's previous year's W-2 form and an annual Transmittal of Income and Tax Statement (Form W-3) to the Social Security Administration on or before the last day of February following the close of the calendar year.

2. State Employment Taxes and Forms

a. Employer Registration Form

Nonprofit corporations with employees must register with the California Employment Development Department within 15 days of becoming subject to the California Unemployment Insurance Code or to California personal income tax withholding provisions. Since this happens, for most nonprofit corporations, once wages in excess of $100 in a calendar quarter are paid, you should register right away if you plan to have any employees. Do this by preparing and submitting Employer's Registration Form DE-1, available from the local Employment Tax District offices listed in the state DE-44 publication.

Note: If you plan to apply for a Sales Tax Permit (see Section F, below), your permit application can also serve as your employer registration form.

b. Personal Income Tax Withholding

The corporation must withhold California personal income taxes from employees' wages according to the tax tables in Publication DE-44. The tables take into account the marital status, claimed allowances, and wage level of the employee. These tables automatically allow for applicable exemptions and the state's standard deduction.

c. California Unemployment and Disability Insurance

Generally, nonprofit 501(c)(3) tax-exempt corporations are subject to California Unemployment and Disability Insurance tax contributions and withholding. Certain churches or religious nonprofit corporations and schools which are a part of a church or religious nonprofit corporation are not subject to unemployment and disability insurance taxes. Rates change constantly . For further information, consult the DE-4525 publication listed above. If you have any questions, call your local Employment Tax office.

Also, certain types of services performed for 501(c)(3) tax-exempt nonprofit groups are not subject to state unemployment and disability coverage unless elected. The California Employment Development Department should mail Form DE-1-NP which lists these excluded services and allows you to elect coverage for any which apply to you. California Unemployment Insurance can be paid by 501(c)(3) groups in one of two ways: 1) the regular contribution rate method, or 2) a prorated cost of benefits paid. Form DE-1-NP, referred to above, allows you to select which payment method you want to use.

Under the regular contribution rate method, unemployment insurance contributions are paid by the corporation at its "employer contribution rate" shown on the Quarterly Withholding Return (DE-3) discussed below.

Under the "prorated cost of benefits" method, the corporation pays the actual amount of unemployment benefits received by ex-employees who receive such benefits, to the extent that such benefits are attributable to "base period" wages paid by the corporation to the ex-employee. Ask the local Employment Tax office for Form DE-1378-F which contains examples of your potential liability under this method.

Disability insurance contributions are paid by the employee and withheld, reported and submitted to the state by the corporation. Again, rates change—check your DE-4525 pamphlet.

d. Withholding Returns

A corporation is required in most cases to file monthly returns with the state, reporting and paying personal income tax withholding and disability and unemployment tax contributions for each employee.

The corporation must file a quarterly return, reporting the employment taxes mentioned above for the previous quarter and pay any balance not already paid with monthly returns. For specifics, consult the DE-4525 pamphlet.[6]

e. Annual Wage and Tax Statement

The corporation should prepare a six-part combined federal/state Wage and Tax Statement, IRS Form W-2. This form indicates total annual state personal income tax and state disability insurance withholding. Copies of this form should be provided to the employee.

f. Annual Reconciliation of Income Tax Withholding Form

The corporation must prepare and file a completed Reconciliation of Income Tax Withheld, Form DE-43, with the Employment Development Department annually, before February 28 following

---

[6]Note: Section 1735 of the California Unemployment Insurance Code specifically holds the officers and other persons in charge of corporate affairs personally liable for taxes, interest, and penalties owed by the corporation.

the close of the calendar year, attaching one copy of each employee's W-2 and a totaled listing of the California personal income tax amounts withheld as shown on the attached W-2s.

E. Employee Returns—A Short Note

Corporate directors, officers, and other compensated corporate personnel must, of course, report employment compensation on their individual annual federal and state income tax returns (IRS Form 1040; state Form 540).

F. Sales Tax Forms and Exemption from Sales Tax

1. Sales Tax

Subject to a few special exceptions, every nonprofit corporation which has gross receipts from the sale of tangible personal property (e.g., merchandise sold to customers) in California must apply for a Sales Tax Seller's Permit by filing an application (Form BT-400) with the nearest office of the California Board of Equalization. Even groups exempt from collecting sales tax, as described below, must obtain a Seller's Permit. As mentioned in Section D2a above, this application may also serve as an employer registration form with the Employment Development Department.

No fee is required for applying for or obtaining a Sales Tax (Seller's) Permit. Some applicants, however, may be required to post a bond or other security for payment of future sales taxes. A separate permit is required for each place of business at which transactions relating to sales tax are customarily entered into with customers. Sales tax is added to the price of certain goods and is collected from the purchaser. Wholesalers, as well as retailers, must obtain a permit. A wholesaler, however, is not required to collect sales tax from a retailer who holds a valid Seller's Permit and who buys items for resale to customers, provided a resale certificate is completed in connection with the transaction.

Sellers must file periodic sales and use tax returns, reporting and paying sales tax collected from customers. A seller must keep complete records of all business transactions, including sales, purchases, and other expenditures and have them available for inspection by the Board of Equalization at all times.

2. Exemption from Collecting and Submitting Sales Tax

A few tax-exempt nonprofit corporations are exempt from collecting sales tax and preparing the quarterly report. To be eligible for the exemption, a nonprofit corporation must meet the following (stringent) requirements:

• The organization must be formed and operated for charitable purposes, and must qualify for the "welfare exemption" from property taxation provided by Section 214 of the California Revenue and Taxation Code. If the corporation owns the retail location, it must have obtained the welfare exemption for the real property at this location. If it leases the premises, it must have obtained the welfare exemption on the personal property (inventory, furnishings, etc.) at this location;

• The organization must be engaged in the relief of poverty and distress and the sales must be made principally as a matter of assistance to purchasers in a distressed financial condition. These conditions are fulfilled if the corporation sells its goods at reduced prices so as "to be of real assistance to purchasers." Incidental sales to persons other than low income consumers will not prevent the organization from obtaining the sales tax exemption; and

• The property sold must have been made, prepared, assembled or manufactured by the organization. This condition will be satisfied when the property is picked up at various locations and assembled at one or more locations for purposes of sale, even though nothing other than assembling needs to be done to place it in saleable condition. Property is considered "prepared" when it is made ready for sale by such processes as cleaning, repairing or reconditioning.

A nonprofit corporation seeking to obtain this exemption from sales tax collection and reporting must, as we've said, still apply for a Seller's Permit by filing Form BT-400, attaching to it a Certificate of Exemption—Charitable Organizations, Form BT-719, also available at the nearest Board of Equalization office. Applicants should also request an information sheet relating to the exemption, Form BT-719-A.[7]

G. Licenses and Permits

Many businesses, whether operating as profit or nonprofit corporations, partnerships, etc., are required to obtain state licenses and permits before commencing business. So, while you may not be subject to the usual kind of red tape applicable to strictly profit-making enterprises (e.g., contractors, real estate brokers, etc.), you should check with your local Department of Consumer Affairs office for information concerning any state licensing requirements for your activities or type of organization.[8] If

---

[7]Note: Special transactions are exempt from the collection of sales tax (purchase of art which will be loaned by certain nonprofits; purchase of art by government entities which will be displayed to the public). Certain transactions entered into by any kind of organization (profit or nonprofit) are not subject to the collection of sales tax. Examples are sales of personal property shipped out of state and certain sales incidental to the performance of services. Other special sales tax exemptions exist for special nonprofit groups (e.g., certain nonprofit cooperative nursery schools are exempt). Call a Board of Equalization office for further information.

[8]The *California License Handbook*, published by the California Department of Economic and Business Development, is a comprehensive guide to California license requirements, as well as a thorough sourcebook on California's regulatory agencies and

one of the boards does not regulate your activities, they may be able to refer you to the particular state agency which oversees your operations. Many nonprofit institutions, for example schools or hospitals, will, of course, need to comply with a number of registration and reporting requirements administered by the state and, possibly, the federal government. A local business license or permit may also be required for your activities—check with your city business license department.

Newly incorporated groups which have held licenses or permits for previous activities or operations should check to see if special corporate licensing requirements apply to their activities. In some cases a separate corporate license must be taken out in the corporate name; in others a corporate license must be obtained in the name of supervisory corporate personnel.

You should also check to see if the city and county where your principal place of business is located (and other places where you plan to conduct activities) require you to obtain a permit for soliciting funds for charitable purposes. Many cities and counties have enacted permit (or other) requirements of this type.

H. Workers' Compensation

With some exceptions, employees of a nonprofit corporation, whether officers or otherwise, are required to be covered by Workers' Compensation Insurance. Rates vary depending on the salary level and risk associated with an employee's job. Generally, if directors are only paid travel expenses for attending meetings, they may be exempt from coverage (although flat per-meeting payments will generally make them subject to coverage). This is a blurry area so check with your insurance agent or

broker (or your local State Compensation Insurance Commission) for names of carriers, rates, and extent of required coverage in all cases.

I. Private Insurance Coverage

Nonprofit corporations, like other organizations, should carry the usual kinds of commercial insurance to prevent undue loss in the event of an accident, fire, theft, etc. Although the corporate form may insulate directors, officers, etc. from personal loss, it won't prevent corporate assets from being jeopardized by such eventualities. Coverage for general liability, product liability, and fire and theft should be looked into. Liability insurance for directors and officers should also be looked into, particularly if your nonprofit corporation wants to reassure any "passive" directors which it has nominated that they will be protected from personal liability in the event of a lawsuit. **Also note:** To take advantage of California's volunteer director and officer immunity provisions, adequate director and officer liability insurance must be obtained (or be proven to be unobtainable)—see Chapter 2, Sections E and F.

---

the red tape involved in doing business in California. Call their office in Sacramento to obtain ordering information.

Chapter 12

LAWYERS AND ACCOUNTANTS

WHILE WE OBVIOUSLY BELIEVE you can take care of the bulk of the work associated with organizing and operating your nonprofit corporation, you may need to consult a lawyer or accountant on complicated or special issues. Furthermore, it often makes sense to have another person experienced in forming non-profits and preparing tax exemption applications look your papers over. Reviewing your incorporation papers with an attorney or accountant is a sensible way to insure that all of your papers are up-to-date and meet your specialized needs. The professional should have experience in nonprofit incorporations and tax exemption applications, and should be prepared to answer your specific, informed questions and review, not rewrite, the forms you have prepared.

The next two sections provide a few general suggestions on finding the right lawyer or tax advisor and, if you wish to do your own legal research, how to find the law.

A. Lawyers

Finding the right lawyer is not always easy. Obviously, the best lawyer to choose is someone you personally know and trust and who has lots of experience advising smaller nonprofits. This, of course, may be a tall order. The next best is a non-profit advisor whom a friend, another nonprofit incorporator, or someone in your nonprofit network recommends. A local nonprofit resource center, for example, may be able to steer you to one or more lawyers who maintain an active nonprofit practice. With patience and persistence (and enough phone calls), this second word-of-mouth approach almost always brings positive results.

Another approach is to locate a local nonprofit legal referral panel. Panels of this sort are typically run by a local bar association or another nonprofit organization. One in your area may be able to give you the names of lawyers who are experienced in nonprofit law and practice and who offer a discount or free consultation as part of the referral panel program. Ask about and try to avoid referral services which are operated on a strict rotating basis. In this case you'll get the name of the next lawyer on the list, not necessarily one with nonprofit experience. Also watch out for private (and highly suspect) commercial referral services that often refer lawyers to themselves—you'll want to avoid these.

When you call a prospective lawyer, speak with the lawyer personally, not just the reception desk. You can probably get a good idea of how the person operates by paying close attention to the way your call is handled. Is the lawyer available, or is your call returned promptly? Is the lawyer willing to spend at least a few minutes talking to you to determine if she is really the best person for the job? Does the lawyer seem sympathetic to, and compatible with, the nonprofit goals of your group? Do you get a good personal feeling from your conversation? Oh, and one more thing: Be sure to get the hourly rate the lawyer will charge set in advance. If you are using this book, you will probably want to eliminate lawyers who charge $200 per hour to support an office on top of the tallest building in town.

What About Lost-Cost Law Clinics?

Law clinics advertise their services regularly on TV and radio. Can they help your form a nonprofit organization? Perhaps, but usually at a rate well above their initial low consultation rate. Since the lawyer turnover rate at these clinics is high and the degree of familiarity with nonprofit legal and tax issues is usually low, we recommend you spend your money more wisely by finding a reasonably-priced nonprofit lawyer elsewhere.

Looking Up the Law Yourself: Many incorporators may wish to research legal information on their own. County law libraries are open to the public (you need not be a lawyer to use them) and are not difficult to use once you understand how the information is categorized and stored. They are an invaluable source of nonprofit and profit corporation and general business forms, corporate tax procedures and information, etc. Research librarians will usually go out of their way to help you find the right statute, form or background reading on any corporate or tax issue. If you are interested in doing self-help legal research, an excellent source of information is *Legal Research: How to Find and Understand the Law* by Elias (Nolo Press). Also, you may wish to obtain a copy of the California Corporations Code to look up code sections yourself (an edition published by West Publishing Co. is available through Nolo Press).

B. Accountants

As you already know, organizing and operating a nonprofit corporation involves a significant amount of financial and tax work. While much of it easy, a nit-picking attention to definitions, cross references, formulas and other elusive or downright boring details is required, particularly when preparing your federal 1023 tax exemption application. As we often suggest in the book, you may find it sensible to seek advice from an accountant or other tax advisor when organizing your nonprofit corporation. For example, you may need help preparing the income statements, balance sheets and other financial and tax information submitted with your IRS tax exemption application. Also, if your organization will handle any significant amount of money, you will need an accountant or bookkeeper to set up your double-entry accounting books (cash receipts and disbursement journals, general ledger, etc.). Double entry accounting techniques are particularly important to nonprofits that receive federal or private grant or program funds—accounting for these "restricted

funds" is a special area of accounting that usually requires assistance to implement. Nonprofit corporation account books should be designed to allow for easily transferring financial data to state and federal nonprofit corporate tax returns and disclosure statements and to provide an easy way to determine, at any time, whether receipts and expenditures fall into the categories proper to maintaining your 501(c)(3) tax exemption, public charity status, and grant or program eligibility. You will also want to know whether your operations are likely to subject you to an unrelated business income tax under federal and state rules.

Once your corporation is organized and your books are set up, the ongoing work of keeping books and filing tax forms may be performed by corporate personnel with experience in bookkeeping and nonprofit tax matters. Whatever your arrangement, make sure to at least obtain the tax publications listed at the beginning of Chapter 11. These pamphlets contain essential information on preparing and filing IRS corporation and employment tax returns.

When you select an accountant or bookkeeper, the same considerations apply as when selecting a lawyer. Choose someone you know or whom a friend or nonprofit contact recommends. Be as specific as you can regarding the services you wish performed and make sure the advisor has had experience with nonprofit taxation and tax exemption applications as well as regular payroll, tax and accounting procedures. Many nonprofit bookkeepers work part-time for several nonprofit organizations. Again, calling people in your nonprofit network is often the best way to find this type of person.

APPENDIX—7TH EDITION

Incorporation Checklist

Application for Reservation of Corporate Name

Articles of Incorporation of California Public Benefit Corporation

Articles of Incorporation of California Religious Corporation

Bylaws of California Public Benefit Corporation

Membership Provisions of California Public Benefit Corporation

Bylaws of California Religious Corporation

Membership Provisions of California Religious Corporation

Cover Letter to Secretary of State

IRS Form 8718, User Fee for Exempt Organization Determination Letter Request

Waiver of Notice and Consent to Holding of First Meeting of Board of Directors

Minutes of First Meeting of Board of Directors

California Nonprofit Corporation Resource List

INCORPORATION CHECKLIST

Chapter	Step	Page	New* Groups	Existing* Groups	Optional**	Step Name	My Group	Done
6	1	6/2	√	√		Choose a Corporate Name		
	2	6/12	√	√		Prepare Articles of Incorporation		
	3	6/22		√	√	Prepare Articles for Unincorporated Association		
	4	6/25	√	√	√	File Articles Early		
	5	6/25	√	√		Prepare Bylaws		
7	6	7/2	√	√		Prepare State Tax Exemption Application		
8	7	8/2	√	√		Consolidate Paperwork		
	8	8/2	√	√		Make Copies		
	9	8/3	√	√		File State Tax Exemption and Articles		
9	10	9/2	√	√		Prepare and File Federal Tax Exemption Application		
10	11	10/2	√	√		Mail IRS Letter to Franchise Tax Board		
	12	10/2	√	√		Set Up Corporate Records Book		
	13	10/5		√	√	Prepare Offer to Transfer Assets		
	14	10/11		√		Prepare Minutes of First Board Meeting		
	15	10/19	√	√		Place Minutes and Attachments in Corporate Records		
	16	10/19		√	√	Comply with Bulk Sales Law		
	17	10/20		√	√	Prepare Bill of Sale for Assets		
	18	10/23		√	√	Prepare Assignments of Leases and Deeds		
	19	10/23		√	√	File Final Papers for Prior Organization		
	20	10/23		√	√	Notify Creditors of Prior Organization		
	21	10/24	√	√	√	File Fictitious Business Name Statement		
	22	10/24	√	√	√	Apply for Nonprofit Mailing Permit		
	23	10/25	√	√	√	Apply for Property Tax Exemption		
	24	10/25	√	√		File Domestic Corporation Statement		
	25	10/27	√	√	√	Register with Attorney General (Public Benefit Corps)		
	26	10/28	√	√	√	Issue Membership Certificates		
	27	10/28		√	√	File Articles with County Recorder		
	28	10/29	√	√	√	Register with Fair Political Practices Commission		

* **New** = Groups starting operations as a newly-formed corporation.
* **Existing** = Groups in operation prior to incorporation.
** **Optional** = 1) optional step may be elected by new or existing groups or
2) step must be followed by some (but not all) new or existing groups to which step applies.

from *The California Nonprofit Corporation Handbook*
Copyright © 1989 -1992 by Anthony Mancuso
Published by Nolo Press, Berkeley, CA (415) 549-1976

APPLICATION FOR RESERVATION OF CORPORATE NAME

_____

_____

_____

Secretary of State
Corporate Name Availability Section
1500 11th Street
Sacramento, CA 95814-2974

Dear Secretary of State:

Please reserve a corporate name for use of the undersigned for sixty days following the issuance of your certificate of reservation of name.

The name desired is one of the following, listed in order of preference:

1. _____

2. _____

3. _____

4. _____

I enclose the required fee for the certificate of reservation to be issued.

Sincerely,

_____

ARTICLES OF INCORPORATION

ONE: The name of this corporation is _____
_____.

TWO: This corporation is a nonprofit public benefit corporation and is not organized for the private gain of any person. It is organized under the Nonprofit Public Benefit Corporation Law for charitable purposes. The specific purposes for which this corporation is organized are

_____

_____
_____
_____
_____
_____.

THREE: The name and address in the State of California of this corporation's initial agent for service of process is _____
_____.

FOUR: (a) This corporation is organized and operated exclusively for _____
_____
purposes within the meaning of Section 501(c)(3) of the Internal Revenue Code.

(b) Notwithstanding any other provision of these Articles, the corporation shall not carry on any other activities not permitted to be carried on (1) by a corporation exempt from federal income tax under Section 501(c)(3) of the Internal Revenue Code or (2) by a corporation contributions to which are deductible under Section 170(c)(2) of the Internal Revenue Code.

(c) No substantial part of the activities of this corporation shall consist of carrying on propaganda, or otherwise attempting to influence legislation, and the corporation shall not participate or intervene in any political campaign (including the publishing or distribution of statements) on behalf of, or in opposition to, any candidate for public office.

FIVE: The names and addresses of the persons appointed to act as the initial Directors of this corporation are:

Name   Address

_____   _____

_____   _____

_____   _____

_____   _____

_____   _____

SIX: The property of this corporation is irrevocably dedicated to _____
_____ and no part of the net income or
assets of the organization shall ever inure to the benefit of any director, officer or member thereof
or to the benefit of any private person.

On the dissolution or winding up of the corporation, its assets remaining after payment of, or
provision for payment of, all debts and liabilities of this corporation, shall be distributed to a
nonprofit fund, foundation, or corporation which is organized and operated exclusively
for_____ and
which has established its tax-exempt status under Section 501(c)(3) of the Internal Revenue Code.

Date: _____

_____ , Director

_____ , Director

_____ , Director

_____ , Director

_____ , Director

We, the above-mentioned initial directors of this corporation, hereby declare that we are the
persons who executed the foregoing Articles of Incorporation, which execution is our act and
deed.

_____ , Director

_____ , Director

_____ , Director

_____ , Director

_____ , Director

ARTICLES OF INCORPORATION

ONE: The name of this corporation is _____
_____

TWO: This corporation is a nonprofit religious corporation and is not organized for the private gain of any person. It is organized under the Nonprofit Religious Corporation Law primarily for religious purposes. The specific purposes for which this corporation is organized are

_____
_____
_____
_____
_____.

THREE: The name and address in the State of California of this corporation's initial agent for service of process is _____
_____.

FOUR: (a) This corporation is organized and operated exclusively for religious purposes within the meaning of Section 501(c)(3) of the Internal Revenue Code.

(b) Notwithstanding any other provision of these Articles, the corporation shall not carry on any other activities not permitted to be carried on (1) by a corporation exempt from federal income tax under Section 501(c)(3) of the Internal Revenue Code or (2) by a corporation contributions to which are deductible under Section 170(c)(2) of the Internal Revenue Code.

(c) No substantial part of the activities of this corporation shall consist of carrying on propaganda, or otherwise attempting to influence legislation, and the corporation shall not participate or intervene in any political campaign (including the publishing or distribution of statements) on behalf of, or in opposition to, any candidate for public office.

FIVE: The names and addresses of the persons appointed to act as the initial directors of this corporation are:

Name   Address

_____   _____

_____   _____

_____   _____

_____   _____

_____   _____

SIX: The property of this corporation is irrevocably dedicated to religious purposes and no part of the net income or assets of the organization shall ever inure to the benefit of any director, officer or member thereof or to the benefit of any private person.

On the dissolution or winding up of the corporation, its assets remaining after payment of, or provision for payment of, all debts and liabilities of this corporation, shall be distributed to a nonprofit fund, foundation, or corporation which is organized and operated exclusively for religious purposes and which has established its tax-exempt status under Section 501(c)(3) of the Internal Revenue Code.

Date: _____

_____
, Director

_____
, Director

_____
, Director

_____
, Director

_____
, Director

We, the above-mentioned initial directors of this corporation, hereby declare that we are the persons who executed the foregoing Articles of Incorporation, which execution is our act and deed.

_____
, Director

_____
, Director

_____
, Director

_____
, Director

_____
, Director

BYLAWS

OF

_____

A CALIFORNIA PUBLIC BENEFIT CORPORATION

ARTICLE 1
OFFICES

SECTION 1. PRINCIPAL OFFICE

The principal office of the corporation for the transaction of its business is located in _____ County, California.

SECTION 2. CHANGE OF ADDRESS

The county of the corporation's principal office can be changed only by amendment of these Bylaws and not otherwise. The Board of Directors may, however, change the principal office from one location to another within the named county by noting the changed address and effective date below, and such changes of address shall not be deemed an amendment of these Bylaws:

_____   Dated: _____, 19__

_____   Dated: _____, 19__

_____   Dated: _____, 19__

SECTION 3. OTHER OFFICES

The corporation may also have offices at such other places, within or without the State of California, where it is qualified to do business, as its business may require and as the board of directors may, from time to time, designate.

ARTICLE 2
PURPOSES

SECTION 1. OBJECTIVES AND PURPOSES

The primary objectives and purposes of this corporation shall be:

ARTICLE 3
DIRECTORS

SECTION 1. NUMBER

The corporation shall have _____ directors and collectively they shall be known as the Board of Directors. The number may be changed by amendment of this Bylaw, or by repeal of this Bylaw and adoption of a new Bylaw, as provided in these Bylaws.

SECTION 2. POWERS

Subject to the provisions of the California Nonprofit Public Benefit Corporation law and any limitations in the Articles of Incorporation and Bylaws relating to action required or permitted to be taken or approved by the members, if any, of this corporation, the activities and affairs of this corporation shall be conducted and all corporate powers shall be exercised by or under the direction of the Board of Directors.

SECTION 3. DUTIES

It shall be the duty of the directors to:

(a) Perform any and all duties imposed on them collectively or individually by law, by the Articles of Incorporation of this corporation, or by these Bylaws;

(b) Appoint and remove, employ and discharge, and, except as otherwise provided in these Bylaws, prescribe the duties and fix the compensation, if any, of all officers, agents and employees of the corporation;

(c) Supervise all officers, agents and employees of the corporation to assure that their duties are performed properly;

(d) Meet at such times and places as required by these Bylaws;

(e) Register their addresses with the Secretary of the corporation and notices of meetings mailed or telegraphed to them at such addresses shall be valid notices thereof.

SECTION 4. TERMS OF OFFICE

Each director shall hold office until the next annual meeting for election of the Board of Directors as specified in these Bylaws, and until his or her successor is elected and qualifies.

SECTION 5. COMPENSATION

Directors shall serve without compensation except that they shall be allowed and paid

_____.

In addition, they shall be allowed reasonable advancement or reimbursement of expenses incurred in the performance of their regular duties as specified in Section 3 of this Article. Directors may not be compensated for rendering services to the corporation in any capacity other than director unless such other compensation is reasonable and is allowable under the provisions of Section 6 of this Article.

SECTION 6. RESTRICTION REGARDING INTERESTED DIRECTORS

Notwithstanding any other provision of these Bylaws, not more than forty-nine percent (49%) of the persons serving on the board may be interested persons. For purposes of this Section, "interested persons" means either:

(a) Any person currently being compensated by the corporation for services rendered it within the previous twelve (12) months, whether as a full- or part-time officer or other employee, independent contractor, or otherwise, excluding any reasonable compensation paid to a director as director; or

(b) Any brother, sister, ancestor, descendant, spouse, brother-in-law, sister-in-law, son-in-law, daughter-in-law, mother-in-law, or father-in-law of any such person.

SECTION 7. PLACE OF MEETINGS

Meetings shall be held at the principal office of the corporation unless otherwise provided by the board or at such place within or without the State of California which has been designated from time to time by resolution of the Board of Directors. In the absence of such designation, any meeting not held at the principal office of the corporation shall be valid only if held on the written consent of all directors given either before or after the meeting and filed with the Secretary of the corporation or after all board members have been given written notice of the meeting as hereinafter provided for special meetings of the board. Any meeting, regular or special, may be held by conference telephone or similar communications equipment, so as long as all directors participating in such meeting can hear one another.

SECTION 8. REGULAR AND ANNUAL MEETINGS

Regular meetings of Directors shall be held on _____
_____ at _____ _M, unless such day falls on a legal holiday, in which event the regular meeting shall be held at the same hour and place on the next business day.

If this corporation makes no provision for members, then, at the annual meeting of directors held on _____, directors shall be elected by the Board of Directors in accordance with this section. Cumulative voting by directors for the election of directors shall not be permitted. The candidates receiving the highest number of votes up to the number of directors to be elected shall be elected. Each director shall cast one vote, with voting being by ballot only.

SECTION 9. SPECIAL MEETINGS

Special meetings of the Board of Directors may be called by the Chairperson of the board, the President, the Vice President, the Secretary, or by any two directors, and such meetings shall be held at the place, within or without the State of California, designated by the person or persons calling the meeting, and in the absence of such designation, at the principal office of the corporation.

SECTION 10. NOTICE OF MEETINGS

Regular meetings of the board may be held without notice. Special meetings of the board shall be held upon four (4) days' notice by first-class mail or forty-eight (48) hours' notice delivered personally or by telephone or telegraph. If sent by mail or telegraph, the notice shall be deemed to be delivered on its deposit in the mails or on its delivery to the telegraph company. Such notices shall be addressed to each director at his or her address as shown on the books of the corporation. Notice of the time and place of holding an adjourned meeting need not be given to absent directors if the time and place of the adjourned meeting are fixed at the meeting adjourned and if such adjourned meeting is held no more than twenty-four (24) hours from the time of the original meeting. Notice shall be given of any adjourned regular or special meeting to directors absent from the original meeting if the adjourned meeting is held more than twenty-four (24) hours from the time of the original meeting.

SECTION 11. CONTENTS OF NOTICE

Notice of meetings not herein dispensed with shall specify the place, day and hour of the meeting. The purpose of any board meeting need not be specified in the notice.

SECTION 12. WAIVER OF NOTICE AND CONSENT TO HOLDING MEETINGS

The transactions of any meeting of the board, however called and noticed or wherever held, are as valid as though the meeting had been duly held after proper call and notice, provided a quorum, as hereinafter defined, is present and provided that either before or after the meeting each director not present signs a waiver of notice, a consent to holding the meeting, or an approval of the minutes thereof. All such waivers, consents, or approvals shall be filed with the corporate records or made a part of the minutes of the meeting.

SECTION 13. QUORUM FOR MEETINGS

A quorum shall consist of _____ Directors.

Except as otherwise provided in these Bylaws or in the Articles of Incorporation of this corporation, or by law, no business shall be considered by the board at any meeting at which a quorum, as hereinafter defined, is not present, and the only motion which the Chair shall entertain at such meeting is a motion to adjourn. However, a majority of the directors present at such meeting may adjourn from time to time until the time fixed for the next regular meeting of the board.

When a meeting is adjourned for lack of a quorum, it shall not be necessary to give any notice of the time and place of the adjourned meeting or of the business to be transacted at such meeting, other than by announcement at the meeting at which the adjournment is taken, except as provided in Section 10 of this Article.

The directors present at a duly called and held meeting at which a quorum is initially present may continue to do business notwithstanding the loss of a quorum at the meeting due to a withdrawal of directors from the meeting, provided that any action thereafter taken must be approved by at least a majority of the required quorum for such meeting or such greater percentage as may be required by law, or the Articles of Incorporation or Bylaws of this corporation.

SECTION 14. MAJORITY ACTION AS BOARD ACTION

Every act or decision done or made by a majority of the directors present at a meeting duly held at which a quorum is present is the act of the Board of Directors, unless the Articles of Incorporation or Bylaws of this corporation, or provisions of the California Nonprofit Public Benefit Corporation Law, particularly those provisions relating to appointment of committees (Section 5212), approval of contracts or transactions in which a director has a material financial interest (Section 5233) and indemnification of directors (Section 5238e), require a greater percentage or different voting rules for approval of a matter by the board.

SECTION 15. CONDUCT OF MEETINGS

Meetings of the Board of Directors shall be presided over by the Chairperson of the Board, or, if no such person has been so designated or, in his or her absence, the President of the corporation or, in his or her absence, by the Vice President of the corporation or, in the absence of each of these persons, by a Chairperson chosen by a majority of the directors present at the meeting. The Secretary of the corporation shall act as secretary of all meetings of the board, provided that, in his or her absence, the presiding officer shall appoint another person to act as Secretary of the Meeting.

Meetings shall be governed by _____
_____, as such rules may be revised from

time to time, insofar as such rules are not inconsistent with or in conflict with these Bylaws, with the Articles of Incorporation of this corporation, or with provisions of law.

SECTION 16. ACTION BY UNANIMOUS WRITTEN CONSENT WITHOUT MEETING

Any action required or permitted to be taken by the Board of Directors under any provision of law may be taken without a meeting, if all members of the board shall individually or collectively consent in writing to such action. For the purposes of this Section only, "all members of the board" shall not include any "interested director" as defined in Section 5233 of the California Nonprofit Public Benefit Corporation Law. Such written consent or consents shall be filed with the minutes of the proceedings of the board. Such action by written consent shall have the same force and effect as the unanimous vote of the directors. Any certificate or other document filed under any provision of law which relates to action so taken shall state that the action was taken by unanimous written consent of the Board of Directors without a meeting and that the Bylaws of this corporation authorize the directors to so act, and such statement shall be prima facie evidence of such authority.

SECTION 17. VACANCIES

Vacancies on the Board of Directors shall exist (1) on the death, resignation or removal of any director, and (2) whenever the number of authorized directors is increased.

The Board of Directors may declare vacant the office of a director who has been declared of unsound mind by a final order of court, or convicted of a felony, or been found by a final order or judgment of any court to have breached any duty under Section 5230 and following of the California Nonprofit Public Benefit Corporation Law.

If this corporation has any members, then, if the corporation has less than fifty (50) members, directors may be removed without cause by a majority of all members, or, if the corporation has fifty (50) or more members, by vote of a majority of the votes represented at a membership meeting at which a quorum is present.

If this corporation has no members, directors may be removed without cause by a majority of the directors then in office.

Any director may resign effective upon giving written notice to the Chairperson of the Board, the President, the Secretary, or the Board of Directors, unless the notice specifies a later time for the effectiveness of such resignation. No director may resign if the corporation would then be left without a duly elected director or directors in charge of its affairs, except upon notice to the Attorney General.

Vacancies on the board may be filled by approval of the board or, if the number of directors then in office is less than a quorum, by (1) the unanimous written consent of the directors then in office, (2) the affirmative vote of a majority of the directors then in office at a meeting held pursuant to notice or waivers of notice complying with this Article of these Bylaws, or (3) a sole remaining director. If this corporation has members, however, vacancies created by the removal of a director may be filled only by the approval of the members. The members, if any, of this corporation may elect a director at any time to fill any vacancy not filled by the directors.

A person elected to fill a vacancy as provided by this Section shall hold office until the next annual election of the Board of Directors or until his or her death, resignation or removal from office.

SECTION 18. NON-LIABILITY OF DIRECTORS

The directors shall not be personally liable for the debts, liabilities, or other obligations of the corporation.

SECTION 19. INDEMNIFICATION BY CORPORATION OF DIRECTORS, OFFICERS, EMPLOYEES AND OTHER AGENTS

To the extent that a person who is, or was, a director, officer, employee or other agent of this corporation has been successful on the merits in defense of any civil, criminal, administrative or investigative proceeding brought to procure a judgment against such person by reason of the fact that he or she is, or was, an agent of the corporation, or has been successful in defense of any claim, issue or matter, therein, such person shall be indemnified against expenses actually and reasonably incurred by the person in connection with such proceeding.

If such person either settles any such claim or sustains a judgment against him or her, then indemnification against expenses, judgments, fines, settlements and other amounts reasonably incurred in connection with such proceedings shall be provided by this corporation but only to the extent allowed by, and in accordance with the requirements of, Section 5238 of the California Nonprofit Public Benefit Corporation Law.

SECTION 20. INSURANCE FOR CORPORATE AGENTS

The Board of Directors may adopt a resolution authorizing the purchase and maintenance of insurance on behalf of any agent of the corporation (including a director, officer, employee or other agent of the corporation) against any liability other than for violating provisions of law relating to self-dealing (Section 5233 of the California Nonprofit Public Benefit Corporation Law) asserted against or incurred by the agent in such capacity or arising out of the agent's status as such, whether or not the corporation would have the power to indemnify the agent against such liability under the provisions of Section 5238 of the California Nonprofit Public Benefit Corporation Law.

ARTICLE 4
OFFICERS

SECTION 1. NUMBER OF OFFICERS

The officers of the corporation shall be a President, a Secretary, and a Chief Financial Officer who shall be designated the Treasurer. The corporation may also have, as determined by the Board of Directors, a Chairperson of the Board, one or more Vice Presidents, Assistant Secretaries, Assistant Treasurers, or other officers. Any number of offices may be held by the same person except that neither the Secretary nor the Treasurer may serve as the President or Chairperson of the Board.

SECTION 2. QUALIFICATION, ELECTION, AND TERM OF OFFICE

Any person may serve as officer of this corporation. Officers shall be elected by the Board of Directors, at any time, and each officer shall hold office until he or she resigns or is removed or is otherwise disqualified to serve, or until his or her successor shall be elected and qualified, whichever occurs first.

SECTION 3. SUBORDINATE OFFICERS

The Board of Directors may appoint such other officers or agents as it may deem desirable, and such officers shall serve such terms, have such authority, and perform such duties as may be prescribed from time to time by the Board of Directors.

SECTION 4. REMOVAL AND RESIGNATION

Any officer may be removed, either with or without cause, by the Board of Directors, at any time. Any officer may resign at any time by giving written notice to the Board of Directors or to the President or Secretary of the corporation. Any such resignation shall take effect at the date of receipt of such notice or at any later date specified therein, and, unless otherwise specified therein, the acceptance of such resignation shall not be necessary to make it effective. The above provisions of this Section shall be superseded by any conflicting terms of a contract which has been approved or ratified by the Board of Directors relating to the employment of any officer of the corporation.

SECTION 5. VACANCIES

Any vacancy caused by the death, resignation, removal, disqualification, or otherwise, of any officer shall be filled by the Board of Directors. In the event of a vacancy in any office other than that of President, such vacancy may be filled temporarily by appointment by the President until such time as the Board shall fill the vacancy. Vacancies occurring in offices of officers appointed at the discretion of the board may or may not be filled as the board shall determine.

SECTION 6. DUTIES OF PRESIDENT

The President shall be the chief executive officer of the corporation and shall, subject to the control of the Board of Directors, supervise and control the affairs of the corporation and the activities of the officers. He or she shall perform all duties incident to his or her office and such other duties as may be required by law, by the Articles of Incorporation of this corporation, or by these Bylaws, or which may be prescribed from time to time by the Board of Directors. Unless another person is specifically appointed as Chairperson of the Board of Directors, he or she shall preside at all meetings of the Board of Directors. If applicable, the President shall preside at all meetings of the members. Except as otherwise expressly provided by law, by the Articles of Incorporation, or by these Bylaws, he or she shall, in the name of the corporation, execute such deeds, mortgages, bonds, contracts, checks, or other instruments which may from time to time be authorized by the Board of Directors.

SECTION 7. DUTIES OF VICE PRESIDENT

In the absence of the President, or in the event of his or her inability or refusal to act, the Vice President shall perform all the duties of the President, and when so acting shall have all the powers of, and be subject to all the restrictions on, the President. The Vice President shall have other powers and perform such other duties as may be prescribed by law, by the Articles of Incorporation, or by these Bylaws, or as may be prescribed by the Board of Directors.

SECTION 8. DUTIES OF SECRETARY

The Secretary shall:

Certify and keep at the principal office of the corporation the original, or a copy of these Bylaws as amended or otherwise altered to date.

Keep at the principal office of the corporation or at such other place as the board may determine, a book of minutes of all meetings of the directors, and, if applicable, meetings of committees of directors and of members, recording therein the time and place of holding, whether regular or special, how called, how notice thereof was given, the names of those present or represented at the meeting, and the proceedings thereof.

See that all notices are duly given in accordance with the provisions of these Bylaws or as required by law.

Be custodian of the records and of the seal of the corporation and see that the seal is affixed to all duly executed documents, the execution of which on behalf of the corporation under its seal is authorized by law or these Bylaws.

Keep at the principal office of the corporation a membership book containing the name and address of each and any members, and, in the case where any membership has been terminated, he or she shall record such fact in the membership book together with the date on which such membership ceased.

Exhibit at all reasonable times to any director of the corporation, or to his or her agent or attorney, on request therefor, the Bylaws, the membership book, and the minutes of the proceedings of the directors of the corporation.

In general, perform all duties incident to the office of Secretary and such other duties as may be required by law, by the Articles of Incorporation of this corporation, or by these Bylaws, or which may be assigned to him or her from time to time by the Board of Directors.

SECTION 9. DUTIES OF TREASURER

Subject to the provisions of these Bylaws relating to the "Execution of Instruments, Deposits and Funds," the Treasurer shall:

Have charge and custody of, and be responsible for, all funds and securities of the corporation, and deposit all such funds in the name of the corporation in such banks, trust companies, or other depositories as shall be selected by the Board of Directors.

Receive, and give receipt for, monies due and payable to the corporation from any source whatsoever.

Disburse, or cause to be disbursed, the funds of the corporation as may be directed by the Board of Directors, taking proper vouchers for such disbursements.

Keep and maintain adequate and correct accounts of the corporation's properties and business transactions, including accounts of its assets, liabilities, receipts, disbursements, gains and losses.

Exhibit at all reasonable times the books of account and financial records to any director of the corporation, or to his or her agent or attorney, on request therefor.

Render to the President and directors, whenever requested, an account of any or all of his or her transactions as Treasurer and of the financial condition of the corporation.

Prepare, or cause to be prepared, and certify, or cause to be certified, the financial statements to be included in any required reports.

In general, perform all duties incident to the office of Treasurer and such other duties as may be required by law, by the Articles of Incorporation of the corporation, or by these Bylaws, or which may be assigned to him or her from time to time by the Board of Directors.

SECTION 10. COMPENSATION

The salaries of the officers, if any, shall be fixed from time to time by resolution of the Board of Directors, and no officer shall be prevented from receiving such salary by reason of the fact that he or she is also a director of the corporation, provided, however, that such compensation paid a director for serving as an officer of this corporation shall only be allowed if permitted under the provisions of Article 3, Section 6 of these Bylaws. In all cases, any salaries received by officers of this corporation shall be reasonable and given in return for services actually rendered for the corporation which relate to the performance of the charitable or public purposes of this corporation.

ARTICLE 5
COMMITTEES

SECTION 1. EXECUTIVE COMMITTEE

The Board of Directors may, by a majority vote of directors, designate two (2) or more of its members (who may also be serving as officers of this corporation) to constitute an Executive Committee and delegate to such Committee any of the powers and authority of the board in the management of the business and affairs of the corporation, except with respect to:

(a) The approval of any action which, under law or the provisions of these Bylaws, requires the approval of the members or of a majority of all of the members.

(b) The filling of vacancies on the board or on any committee which has the authority of the board.

(c) The fixing of compensation of the directors for serving on the board or on any committee.

(d) The amendment or repeal of Bylaws or the adoption of new Bylaws.

(e) The amendment or repeal or any resolution of the board which by its express terms is not so amendable or repealable.

(f) The appointment of committees of the board or the members thereof.

(g) The expenditure of corporate funds to support a nominee for director after there are more people nominated for director than can be elected.

(h) The approval of any transaction to which this corporation is a party and in which one or more of the directors has a material financial interest, except as expressly provided in Section 5233(d)(3) of the California Nonprofit Public Benefit Corporation Law.

By a majority vote of its members then in office, the board may at any time revoke or modify any or all of the authority so delegated, increase or decrease but not below two (2) the number of its members, and fill vacancies therein from the members of the board. The Committee shall keep regular minutes of its proceedings, cause them to be filed with the corporate records, and report the same to the board from time to time as the board may require.

SECTION 2. OTHER COMMITTEES

The corporation shall have such other committees as may from time to time be designated by resolution of the Board of Directors. Such other committees may consist of persons who are not also members of the board. These additional committees shall act in an advisory capacity only to the board and shall be clearly titled as "advisory" committees.

SECTION 3. MEETINGS AND ACTION OF COMMITTEES

Meetings and action of committees shall be governed by, noticed, held and taken in accordance with the provisions of these Bylaws concerning meetings of the Board of Directors, with such changes in the context of such Bylaw provisions as are necessary to substitute the committee and its members for the Board of Directors and its members, except that the time for regular meetings of committees may be fixed by resolution of the Board of Directors or by the committee. The time for special meetings of committees may also be fixed by the Board of Directors. The Board of Directors may also adopt rules and regulations pertaining to the conduct of meetings of committees to the extent that such rules and regulations are not inconsistent with the provisions of these Bylaws.

ARTICLE 6
EXECUTION OF INSTRUMENTS, DEPOSITS AND FUNDS

SECTION 1. EXECUTION OF INSTRUMENTS

The Board of Directors, except as otherwise provided in these Bylaws, may by resolution authorize any officer or agent of the corporation to enter into any contract or execute and deliver any instrument in the name of and on behalf of the corporation, and such authority may be general or confined to specific instances. Unless so authorized, no officer, agent, or employee shall have any power or authority to bind the corporation by any contract or engagement or to pledge its credit or to render it liable monetarily for any purpose or in any amount.

SECTION 2. CHECKS AND NOTES

Except as otherwise specifically determined by resolution of the Board of Directors, or as otherwise required by law, checks, drafts, promissory notes, orders for the payment of money, and other evidence of indebtedness of the corporation shall be signed by the Treasurer and countersigned by the President of the corporation.

SECTION 3. DEPOSITS

All funds of the corporation shall be deposited from time to time to the credit of the corporation in such banks, trust companies, or other depositories as the Board of Directors may select.

SECTION 4. GIFTS

The Board of Directors may accept on behalf of the corporation any contribution, gift, bequest, or devise for the charitable or public purposes of this corporation.

ARTICLE 7
CORPORATE RECORDS, REPORTS AND SEAL

SECTION 1. MAINTENANCE OF CORPORATE RECORDS

The corporation shall keep at its principal office in the State of California:

(a) Minutes of all meetings of directors, committees of the board and, if this corporation has members, of all meetings of members, indicating the time and place of holding such meetings, whether regular or special, how called, the notice given, and the names of those present and the proceedings thereof;

(b) Adequate and correct books and records of account, including accounts of its properties and business transactions and accounts of its assets, liabilities, receipts, disbursements, gains and losses;

(c) A record of its members, if any, indicating their names and addresses and, if applicable, the class of membership held by each member and the termination date of any membership;

(d) A copy of the corporation's Articles of Incorporation and Bylaws as amended to date, which shall be open to inspection by the members, if any, of the corporation at all reasonable times during office hours.

SECTION 2. CORPORATE SEAL

The Board of Directors may adopt, use, and at will alter, a corporate seal. Such seal shall be kept at the principal office of the corporation. Failure to affix the seal to corporate instruments, however, shall not affect the validity of any such instrument.

SECTION 3. DIRECTORS' INSPECTION RIGHTS

Every director shall have the absolute right at any reasonable time to inspect and copy all books, records and documents of every kind and to inspect the physical properties of the corporation.

SECTION 4. MEMBERS' INSPECTION RIGHTS

If this corporation has any members, then each and every member shall have the following inspection rights, for a purpose reasonably related to the person's interest as a member:

(a) To inspect and copy the record of all members' names, addresses and voting rights, at reasonable times, upon five (5) business days' prior written demand on the corporation, which demand shall state the purpose for which the inspection rights are requested.

(b) To obtain from the Secretary of the corporation, upon written demand and payment of a reasonable charge, an alphabetized list of the names, addresses and voting rights of those members entitled to vote for the election of directors as of the most recent record date for which the list has been compiled or as of the date specified by the member subsequent to the date of demand. The demand shall state the purpose for which the list is requested. The membership list shall be made available on or before the later of ten (10) business days after the demand is received or after the date specified therein as of which the list is to be compiled.

(c) To inspect at any reasonable time the books, records, or minutes of proceedings of the members or of the board or committees of the board, upon written demand on the corporation by the member, for a purpose reasonably related to such person's interests as a member.

SECTION 5. RIGHT TO COPY AND MAKE EXTRACTS

Any inspection under the provisions of this Article may be made in person or by agent or attorney and the right to inspection includes the right to copy and make extracts.

SECTION 6. ANNUAL REPORT

The board shall cause an annual report to be furnished not later than one hundred and twenty (120) days after the close of the corporation's fiscal year to all directors of the corporation and, if this corporation has members, to any member who requests it in writing, which report shall contain the following information in appropriate detail:

(a) The assets and liabilities, including the trust funds, of the corporation as of the end of the fiscal year;

(b) The principal changes in assets and liabilities, including trust funds, during the fiscal year;

(c) The revenue or receipts of the corporation , both unrestricted and restricted to particular purposes, for the fiscal year;

(d) The expenses or disbursements of the corporation, for both general and restricted purposes, during the fiscal year;

(e) Any information required by Section 7 of this Article.

The annual report shall be accompanied by any report thereon of independent accountants, or, if there is no such report, the certificate of an authorized officer of the corporation that such statements were prepared without audit from the books and records of the corporation.

If this corporation has members, then, if this corporation receives TWENTY-FIVE THOUSAND DOLLARS ($25,000), or more, in gross revenues or receipts during the fiscal year, this corporation shall automatically send the above annual report to all members, in such manner, at such time, and with such contents, including an accompanying report from independent accountants or certification of a corporate officer, as specified by the above provisions of this Section relating to the annual report.

SECTION 7. ANNUAL STATEMENT OF SPECIFIC TRANSACTIONS TO MEMBERS

This corporation shall mail or deliver to all directors and any and all members a statement within one hundred and twenty (120) days after the close of its fiscal year which briefly describes the amount and circumstances of any indemnification or transaction of the following kind:

(a) Any transaction in which the corporation, or its parent or its subsidiary, was a party, and in which either of the following had a direct or indirect material financial interest:

(1) Any director or officer of the corporation, or its parent or subsidiary (a mere common directorship shall not be considered a material financial interest); or

(2) Any holder of more than ten percent (10%) of the voting power of the corporation, its parent or its subsidiary.

The above statement need only be provided with respect to a transaction during the previous fiscal year involving more than FIFTY THOUSAND DOLLARS ($50,000) or which was one of a number of transactions with the same persons involving, in the aggregate, more than FIFTY THOUSAND DOLLARS ($50,000).

Similarly, the statement need only be provided with respect to indemnifications or advances aggregating more than TEN THOUSAND DOLLARS ($10,000) paid during the previous fiscal year to any director or officer, except that no such statement need be made if such indemnification was approved by the members pursuant to Section 5238(e)(2) of the California Nonprofit Public Benefit Corporation Law.

Any statement required by this Section shall briefly describe the names of the interested persons involved in such transactions, stating each person's relationship to the corporation, the nature of such person's interest in the transaction and, where practical, the amount of such interest, provided that in the case of a transaction with a partnership of which such person is a partner, only the interest of the partnership need be stated.

If this corporation has any members and provides all members with an annual report according to the provisions of Section 6 of this Article, then such annual report shall include the information required by this Section.

ARTICLE 8
FISCAL YEAR

SECTION 1. FISCAL YEAR OF THE CORPORATION

The fiscal year of the corporation shall begin on the _____
_____ and end on the _____
_____ in each year.

ARTICLE 9
AMENDMENT OF BYLAWS

SECTION 1. AMENDMENT

Subject to any provision of law applicable to the amendment of Bylaws of public benefit nonprofit corporations, these Bylaws, or any of them, may be altered, amended, or repealed and new Bylaws adopted as follows:

(a) Subject to the power of members, if any, to change or repeal these Bylaws under Section 5150 of the Corporations Code, by approval of the Board of Directors unless the Bylaw amendment would materially and adversely affect the rights of members, if any, as to voting or transfer, provided, however, if this corporation has admitted any members, then a Bylaw specifying or changing the fixed number of directors of the corporation, the maximum or minimum number of directors, or changing from a fixed to variable board or vice versa, may not be adopted, amended, or repealed except as provided in subparagraph (b) of this Section; or

(b) By approval of the members, if any, of this corporation.

ARTICLE 10
AMENDMENT OF ARTICLES

SECTION 1. AMENDMENT OF ARTICLES BEFORE ADMISSION OF MEMBERS

Before any members have been admitted to the corporation, any amendment of the Articles of Incorporation may be adopted by approval of the Board of Directors.

SECTION 2. AMENDMENT OF ARTICLES AFTER ADMISSION OF MEMBERS

After members, if any, have been admitted to the corporation, amendment of the Articles of Incorporation may be adopted by the approval of the Board of Directors and by the approval of the members of this corporation.

SECTION 3. CERTAIN AMENDMENTS

Notwithstanding the above Sections of this Article, this corporation shall not amend its Articles of Incorporation to alter any statement which appears in the original Articles of Incorporation of the names and addresses of the first directors of this corporation, nor the name and address of its initial agent, except to correct an error in such statement or to delete such statement after the corporation has filed a "Statement by a Domestic Non-Profit Corporation" pursuant to Section 6210 of the California Nonprofit Corporation Law.

ARTICLE 11
PROHIBITION AGAINST SHARING CORPORATE PROFITS AND ASSETS

SECTION 1. PROHIBITION AGAINST SHARING CORPORATE PROFITS AND ASSETS

No member, director, officer, employee, or other person connected with this corporation, or any private individual, shall receive at any time any of the net earnings or pecuniary profit from the operations of the corporation, provided, however, that this provision shall not prevent payment to any such person of reasonable compensation for services performed for the corporation in effecting any of its public or charitable purposes, provided that such compensation is otherwise permitted by these Bylaws and is fixed by resolution of the Board of Directors; and no such person or persons shall be entitled to share in the distribution of, and shall not receive, any of the corporate assets on dissolution of the corporation. All members, if any, of the corporation shall be deemed to have expressly consented and agreed that on such dissolution or winding up of the affairs of the corporation, whether voluntarily or involuntarily, the assets of the corporation, after all debts have been satisfied, shall be distributed as required by the Articles of Incorporation of this corporation and not otherwise.

ARTICLE 12

MEMBERS

SECTION 1. DETERMINATION OF MEMBERS

If this corporation makes no provision for members, then, pursuant to Section 5310(b) of the Nonprofit Public Benefit Corporation Law of the State of California, any action which would otherwise, under law or the provisions of the Articles of Incorporation or Bylaws of this corporation, require approval by a majority of all members or approval by the members, shall only require the approval of the Board of Directors.

WRITTEN CONSENT OF DIRECTORS ADOPTING BYLAWS

We, the undersigned, are all of the persons named as the initial directors in the Articles of Incorporation of _____,
a California nonprofit corporation, and, pursuant to the authority granted to the directors by these Bylaws to take action by unanimous written consent without a meeting, consent to, and hereby do, adopt the foregoing Bylaws, consisting of _____ pages, as the Bylaws of this corporation.

Dated: _____

_____
, Director

_____
, Director

_____
, Director

_____
, Director

_____
, Director

CERTIFICATE

This is to certify that the foregoing is a true and correct copy of the Bylaws of the corporation named in the title thereto and that such Bylaws were duly adopted by the Board of Directors of said corporation

Dated: _____

_____
, Secretary

_____

A CALIFORNIA PUBLIC BENEFIT CORPORATION

ARTICLE 12
MEMBERS

SECTION 1. DETERMINATION AND RIGHTS OF MEMBERS

The corporation shall have only one class of members. No member shall hold more than one membership in the corporation. Except as expressly provided in or authorized by the Articles of Incorporation or Bylaws of this corporation, all memberships shall have the same rights, privileges, restrictions and conditions.

SECTION 2. QUALIFICATIONS OF MEMBERS

The qualifications for membership in this corporation are as follows: _____

_____

SECTION 3. ADMISSION OF MEMBERS

Applicants shall be admitted to membership _____

_____
_____
_____

SECTION 4. FEES, DUES AND ASSESSMENTS

(a) The following fee shall be charged for making application for membership in the corporation:

_____
_____
_____.

(b) The annual dues payable to the corporation by members shall be _____

_____
_____.

(c) Memberships shall be nonassessable.

SECTION 5. NUMBER OF MEMBERS

There is no limit on the number of members the corporation may admit.

SECTION 6. MEMBERSHIP BOOK

The corporation shall keep a membership book containing the name and address of each member. Termination of the membership of any member shall be recorded in the book, together with the date of termination of such membership. Such book shall be kept at the corporation's principal office and shall be available for inspection by any director or member of the corporation during regular business hours.

The record of names and addresses of the members of this corporation shall constitute the membership list of this corporation and shall not be used, in whole or part, by any person for any purpose not reasonably related to a member's interest as a member.

SECTION 7. NONLIABILITY OF MEMBERS

A member of this corporation is not, as such, personally liable for the debts, liabilities, or obligations of the corporation.

SECTION 8. NONTRANSFERABILITY OF MEMBERSHIPS

No member may transfer a membership or any right arising therefrom. All rights of membership cease upon the member's death.

SECTION 9. TERMINATION OF MEMBERSHIP

(a) Grounds for Termination. The membership of a member shall terminate upon the occurrence of any of the following events:

(1) Upon his or her notice of such termination delivered to the President of Secretary of the corporation personally or by mail, such membership to terminate upon the date of delivery of the notice or date of deposit in the mail.

(2) Upon a determination by the Board of Directors that the member has engaged in conduct materially and seriously prejudicial to the interests or purposes of the corporation.

(3) If this corporation has provided for the payment of dues by members, upon a failure to renew his or her membership by paying dues on or before their due date, such termination to be effective thirty (30) days after a written notification of delinquency is given personally or mailed to such member by the Secretary of the corporation. A member may avoid such termination by paying the amount of delinquent dues within a thirty (30)-day period following the member's receipt of the written notification of delinquency.

(b) Procedure for Expulsion. Following the determination that a member should be expelled under subparagraph (a)(2) of this section, the following procedure shall be implemented:

(1) A notice shall be sent by first-class or registered mail to the last address of the member as shown on the corporation's records, setting forth the expulsion and the reasons therefor. Such notice shall be sent at least fifteen (15) days before the proposed effective date of the expulsion.

(2) The member being expelled shall be given an opportunity to be heard, either orally or in writing, at a hearing to be held not less than five (5) days before the effective date of the proposed expulsion. The hearing will be held by the Board of Directors in accordance with the quorum and voting rules set forth in these Bylaws applicable to the meetings of the Board. The notice to the member of his or her proposed expulsion shall state the date, time, and place of the hearing on his or her proposed expulsion.

(3) Following the hearing, the Board of Directors shall decide whether or not the member should in fact be expelled, suspended, or sanctioned in some other way. The decision of the Board shall be final.

(4) If this corporation has provided for the payment of dues by members, any person expelled from the corporation shall receive a refund of dues already paid. The refund shall be pro-rated to return only the unaccrued balance remaining for the period of the dues payment.

SECTION 10. RIGHTS ON TERMINATION OF MEMBERSHIP

All rights of a member in the corporation shall cease on termination of membership as herein provided.

SECTION 11. AMENDMENTS RESULTING IN THE TERMINATION OF MEMBERSHIPS

Notwithstanding any other provision of these Bylaws, if any amendment of the Articles of Incorporation or of the Bylaws of this corporation would result in the termination of all memberships or any class of memberships, then such amendment or amendments shall be effected only in accordance with the provisions of Section 5342 of the California Nonprofit Public Benefit Corporation Law.

ARTICLE 13
MEETINGS OF MEMBERS

SECTION 1. PLACE OF MEETINGS

Meetings of members shall be held at the principal office of the corporation or at such other place or places within or without the State of California as may be designated from time to time by resolution of the Board of Directors.

SECTION 2. ANNUAL AND OTHER REGULAR MEETINGS

The members shall meet annually on _____
_____ in each year, at _____ _M, for the purpose of electing directors and transacting other business as may come before the meeting. Cumulative voting for the election of directors shall not be permitted. The candidates receiving the highest number of votes up to the number of directors to be elected shall be elected. Each voting member shall cast one vote, with voting being by ballot only. The annual meeting of members for the purpose of electing directors shall be deemed a regular meeting and any reference in these Bylaws to regular meetings of members refers to this annual meeting.

Other regular meetings of the members shall be held on _____, at _____ M.

If the day fixed for the annual meeting or other regular meetings falls on a legal holiday, such meeting shall be held at the same hour and place on the next business day.

SECTION 3. SPECIAL MEETINGS OF MEMBERS

(a) Persons Who May Call Special Meetings of Members. Special meetings of the members shall be called by the Board of Directors, the Chairperson of the Board, or the President of the corporation. In addition, special meetings of the members for any lawful purpose may be called by five percent (5%) or more of the members.

SECTION 4. NOTICE OF MEETINGS

(a) Time of Notice. Whenever members are required or permitted to take action at a meeting, a written notice of the meeting shall be given by the Secretary of the corporation not less than ten (10) nor more than ninety (90) days before the date of the meeting to each member who, on the record date for the notice of the meeting, is entitled to vote thereat, provided, however, that if notice is given by mail, and the notice is not mailed by first-class, registered, or certified mail, that notice shall be given twenty (20) days before the meeting.

(b) Manner of Giving Notice. Notice of a members' meeting or any report shall be given either personally or by mail or other means of written communication, addressed to the member at the address of such member appearing on the books of the corporation or given by the member to the corporation for the purpose of notice; or if no address appears or is given, at the place where the principal office of the corporation is located or by publication of notice of the meeting at least once in a newspaper of general circulation in the county in which the principal office is located. Notice shall be deemed to have been given at the time when delivered personally or deposited in the mail or sent by telegram or other means of written communication.

(c) Contents of Notice. Notice of a membership meeting shall state the place, date, and time of the meeting and (1) in the case of a special meeting, the general nature of the business to be transacted, and no other business may be transacted, or (2) in the case of a regular meeting, those matters which the Board, at the time notice is given, intends to present for action by the members. Subject to any provision to the contrary contained in these Bylaws, however, any proper matter may be presented at a regular meeting for such action. The notice of any meeting of members at which directors are to be elected shall include the names of all those who are nominees at the time notice is given to members.

(d) Notice of Meetings Called by Members. If a special meeting is called by members as authorized by these Bylaws, the request for the meeting shall be submitted in writing, specifying the general nature of the business proposed to be transacted and shall be delivered personally or sent by registered mail or by telegraph to the Chairperson of the Board, President, Vice President or Secretary of the corporation. The officer receiving the request shall promptly cause notice to be given to the members entitled to vote that a meeting will be held, stating the date of the meeting. The date for such meeting shall be fixed by the Board and shall not be less than thirty-five (35) nor more than ninety (90) days after the receipt of the request for the meeting by the officer. If the notice is not given within twenty (20) days after the receipt of the request, persons calling the meeting may give the notice themselves.

(e) Waiver of Notice of Meetings. The transactions of any meeting of members, however called and noticed, and wherever held, shall be as valid as though taken at a meeting duly held after regular call and notice, if a quorum is present either in person or by proxy, and if, either before or after the meeting, each of the persons entitled to vote, not present in person or by proxy, signs a written waiver of notice or a consent to the holding of the meeting or an approval of the minutes thereof. All such waivers, consents and approvals shall be filed with the corporate records or made a part of the minutes of the meeting. Waiver of notices or consents need not specify either the business to be transacted or the purpose of any regular or special meeting of members, except that if action is taken or proposed to be taken for approval of any of the matters specified in subparagraph (f) of this section, the waiver of notice or consent shall state the general nature of the proposal.

(f) Special Notice Rules for Approving Certain Proposals. If action is proposed to be taken or is taken with respect to the following proposals, such action shall be invalid unless unanimously approved by those entitled to vote or unless the general nature of the proposal is stated in the notice of meeting or in any written waiver of notice:

1. Removal of directors without cause;

2. Filling of vacancies on the Board by members;

3. Amending the Articles of Incorporation; and

4. An election to voluntarily wind up and dissolve the corporation.

SECTION 5. QUORUM FOR MEETINGS

A quorum shall consist of _____ of the voting members of the corporation.

The members present at a duly called and held meeting at which a quorum is initially present may continue to do business notwithstanding the loss of a quorum at the meeting due to a withdrawal of members from the meeting provided that any action taken after the loss of a quorum must be approved by at least a majority of the members required to constitute a quorum.

In the absence of a quorum, any meeting of the members may be adjourned from time to time by the vote of a majority of the votes represented in person or by proxy at the meeting, but no other business shall be transacted at such meeting.

When a meeting is adjourned for lack of a sufficient number of members at the meeting or otherwise, it shall not be necessary to give any notice of the time and place of the adjourned meeting or of the business to be transacted at such meeting other than by announcement at the meeting at which the adjournment is taken of the time and place of the adjourned meeting. However, if after the adjournment a new record date is fixed for notice or voting, a notice of the adjourned meeting shall be given to each member who, on the record date for notice of the meeting, is entitled to vote at the meeting. A meeting shall not be adjourned for more than forty-five (45) days.

Notwithstanding any other provision of this Article, if this corporation authorizes members to conduct a meeting with a quorum of less than one-third (1/3) of the voting power, then, if less than one-third (1/3) of the voting power actually attends a regular meeting, in person or by proxy, then no action may be taken on a matter unless the general nature of the matter was stated in the notice of the regular meeting.

SECTION 6. MAJORITY ACTION AS MEMBERSHIP ACTION

Every act or decision done or made by a majority of voting members present in person or by proxy at a duly held meeting at which a quorum is present is the act of the members, unless the law, the Articles of Incorporation of this corporation, or these Bylaws require a greater number.

SECTION 7. VOTING RIGHTS

Each member is entitled to one vote on each matter submitted to a vote by the members. Voting at duly held meetings shall be by voice vote. Election of Directors, however, shall be by ballot.

SECTION 8. PROXY VOTING

Members entitled to vote _____ be permitted to vote or act by proxy. If membership voting by proxy is not allowed by the preceding sentence, no provision in this or other sections of these Bylaws referring to proxy voting shall be construed to permit any member to vote or act by proxy.

If membership voting by proxy is allowed, members entitled to vote shall have the right to vote either in person or by a written proxy executed by such person or by his or her duly authorized agent and filed with the Secretary of the corporation, provided, however, that no proxy shall be valid after eleven (11) months from the date of its execution unless otherwise provided in the proxy. In any case, however, the maximum term of any proxy shall be three (3) years from the date of its execution. No proxy shall be irrevocable and may be revoked following the procedures given in Section 5613 of the California Nonprofit Public Benefit Corporation Law.

If membership voting by proxy is allowed, all proxies shall state the general nature of the matter to be voted on and, in the case of a proxy given to vote for the election of directors, shall list those persons who were nominees at the time the notice of the vote for election of directors was given to the members. In any election of directors, any proxy which is marked by a member "withhold" or otherwise marked in a manner indicating that the authority to vote for the election of directors is withheld shall not be voted either for or against the election of a director.

If membership voting by proxy is allowed, proxies shall afford an opportunity for the member to specify a choice between approval and disapproval for each matter or group of related matters intended, at the time the proxy is distributed, to be acted upon at the meeting for which the proxy is solicited. The proxy shall also provide that when the person solicited specifies a choice with respect to any such matter, the vote shall be cast in accordance therewith.

SECTION 9. CONDUCT OF MEETINGS

Meetings of members shall be presided over by the Chairperson of the Board, or, if there is no Chairperson, by the President of the corporation or, in his or her absence, by the Vice President of the corporation or, in the absence of all of these persons, by a Chairperson chosen by a majority of the voting members, present in person or by proxy. The Secretary of the corporation shall act as Secretary of all meetings of members, provided that, in his or her absence, the presiding officer shall appoint another person to act as Secretary of the Meeting.

Meetings shall be governed by _____
_____, as such rules may be revised from time to time, insofar as such rules are not inconsistent with or in conflict with these Bylaws, with the Articles of Incorporation of this corporation, or with any provision of law.

SECTION 10. ACTION BY WRITTEN BALLOT WITHOUT A MEETING

Any action which may be taken at any regular or special meeting of members may be taken without a meeting if the corporation distributes a written ballot to each member entitled to vote on the matter. The ballot shall set forth the proposed action, provide an opportunity to specify approval or disapproval of each proposal, provide that where the person solicited specifies a choice with respect to any such proposal the vote shall be cast in accordance therewith, and provide a reasonable time within which to return the ballot to the corporation. Ballots shall be mailed or delivered in the manner required for giving notice of meetings specified in Section 4(b) of this Article.

All written ballots shall also indicate the number of responses needed to meet the quorum requirement and, except for ballots soliciting votes for the election of directors, shall state the percentage of approvals necessary to pass the measure submitted. The ballots must specify the time by which they must be received by the corporation in order to be counted.

Approval of action by written ballot shall be valid only when the number of votes cast by ballot within the time period specified equals or exceeds the quorum required to be present at a meeting authorizing the action, and the number of approvals equals or exceeds the number of votes that would be required to approve the action at a meeting at which the total number of votes cast was the same as the number of votes cast by ballot.

Directors may be elected by written ballot. Such ballots for the election of directors shall list the persons nominated at the time the ballots are mailed or delivered. If any such ballots are marked "withhold" or otherwise marked in a manner indicating that the authority to vote for the election of directors is withheld, they shall not be counted as votes either for or against the election of a director.

A written ballot may not be revoked after its receipt by the corporation or its deposit in the mail, whichever occurs first.

SECTION 11. REASONABLE NOMINATION AND ELECTION PROCEDURES

This corporation shall make available to members reasonable nomination and election procedures with respect to the election of directors by members. Such procedures shall be reasonable given the nature, size and operations of the corporation, and shall include:

    (a) A reasonable means of nominating persons for election as directors.

    (b) A reasonable opportunity for a nominee to communicate to the members the nominee's qualifications and the reasons for the nominee's candidacy.

    (c) A reasonable opportunity for all nominees to solicit votes.

    (d) A reasonable opportunity for all members to choose among the nominees.

Upon the written request by any nominee for election to the Board and the payment with such request of the reasonable costs of mailing (including postage), the corporation shall, within ten (10) business days after such request (provided payment has been made) mail to all members or such portion of them that the nominee may reasonably specify, any material which the nominee shall furnish and which is reasonably related to the election, unless the corporation within five (5) business days after the request allows the nominee, at the corporation's option, the right to do either of the following:

    1. inspect and copy the record of all members' names, addresses and voting rights, at reasonable times, upon five (5) business days' prior written demand upon the corporation, which demand shall state the purpose for which the inspection rights are requested; or

    2. obtain from the Secretary, upon written demand and payment of a reasonable charge, a list of the names, addresses and voting rights of those members entitled to vote for the election of directors, as of the most recent record date for which it has been compiled or as of any date specified by the nominee subsequent to the date of demand.

The demand shall state the purpose for which the list is requested and the membership list shall be made available on or before the later of ten (10) business days after the demand is received or after the date specified therein as the date as of which the list is to be compiled.

If the corporation distributes any written election material soliciting votes for any nominee for director at the corporation's expense, it shall make available, at the corporation's expense, to each other nominee, in or with the same material, the same amount of space that is provided any other nominee, with equal prominence, to be used by the nominee for a purpose reasonably related to the election.

Generally, any person who is qualified to be elected to the Board of Directors shall be nominated at the annual meeting of members held for the purpose of electing directors by any member present at the meeting in person or by proxy. However, if the corporation has five hundred (500) or more members, any of the additional nomination procedures specified in subsections (a) and (b) of Section 5221 of the California Nonprofit Public Benefit Corporation Law may be used to nominate persons for election to the Board of Directors.

If this corporation has five thousand (5,000) or more members, then the nomination and election procedures specified in Section 5522 of the California Nonprofit Corporation Law shall be followed by this corporation in nominating and electing persons to the Board of Directors.

SECTION 12. ACTION BY UNANIMOUS WRITTEN CONSENT WITHOUT MEETING

Except as otherwise provided in these Bylaws, any action required or permitted to be taken by the members may be taken without a meeting, if all members shall individually or collectively consent in writing to the action. The written consent or consents shall be filed with the minutes of the proceedings of the members. The action by written consent shall have the same force and effect as the unanimous vote of the members.

SECTION 13. RECORD DATE FOR MEETINGS

The record date for purposes of determining the members entitled to notice, voting rights, written ballot rights, or any other right with respect to a meeting of members or any other lawful membership action, shall be fixed pursuant to Section 5611 of the California Nonprofit Public Benefit Corporation Law.

WRITTEN CONSENT OF DIRECTORS ADOPTING BYLAWS

We, the undersigned, are all of the persons named as the initial directors in the Articles of Incorporation of _____

_____, a California nonprofit corporation, and, pursuant to the authority granted to the directors by these Bylaws to take action by unanimous written consent without a meeting, consent to, and hereby do, adopt the foregoing Bylaws, consisting of _____ pages, as the Bylaws of this corporation.

Dated: _____

_____

, Director

_____

, Director

_____

, Director

_____

, Director

_____

, Director

CERTIFICATE

This is to certify that the foregoing is a true and correct copy of the Bylaws of the corporation named in the title thereto and that such Bylaws were duly adopted by the Board of Directors of said corporation

Dated: _____

_____

, Secretary

BYLAWS

OF

_____

A CALIFORNIA RELIGIOUS CORPORATION

ARTICLE 1
OFFICES

SECTION 1. PRINCIPAL OFFICE

The principal office of the corporation for the transaction of its business is located in
_____County, California.

SECTION 2. CHANGE OF ADDRESS

The county of the corporation's principal office can be changed only by amendment of these Bylaws and not otherwise. The Board of Directors may, however, change the principal office from one location to another within the named county by noting the changed address and effective date below, and such changes of address shall not be deemed an amendment of these Bylaws:

_____	Dated: _____, 19__
_____	Dated: _____, 19__
_____	Dated: _____, 19__

SECTION 3. OTHER OFFICES

The corporation may also have offices at such other places, within or without the State of California, where it is qualified to do business, as its business may require and as the Board of Directors may, from time to time, designate.

ARTICLE 2
PURPOSES

SECTION 1. OBJECTIVES AND PURPOSES

The primary objectives and purposes of this corporation shall be:

ARTICLE 3
DIRECTORS

SECTION 1. NUMBER

The corporation shall have _____ directors and collectively they shall be known as the Board of Directors. The number may be changed by amendment of this Bylaw, or by repeal of this Bylaw and adoption of a new Bylaw, as provided in these Bylaws.

SECTION 2. POWERS

Subject to the provisions of the California Nonprofit Religious Corporation law and any limitations in the Articles of Incorporation and Bylaws relating to action required or permitted to be taken or approved by the members, if any, of this corporation, the activities and affairs of this corporation shall be conducted and all corporate powers shall be exercised by or under the direction of the Board of Directors.

SECTION 3. DUTIES

It shall be the duty of the directors to:

(a) Perform any and all duties imposed on them collectively or individually by law, by the Articles of Incorporation of this corporation, or by these Bylaws;

(b) Appoint and remove, employ and discharge, and, except as otherwise provided in these Bylaws, prescribe the duties and fix the compensation, if any, of all officers, agents and employees of the corporation;

(c) Supervise all officers, agents and employees of the corporation to assure that their duties are performed properly;

(d) Meet at such times and places as required by these Bylaws;

(e) Register their addresses with the Secretary of the corporation and notices of meetings mailed or telegraphed to them at such addresses shall be valid notices thereof.

SECTION 4. TERMS OF OFFICE

Each director shall hold office until the next annual meeting for election of the Board of Directors as specified in these Bylaws, and until his or her successor is elected and qualifies.

SECTION 5. COMPENSATION

Directors shall serve without compensation except that they shall be allowed and paid

_____

_____. In addition, they shall be allowed reasonable advancement or reimbursement of expenses incurred in the performance of their regular duties as specified in Section 3 of this Article.

SECTION 6. PLACE OF MEETINGS

Meetings shall be held at the principal office of the corporation unless otherwise provided by the Board or at such place within or without the State of California which has been designated from time to time by resolution of the Board of Directors. In the absence of such designation, any meeting not held at the principal office of the corporation shall be valid only if held on the written consent of all directors given either before or after the meeting and filed with the Secretary of the corporation or after all Board members have been given written notice of the meeting as hereinafter provided for special meetings of the Board. Any meeting, regular or special, may be held by conference telephone or similar communications equipment, so as long as all directors participating in such meeting can hear one another.

SECTION 7. REGULAR AND ANNUAL MEETINGS

Regular meetings of Directors shall be held on _____
_____ at _____ _M, unless such day falls on a legal

holiday, in which event the regular meeting shall be held at the same hour and place on the next business day.

If this corporation makes no provision for members, then, at the annual meeting of directors held on _____, directors shall be elected by the Board of Directors in accordance with this section. Cumulative voting by directors for the election of directors shall not be permitted. The candidates receiving the highest number of votes up to the number of directors to be elected shall be elected. Each director shall cast one vote, with voting being by ballot only.

SECTION 8. SPECIAL MEETINGS

Special meetings of the Board of Directors may be called by the Chairperson of the Board, the President, the Vice President, the Secretary, or by any two directors, and such meetings shall be held at the place, within or without the State of California, designated by the person or persons calling the meeting, and in the absence of such designation, at the principal office of the corporation.

SECTION 9. NOTICE OF MEETINGS

Regular meetings of the Board may be held without notice. Special meetings of the Board shall be held upon four (4) days' notice by first-class mail or forty-eight (48) hours' notice delivered personally or by telephone or telegraph. If sent by mail or telegraph, the notice shall be deemed to be delivered on its deposit in the mails or on its delivery to the telegraph company. Such notices shall be addressed to each director at his or her address as shown on the books of the corporation. Notice of the time and place of holding an adjourned meeting need not be given to absent directors if the time and place of the adjourned meeting are fixed at the meeting adjourned and if such adjourned meeting is held no more than twenty-four (24) hours from the time of the original meeting. Notice shall be given of any adjourned regular or special meeting to directors absent from the original meeting if the adjourned meeting is held more than twenty-four (24) hours from the time of the original meeting.

SECTION 10. CONTENTS OF NOTICE

Notice of meetings not herein dispensed with shall specify the place, day and hour of the meeting. The purpose of any Board meeting need not be specified in the notice.

SECTION 11. WAIVER OF NOTICE AND CONSENT TO HOLDING MEETINGS

The transactions of any meeting of the Board, however called and noticed or wherever held, are as valid as though the meeting had been duly held after proper call and notice, provided a quorum, as hereinafter defined, is present and provided that either before or after the meeting each director not present signs a waiver of notice, a consent to holding the meeting, or an approval of the minutes thereof. All such waivers, consents, or approvals shall be filed with the corporate records or made a part of the minutes of the meeting.

SECTION 12. QUORUM FOR MEETINGS

A quorum shall consist of _____ Directors.

Except as otherwise provided in these Bylaws or in the Articles of Incorporation of this corporation, or by law, no business shall be considered by the Board at any meeting at which a quorum, as hereinafter defined, is not present, and the only motion which the Chair shall entertain at such meeting is a motion to adjourn. However, a majority of the directors present at such meeting may adjourn from time to time until the time fixed for the next regular meeting of the Board.

When a meeting is adjourned for lack of a quorum, it shall not be necessary to give any notice of the time and place of the adjourned meeting or of the business to be transacted at such meeting, other than by announcement at the meeting at which the adjournment is taken, except as provided in Section 9 of this Article.

The directors present at a duly called and held meeting at which a quorum is initially present may continue to do business notwithstanding the loss of a quorum at the meeting due to a withdrawal of directors from the meeting, provided that any action thereafter taken must be approved by at least a majority of the required quorum for such meeting or such greater percentage as may be required by law, or the Articles of Incorporation or Bylaws of this corporation.

SECTION 13. MAJORITY ACTION AS BOARD ACTION

Every act or decision done or made by a majority of the directors present at a meeting duly held at which a quorum is present is the act of the Board of Directors, unless the Articles of Incorporation or Bylaws of this corporation, or provisions of the California Nonprofit Religious Corporation Law, particularly those provisions relating to appointment of committees (Section 9212), approval of contracts or transactions in which a director has a material financial interest (Section 9243) and indemnification of directors (Section 9246e), require a greater percentage or different voting rules for approval of a matter by the Board.

SECTION 14. CONDUCT OF MEETINGS

Meetings of the Board of Directors shall be presided over by the Chairperson of the Board, or, if no such person has been so designated or, in his or her absence, the President of the corporation or, in his or her absence, by the Vice President of the corporation or, in the absence of each of these persons, by a Chairperson chosen by a majority of the directors present at the meeting. The Secretary of the corporation shall act as secretary of all meetings of the Board, provided that, in his or her absence, the presiding officer shall appoint another person to act as Secretary of the Meeting.

Meetings shall be governed by

_____

_____, as such rules may be revised from time to time, insofar as such rules are not inconsistent with or in conflict with these Bylaws, with the Articles of Incorporation of this corporation, or with provisions of law.

SECTION 15. ACTION BY UNANIMOUS WRITTEN CONSENT WITHOUT MEETING

Any action required or permitted to be taken by the Board of Directors under any provision of law may be taken without a meeting, if all members of the Board shall individually or collectively consent in writing to such action. Such written consent or consents shall be filed with the minutes of the proceedings of the Board. Such action by written consent shall have the same force and effect as the unanimous vote of the directors. Any certificate or other document filed under any provision of law which relates to action so taken shall state that the action was taken by unanimous written consent of the Board of Directors without a meeting and that the Bylaws of this corporation authorize the directors to so act, and such statement shall be prima facie evidence of such authority.

SECTION 16. VACANCIES

Vacancies on the Board of Directors shall exist (1) on the death, resignation or removal of any director, and (2) whenever the number of authorized directors is increased.

The Board of Directors may declare vacant the office of a director who has been declared of unsound mind by a final order of court, or convicted of a felony, or has been removed from office by order of the Superior Court for engaging in fraudulent acts pursuant to Section 9223 of the California Nonprofit Religious Corporation Law.

If this corporation has any members, directors may be removed without cause if such removal is approved by the members.

Any director may resign effective upon giving written notice to the Chairperson of the Board, the President, the Secretary, or the Board of Directors, unless the notice specifies a later time for the effectiveness of such resignation. No director may resign if the corporation would then be left without a duly elected director or directors in charge of its affairs.

Except for a vacancy created by the removal of a director by the members, if any, of this corporation, vacancies on the Board may be filled by approval of the Board or, if the number of directors then in office is less than a quorum, by (1) the unanimous written consent of the directors then in office, (2) the affirmative vote of a majority of the directors then in office at a meeting held pursuant to notice or waiver of notice complying with this Article of these Bylaws, or (3) a sole remaining director. The members, if any, of this corporation may elect a director at any time to fill any vacancy not filled by the directors.

A person elected to fill a vacancy as provided by this section shall hold office until the next annual election of the Board of Directors or until his or her death, resignation or removal from office.

SECTION 17. NON-LIABILITY OF DIRECTORS

The directors shall not be personally liable for the debts, liabilities, or other obligations of the corporation.

SECTION 18. INDEMNIFICATION BY CORPORATION OF DIRECTORS, OFFICERS, EMPLOYEES AND OTHER AGENTS

To the extent that a person who is, or was, a director, officer, employee or other agent of this corporation has been successful on the merits in defense of any civil, criminal, administrative or investigative proceeding brought to procure a judgment against such person by reason of the fact that he or she is, or was, an agent of the corporation, or has been successful in defense of any claim, issue or matter, therein, such person shall be indemnified against expenses actually and reasonably incurred by the person in connection with such proceeding.

If such person either settles any such claim or sustains a judgment against him or her, then indemnification against expenses, judgments, fines, settlements and other amounts reasonably incurred in connection with such proceedings shall be provided by this corporation but only to the extent allowed by, and in accordance with the requirements of, Section 9246 of the California Nonprofit Religious Corporation Law.

SECTION 19. INSURANCE FOR CORPORATE AGENTS

The Board of Directors may adopt a resolution authorizing the purchase and maintenance of insurance on behalf of any agent of the corporation (including a director, officer, employee or other agent of the corporation) against any liability other than for violating provisions of law relating to self-dealing (Section 9243 of the California Nonprofit Religious Corporation Law) asserted against or incurred by the agent in such capacity or arising out of the agent's status as such, whether or not the corporation would have the power to indemnify the agent against such liability under the provisions of Section 9246 of the California Nonprofit Religious Corporation Law.

ARTICLE 4
OFFICERS

SECTION 1. NUMBER OF OFFICERS

The officers of the corporation shall be a President, a Secretary, and a Chief Financial Officer who shall be designated the Treasurer. The corporation may also have, as determined by the Board of Directors, a Chairperson of the Board, one or more Vice Presidents, Assistant Secretaries, Assistant Treasurers, or other officers. Any number of offices may be held by the same person except that neither the Secretary nor the Treasurer may serve as the President or Chairperson of the Board.

SECTION 2. QUALIFICATION, ELECTION, AND TERM OF OFFICE

Any person may serve as officer of this corporation. Officers shall be elected by the Board of Directors, at any time, and each officer shall hold office until he or she resigns or is removed or is otherwise disqualified to serve, or until his or her successor shall be elected and qualified, whichever occurs first.

SECTION 3. SUBORDINATE OFFICERS

The Board of Directors may appoint such other officers or agents as it may deem desirable, and such officers shall serve such terms, have such authority, and perform such duties as may be prescribed from time to time by the Board of Directors.

SECTION 4. REMOVAL AND RESIGNATION

Any officer may be removed, either with or without cause, by the Board of Directors, at any time. Any officer may resign at any time by giving written notice to the Board of Directors or to the President or Secretary of the corporation. Any such resignation shall take effect at the date of receipt of such notice or at any later date specified therein, and, unless otherwise specified therein, the acceptance of such resignation shall not be necessary to make it effective. The above provisions of this section shall be superseded by any conflicting terms of a contract which has been approved or ratified by the Board of Directors relating to the employment of any officer of the corporation.

SECTION 5. VACANCIES

Any vacancy caused by the death, resignation, removal, disqualification, or otherwise, of any officer shall be filled by the Board of Directors. In the event of a vacancy in any office other than that of President, such vacancy may be filled temporarily by appointment by the President until such time as the Board shall fill the vacancy. Vacancies occurring in offices of officers appointed at the discretion of the Board may or may not be filled as the Board shall determine.

SECTION 6. DUTIES OF PRESIDENT

The President shall be the chief executive officer of the corporation and shall, subject to the control of the Board of Directors, supervise and control the affairs of the corporation and the activities of the officers. He or she shall perform all duties incident to his or her office and such other duties as may be required by law, by the Articles of Incorporation of this corporation, or by these Bylaws, or which may be prescribed from time to time by the Board of Directors. Unless another person is specifically appointed as Chairperson of the Board of Directors, he or she shall preside at all meetings of the Board of Directors. If applicable, the President shall preside at all meetings of the members. Except as otherwise expressly provided by law, by the Articles of Incorporation, or by these Bylaws, he or she shall, in the name of the corporation, execute such deeds, mortgages, bonds, contracts, checks, or other instruments which may from time to time be authorized by the Board of Directors.

SECTION 7. DUTIES OF VICE PRESIDENT

In the absence of the President, or in the event of his or her inability or refusal to act, the Vice President shall perform all the duties of the President, and when so acting shall have all the powers of, and be subject to all the restrictions on, the President. The Vice President shall have other powers and perform such other duties as may be prescribed by law, by the Articles of Incorporation, or by these Bylaws, or as may be prescribed by the Board of Directors.

SECTION 8. DUTIES OF SECRETARY

The Secretary shall:

Certify and keep at the principal office of the corporation the original, or a copy of these Bylaws as amended or otherwise altered to date.

Keep at the principal office of the corporation or at such other place as the Board may determine, a book of minutes of all meetings of the directors, and, if applicable, meetings of committees of directors and of members, recording therein the time and place of holding, whether regular or special, how called, how notice thereof was given, the names of those present or represented at the meeting, and the proceedings thereof.

See that all notices are duly given in accordance with the provisions of these Bylaws or as required by law.

Be custodian of the records and of the seal of the corporation and see that the seal is affixed to all duly executed documents, the execution of which on behalf of the corporation under its seal is authorized by law or these Bylaws.

Keep at the principal office of the corporation a membership book containing the name and address of each and any members, and, in the case where any membership has been terminated, he or she shall record such fact in the membership book together with the date on which such membership ceased.

Exhibit at all reasonable times to any director of the corporation, or to his or her agent or attorney, on request therefor, the Bylaws, the membership book, and the minutes of the proceedings of the directors of the corporation.

In general, perform all duties incident to the office of Secretary and such other duties as may be required by law, by the Articles of Incorporation of this corporation, or by these Bylaws, or which may be assigned to him or her from time to time by the Board of Directors.

SECTION 9. DUTIES OF TREASURER

Subject to the provisions of these Bylaws relating to the "Execution of Instruments, Deposits and Funds," the Treasurer shall:

Have charge and custody of, and be responsible for, all funds and securities of the corporation, and deposit all such funds in the name of the corporation in such banks, trust companies, or other depositories as shall be selected by the Board of Directors.

Receive, and give receipt for, monies due and payable to the corporation from any source whatsoever.

Disburse, or cause to be disbursed, the funds of the corporation as may be directed by the Board of Directors, taking proper vouchers for such disbursements.

Keep and maintain adequate and correct accounts of the corporation's properties and business transactions, including accounts of its assets, liabilities, receipts, disbursements, gains and losses.

Exhibit at all reasonable times the books of account and financial records to any director of the corporation, or to his or her agent or attorney, on request therefor.

Render to the President and directors, whenever requested, an account of any or all of his or her transactions as Treasurer and of the financial condition of the corporation.

Prepare, or cause to be prepared, and certify, or cause to be certified, the financial statements to be included in any required reports.

In general, perform all duties incident to the office of Treasurer and such other duties as may be required by law, by the Articles of Incorporation of the corporation, or by these Bylaws, or which may be assigned to him or her from time to time by the Board of Directors.

SECTION 10. COMPENSATION

The salaries of the officers, if any, shall be fixed from time to time by resolution of the Board of Directors, and no officer shall be prevented from receiving such salary by reason of the fact that he or she is also a director of the corporation. In all cases, any salaries received by officers of this corporation shall be reasonable and given in return for services actually rendered the corporation which relate to the performance of the religious purposes of this corporation.

ARTICLE 5
COMMITTEES

SECTION 1. EXECUTIVE COMMITTEE

The Board of Directors may, by a majority vote of directors, designate two (2) or more of its members (who may also be serving as officers of this corporation) to constitute an Executive Committee and delegate to such Committee any of the powers and authority of the Board in the management of the business and affairs of the corporation, except with respect to:

(a) The approval of any action which, under law or the provisions of these Bylaws, requires the approval of the members or of a majority of all of the members.

(b) The filling of vacancies on the Board or on any committee which has the authority of the Board.

(c) The fixing of compensation of the directors for serving on the Board or on any committee.

(d) The amendment or repeal of Bylaws or the adoption of new Bylaws.

(e) The amendment or repeal or any resolution of the Board which by its express terms is not so amendable or repealable.

(f) The appointment of committees of the Board or the members thereof.

By a majority vote of its members then in office, the Board may at any time revoke or modify any or all of the authority so delegated, increase or decrease but not below two (2) the number of its members, and fill vacancies therein from the members of the Board. The Committee shall keep regular minutes of its proceedings, cause them to be filed with the corporate records, and report the same to the Board from time to time as the Board may require.

SECTION 2. OTHER COMMITTEES

The corporation shall have such other committees as may from time to time be designated by resolution of the Board of Directors. Such other committees may consist of persons who are not also members of the Board. These additional committees shall act in an advisory capacity only to the Board and shall be clearly titled as "advisory" committees.

SECTION 3. MEETINGS AND ACTION OF COMMITTEES

Meetings and action of committees shall be governed by, noticed, held and taken in accordance with the provisions of these Bylaws concerning meetings of the Board of Directors, with such changes in the context of such Bylaw provisions as are necessary to substitute the committee and its members for the Board of Directors and its members, except that the time for regular meetings of committees may be fixed by resolution of the Board of Directors or by the committee. The time for special meetings of committees may also be fixed by the Board of Directors. The Board of Directors may also adopt rules and regulations pertaining to the conduct of meetings of committees to the extent that such rules and regulations are not inconsistent with the provisions of these Bylaws.

ARTICLE 6
EXECUTION OF INSTRUMENTS, DEPOSITS AND FUNDS

SECTION 1. EXECUTION OF INSTRUMENTS

The Board of Directors, except as otherwise provided in these Bylaws, may by resolution authorize any officer or agent of the corporation to enter into any contract or execute and deliver any instrument in the name of and on behalf of the corporation, and such authority may be general or confined to specific instances. Unless so authorized, no officer, agent, or employee shall have any power or authority to bind the corporation by any contract or engagement or to pledge its credit or to render it liable monetarily for any purpose or in any amount.

SECTION 2. CHECKS AND NOTES

Except as otherwise specifically determined by resolution of the Board of Directors, or as otherwise required by law, checks, drafts, promissory notes, orders for the payment of money, and other evidence of indebtedness of the corporation shall be signed by the Treasurer and countersigned by the President of the corporation.

SECTION 3. DEPOSITS

All funds of the corporation shall be deposited from time to time to the credit of the corporation in such banks, trust companies, or other depositories as the Board of Directors may select.

SECTION 4. GIFTS

The Board of Directors may accept on behalf of the corporation any contribution, gift, bequest, or devise for the religious purposes of this corporation.

ARTICLE 7
CORPORATE RECORDS, REPORTS AND SEAL

SECTION 1. MAINTENANCE OF CORPORATE RECORDS

The corporation shall keep at its principal office in the State of California:

(a) Minutes of all meetings of directors, committees of the Board and, if this corporation has members, of all meetings of members, indicating the time and place of holding such meetings, whether regular or special, how called, the notice given, and the names of those present and the proceedings thereof;

(b) Adequate and correct books and records of account, including accounts of its properties and business transactions and accounts of its assets, liabilities, receipts, disbursements, gains and losses;

(c) A record of its members, if any, indicating their names and addresses and, if applicable, the class of membership held by each member and the termination date of any membership;

(d) A copy of the corporation's Articles of Incorporation and Bylaws as amended to date, which shall be open to inspection by the members, if any, of the corporation at all reasonable times during office hours.

SECTION 2. CORPORATE SEAL

The Board of Directors may adopt, use, and at will alter, a corporate seal. Such seal shall be kept at the principal office of the corporation. Failure to affix the seal to corporate instruments, however, shall not affect the validity of any such instrument.

SECTION 3. DIRECTORS' INSPECTION RIGHTS

Every director shall have the absolute right at any reasonable time to inspect and copy all books, records and documents of every kind and to inspect the physical properties of the corporation.

SECTION 4. MEMBERS' INSPECTION RIGHTS

If this corporation has any members, then each and every member shall have the following inspection rights, for a purpose reasonably related to such person's interest as a member:

(a) To inspect and copy the record of all members' names, addresses and voting rights, at reasonable times, upon five (5) business days' prior written demand on the corporation, which demand shall state the purpose for which the inspection rights are requested.

(b) To inspect at any reasonable time the books, records, or minutes of proceedings of the members or of the Board or committees of the Board, upon written demand on the corporation by the member, for a purpose reasonably related to such person's interests as a member.

SECTION 5. RIGHT TO COPY AND MAKE EXTRACTS

Any inspection under the provisions of this Article may be made in person or by agent or attorney and the right to inspection includes the right to copy and make extracts.

ARTICLE 8
FISCAL YEAR

SECTION 1. FISCAL YEAR OF THE CORPORATION

The fiscal year of the corporation shall begin on the _____
_____ and end on the _____
_____ in each year.

ARTICLE 9

AMENDMENT OF BYLAWS

SECTION 1. AMENDMENT

Subject to any provision of law applicable to the amendment of Bylaws of religious nonprofit corporations, these Bylaws, or any of them, may be altered, amended, or repealed and new Bylaws adopted as follows:

(a) Subject to the power of members, if any, to change or repeal these Bylaws under Section 9150 of the Corporations Code, by approval of the Board of Directors unless the Bylaw amendment would materially and adversely affect the rights of members, if any, as to voting or transfer, provided, however, if this corporation has admitted any members, then a Bylaw specifying or changing the fixed number of directors of the corporation, the maximum or minimum number of directors, or changing from a fixed to variable Board or vice versa, may not be adopted, amended, or repealed except as provided in subparagraph (b) of this section; or

(b) By approval of the members, if any, of this corporation.

ARTICLE 10
AMENDMENT OF ARTICLES

SECTION 1. AMENDMENT OF ARTICLES BEFORE ADMISSION OF MEMBERS

Before any members have been admitted to the corporation, any amendment of the Articles of Incorporation may be adopted by approval of the Board of Directors.

SECTION 2. AMENDMENT OF ARTICLES AFTER ADMISSION OF MEMBERS

After members, if any, have been admitted to the corporation, amendment of the Articles of Incorporation may be adopted by the approval of the Board of Directors and by the approval of the members of this corporation.

SECTION 3. CERTAIN AMENDMENTS

Notwithstanding the above Sections of this Article, this corporation shall not amend its Articles of Incorporation to alter any statement which appears in the original Articles of Incorporation of the names and addresses of the first directors of this corporation, nor the name and address of its initial agent, except to correct an error in such statement or to delete such statement after the corporation has filed a "Statement by a Domestic Non-Profit Corporation" pursuant to Section 6210 of the California Nonprofit Corporation Law.

ARTICLE 11
PROHIBITION AGAINST SHARING CORPORATE PROFITS AND ASSETS

SECTION 1. PROHIBITION AGAINST SHARING CORPORATE PROFITS AND ASSETS

No member, director, officer, employee, or other person connected with this corporation, or any private individual, shall receive at any time any of the net earnings or pecuniary profit from the operations of the corporation, provided, however, that this provision shall not prevent payment to any such person of reasonable compensation for services performed for the corporation in effecting any of its religious purposes, provided that such compensation is otherwise permitted by these Bylaws and is fixed by resolution of the Board of Directors; and no such person or persons shall be entitled to share in the distribution of, and shall not receive, any of the corporate assets on dissolution of the corporation. All members, if any, of the corporation shall be deemed to have expressly consented and agreed that on such dissolution or winding up of the affairs of the corporation, whether voluntarily or involuntarily, the assets of the corporation, after all debts have been satisfied, shall be distributed as required by the Articles of Incorporation of this corporation and not otherwise.

ARTICLE 12
MEMBERS

SECTION 1. DETERMINATION OF MEMBERS

If this corporation makes no provision for members, then, pursuant to Section 9310(b) of the Nonprofit Religious Corporation Law of the State of California, any action which would otherwise, under law or the provisions of the Articles of Incorporation or Bylaws of this corporation, require approval by a majority of all members or approval by the members, shall only require the approval of the Board of Directors.

WRITTEN CONSENT OF DIRECTORS ADOPTING BYLAWS

We, the undersigned, are all of the persons named as the initial directors in the Articles of Incorporation of _____, a California nonprofit corporation, and, pursuant to the authority granted to the directors by these Bylaws to take action by unanimous written consent without a meeting, consent to, and hereby do, adopt the foregoing Bylaws, consisting of _____ pages, as the Bylaws of this corporation.

Dated: _____

_____
, Director

_____
, Director

_____
, Director

_____
, Director

_____
, Director

CERTIFICATE

This is to certify that the foregoing is a true and correct copy of the Bylaws of the corporation named in the title thereto and that such Bylaws were duly adopted by the Board of Directors of said corporation.

Dated: _____

_____
, Secretary

MEMBERSHIP PROVISIONS

OF

_____

A CALIFORNIA RELIGIOUS CORPORATION

ARTICLE 12
MEMBERS

SECTION 1. DETERMINATION AND RIGHTS OF MEMBERS

The corporation shall have only one class of members. No member shall hold more than one membership in the corporation. Except as expressly provided in or authorized by the Articles of Incorporation or Bylaws of this corporation, all memberships shall have the same rights, privileges, restrictions and conditions.

SECTION 2. QUALIFICATIONS OF MEMBERS

The qualifications for membership in this corporation are as follows: _____
_____.

SECTION 3. ADMISSION OF MEMBERS

Applicants shall be admitted to membership _____
_____
_____
_____.

SECTION 4. FEES, DUES AND ASSESSMENTS

(a) The following fee shall be charged for making application for membership in the corporation:
_____
_____
_____.

(b) The annual dues payable to the corporation by members shall be _____
_____
_____.

(c) Memberships shall be nonassessable.

SECTION 5. NUMBER OF MEMBERS

There is no limit on the number of members the corporation may admit.

SECTION 6. MEMBERSHIP BOOK

The corporation shall keep a membership book containing the name and address of each member. Termination of the membership of any member shall be recorded in the book, together with the date of termination of such membership. Such book shall be kept at the corporation's principal office and shall be available for inspection by any director or member of the corporation during regular business hours.

The record of names and addresses of the members of this corporation shall constitute the membership list of this corporation and shall not be used, in whole or part, by any person for any purpose not reasonably related to a member's interest as a member.

SECTION 7. NONLIABILITY OF MEMBERS

A member of this corporation is not, as such, personally liable for the debts, liabilities, or obligations of the corporation.

SECTION 8. NONTRANSFERABILITY OF MEMBERSHIPS

No member may transfer a membership or any right arising therefrom. All rights of membership cease upon the member's death.

SECTION 9. TERMINATION OF MEMBERSHIP

(a) Grounds for Termination. The membership of a member shall terminate upon the occurrence of any of the following events:

(1) Upon his or her notice of such termination delivered to the President of Secretary of the corporation personally or by mail, such membership to terminate upon the date of delivery of the notice or date of deposit in the mail.

(2) Upon a determination by the Board of Directors that the member has engaged in conduct materially and seriously prejudicial to the interests or purposes of the corporation.

(3) If this corporation has provided for the payment of dues by members, upon a failure to renew his or her membership by paying dues on or before their due date, such termination to be effective thirty (30) days after a written notification of delinquency is given personally or mailed to such member by the Secretary of the corporation. A member may avoid such termination by paying the amount of delinquent dues within a thirty (30)-day period following the member's receipt of the written notification of delinquency.

(b) Procedure for Expulsion. Following the determination that a member should be expelled under subparagraph (a)(2) of this section, the following procedure shall be implemented:

(1) A notice shall be sent by first-class or registered mail to the last address of the member as shown on the corporation's records, setting forth the expulsion and the reasons therefor. Such notice shall be sent at least fifteen (15) days before the proposed effective date of the expulsion.

(2) The member being expelled shall be given an opportunity to be heard, either orally or in writing, at a hearing to be held not less than five (5) days before the effective date of the proposed expulsion. The hearing will be held by the Board of Directors in accordance with the quorum and voting rules set forth in these Bylaws applicable to the meetings of the Board. The notice to the member of his or her proposed expulsion shall state the date, time, and place of the hearing on his or her proposed expulsion.

(3) Following the hearing, the Board of Directors shall decide whether or not the member should in fact be expelled, suspended, or sanctioned in some other way. The decision of the Board shall be final.

(4) If this corporation has provided for the payment of dues by members, any person expelled from the corporation shall receive a refund of dues already paid. The refund shall be pro-rated to return only the unaccrued balance remaining for the period of the dues payment.

SECTION 10. RIGHTS ON TERMINATION OF MEMBERSHIP

All rights of a member in the corporation shall cease on termination of membership as herein provided.

ARTICLE 13
MEETINGS OF MEMBERS

SECTION 1. PLACE OF MEETINGS

Meetings of members shall be held at the principal office of the corporation or at such other place or places within or without the State of California as may be designated from time to time by resolution of the Board of Directors.

SECTION 2. ANNUAL AND OTHER REGULAR MEETINGS

The members shall meet annually on _____
_____ in each year, at _____ _M, for the purpose of electing directors and transacting other business as may come before the meeting. Cumulative voting for the election of directors shall not be permitted. The candidates receiving the highest number of votes up to the number of directors to be elected shall be elected. Each voting member shall cast one vote, with voting being by ballot only. The annual meeting of members for the purpose of electing directors shall be deemed a regular meeting and any reference in these Bylaws to regular meetings of members refers to this annual meeting.

Other regular meetings of the members shall be held on _____, at _____ M.

If the day fixed for the annual meeting or other regular meetings falls on a legal holiday, such meeting shall be held at the same hour and place on the next business day.

SECTION 3. SPECIAL MEETINGS OF MEMBERS

(a) Persons Who May Call Special Meetings of Members. Special meetings of the members shall be called by the Board of Directors, the Chairperson of the Board, or the President of the corporation. In addition, special meetings of the members for any lawful purpose may be called by five percent (5%) or more of the members.

SECTION 4. NOTICE OF MEETINGS

(a) Time of Notice. Whenever members are required or permitted to take action at a meeting, a written notice of the meeting shall be given by the Secretary of the corporation not less than ten (10) nor more than ninety (90) days before the date of the meeting to each member who, on the record date for the notice of the meeting, is entitled to vote thereat, provided, however, that if notice is given by mail, and the notice is not mailed by first-class, registered, or certified mail, that notice shall be given twenty (20) days before the meeting.

(b) Manner of Giving Notice. Notice of a members' meeting or any report shall be given either personally or by mail or other means of written communication, addressed to the member at the address of such member appearing on the books of the corporation or given by the member to the corporation for the purpose of notice; or if no address appears or is given, at the place where the principal office of the corporation is located or by publication of notice of the meeting at least once in a newspaper of general circulation in the county in which the principal office is located. Notice shall be deemed to have been given at the time when delivered personally or deposited in the mail or sent by telegram or other means of written communication.

(c) <u>Contents of Notice</u>. Notice of a membership meeting shall state the place, date, and time of the meeting and (1) in the case of a special meeting, the general nature of the business to be transacted, and no other business may be transacted, or (2) in the case of a regular meeting, those matters which the Board, at the time notice is given, intends to present for action by the members. Subject to any provision to the contrary contained in these Bylaws, however, any proper matter may be presented at a regular meeting for such action. The notice of any meeting of members at which directors are to be elected shall include the names of all those who are nominees at the time notice is given to members.

(d) <u>Notice of Meetings Called by Members</u>. If a special meeting is called by members as authorized by these Bylaws, the request for the meeting shall be submitted in writing, specifying the general nature of the business proposed to be transacted and shall be delivered personally or sent by registered mail or by telegraph to the Chairperson of the Board, President, Vice President or Secretary of the corporation. The officer receiving the request shall promptly cause notice to be given to the members entitled to vote that a meeting will be held, stating the date of the meeting. The date for such meeting shall be fixed by the Board and shall not be less than thirty-five (35) nor more than ninety (90) days after the receipt of the request for the meeting by the officer. If the notice is not given within twenty (20) days after the receipt of the request, persons calling the meeting may give the notice themselves.

(e) <u>Waiver of Notice of Meetings</u>. The transactions of any meeting of members, however called and noticed, and wherever held, shall be as valid as though taken at a meeting duly held after regular call and notice, if a quorum is present either in person or by proxy, and if, either before or after the meeting, each of the persons entitled to vote, not present in person or by proxy, signs a written waiver of notice or a consent to the holding of the meeting or an approval of the minutes thereof. All such waivers, consents and approvals shall be filed with the corporate records or made a part of the minutes of the meeting. Waiver of notices or consents need not specify either the business to be transacted or the purpose of any regular or special meeting of members, except that if action is taken or proposed to be taken for approval of any of the matters specified in subparagraph (f) of this section, the waiver of notice or consent shall state the general nature of the proposal.

(f) <u>Special Notice Rules for Approving Certain Proposals</u>. If action is proposed to be taken or is taken with respect to the following proposals, such action shall be invalid unless unanimously approved by those entitled to vote or unless the general nature of the proposal is stated in the notice of meeting or in any written waiver of notice:

1. Adoption, amendment or repeal the Bylaws pursuant to Section 9150(b) of the California Corporations Code;

2. Removal of directors pursuant to Section 9222 of the California Corporations Code;

3. Amendment of the Articles of Incorporation pursuant to Sections 9620 and 5812 of the California Corporations Code;

4. Disposal of all, or substantially all, corporate assets pursuant to Section 9631(a) of the California Corporations Code;

5. Approval of the principal terms of a merger pursuant to Section 9640(c) of the California Corporations Code;

6. Amendments to an agreement of merger pursuant to Section 6015(a) and 9640 of the California Corporations Code; and

7. An election to voluntarily wind up and dissolve the corporation pursuant to Section 9680(b) of the California Corporations Code.

SECTION 5. QUORUM FOR MEETINGS

A quorum shall consist of a majority of the voting power of the corporation.

The members present at a duly called and held meeting at which a quorum is initially present may continue to do business notwithstanding the loss of a quorum at the meeting due to a withdrawal of members from the meeting provided that any action taken after the loss of a quorum must be approved by at least a majority of the members required to constitute a quorum.

In the absence of a quorum, any meeting of the members may be adjourned from time to time by the vote of a majority of the votes represented in person or by proxy at the meeting, but no other business shall be transacted at such meeting.

When a meeting is adjourned for lack of a sufficient number of members at the meeting or otherwise, it shall not be necessary to give any notice of the time and place of the adjourned meeting or of the business to be transacted at such meeting other than by announcement at the meeting at which the adjournment is taken of the time and place of the adjourned meeting. However, if after the adjournment a new record date is fixed for notice or voting, a notice of the adjourned meeting shall be given to each member who, on the record date for notice of the meeting, is entitled to vote at the meeting. A meeting shall not be adjourned for more than forty-five (45) days.

SECTION 6. MAJORITY ACTION AS MEMBERSHIP ACTION

Every act or decision done or made by a majority of the voting power present in person or by proxy at a duly held meeting at which a quorum is present is the act of the members, unless the law, the Articles of Incorporation of this corporation, or these Bylaws require a greater number.

SECTION 7. VOTING RIGHTS

Each member is entitled to one vote on each matter submitted to a vote by the members. Voting at duly held meetings shall be by voice vote. Election of Directors, however, shall be by ballot.

SECTION 8. PROXY VOTING

Members entitled to vote _____ be permitted to vote or act by proxy. If membership voting by proxy is not allowed by the preceding sentence, no provision in this or other sections of these Bylaws referring to proxy voting shall be construed to permit any member to vote or act by proxy.

If membership voting by proxy is allowed, members entitled to vote shall have the right to vote either in person or by a written proxy executed by such person or by his or her duly authorized agent and filed with the Secretary of the corporation, provided, however, that no proxy shall be valid after eleven (11) months from the date of its execution unless otherwise provided in the proxy. In any case, however, the maximum term of any proxy shall be three (3) years from the date of its execution. No proxy shall be irrevocable and may be revoked following the procedures given in Section 9417 of the California Nonprofit Religious Corporation Law.

If membership voting by proxy is allowed, all proxies shall state the general nature of the matter to be voted on and, in the case of a proxy given to vote for the election of directors, shall list those persons who were nominees at the time the notice of the vote for election of directors was given to the members. In any election of directors, any proxy which is marked by a member "withhold" or otherwise marked in a manner indicating that the authority to vote for the election of directors is withheld shall not be voted either for or against the election of a director.

If membership voting by proxy is allowed, proxies shall afford an opportunity for the member to specify a choice between approval and disapproval for each matter or group of related matters intended, at the time the proxy is distributed, to be acted upon at the meeting for which the proxy is solicited. The proxy shall also provide that when the person solicited specifies a choice with respect to any such matter, the vote shall be cast in accordance therewith.

SECTION 9. CONDUCT OF MEETINGS

Meetings of members shall be presided over by the Chairperson of the Board, or, if there is no Chairperson, by the President of the corporation or, in his or her absence, by the Vice President of the corporation or, in the absence of all of these persons, by a Chairperson chosen by a majority of the voting members, present in person or by proxy. The Secretary of the corporation shall act as Secretary of all meetings of members, provided that, in his or her absence, the presiding officer shall appoint another person to act as Secretary of the Meeting.

Meetings shall be governed by _____
_____, as such rules may be revised from time to time, insofar as such rules are not inconsistent with or in conflict with these Bylaws, with the Articles of Incorporation of this corporation, or with any provision of law.

SECTION 10. ACTION BY WRITTEN BALLOT WITHOUT A MEETING

Any action which may be taken at any regular or special meeting of members may be taken without a meeting if the corporation distributes a written ballot to each member entitled to vote on the matter. The ballot shall set forth the proposed action, provide an opportunity to specify approval or disapproval of each proposal, provide that where the person solicited specifies a choice with respect to any such proposal the vote shall be cast in accordance therewith, and provide a reasonable time within which to return the ballot to the corporation. Ballots shall be mailed or delivered in the manner required for giving notice of meetings specified in Section 4(b) of this Article.

All written ballots shall also indicate the number of responses needed to meet the quorum requirement and, except for ballots soliciting votes for the election of directors, shall state the percentage of approvals necessary to pass the measure submitted. The ballots must specify the time by which they must be received by the corporation in order to be counted.

Approval of action by written ballot shall be valid only when the number of votes cast by ballot within the time period specified equals or exceeds the quorum required to be present at a meeting authorizing the action, and the number of approvals equals or exceeds the number of votes that would be required to approve the action at a meeting at which the total number of votes cast was the same as the number of votes cast by ballot.

Directors may be elected by written ballot. Such ballots for the election of directors shall list the persons nominated at the time the ballots are mailed or delivered. If any such ballots are marked "withhold" or otherwise marked in a manner indicating that the authority to vote for the election of directors is withheld, they shall not be counted as votes either for or against the election of a director.

A written ballot may not be revoked after its receipt by the corporation or its deposit in the mail, whichever occurs first.

SECTION 11. ACTION BY UNANIMOUS WRITTEN CONSENT WITHOUT MEETING

Except as otherwise provided in these Bylaws, any action required or permitted to be taken by the members may be taken without a meeting, if all members shall individually or collectively consent in writing to the action. The written consent or consents shall be filed with the minutes of the proceedings of the members. The action by written consent shall have the same force and effect as the unanimous vote of the members.

WRITTEN CONSENT OF DIRECTORS ADOPTING BYLAWS

We, the undersigned, are all of the persons named as the initial directors in the Articles of Incorporation of _____

_____, a California nonprofit corporation, and, pursuant to the authority granted to the directors by these Bylaws to take action by unanimous written consent without a meeting, consent to, and hereby do, adopt the foregoing Bylaws, consisting of _____ pages, as the Bylaws of this corporation.

Dated: _____

_____
, Director

_____
, Director

_____
, Director

_____
, Director

_____
, Director

CERTIFICATE

This is to certify that the foregoing is a true and correct copy of the Bylaws of the corporation named in the title thereto and that such Bylaws were duly adopted by the Board of Directors of said corporation.

Dated: _____

_____
, Secretary

COVER LETTER TO SECRETARY OF STATE

_____

_____

_____

Secretary of State
Corporate Filing Division
1500 11th Street
Sacramento, California 95814-2974

Dear Secretary of State:

I enclose an original and _____ copies of the proposed Articles of Incorporation of

_____

_____, a proposed California nonprofit

_____ corporation, together with the California Franchise Tax
Board Exemption Application, application fee and its attachments, fastened separately.

Please forward the exemption application materials to the Franchise Tax Board and, upon
exemption approval, file the enclosed original Articles of Incorporation. After filing, please return
to me, at the above address, two of the enclosed copies of the Articles, compared and certified by
your office. A check in the amount of $30, made payable to your office, for filing Articles for the
above nonprofit corporation is also enclosed.

Sincerely,

Form **8718**
(Rev. January 1996)

Department of the Treasury
Internal Revenue Service

User Fee for Exempt Organization Determination Letter Request

▶ Attach this form to determination letter application.
(Form 8718 is NOT a determination letter application.)

1 Name of organization	2 Employer Identification Number

Caution: *Do not attach Form 8718 to an application for a pension plan determination letter. Use Form 8717 instead.*

3 Type of request   **Fee**

a ☐ Initial request for a determination letter for:

• An exempt organization that has had annual gross receipts averaging not more than $10,000 during the preceding 4 years, or

• A new organization that anticipates gross receipts averaging not more than $10,000 during its first 4 years ▶ $150

Note: *If you checked box 3a, you must complete the Certification below.*

Certification

I certify that the annual gross receipts of ....
name of organization

have averaged (or are expected to average) not more than $10,000 during the preceding 4 (or the first 4) years of operation.

Signature ▶   Title ▶

b ☐ Initial request for a determination letter for:

• An exempt organization that has had annual gross receipts averaging more than $10,000 during the preceding 4 years, or

• A new organization that anticipates gross receipts averaging more than $10,000 during its first 4 years   . ▶ $465

c ☐ Group exemption letters .   .   .   . ▶ $500

Instructions

The law requires payment of a user fee with each application for a determination letter. The user fees are listed on line 3 above. For more information, see Rev. Proc. 96-8, 1996-1 I.R.B. 187.

Check the box on line 3 for the type of application you are submitting. If you check box 3a, you must complete and sign the certification statement that appears under line 3a.

Attach to Form 8718 a check or money order payable to the Internal Revenue Service for the full amount of the user fee. If you do not include the full amount, your application will be returned. Attach Form 8718 to your determination letter application.

To avoid delays, send the determination letter application and Form 8718 to the applicable IRS address shown below. Use the address below even if a different address appears in another form or publication.

If the organization is in	Send fee and request for determination letter to
Connecticut, Maine, Massachusetts, New Hampshire, New York, Rhode Island, Vermont	Internal Revenue Service EP/EO Division P. O. Box 1680, GPO Brooklyn, NY 11202
Delaware, District of Columbia, Maryland, New Jersey, Pennsylvania, Virginia, any U.S. possession or foreign country	Internal Revenue Service EP/EO Division P. O. Box 17010 Baltimore, MD 21203
Indiana, Kentucky, Michigan, Ohio, West Virginia	Internal Revenue Service P. O. Box 192 Covington, KY 41012-0192
Arizona, Colorado, Kansas, Oklahoma, New Mexico, Texas, Utah, Wyoming	Internal Revenue Service EP/EO Division Mail Code 4950 DAL 1100 Commerce Street Dallas, TX 75242
Alabama, Arkansas, Florida, Georgia, Louisiana, Mississippi, North Carolina, South Carolina, Tennessee	Internal Revenue Service EP/EO Division P.O. Box 941 Atlanta, GA 30370
Alaska, California, Hawaii, Idaho, Nevada, Oregon, Washington	Internal Revenue Service EO Application EP/EO Division McCaslin Industrial Park 2 Cupania Circle Monterey Park, CA 91755-7406
Illinois, Iowa, Minnesota, Missouri, Montana, Nebraska, North Dakota, South Dakota, Wisconsin	Internal Revenue Service EP/EO Division 230 S. Dearborn DPN 20-5 Chicago, IL 60604

Attach Check or Money Order Here

WAIVER OF NOTICE AND CONSENT TO HOLDING
OF FIRST MEETING OF BOARD OF DIRECTORS
OF

_____

A CALIFORNIA NONPROFIT _____ **CORPORATION**

We, the undersigned, being all the directors of _____,
a California nonprofit _____ corporation, hereby
waive notice of the first meeting of the Board of Directors of the corporation and consent to the
holding of said meeting at _____
_____, California, on _____, 19__, at _____ _M.,
and consent to the transaction of any and all business by the directors at the meeting, including,
without limitation, the adoption of Bylaws, the election of officers and the selection of the place
where the corporation's bank account will be maintained.

Dated: _____

_____
, Director

_____
, Director

_____
, Director

_____
, Director

_____
, Director

MINUTES OF FIRST MEETING OF BOARD OF DIRECTORS
OF

_____

A CALIFORNIA NONPROFIT _____ CORPORATION

The Board of Directors of _____ held its first meeting
on _____, 19__ at _____
_____, California.
Written waiver of notice was signed by all of the directors.

The following directors, constituting a quorum of the full board, were present at the meeting:

_____

_____

_____

_____

_____

There were absent:

_____

_____

_____

_____

_____

On motion and by unanimous vote, _____ was elected
temporary Chairperson and then presided over the meeting.
_____ was elected temporary Secretary of the meeting.

The Chairperson announced that the meeting was held pursuant to written waiver of notice
signed by each of the directors. Upon a motion duly made, seconded and unanimously carried,
the waiver was made a part of the records of the meeting; it now precedes the minutes of this
meeting in the Corporate Records Book.

BYLAWS

There was then presented to the meeting for adoption a proposed sets of Bylaws of the
corporation. The Bylaws were considered and discussed and, on motion duly made and
seconded, it was unanimously

RESOLVED, that the Bylaws presented to this meeting be and hereby are adopted as the Bylaws
of the corporation;

RESOLVED FURTHER, that the Secretary insert a copy of the Bylaws in the Corporate Records
Book and see that a copy of the Bylaws is kept at the corporation's principal office as required by
law.

CALIFORNIA AND FEDERAL TAX EXEMPTIONS

The Chairperson announced that, upon application previously submitted to the California Franchise Tax Board, the corporation was determined to be exempt from payment of state corporate franchise taxes as a/n _____ organization under Section 23701(d) of the California Revenue and Taxation Code per Franchise Tax Board determination letter dated _____, 19__. The Chairperson also announced that, upon application previously submitted to the Internal Revenue Service, the corporation was determined to be exempt from payment of federal corporate income taxes as a/n _____ organization under Section 501(c)(3) of the Internal Revenue Code per Internal Revenue Service determination letter dated _____, 19__ and, further, that the corporation has been classified as a public charity under Section _____ of the Internal Revenue Code.

☐ The corporation has obtained an advance ruling of its federal public charity classification. The advance ruling period ends _____.

The Chairperson then presented the originals of both state and federal tax-exemption determination letters, and the Secretary was instructed to insert these documents in the Corporate Records Book.

ELECTION OF OFFICERS

The Chairperson then announced that the next item of business was the election of officers. Upon motion, the following persons were unanimously elected to the offices shown after their names:

_____President

_____Vice President

_____Secretary

_____Treasurer

Each officer who was present accepted his or her office. Thereafter, the President presided at the meeting as Chairperson, and the Secretary acted as Secretary.

COMPENSATION OF OFFICERS

There followed a discussion concerning the compensation to be paid by the corporation to its officers. Upon motion duly made and seconded, it was unanimously

RESOLVED, that the following annual salaries be paid to the officers of this corporation:

President $_____

Vice President $_____

Secretary $_____

Treasurer $_____

CORPORATE SEAL

The Secretary presented to the meeting for adoption a proposed form of seal of the corporation. Upon motion duly made and seconded, it was:

RESOLVED, that the form of corporate seal presented to this meeting be and hereby is adopted as the seal of this corporation, and the Secretary of the corporation is directed to place an impression thereof in the space next to this resolution.

PRINCIPAL OFFICE

After discussion as to the exact location of the corporation's principal office for the transaction of business in the county named in the Bylaws, upon motion duly made and seconded, it was

RESOLVED, that the principal office for the transaction of business of the corporation shall be at

_____, in

_____, California.

BANK ACCOUNT

Upon motion duly made and seconded, it was

RESOLVED, that the funds of this corporation shall be deposited with _____
_____.

RESOLVED FURTHER, that the Treasurer of this corporation be and hereby is authorized and directed to establish an account with said bank and to deposit the funds of this corporation therein.

RESOLVED FURTHER, that any officer, employee or agent of this corporation be and is authorized to endorse checks, drafts or other evidences of indebtedness made payable to this corporation, but only for the purpose of deposit.

RESOLVED FURTHER, that all checks, drafts and other instruments obligating this corporation to pay money shall be signed on behalf of this corporation by any _____ of the following:

_____

_____

_____

RESOLVED FURTHER, that said bank be and hereby is authorized to honor and pay all checks and drafts of this corporation signed as provided herein.

RESOLVED FURTHER, that the authority hereby conferred shall remain in force until revoked by the Board of Directors of this corporation and until written notice of such revocation shall have been received by said bank.

RESOLVED FURTHER, that the Secretary of this corporation be and hereby is authorized to certify as to the continuing authority of these resolutions, the persons authorized to sign on behalf of this corporation and the adoption of said bank's standard form of resolution, provided that said form does not vary materially from the terms of the foregoing resolutions.

CORPORATE CERTIFICATES

The Secretary then presented to the meeting proposed director, sponsor, membership or other forms of corporate certificates for approval by the board. Upon motion duly made and seconded, it was

RESOLVED, that the form of certificates presented to this meeting are hereby adopted for use by this corporation and the Secretary is directed to attach a copy of each form of certificate to the minutes of this meeting.

ISSUANCE OF MEMBERSHIPS

The board next took up the matter of issuance of memberships in the corporation.

Upon motion duly made and seconded, it was unanimously

RESOLVED, that upon _____

_____

_____

_____ ,

members shall be admitted to the corporation and shall be entitled to all rights and privileges and subject to all the obligations, restrictions and limitations applicable to such membership in the corporation as set forth in the Articles of Incorporation and Bylaws of the corporation and subsequent amendments and changes thereto, and subject to any further limitations as resolved from time to time by the board of directors.

RESOLVED FURTHER, that the Secretary of the corporation shall record the name and address of each member in the membership book of the corporation and, upon the termination of any membership in accordance with the termination procedures specified in the Bylaws of the corporation, the Secretary shall record the date of termination of such membership in the membership book.

ACCEPTANCE OF OFFER TO TRANSFER ASSETS AND LIABILITIES
OF PREDECESSOR ORGANIZATION

Upon motion duly made and seconded, it was unanimously

RESOLVED, that the corporation accept the written offer dated _____, 19__ to transfer the assets and liabilities of the predecessor organization, _____

_____, in accordance with the terms of said offer, a copy of which precedes the minutes of this meeting in the Corporate Records Book.

RESOLVED FURTHER, that the appropriate officers of this corporation are authorized and directed to take such actions and execute such documents as they deem necessary or appropriate to effect the transfer of said business to this corporation.

Since there was no further business to come before the meeting, on motion duly made and seconded, the meeting was adjourned.

Dated: _____   _____
                                                          , Secretary

CALIFORNIA NONPROFIT CORPORATION RESOURCE LIST

The following is a list of resource organizations for California nonprofit corporations. This is a short, starting list and will be updated and expanded with each edition. Please fill in the reader registration card inserted in this book and let us know of any legal, financial or other nonprofit resource you've found to be helpful. Phone numbers and street addresses are not included.

Organization	Description	Resources/Services
California Lawyers for the Arts San Francisco	Seminars, clinics, publications and lawyer referral panel.	Publisher of *The Working Arts*. Facilities include nonprofit resource library—free use to members.
The Grantsmanship Center Los Angeles	Training programs and publications for nonprofit organizations.	Various programs, support services and publications. Call or write to obtain free issue of the *Whole Nonprofit Catalog*, the Center's newsletter and program guide, published three times each year.
Lai Insurance Agents & Brokers Oakland	Insurance Agency specializing in insurance for nonprofit organizations and their directors, officers and volunteers.	
The National Association for Independent Paralegals Sonoma	Referrals to local typing service; nonprofit seminars and assistance.	Includes assistance with nonprofit recordkeeping and organizational steps.
The Management Center San Francisco	Management consulting services, information and publications for nonprofits.	Publisher of *Guide to the California Nonprofit Public Benefit Corporation Law*.
Public Interest Clearing House San Francisco	Information and support for the public interest community (legal service programs, public interest law firms, pro bono attorneys, community activists, law students).	Public Interest Employment Service, Computer Users Group, Law Program, Legal Services Coordination Project, Directory of Bay Area Public Interest Organizations, Publications.
Support Center of San Francisco	Management and computer workshops for nonprofits.	The Support Center is, itself, a 501(c)(3) organization. It also provides on-site training and volunteer consultants to nonprofits and has offices in cities throughout the US.

THE NONPROFIT CORPORATION LAW—
AN OVERVIEW OF THE CHANGES

This supplement provides an overview of some of the basic differences between the old California nonprofit law (in effect prior to 1980) and the California Nonprofit Corporation Law (effective January 1, 1980). This information applies to California nonprofit corporations classified by the Secretary of State as public benefit or religious corporations (your corporation should have received a notice at the close of 1979 indicating which category you are now considered to fall in). This information does not necessarily apply to California mutual benefit corporations.

Most nonprofit corporations in existence at the end of 1979 will wish to amend their Bylaws to make sure they conform to the current law. Note: some changes may occur in the Nonprofit Corporation Law provisions listed below—check a current version of the California Corporations Code for the latest rules.

Old Law	**Nonprofit Corporation Law**
Needed at least 3 directors.	1-director corporations are permitted.
Variable board permitted if minimum number of directors not less than 5 and maximum number no more than minimum number plus 3. Exact number within these limits required to be specified in bylaws.	Variable board permitted with no restriction as to minimum or maximum limits. Exact number must be specified in bylaws.
All directors could be paid by the corporation in some other capacity (e.g., salaried officers, regular employees).	51% of the board can't be paid in any other capacity (even as independent contractors) and/or can't be related to any other person paid by the corporation. These restrictions don't apply to religious corporations.
Directors could serve on the board for an unlimited term.	Maximum term for directors of membership corporations is 3 years (for non-membership corporations the maximum term is 6 years). One-year director term for religious corporations (waivable).
Directors considered the "members" of non-membership corporations.	True non-membership corporations authorized. Fiction of directors being considered "members" of non-membership corporations dispensed with. No need for directors to hold "membership" meetings to approve certain matters in non-membership corporations.
No minimum quorum rule for directors' meetings.	Quorum for directors' meetings cannot be less than 1/5 the authorized number of directors or two, whichever is larger (one, in the case of a one-director corporation). Majority quorum rule for religious corporations (waivable).

Old Law	Nonprofit Corporation Law
No minimum quorum rule for members' meetings.	No minimum quorum for members' meetings. However, for public benefit corporations, if quorum is less than 1/3, special notice of meeting requirements must be met if less than 1/3 of the members actually attend the meeting.
Minimum number of officers: President, Vice President, Secretary and Treasurer. One person could hold two or more offices, except those of President and Secretary could not be held by the same person.	Need President (or Chairman of the Board), Secretary and Chief Financial Officer. One person can hold two or more offices, except the same person cannot serve as President (or Chairman of the Board) and as either the Secretary or Chief Financial Officer.
Voting rules for directors' and members' meetings flexible.	Action at directors' or members' meetings must be approved by a majority of those present at meeting (at which a quorum is initially present) and cannot be approved by less than a majority of a quorum (added flexibility with respect to membership voting in religious corporations).
Financial reporting requirements to directors and members optional.	Public benefit corporations must, generally, submit detailed annual financial statements to directors and members and annual statements of specific transactions to directors and members.
Manner of calling, providing notice for, and holding regular and special meetings of directors and members left, generally, to the corporation—no specific guidelines.	Specific provisions detailing manner of calling, noticing and holding meetings of directors and members. Detailed rules regarding calling, noticing, and holding of members' meetings generally nonwaivable—must be followed (religious corporations allowed greater flexibility).
No restrictions regarding date of adjourned members' meetings.	Public benefit corporations cannot adjourn members' meetings for more than 45 days.
Confusion regarding directors' duty of care, duty of loyalty in self-dealing transactions, and director investment standards.	Specific statutory language detailing standards for director action in these areas.
No statutory standards regarding expulsion of members.	Specific statutory standards and specific "safe-harbor" procedure for expulsion of members of public benefit corporations.
No standards or procedural rules for nomination and election of directors by members.	Specific standards and rules to ensure reasonable election and nomination procedures for public benefit corporations.

Caution: The repeal of your old bylaws and the adoption of new bylaws may trigger special notice or voting requirements. Before adopting your new bylaws, we suggest you have a lawyer look over your bylaw changes and bylaw amendment procedure.

INDEX

CATALOG

...more from Nolo Press

◪ Book with disk

CALL 800-992-6656 OR USE THE ORDER FORM IN THE BACK OF THE BOOK

	EDITION	PRICE	CODE
Tax Savvy for Small Business	1st	$26.95	SAVVY
Trademark: How to Name Your Business & Product	2nd	$29.95	TRD
Workers' Comp for Employers	2nd	$29.95	CNTRL
Your Rights in the Workplace	3rd	$18.95	YRW

CONSUMER

	EDITION	PRICE	CODE
Fed Up With the Legal System: What's Wrong & How to Fix It	2nd	$9.95	LEG
Glossary of Insurance Terms	5th	$14.95	GLINT
How to Insure Your Car	1st	$12.95	INCAR
How to Win Your Personal Injury Claim	2nd	$24.95	PICL
Nolo's Pocket Guide to California Law	4th	$10.95	CLAW
Nolo's Pocket Guide to Consumer Rights	2nd	$12.95	CAG
The Over 50 Insurance Survival Guide	1st	$16.95	OVER50
Trouble-Free Travel...And What to Do When Things Go Wrong	1st	$14.95	TRAV
True Odds: How Risk Affects Your Everyday Life	1st	$19.95	TROD
What Do You Mean It's Not Covered?	1st	$19.95	COVER

ESTATE PLANNING & PROBATE

	EDITION	PRICE	CODE
How to Probate an Estate (California Edition)	8th	$34.95	PAE
Make Your Own Living Trust	2nd	$21.95	LITR
Nolo's Simple Will Book	2nd	$17.95	SWIL
Plan Your Estate	3rd	$24.95	NEST
The Quick and Legal Will Book	1st	$15.95	QUIC
Nolo's Law Form Kit: Wills	1st	$14.95	KWL

FAMILY MATTERS

	EDITION	PRICE	CODE
A Legal Guide for Lesbian and Gay Couples	9th	$24.95	LG
California Marriage Law	12th	$19.95	MARR
Child Custody: Building Agreements That Work	2nd	$24.95	CUST
Divorce & Money: How to Make the Best Financial Decisions During Divorce	3rd	$24.95	DIMO
Get A Life: You Don't Need a Million to Retire	1st	$18.95	LIFE
The Guardianship Book (California Edition)	2nd	$24.95	GB
How to Adopt Your Stepchild in California	4th	$22.95	ADOP
How to Do Your Own Divorce in California	21st	$24.95	CDIV
How to Do Your Own Divorce in Texas	6th	$19.95	TDIV
How to Raise or Lower Child Support in California	3rd	$18.95	CHLD
The Living Together Kit	7th	$24.95	LTK
Nolo's Pocket Guide to Family Law	4th	$14.95	FLD
Practical Divorce Solutions	1st	$14.95	PDS

GOING TO COURT

	EDITION	PRICE	CODE
Collect Your Court Judgment (California Edition	2nd	$19.95	JUDG
The Criminal Records Book (California Edition)	5th	$21.95	CRIM
How to Sue For Up to 25,000...and Win!	2nd	$29.95	MUNI

▣ Book with disk

	EDITION	PRICE	CODE
Everybody's Guide to Small Claims Court (California Edition) 12th	$18.95	CSCC
Everybody's Guide to Small Claims Court (National Edition) 6th	$18.95	NSCC
Fight Your Ticket ... and Win! (California Edition) 6th	$19.95	FYT
How to Change Your Name (California Edition) 6th	$24.95	NAME
Mad at Your Lawyer 1st	$21.95	MAD
Represent Yourself in Court: How to Prepare & Try a Winning Case 1st	$29.95	RYC
Taming the Lawyers 1st	$19.95	TAME

HOMEOWNERS, LANDLORDS & TENANTS

The Deeds Book (California Edition) 3rd	$16.95	DEED
Dog Law 2nd	$12.95	DOG
⬜ Every Landlord's Legal Guide (National Edition) 1st	$29.95	ELLI
For Sale by Owner (California Edition) 2nd	$24.95	FSBO
Homestead Your House (California Edition) 8th	$9.95	HOME
How to Buy a House in California 4th	$24.95	BHCA
The Landlord's Law Book, Vol. 1: Rights & Responsibilities (California Edition) 5th	$34.95	LBRT
The Landlord's Law Book, Vol. 2: Evictions (California Edition) 5th	$34.95	LBEV
Neighbor Law: Fences, Trees, Boundaries & Noise 2nd	$16.95	NEI
Safe Homes, Safe Neighborhoods: Stopping Crime Where You Live 1st	$14.95	SAFE
Tenants' Rights (California Edition) 12th	$18.95	CTEN

HUMOR

29 Reasons Not to Go to Law School 1st	$9.95	29R
Poetic Justice 1st	$9.95	PJ

IMMIGRATION

How to Become a United States Citizen 5th	$14.95	CIT
How to Get a Green Card: Legal Ways to Stay in the U.S.A. 2nd	$24.95	GRN
U.S. Immigration Made Easy 5th	$39.95	IMEZ

MONEY MATTERS

Building Your Nest Egg With Your 401(k) 1st	$16.95	EGG
Chapter 13 Bankruptcy: Repay Your Debts 2nd	$29.95	CH13
How to File for Bankruptcy 6th	$26.95	HFB
Money Troubles: Legal Strategies to Cope With Your Debts 4th	$19.95	MT
Nolo's Law Form Kit: Personal Bankruptcy 1st	$14.95	KBNK
Nolo's Law Form Kit: Rebuild Your Credit 1st	$14.95	KCRD
Simple Contracts for Personal Use 2nd	$16.95	CONT
Smart Ways to Save Money During and After Divorce 1st	$14.95	SAVMO
Stand Up to the IRS 3rd	$24.95	SIRS
The Under 40 Financial Planning Guide 1st	$19.95	UN40

PATENTS AND COPYRIGHTS

The Copyright Handbook: How to Protect and Use Written Works 3rd	$24.95	COHA
Copyright Your Software 1st	$39.95	CYS

⬜ Book with disk

CALL 800-992-6656 OR USE THE ORDER FORM IN THE BACK OF THE BOOK

	EDITION	PRICE	CODE
Patent, Copyright & Trademark: A Desk Reference to Intellectual Property Law	1st	$24.95	PCTM
Patent It Yourself	5th	$44.95	PAT
 Software Development: A Legal Guide (Book with disk—PC)	1st	$44.95	SFT
The Inventor's Notebook	1st	$19.95	INOT

RESEARCH & REFERENCE

	EDITION	PRICE	CODE
Law on the Net	1st	$39.95	LAWN
Legal Research: How to Find & Understand the Law	4th	$19.95	LRES
Legal Research Made Easy (Video)	1st	$89.95	LRME

SENIORS

	EDITION	PRICE	CODE
Beat the Nursing Home Trap: A Consumer's Guide	2nd	$18.95	ELD
Social Security, Medicare & Pensions	6th	$19.95	SOA
The Conservatorship Book (California Edition)	2nd	$29.95	CNSV

SOFTWARE

	EDITION	PRICE	CODE
California Incorporator 2.0—DOS	2.0	$47.97	INCI2
Living Trust Maker 2.0—Macintosh	2.0	$47.97	LTM2
Living Trust Maker 2.0—Windows	2.0	$47.97	LTWI2
Small Business Legal Pro—Macintosh	2.0	$25.97	SBM2
Small Business Legal Pro—Windows	2.0	$25.97	SBW2
Small Business Legal Pro Deluxe CD—Windows/Macintosh CD-ROM	2.0	$35.97	SBCD
Nolo's Partnership Maker 1.0—DOS	1.0	$47.97	PAGI1
Personal RecordKeeper 4.0—Macintosh	4.0	$29.97	RKM4
Personal RecordKeeper 4.0—Windows	4.0	$29.97	RKP4
Patent It Yourself 1.0—Windows	1.0	$149.97	PYW1
WillMaker 6.0—Macintosh	6.0	$41.97	WM6
WillMaker 6.0—Windows	6.0	$41.97	WIW6

Book with disk

ORDER FORM

Code	Quantity	Title	Unit price	Total
		Subtotal		
		California residents add Sales Tax		
Basic Shipping ($5.50 for 1 item; $6.50 for 2-3 items, $7.50 for 4 or more)				
		UPS RUSH delivery $7.50–any size order*		
		TOTAL		

Name _____

Address _____

_____

(UPS to street address, Priority Mail to P.O. boxes) * Delivered in 3 business days from receipt of order.
S.F. Bay area use regular shipping.

FOR FASTER SERVICE, USE YOUR CREDIT CARD AND OUR TOLL-FREE NUMBERS

Order 24 hours a day	1-800-992-6656
Fax your order	1-800-645-0895
e-mail	cs@nolo.com
General Information	1-510-549-1976
Customer Service	1-800-728-3555, Mon.-Fri. 9am-5pm, PST

METHOD OF PAYMENT

☐ Check enclosed
☐ VISA ☐ MasterCard ☐ Discover Card ☐ American Express

Account # _____ Expiration Date _____

Authorizing Signature _____

Daytime Phone _____

PRICES SUBJECT TO CHANGE.

VISIT OUR OUTLET STORES!

You'll find our complete line of books and software, all at a discount.

BERKELEY
950 Parker Street
Berkeley, CA 94720

SAN JOSE
111 N. Market Street, #115
San Jose, CA 95113

VISIT US ONLINE

on **AOL** — keyword: NOLO   on the **INTERNET** — www.nolo.com

NOLO PRESS 950 PARKER ST., BERKELEY, CA 94710

NONPROFIT CORPORATE KITS

Ex Libris® and Centennial® are registered trademarks of Julius Blumberg, Inc.

Nolo Press, in cooperation with Julius Blumberg, Inc. offers two superior corporate kits. The kits are fully described in Chapter 10, Step 12B. The Ex Libris® and Centennial® kits include:

• A corporate records book with minute paper and index dividers for Articles of Incorporation, Bylaws, Minutes and Corporate Certificates. We are partial to the Centennial book which features a handcrafted, red and black simulated leather binder with your corporate name embossed in gold on the spine.

• A metal corporate seal designed to emboss your corporate name and year of incorporation on important corporate documents.

• IRS Package 1023—the 501(c)(3) tax exemption application—plus IRS Forms 8718 and SS-4.

• 20 lithographed Director Certificates printed with your corporate name. An option is provided for you to add 20 Sponsor Certificates.

• An option is included to order membership materials consisting of a membership index and roll sheets, plus 40 lithographed membership certificates.

- -

ORDER COUPON *The California Nonprofit Corporation Handbook*

Name of Corporation (print exactly as on Articles of Incorporation). Put one character per space (including punctuation and spaces). BE SURE CAPITAL AND LOWER CASE LETTERS ARE CLEAR AND SPELLING IS ACCURATE. CORPORATE KITS ARE NONREFUNDABLE.

45

Year of Incorporation: _____   State of Incorporation: CALIFORNIA

☐ Ex Libris Kit $74.95 (100 DRNL)   ☐ Centennial Kit $84.95 (930 DRNL) .... $_____
Each kit includes 20 Director Certificates

☐ Ex Libris Kit $84.95 (100 DRSP)   ☐ Centennial Kit $94.95 (930 DRSP) .... $_____
Each kit includes 20 Director Certificates plus 20 Sponsor Certificates

☐ Membership Materials including 40 Membership Certificates—add $40.00 (9MEMNL) .... $_____

Long corporate names (over 45 characters) cost an additional $25.00 .... $_____

California Residents Only: Add your local Sales Tax .... $_____

Shipping Charges   ☐ $10.00 *or* ☐ $25.00 .... $_____
Regular delivery by ground costs $10.00 and is within 10-12 business days;
Air delivery is within 4 business days and costs $25.00*

TOTAL ENCLOSED .... $_____

METHOD OF PAYMENT   ☐ Check enclosed   ☐ VISA   ☐ Mastercard   ☐ Discover Card   ☐ American Express

NAME _____

STREET ADDRESS (NO PO BOXES) _____

CITY _____ STATE _____ ZIP _____ PHONE _____

SIGNATURE _____ ACCOUNT # _____ EXP. DATE _____

EXTRA STOCK CERTIFICATES: $39.00 for 20 extra stock certificates, plus 50¢ for each additional certificate above this amount, plus half the corporate kit
(with Kit purchase)   shipping price. Please indicate the numbers to be printed on the extra stock certificates.

CORPORATE SEAL ONLY: $30.00 each plus half the corporate kit shipping price.

*All delivery dates are calculated from the day after we receive your order. Prices are subject to change without notice.

SORRY, WE DO NOT ACCEPT TELEPHONE ORDERS FOR CORPORATE KITS.

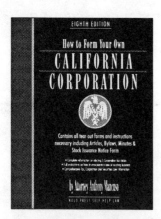
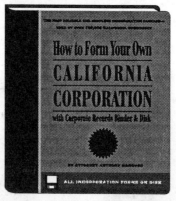

Take 2 minutes & Get a 2-year NOLO *News* subscription free!*

CALL
1-800-992-6656

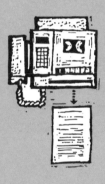

FAX
1-800-645-0895

E-MAIL
NOLOSUB@NOLOPRESS.com

OR MAIL US THIS POSTAGE-PAID REGISTRATION CARD

With our quarterly magazine, the **NOLO** *News*, you'll

- **Learn** about important legal changes that affect you
- **Find out first** about new Nolo products
- **Keep current** with practical articles on everyday law
- **Get answers** to your legal questions in *Ask Auntie Nolo's* advice column

- **Save money** with special Subscriber Only discounts
- **Tickle your funny bone** with our famous *Lawyer Joke* column.

It only takes 2 minutes to reserve your free 2-year subscription or to extend your **NOLO** *News* subscription.

REGISTRATION CARD

NAME _____ DATE _____

ADDRESS _____

_____ PHONE NUMBER _____

CITY _____ STATE _____ ZIP _____

WHERE DID YOU HEAR ABOUT THIS BOOK? _____

WHERE DID YOU PURCHASE THIS PRODUCT? _____

DID YOU CONSULT A LAWYER? (PLEASE CIRCLE ONE)   YES   NO   NOT APPLICABLE

DID YOU FIND THIS BOOK HELPFUL?   (VERY)   5   4   3   2   1   (NOT AT ALL)

SUGGESTIONS FOR IMPROVING THIS PRODUCT _____

_____

WAS IT EASY TO USE?   (VERY EASY)   5   4   3   2   1   (VERY DIFFICULT)

DO YOU OWN A COMPUTER? IF SO, WHICH FORMAT? (PLEASE CIRCLE ONE)   WINDOWS   DOS   MAC

NON 7.2

We occasionally make our mailing list available to carefully selected companies whose products may be of interest to you. If you do not wish to receive mailings from these companies, please check this box ❑

"Nolo helps lay people perform legal tasks without the aid—or fees—of lawyers."

—USA TODAY

[Nolo books are ..."written in plain language, free of legal mumbo jumbo, and spiced with witty personal observations."

—ASSOCIATED PRESS

"...Nolo publications...guide people simply through the how, when, where and why of law."

—WASHINGTON POST

"Increasingly, people who are not lawyers are performing tasks usually regarded as legal work... And consumers, using books like Nolo's, do routine legal work themselves."

—NEW YORK TIMES

"...All of [Nolo's] books are easy-to-understand, are updated regularly, provide pull-out forms...and are often quite moving in their sense of compassion for the struggles of the lay reader."

—SAN FRANCISCO CHRONICLE